The ONE YEAR®

GOD'S GREAT BLESSINGS
DEVOTIONAL *a daily guide*

PATRICIA RAYBON

TYNDALE™
MOMENTUM

An Imprint of
Tyndale House Publishers, Inc.

Visit Tyndale online at www.tyndale.com.

Visit Tyndale Momentum online at www.tyndalemomentum.com.

TYNDALE, The One Year, One Year, and *LeatherLike* are registered trademarks of Tyndale House Publishers, Inc. *Tyndale Momentum,* the Tyndale Momentum logo, and The One Year logo are trademarks of Tyndale House Publishers, Inc. Tyndale Momentum is an imprint of Tyndale House Publishers, Inc.

The One Year God's Great Blessings Devotional

Designed by Beth Sparkman

Published in association with the literary agency of Ann Spangler and Company, 1420 Pontiac Road SE, Grand Rapids, MI 49506.

Unless otherwise indicated, all Scripture quotations are taken from the *Holy Bible*, New Living Translation, second edition, copyright © 1996, 2004, 2007 by Tyndale House Foundation. (Some quotations may be from the NLT, first edition, copyright © 1996.) Used by permission of Tyndale House Publishers, Inc., Carol Stream, Illinois 60188. All rights reserved.

Scripture quotations marked NIV are taken from the Holy Bible, *New International Version,® NIV.®* Copyright © 1973, 1978, 1984 by Biblica, Inc.™ Used by permission of Zondervan. All rights reserved worldwide. www.zondervan.com.

Scripture quotations marked TNIV are taken from the Holy Bible, *Today's New International Version,® TNIV.®* Copyright © 2001, 2005 by Biblica, Inc.™ Used by permission of Zondervan. All rights reserved worldwide. www.zondervan.com.

Scripture quotations marked NASB are taken from the New American Standard Bible,® copyright © 1960, 1962, 1963, 1968, 1971, 1972, 1973, 1975, 1977, 1995 by The Lockman Foundation. Used by permission.

Scripture quotations marked KJV are taken from the *Holy Bible*, King James Version.

Scripture quotations marked NKJV are taken from the New King James Version.® Copyright © 1982 by Thomas Nelson, Inc. Used by permission. All rights reserved.

Scripture quotations marked *The Message* are taken from *The Message* by Eugene H. Peterson, copyright © 1993, 1994, 1995, 1996, 2000, 2001, 2002. Used by permission of NavPress Publishing Group. All rights reserved.

ISBN 978-1-4143-3871-2 (LeatherLike)

Printed in China

19	18	17	16	15	14	13
8	7	6	5	4	3	2

To my husband, Dan—
for always believing, always helping, always praying.

ACKNOWLEDGMENTS

Many great people make up a great book team. I'm honored to acknowledge this book's circle of champions: my husband, Dan, and my encouraging family for loving me as though I'm worth it; my church family in Denver—and to the many "praying grounds" all over the country where I have been welcomed, taught, challenged, and lifted; author Chris Tiegreen for his wise and generous advice on the writing of devotionals; the expert editors, designers, and sales staff at Tyndale House who steered this devotional into fruition and onto bookshelves; associate publisher Jan Long Harris and book editor Kim Miller (both also at Tyndale), whose love and respect for readers and authors pushed me to reach higher, search deeper, and go further; and my friend and agent, Ann Spangler, who never fails to advise me with love, insight, humor, and common sense. To each of you, thank you for blessing this journey. I am grateful.

INTRODUCTION

I DIDN'T KNOW I WAS BLESSED. Never even imagined it. Never dared to guess it. Not all the time, anyway. Instead, like most of us, I lived in a warm house, cooked in a decent kitchen, slept every night on a clean bed. Yet I complained about life. Not enough of this. Not enough of that.

Then one evening, while sharing a dinner with friends, I looked at their photos from a trip to Ghana and saw what I was missing. A smart three-year-old child—taking a soapy bath in a bucket outdoors in a nice rain—looked in the camera's eye and grinned, laughing about it all. On her face? A confident look of blessed joy.

Her humble village had only one deep well. "Children walked for miles every day to bring back their family's water," my friend said.

So when the skies suddenly opened and poured down rain, "everybody grabbed buckets and bowls, catching the water." Then on cue the little girl's mother handed her soap and a towel, "and the child tore off her clothes, scrambled into a bucket, and before you knew it, she was soapy from head to toe." And laughing about it all.

The child had a job to do in a big storm, but she obeyed and worked through the inconvenience, the downpour—not to mention the lack of plumbing—and she found joy. Showered with blessings.

That's what I was seeking when I started this devotional: to be showered with God's best blessings—but not as the world thinks, in material ways. I longed to be showered with God's highest, simplest, and greatest blessings, then get refreshed on the journey—even in a storm.

A simple but brave request? In fact, the path I was looking for was sitting on my shelf, waiting for me to launch ahead. It was *The One Year Bible*—a Christmas gift from the year before, still unwrapped, still bound in its cellophane wrapper. Then finally, worn out on what theologian A. W. Tozer called "the frivolous character of much that passes for Christianity among us," I sat down to open my new Bible.

My plan? I would launch a deliberate, purposeful journey through the fresh wind of God's Word, turning to the sweet truth of God's great and quiet blessings.

But God wasn't so quiet.

Instead, God wrote in loud words. With exclamation points.

Use common sense!

I sat back and squinted. Started reading some more.

Be content!

I nodded slowly, knowing I'd heard such timely advice before—heard it in sermons and Sunday school lessons, in church groups and Bible studies, on back porch swings and front porch stoops, in planes, trains, and automobiles, not to mention on countless long and winding walks.

But for some reason on this trip through the Bible, I was seeing and hearing such urgings in a different way.

I even found myself shaking my head when I read: Don't talk too much! Or as Proverbs 10:19 puts it: "Don't talk too much, for it fosters sin. Be sensible and turn off the flow!"

Exclamation point.

God seemed, indeed, to be personally teaching His own rules for blessings—timeless, smart, life-giving principles of both promise and joy. But I was hearing them with an unusual urgency, and seeing them in a new way.

Thus, I discovered this simple but winsome promise: "Godliness leads to happiness." That's Proverbs 10:28, or my paraphrase of it. So I pondered its simple beauty awhile—long enough to stumble onto yet another provocative promise: "Good-hearted people . . . produce a huge harvest" (Luke 8:15).

This was getting interesting. I started making notes:

"Gentleness makes us great" (see Psalm 18:35).

"God answers prayers when we trust Him" (see 1 Chronicles 5:20).

But of course, I almost said. Then I realized something deeper was percolating. So I wrote down a question: What am I learning? That's when I really started this book about blessings—by asking myself that question. Already, I had one answer: Use common sense! And more than that: Be content!

Not too long after, I added another: Get wisdom!

Then came: Travel light!

Then next: Know Jesus!

Then: Be righteous!

Also: Choose joy!

Good rules for living, to be sure. But I noticed something more. Something surprising. Something wonderful and great, in fact.

NO ORDINARY BLESSINGS

With each command to seek His high road and follow it, God promised a simple but powerful blessing. Not just an ordinary blessing. Instead, to those who followed His virtuous path, God promised His most grandiose, extravagant, crazy, highest, greatest blessings.

Be generous to the poor? "Then your light will break forth like the dawn, and your healing will quickly appear; then your righteousness will go before you, and the glory of the LORD will be your rear guard. Then you will call, and the LORD will answer; you will cry for help, and he will say: Here am I" (Isaiah 58:8-9, NIV).

I read the words again. Slowly. Could this be right? It had to be because in page after page of my new Bible, I found yet more such virtues that God promised His people He would greatly bless.

Some promises seem lilting and bright, such as:

Delight in the Sabbath: "Then you will find your joy in the LORD, and I will cause you to ride on the heights of the land and to feast on the inheritance of your father Jacob" (Isaiah 58:14, NIV).

Other promises seemed grounded as much in faith, but straightforward and clear.

Be kind, Solomon declared, "and your soul will be nourished" (see Proverbs 11:17).

Or even better, Jesus promised: Believe in me "and you will never die" (see John 11:26).

I was intrigued by these conditional but extravagant connections.

Then one day I saw it. The great irony—that for all the ways we Christians struggle to accomplish our goals, fight our demons, slay our dragons, climb our mountains, and satisfy our longings, God offers all that we desire, plus His blessings, if we choose simply to live right by Him, both in good times and storms.

And, no—this isn't a "works over grace" point of view. Grace assures our eternal salvation, to be sure. But to work in virtue assures us an abundance of unimaginable blessings—right now.

Whether it's raining hard or not.

I thought intently about this.

Instead of struggling to be "good Christians"—trying to get to heaven—we experience a preview of heaven by modeling God's character now. By following His ways. By living out His virtues. By receiving His greatest and highest blessings, but also by enjoying the blessed journey.

In fact, as Psalm 107:29-30 promises: "He calmed the storm to a whisper and stilled the waves. What a blessing was that stillness."

Or as Zechariah 10:1 urges us: "Ask the LORD for rain in the spring, for he makes the storm clouds. And he will send showers of rain." Why? "So every field becomes a lush pasture."

Each one of us, indeed, can become a flowering blessing for God's Kingdom when we determine to walk in His virtuous and blessed path.

The apostle Paul writes of this mystery in his letter to the church at Corinth: "We speak of God's secret wisdom, a wisdom that has been hidden and that God destined for our glory before time began" (1 Corinthians 2:7, NIV). Not even rulers understand it, Paul adds. "However, as it is written: 'No eye has seen, no ear has heard, no mind has conceived what God has prepared for those who love him'" (1 Corinthians 2:8-9, NIV).

I could hear the ancient prayer warriors declaring the same truth. Spiritual abundance, Andrew Murray declared, "will depend on my life." Or as he put it: "If I do what God says, God will do what I say."

Even better, He'll do more.

Why so much blessing for a life of virtue?

I could find only one answer. The blessings bespeak love. Only a God who loves us without limit could bless with such magnificence. Thus, His blessings are glorious. Yet, at the same time, they evoke the essence of His godliness.

LIST OF BLESSINGS

But what, in fact, are God's blessed virtues for life?

As I worked through my *One Year Bible*, I first logged a modest list of ten. But I kept reading. Soon my list grew to twenty virtues. I gave my notes a working title—The Virtues God Blesses. I photocopied the list. Sent it to family and friends. Printed out a list for myself. Thumbtacked it to the wall behind my computer screen.

Over time, during my reading, that list grew to thirty virtues. Then forty. At about forty-five, a little light flashed in my mind—my seeker's mind, that is. What if I devoted a year to focused study of the virtues God blesses—then wrote about them? A fifty-two-week devotional on the virtues God blesses.

At a meeting with my publishing team, I "pitched" my idea. They liked it. Then I went home.

And I froze.

I don't have formal theological training under my belt. Certainly, I don't have a flawless, unblemished life to my credit. I wasn't sure other people would even be drawn to the study of blessings.

I was surprised to learn that the Jewish word for "blessing"—*berakhah* or *brakha*—meaning a short prayer of thanksgiving—isn't so much about getting favored by God, but about blessing God with praise. Thus, like David, I longed through this book to declare, "Bless the LORD, O my soul, and all that is within me" (Psalm 103:1, NASB).

I dared even to imagine how our broken, weary world would be transformed and the cause of Christ advanced—and our own lives made new— if the longing of every Christian was to be showered with blessings, but also to live a life that blesses God and others, while we journey through the storm.

But what about me? Could I follow through with this one-year project? Would I be transformed? Would I finish the trip, blessing God by the effort? I found my answer in my new Bible: "And whatever you do or say, do it as a representative of the Lord Jesus, giving thanks through him to God the Father" (Colossians 3:17). Or in the words of a great and beautiful psalm:

> *Commit everything you do to the LORD.*
> *Trust him, and he will help you.*
> *He will make your innocence radiate like the dawn,*
> *and the justice of your cause will shine like the noonday sun.*
> (Psalm 37:5-6)

A shining book on smart virtues that God blesses seemed a worthy project, to be sure. A devotional format would allow deep and daily study of this blessed kind of life. In fact, for all the memoirs and essays and reflections I have written or read, the biggest day-to-day difference in my life has sprung from getting up every morning to pray and read from devotionals— everything from Oswald Chambers's classic, *My Utmost for His Highest,* to contemporary writer Chris Tiegreen's One Year devotionals with Walk Thru the Bible.

I was blessed, indeed, with this advice from Chris Tiegreen on the writing of daily devotionals: Don't just ask the why of what God tells us, he said. "Sometimes it's most helpful to ask why not."

Or in the case of God's blessings: how?

That's what I offer in this book. It is a one-year devotional study of biblical virtues and blessings, offering the ways and means that God blesses us. It's based on the premise that the secret to every desire of a Christian life—and to every desire of God to bless us—can be found by pursuing His high and blessed path of virtue.

Written from a personal point of view, this devotional explores one virtue per week, one point per day. As I explained to this book's editor: "I covered fifty-two virtues that bless God when we obey Him and bless us because we tried."

But what's the best way to use this devotional?

Take it one day at a time. One week at a time.

Be content—you don't have to digest the entire book whole in one sitting. Instead, go slow, letting God inspire each day's intimate searching and seeking.

Then at the end of each week, take some time to answer the study questions, allowing them to pull you deeper and further into God's blessed path for your life.

What will you and I discover?

I don't hold every answer. But I hear David in Psalm 108: "My heart is confident in you, O God; no wonder I can sing your praises with all my heart!" (v. 1). Still, like David, will we get lost on this journey? Or frustrated? Tired? Afraid?

Or will we stand under God's downpour and enjoy His mighty rain? Already greatly blessed. If so, we will rest in the one who promises to bless our efforts with His presence—and His power—leading us on His journey to a mighty end.

LISTENING

His Promise

Blessed is the man who listens to me.
Proverbs 8:34, NIV

My Prayer

Bless me with the power to listen,
O Mighty God.
Then convince me that it's okay
sometimes to stay quiet.

Listening: To Him

Listen, my child. . . .
Proverbs 1:8-9

It's dark, cold, and early. But I'm excited. On this morning, the most important thing I have to do is hear from God. And not just a little bit. I want to
hear without limits. Isn't that what we're all saying today? That we want to
be blessed by God this year? So we can bless God without limits?

So I sit, like you, Bible in hand—the first chapter of Proverbs staring up
at this new year—looking for some life-changing secret on how to make
such blessings happen.

Instead, Proverbs offers a gracious and quiet word: *Listen.*

It's not a suggestion. It's a plea. Spoken tenderly. Even kindly. "Listen, my
child. . . ." The writer, King Solomon, seems to know most of us *don't* listen
well. We wake up talking, our voices rattling around in our heads, hollering
first and hearing second.

But Solomon says *stop.*

Step off the loud, rusty, ragged treadmills of our lives. This fresh year, he
says, turn from our noise—all the emotional chatter raging in our minds or
spewing from other people. And turn it off.

Listening is serious business, to be sure. Listening to God's Word,
implanted by God's Spirit in our hearts, "has the power to save your souls,"
says James 1:19-21. Why? "My sheep listen to my voice," Jesus answers. "I
know them, and they follow me." When we listen, "I give them eternal life,"
Jesus promises, "and they will never perish. No one can snatch them away
from me" (John 10:27-28). When we listen to God, He knows us. As we
silence ourselves, our prayers don't perish. God may hear us better, plus, He
grants us eternal life. I'm ready to try that this year. Quiet my heart. *And* my
mouth. Then look what I'll discover: God is speaking. 🌿

A good listener is not only popular everywhere,
but after a while he knows something.
WILLIAM MIZNER

Listening: To His Call

Joyful are those who listen to me.
Proverbs 8:34

Get up.

That's the best way to listen to God.

Listening, as it turns out, is an action word. *Draw near to Him.* That's what the Hebrew word for listen—*shama*—fully means. Draw near and look. Then, attuned, we hear God's call: "Come closer, and listen to this . . . I am the LORD your God, who teaches you what is good for you and leads you along the paths you should follow" (Isaiah 48:16-17).

Moses did that. After a plush life in Pharaoh's palace, he got up to defend the helpless—starting a personal journey that led him back to God. But first, he rescued a Hebrew slave. Then he saved seven women from cruel shepherds, watering their thirsty sheep. Then he said yes to marrying one of the women, honoring her grateful father.

Finally, on a humble hillside, tending his father-in-law's flock and far from worldly and inner distractions, he got up to draw near, looking at God's handiwork—a burning bush. At that moment, then, he heard God speak. "Moses! Moses!"

Was it a loud voice? Will you and I hear God—actually calling us by name?

I hear questions like this at a women's prayer retreat.

"I'm a concrete person," one woman says. "What does it mean to listen to God? How can I hear Him?" For answers, we look at Moses. Then we see: Listening to God is getting up with intent. It's going humbly to new places. It's doing plain, hard work—leaving behind the world to go back to church, Bible study, prayer meeting, to all the places His voice is shared. Then we stop trying so hard to hear His call. Instead, we work and walk by His Spirit, in His joy. *Then* He speaks. 🌿

Part of doing something is listening.
MADELEINE L'ENGLE

Listening: For His Spirit

All the people listened closely.
Nehemiah 8:3

Curious business, this godly listening. As I try it, I hear all manner of mysteries. Great advice. Honest truth. Deep desires. So I'm hearing less gossip. Less complaining. Less doubt, fear, worry, and false teaching. I see, in fact, why our enemy overwhelms our ears with noise.

If we listen to ungodly things, we miss one of God's greatest blessings: hearing God's Spirit. So I quiet myself to better hear my Bible, feeling that listening seems too pretty a virtue to unlock God's mighty, delivering, trustworthy, Spirit-filled power. Then I see:

Those who refuse to listen to God prefer to go their own way—to trust in themselves. To be their own god. So God asks something simple—*just listen to Me*—knowing that those who listen truly want to know what His Spirit says.

Yet how do we hear Him?

By listening closely. That's what Jesus taught. *Draw near*, Christ says. Why? He doesn't shout. To hear Him, we sit close, see Him better, and then we learn. "The closer you listen, the more understanding you will be given—and you will receive even more" (Mark 4:24).

Theologian Richard Foster, in his book *Prayer: Finding the Heart's True Home*, describes this close approach to listening to God. "I wait quietly," he says. Tuning his heart to God's voice, he waits as "people and situations spontaneously rise" to his awareness. Letting the Spirit guide his prayer, he then remains quiet for a while, "inviting the Spirit to pray through [him] 'with sighs too deep for words.'" Throughout the day, he jots down brief prayer notes in a small journal.

Dare we do the same? Listen closely enough to hear the Spirit-filled thunder of God's clear voice? Even take notes? I dare you to try it today. Then, in your quiet, God speaks. 🌿

If the key is prayer, the door is Jesus Christ.
RICHARD FOSTER

Listening: To Each Other

Listen, my child, to what your father teaches you.
Proverbs 1:8

In Dale Carnegie's classic self-improvement book, *How to Win Friends and Influence People*, the author describes the concentrated listening style of famed psychiatrist Sigmund Freud. Quoting a man who had met Freud, Carnegie writes: "There was none of that piercing 'soul penetrating gaze' business. His eyes were mild and genial. His voice was low and kind. His gestures were few. But the attention he gave me, his appreciation of what I said, even when I said it badly, was extraordinary."

Or as he concluded: "You've no idea what it meant to be listened to like that."

King Solomon, traditionally credited as the author of Proverbs, seems to say precisely what it means: Good listeners are gracious. Mild and genial. Confident but kind. None of that soul-piercing gaze business. So they listen with love. With patience. With interest. With appreciation. Without judgment. The result? God crowns their listening with His grace (v. 9).

So gracious listeners learn things. We also hear what we desperately need to know.

"Listen to whatever Sarah tells you," God urges Abraham, "because it is through Isaac that your offspring will be reckoned" (Genesis 21:12, NIV). Or when Jacob blesses his sons, first he urges them, "Assemble and listen, sons of Jacob; listen to your father Israel" (Genesis 49:2, NIV). And Moses "listened to his father-in-law and did everything he said" (Exodus 18:24, NIV).

Of course, the model for listening is God Himself. He "listened to Leah, and she became pregnant" (Genesis 30:17, NIV). He listened to Rachel "and opened her womb" (Genesis 30:22, NIV).

I study these stories and the truth becomes clear. If we learn how to listen like God, we hear what matters. 🌿

> You can make more friends in two months by becoming
> more interested in other people than you can in two years
> by trying to get people interested in you.
> DALE CARNEGIE

Listening: With Honor

*Listen, my child, to what your father teaches you. Don't neglect
your mother's teaching. What you learn from them will . . .
clothe you with honor.*
Proverbs 1:8-9

As a young bride, I worked hard to learn the first secret of staying married—
how to listen. To pay attention. To hear feelings, not just words. Then not to
judge—or rush to talk. To let the Holy Spirit empower me to hear. A faith
walk, yes. Listening is like that.

Then in today's Scripture, God raises the stakes—pleading with us to
listen, not just to anybody, but to parents. But the teenager in us reels. Listen
to *parents*? Nothing will be harder. Even if parents are wise. Or loving. Or
perfect. Or even downright bad. Or even downright dangerous.

Yet God says we should listen—not because all parents teach us how to
live—but in the case of ungodly parents, because they teach us how *not* to
live. It's the position of respect that God seems to care most about in this
exchange. That is, we listen to parents—not because they're perfect parents,
but because they are our parents, period. Then as we listen, we release God's
ability to clothe us with His honor.

Thinking on this, I turn to the Ten Commandments, pondering that
provocative promise: "Honor your father and your mother, so that you may
live long in the land the Lord your God is giving you" (Exodus 20:12, NIV).

But surely this isn't just about living a long life. It's about living long in
whatever territory God has set aside for you to serve Him.

If you're not living well in the land God has set aside for you, this Scripture
provides the antidote. Listen to your parents. Still can't? Cry to the Holy
Spirit to empower you. The blessing? You learn to listen to others. To spouses
and to children. To coworkers and to neighbors. To friends. Even to enemies.

In our listening, we learn. But also we gain—a blessed garb of empowered
honor. ❧

The first duty of love is to listen.
PAUL TILLICH

Listening: To Life

Listen to his voice, and hold fast to him. For the LORD is your life.
Deuteronomy 30:20, NIV

Helen Keller couldn't hear. She couldn't see. But early on, the renowned civic servant found a priceless way around those problems. She found a friend who listened. According to Keller's autobiography, *The Story of My Life*, her first little friend—after Keller became deaf and blind following illness at age nineteen months—was the young daughter of the Keller family's cook.

> We spent a great deal of time in the kitchen, kneading dough balls, helping make ice-cream, grinding coffee, quarreling over the cake-bowl, and feeding the hens and turkeys that swarmed about the kitchen steps. . . . I could not tell Martha Washington when I wanted to go egg-hunting, but I would double my hands and put them on the ground, which meant something round in the grass, and Martha always understood.

At least one psychiatrist has said this early friendship—through which Helen Keller perfected some sixty communication signs—was crucial for Keller's later improvements, most notably with her beloved teacher, Anne Sullivan. But what does this story teach us?

We learn, first, that listening takes two—that, indeed, the arithmetic of the gospel is two by two. "Two are better than one" (Ecclesiastes 4:9, NIV). Or as Jesus put it: "Apart from me you can do nothing" (John 15:5). As important, however, we learn that when we work hard to listen well, we don't just gain friends. We gain life.

Helen Keller, in describing her "long night"—that "silent, aimless, day-less life" of her early years—said learning to listen and communicate was like being "restored to my human heritage." Yes, listening to God births life. "Give ear . . . hear me, that your soul may live" (Isaiah 55:3, NIV). That's theological truth. Here's practical truth: listening heals, mends, repairs. So listen to a hurting soul today. God will bless you both with His life. 🔥

Unless we form the habit of going to the Bible in bright moments as well as in trouble, we cannot fully respond to its consolations.
HELEN KELLER

Going Deeper

Blessed . . . are those who hear the word of God and obey it.
Luke 11:28, NIV

Are you a good listener? If not, why not?

If you could make one change this year to listen better to God, what would it be? Explain.

What about listening to other people? What special insight has God taught you this week about listening when others are talking?

If you'd like, write a prayer that reflects your needs regarding the virtue of listening.

Perhaps the best gift we can offer a hurting world
is deep, holy listening.
JOHNNY R. SEARS

LOVING

His Promise

*Above all, clothe yourselves with love, which binds us
all together in perfect harmony.*
Colossians 3:14

My Prayer

Dear Father of love, show me the secret
of loving others, myself, and You,
empowering the holy path to perfect harmony.

8 / Read Zephaniah 3:16-20

Loving: As God Sings

With his love . . . he will rejoice over you with joyful songs.
Zephaniah 3:17

Try hard to love this year.

Even though it's hard. Even though we're stubborn and jealous, fearful and envious. Or plumb crazy. Or on some days, it seems, we're all of these things.

Psychologists say we struggle to love because we don't love ourselves. Jesus says it better, but harder. "Love your neighbor as yourself" (Matthew 22:39). Almost impossible some days, isn't it? So in John 13:34, He issues His disciples an updated commandment: "Love each other. Just as I have loved you."

But how does Jesus love?

He puts others first, of course. But He also loves with delight—making breakfast for His friends on the beach. Washing their feet. Healing old hurts and bad brokenness.

Dare you remind yourself today, then, of His love for *you*? To actually believe, as Christian psychiatrist Curt Thompson says in his book *Anatomy of the Soul*, that Jesus likes you a lot—that He wants to make you breakfast, to wash your weary feet, to heal all your gaping wounds and bruised memories?

Church folks preach to each other about such things all the time. But could you and I today, Thompson urges, simply believe it? To "simply imagine . . . being in God's presence *while he is feeling delighted to be with you, while he is quieting you and rejoicing*" in your presence? Then, Thompson dares to add: "Imagine God singing about you."

That's what Zephaniah did. He told the disobedient children of Israel that despite everything, the Lord God "will take delight in you with gladness. . . . He will rejoice over you with joyful songs" (Zephaniah 3:17).

But what about you? Are you that lovable to God? *Yes.* Don't ever doubt it. He gave all for you. In fact, tell yourself: *He's singing about me.* How often? All the livelong day. 🌿

Our Lord God must be a pious man to be able to love rascals.
MARTIN LUTHER

Loving: As God Deserves

He who pursues righteousness and love finds life, prosperity and honor.
Proverbs 21:21, NIV

The phone rang. An elderly woman—recently moved to town and now a new member at my church—was calling to ask for a ride to an evening church meeting.

"I hate to bother you, sweetie," she said, and I smiled to myself. Just seconds before, I'd finished writing a devotion on loving with excellence—that is, with action. Now here was an opportunity to put it into practice.

"Are you going this evening?" the woman went on. "I don't want to be any trouble."

"No trouble at all," I told her. "I'd be honored to pick you up!" I paused—not sure why I mentioned "honor." As we chatted, in fact, I forgot I'd said it. But when we hung up and I returned to my writing, turning to Proverbs 21, I found today's little nugget—that God's reward for pursuing the righteous way of love is honor.

Certainly, it felt honorable—and right—to drive a few extra blocks to pick up our new church friend. Who treats me like a daughter.

With pet names.

Sweetie. Honey. Sweetheart. My ears soak up this gentle, generous affection from a woman I've only just met. But she needs me. Her eyesight is bad, for one thing. "I'm legally blind, honey," my new friend told me one Sunday. I watched her in our Bible class, holding her Bible up to her face, straining to read the precious words—letting me see with my own eyes, as I helped her into our car after church, that helping her compares nothing to what she is allowing me to get in return. Honor from God. But as I pursue this path, I discover much more. I see that a path of love also brings honor *to* God. So empower us, O God, to walk Your path of love all day. ❧

We are shaped and fashioned by what we love.
JOHANN WOLFGANG GOETHE

Loving: As God Loves

And now I will show you the most excellent way.
1 Corinthians 12:31, NIV

It was a high-profile city. Worldly, too. So maybe Corinth was like the place where you live. Or the place you'd like to live. (Or you think you'd like to live.)

But Corinth, as "happening" as it was—this crossroads of commerce and culture—was also at the center of corruption. A moral cesspool, some called it. The Greeks even had a name—*korinthiazomai*, "to act like a Corinthian." What did it mean? To be sexually immoral. Yes, Corinth was that kind of place.

The church there, in fact, was embedded, tainted, and torn with the spirit of the city. So a sexual scandal was brewing at the church. Spiritual pride thrived there too. With church members from across the globe, all speaking various languages, the Corinthian congregation especially prided "speaking in tongues." It was talking like angels, they said.

But the apostle Paul knew better. So he wrote them a letter. Saying this:

Even if you speak like angels—speaking in tongues—if you don't love like Christ, it counts for nothing. Such fancy talk in God's ears is like a noisy gong or a clanging cymbal.

This surely got their attention. Does it get yours today?

Love is better than talk, in other words.

More than any other spiritual gift, and there are many, love is better. Better than knowledge, tithing, even prophecy. Paul wrote in detail about these gifts and others throughout the book of 1 Corinthians. But in the thirteenth chapter, known sometimes as the love chapter of the Bible, Paul makes a case for love. "The most excellent way."

Why excellent?

Because God *is* love. So love never fails. There's no better way to say it. In any language, love never fails. So bless God today by loving. Then don't forget: let God bless you by loving you back. 🌿

Love first!
KENT HUGHES

Loving: My Spouse

Husbands, love your wives.
Ephesians 5:25, NIV

It's one of those days. And nights. My husband and I are bickering a little. Not seeing eye to eye on some little nothing of an argument. So I hold my tongue. Determined to love. Finally, he asks: "What's wrong?"

It's the question every spouse hears from time to time. What's wrong?

I'm not sure I'm ready to answer. Soon, in fact, the little dustup is over. We've learned after many years to get over it—and get on with it. To let little nothings stay little nothings—and not be more. More than anything, perhaps, both my husband and I keep trying to learn the secret to love "as Christ loved the church," as today's Scripture says.

But this business of married love is complicated, to be sure.

To make it work, psychologist and marriage expert Willard Harley teaches couples how to meet each other's emotional needs by finding out, first, what those needs are. Honesty? Conversation? Sexual intimacy? Financial support? Affection? Family commitment? Love in marriage takes work, starting with each person caring enough to know what the other needs.

That's how Christ loves the church. By caring enough to know us. That's why, during His ministry on earth, He so often asked this knowing question: "What do you want me to do for you?" Too many people, however, don't know themselves well enough even to answer Jesus, let alone their spouses. But knowing matters. Jesus' question proves it. So He kept asking it: *What do you want Me to do for you?*

Husbands ask wives the same question. So why don't we stop hedging and speak the answer? Let ourselves be known, in other words. That's a courageous gift to give a loving man. Then my loving man can love me in return. He who loves his wife, Paul wrote, loves himself. As Jesus loves. By being known. Deeply. Specifically. And right on target. What a wonderful way to give and get real love today. 🌿

> Happily married couples not only put out the effort,
> they also put their effort in the right places.
> WILLARD HARLEY JR.

Loving: With All Knowledge

But the man who loves God is known by God.
1 Corinthians 8:3, NIV

"Remember me?" A visitor at our church is shaking my hand. Big smile. Hearty handshake. I'm smiling back. In my mind, however, I'm lost and embarrassed. Her face is familiar. But in truth, I can't remember how I know her. So we talk awhile. My husband walks up. Greets her too. Knowing him, I can tell he's struggling to put a name with her face. Finally, in the car, it comes to me. "I know her," I tell him, explaining. "She rode our commuter bus." We both smile. Mystery solved.

Or was it? Because I've seen the same quizzical look on others' faces when they can't remember my name or face. I am amazed and humbled, therefore, to love a God who knows me completely—who promises that the very hairs on my head are *all* numbered (Matthew 10:30).

It's such a contrast to human knowledge. The famed nineteenth-century Baptist preacher Charles Spurgeon takes aim at human knowledge this way: "Many men know a great deal, and are all the greater fools for it." He adds: "There is no fool so great a fool as a knowing fool." In fact, the apostle Paul warns about it: If I "knew everything about everything, but didn't love others, what good would I be?" (1 Corinthians 13:2).

So I stop congratulating myself that, finally, I know who the church visitor is. I remember her. But I don't *know* her. Not as God knows her, and not as God knows me.

How can I bless others by knowing them today? I start by loving God as He pleads. *With all your heart, all your soul, all your mind, and all your strength* (Mark 12:30). When I love God that much, I know Him more. Then He blesses me with His power so I may love and know others like He does. 🌿

There is nothing sweeter in this sad world than the sound
of someone you love calling your name.
KATE DICAMILLO

Loving: My Enemies

But love your enemies. . . . Then your reward will be great.
Luke 6:35, NIV

Love my enemies. Sounds so easy. So daring. So sublime. Then last Sunday the FBI came to my neighborhood near Denver to arrest a suspected al-Qaeda terrorist.

He lived a few blocks away. No, not on my street. But his apartment complex was close. *Real* close. Close enough to make Jesus' admonition to love him as a neighbor feel not hypothetical or theological—but like a real-life challenge.

Love my neighbor? A suspected *terrorist?* And, with that, you know where today's commentary is going. Two places, actually.

First, loving any neighbor—as much as I love myself—is hard enough. For starters, I have to love myself without limits to love anybody else without questions. Then when the FBI reported their suspected terrorist had been photographed in a beauty supply warehouse in my hometown—buying "large quantities" of chemicals used to make test batches of explosives, I questioned hate. I questioned love.

But I also questioned evil. How, indeed, can I love an enemy?

For answers, I turn again to Jesus—and to His beautiful and perfect prayer. *Our Father*. His praying started like that. Soon, however, Jesus added: "But deliver us from the evil one. . . ." (Matthew 6:9, 13).

After the FBI arrest in my town, Christ's words rose from rote familiarity to fresh urgency. *Deliver us from evil.* It's no longer an idle request. But how?

How can the Lord confront evil at every hand? And in our world? And in our hearts? And even in a determined young suspect living just blocks away?

On this new day, Jesus still offers His timeless answer. When it comes to enemies—and to neighbors—the Savior empowers only one, blessed, uncompromising, all-availing, sweeter-than-ever remedy.

We can love. 🌿

Those who love to be feared, fear to be loved.
SAINT FRANCIS DE SALES

Going Deeper

*I love the Father and . . . I do exactly what
my Father has commanded me.*
John 14:31, NIV

Do you love yourself? What exactly does that mean to you?

What are ways God has shown His love for you this week?

What can you do today to show love to someone besides yourself?

What special insight has God taught you this week about love?

If you'd like, write a prayer that reflects your needs regarding the
virtue of love.

To love is to make one's heart a swinging door.
HOWARD THURMAN

COMPASSION

His Promise

Therefore, as God's chosen people, holy and dearly loved,
clothe yourselves with compassion . . .
since you know that you will receive an inheritance
from the Lord as a reward.
Colossians 3:12, 24, NIV

My Prayer

O God, strengthen my will, not only
to feel compassion, but also to show it,
as you prepare an inheritance
for me as a reward.

Compassion: For Healing

His father saw him and was filled with compassion.
Luke 15:20, NIV

The 2010 Winter Olympics were under way in Vancouver with the usual gossip, drama, and controversy. But around the world, all eyes focused on a different athlete—a celebrity golfer standing at microphones back in the States, his voice hushed as he admitted marital infidelity and other "failures."

Yet as he finished his remarks, his mother stood from her seat and hugged him. He hugged her back. She held him even closer, reaching up to kiss his face. Watching the scene, and the compassion she showed her son, I immediately thought of Jesus' parable of the Lost Son. While he was still a long way off, says Luke 15:20, "his father saw him coming. Filled with love and compassion, he ran to his son, embraced him, and kissed him."

The Prodigal's father could have lashed out, berating him. Or turned his back. Or locked his door, refusing to welcome his son home. And for good reason. This younger son dishonored his father and family by demanding his inheritance before his older brother. Essentially, he was wishing his father dead. Then he'd squandered his father's hard-earned wealth in "wild living." Now, the boy was back—ragged, dirty, smelly, broke, and broken. Yet, as with the golfer, this boy's parent showed compassion, running to him—even embracing him and kissing him.

Did this gesture of compassion restore the father's money? No. Or restore the golfer's reputation? Or marriage? Or make everything else okay again? No. But compassion does something better. It allows broken people to start healing again. In the parable, the father throws a feast to celebrate. Perhaps the golfer's mother did the same. Compassion doesn't end every family problem. But it is a blessed place to start. 🌿

It is easy enough to . . . criticize and condemn,
but redemption is costly, and comfort draws from the deep.
SAMUEL CHADWICK

Compassion: For Life

"Right!" Jesus told him. "Do this and you will live!"
Luke 10:28

My good friend Denise can cry a good river. Openly. Deeply. Sincerely. In a heartbeat, if she sees anybody or anything hurting—man, animal, or child—her eyes well up, and in an instant, she's reaching out to comfort, wiping away tears—and not just her own. When it comes to compassion—meaning "to suffer with"—she could write the book, and she admits it. "I *know* I feel deeply," she says.

But why don't we all feel such compassion? As in the parable of the Good Samaritan, why are more of us like the indifferent priest and the uncaring Levite—walking past, if not running past, the hurt we see and not stopping to help?

Jesus understood the problem. When an expert in religious law asked how he could obtain eternal life, the Lord offered a subtle question: "What does the law of Moses say?" The scholarly man shot back an answer: "Love God and love your neighbor as yourself," much as any churchgoer would say. We know such love is right, and Jesus agrees. "Right!" But the clever man couldn't let well enough alone. "And who is my neighbor?" Of course, Jesus replied with the parable—a story so familiar that most of us could repeat it from memory. Like the scholarly man, we know this story and its classic theme: compassion.

But Jesus reminds us of something far greater.

This parable is about eternal life. *That* is the blessing and reward for showing compassion, a deeper life in God. That life factor, indeed, prompted the clever man's question. *What must I do to inherit eternal life?* Do compassion, Jesus replies in his parable. Do *this* and you will live. Put others before self, that is—and live. It's neighborly to help. But even better, compassion allows God to bless us with His life. What a gift for sharing what God has already freely given. His compassionate help and power. 🌿

We help, because we were helped.
ANNE LAMOTT

Compassion: That Shares His Light

Even in darkness light dawns for the upright,
for the gracious and compassionate and righteous man.
Psalm 112:4, NIV

The news from Haiti was winding down. A month had passed, in fact, since a powerful earthquake devastated the island nation, killing hundreds of thousands and leaving over a million more homeless. Now the social action pastor at my church in Colorado was juggling details for a welcome celebration for some thirty-two Haitian orphans and their new adoptive families. A whirlwind of a celebration was in the planning.

But my pastor friend was exhausted. Worried, too. "Maybe I should've waited until the families got settled," she said during a hurried phone call pleading for help. The event was two days away, and aside from a local Haitian church and a few other special guests, no one—not even one of the thirty-two adoptive families—had called to accept the invitation. I could feel a heaviness in her voice. A dark cloud of doubt hung over her head—as gray as the overcast, snowy day. She tried to laugh. "Now whose idea was this again?"

Laughing with her, I prayerfully agreed that the welcome celebration would go off without a hitch. And amazingly it did. Looking back, however, I see what lifted it above the problems to a powerful end. It was this pastor's dogged compassion.

Despite snow and cold, her love for the wide-eyed Haitian babies and their determined new parents drew a throng of people—including the Haitian church members, plus choirs from across the city, a dance troupe, elected officials, and a great turnout of the adoptive families, all toting their recently arrived Haitian babies snuggly wrapped in new winter parkas and coats. Donated toys, diapers, and baby formula completed the picture. At the center of it all was my compassionate friend, the light of her passion outshining the weather and the logistics; her calling to suffer for the least and love with the hurting blessing the cold, cloudy day into the power of sunshine. 🌿

Yes, the sun is coming up in me—in me.
SHAUN GROVES

Compassion: That Lives in Truth

The woman whose son was alive was filled with compassion.
1 Kings 3:26, NIV

My husband showed me his photos from the Haitian children's welcome event at our church. In every shot, attentive parents hugged their newly adopted children, looking not into the camera lens but into their children's eyes with love and concern.

The children had endured more than they ever could say in their Creole language—and more than we could understand. For now, however, the big thing was the main thing. *They were alive.*

Like the compassionate mother in today's Scripture, these adoptive parents were powered, not by the death the children had witnessed and escaped, but by the children's need for love and nurturing *now.* These bright-eyed, squealing, squirming, curious babies and toddlers needed parents who recognized their struggle was not just to live but to keep on living.

In the biblical story, the fake mother was willing to see the living child cut in two—a horrifying outcome—just to hold on to what never was hers in the first place. Better dead than alive? She'd accept such a child out of her own selfish needs. But the child's true mother begged the king: "Please, my lord, give her the living baby! Don't kill him!" (v. 26, NIV).

True parents react like that. Their compassion sees not just a baby's present worth but a child's future potential. With children, true compassion means not just putting up with present inconveniences—diapers, pacifiers, late nights, early mornings—but suffering with children through every stage of life. For the Haitian children, their adoptive parents didn't birth them. But their compassion was real. Thus their parenting will be too. May our compassion for others be just as undivided, just as empowered—offered not for ourselves but for the blessing of us all. ❦

What we have to recover is our original unity.
THOMAS MERTON

Compassion: For the Least

"Lord," he said, "my servant lies at home paralyzed
and in terrible suffering."
Matthew 8:6, NIV

It's another marvelous story about faith—but with a twist. In fact, like so many Bible stories about compassionate healing, this moment in the Gospel of Matthew—where a Roman centurion pleads with Jesus to help his suffering servant—is, at its core, about the man's deep faith.

Yet what drove it? His compassion.

A powerful sentiment from a powerful man. Clearly, he realizes that his own compassion, plus his recognition that Jesus is Lord and Healer of all, will compel Jesus to action. "O Lord," he pleads, "my servant lies at home *suffering.*" Nothing is said about his own need to put his servant back to work. Instead, Jesus' ability to render immediate relief is at the forefront. Immediately, indeed, Jesus responds. "I will go and heal him" (v. 7, NIV). No questions. No delay.

This is no small point. As this story teaches, our compassion for the least compels our Lord to action. To faithful compassion, the Great Physician responds with a doctor's greatest blessing: His healing. I will go *and* heal, Jesus says. Are there any better words for a compassionate person to hear from the Lord?

What a powerful lesson. If we want Jesus to heal, we should first focus with compassion on the least. The very idea seems a bit illogical. Shouldn't we ask first for ourselves—seeking relief for our own needs? This story says the opposite. It says no matter our own needs (such as the Roman officer's, to get his servant back to work), it's far more effective to seek the Lord's relief for somebody else. Then something wonderful and blessed happens. By the power of faith, both our needs get met. ❦

> I have this theory that if one person can go out of their way to show compassion, then it will start a chain reaction of the same.
> RACHEL JOY SCOTT

Compassion: In Action

He broke them and gave them to the disciples,
and they in turn to the people.
Matthew 15:36, NIV

The Rwandan boy lost his parents, his home, and finally his eyesight. Then this orphan named Marcel—who suffered from keratoconus, a degenerative eye condition that leads to misshapen corneas and, in Marcel's case, blindness—met a recent high school graduate from Colorado doing missions work in Rwanda.

John, the American boy, e-mailed his father back in the States: "I know this sounds crazy . . . but could he come to America with me when I come back?"

Crazy? John went on: "Tell everyone who knows me that this is what I want for Christmas and my birthday for the next 10 years—for him to have the gift of sight."

Compassion in action. In the case of the nineteen-year-old Rwandan orphan, as told in a *Denver Post* news story, the American boy's compassion actively led to a medical team in Colorado donating their skills, time, and dollars to surgically correct Marcel's eyesight—forever changing the orphaned boy's life. He's now back in Rwanda, where he continues his studies.

Jesus displayed the same kind of compassion after looking out on a great crowd of hungry people. They'd followed after Him for three days as He healed the afflicted. But now, Jesus told His disciples, "I have compassion for these people; they . . . have nothing to eat" (v. 32, NIV). So He blessed some bread and a few fish, giving the food to His disciples, and they in turn to the people. And "they all ate and were satisfied" (v. 37, NIV). Again, compassion in action.

I reflected on this recently while reading a newsletter from a Bible translation organization I support with donations. This time, however, they asked not for donations—but for prayer. Fifteen times, in fact, the newsletter pleaded: *Pray.* So I stopped right then. I prayed. Actively. That's what someone needs you to do today—not to talk about helping, but to act on it. That's a blessing that will bless you back. 🔥

Compassion costs.
SAMUEL CHADWICK

Going Deeper

I have compassion for these people.
Matthew 15:32, NIV

· If compassion is suffering with someone, how has God shown compassion to you?

Whom has God shown you this week who needs your compassion?

How have you responded?

What else—or what more—could you do to demonstrate compassion in this situation?

If you'd like, write a prayer that reflects what God is trying to teach you about the virtue of compassion.

Compassion will cure more sins than condemnation.
HENRY WARD BEECHER

KINDNESS

His Promise

Those who are kind benefit themselves,
but the cruel bring ruin on themselves.
Proverbs 11:17, TNIV

My Prayer

Where there is cruelty in my heart, O God,
replace it with kindness
—for Your glory and for my benefit.

Kindness: To Our Friends

A kindhearted woman gains respect.
Proverbs 11:16, NIV

Breakfast and orange juice and something new—the morning's Dear Amy column, which I usually skim over. But on a recent day, the newspaper on my kitchen table kept attracting my close attention.

> Dear Amy: I'm at a loss as to how to deal with my 16-year-old daughter and to teach her how to "play nice."

The girl was rude and sarcastic, her mother said, and her humor was pointed and hurtful. So the mother's concern was heartfelt. What about her daughter's future?

> I have serious concerns about my daughter's future . . . about her ability to hold a job and get along with co-workers and a boss, her ability to nurture a child.

This mother had good reason to be concerned. Her teenager, eager for peer approval, was "aggressively" trying everything she could think of to gain attention and acceptance except the one thing that would make a difference. Yes, kindness—that thoughtful empathy for others—would have earned her the respect she seemingly was so desperate to achieve.

Dear Amy's columnist said as much. Sign up the teen for volunteer service, she said, offering her "the experience of spending time with people who are immune to her attitude because they've got bigger problems to deal with." In other words, require this troubled teenage girl to offer some basic kindness. "Kind words are like honey—sweet to the soul and healthy for the body," says Proverbs 16:24. Interesting, indeed, that the writer of Proverbs also shows the outcome of such kindness when practiced by a woman. Not that everybody doesn't benefit. But a young woman? She gains what every person craves from the world:

The blessing and power of respect. 🌿

Kindness makes a person attractive.
ALEXANDER MACLAREN

Kindness: Like God

I am the LORD, who exercises kindness.
Jeremiah 9:24, NIV

Bring it on. That's what I say today to the Daniel Fast at my church. But by day four of this Bible-based fasting program, I'm dragging and irritable. I joke about my stomach growling. But I'm not laughing. My husband isn't either. So I offer perspective—or try. "Pastor said it's not about the food."

My husband frowns, one eyebrow arched in doubt. "Then what *is* it about?"

He's sort of laughing in his normally good-natured way. But this fast—our chance to cut junk from our diets—is stressing me to irritation. I sigh.

"It's about drawing closer to God," I finally say to my husband. But as we walk past grocery shelves, reading labels, eliminating "pleasant" foods—such as chocolate chip cookies—he's not drawing nearer to God. Neither am I. Instead, I can read the anxiety gripping my husband—anxiety, yes, attacking this man who admits he loves to eat. Meat, potatoes, and gravy.

I sigh again.

I can imagine twenty-one long days of this—his anxiety, my irritability. So when we return home, I try to pray. After a day of this, after searching my Bible, one word grabs my attention. *Kindness.* Or as the prophet Jeremiah puts it: "This is what the LORD says . . . that I am the LORD, who exercises kindness, justice and righteousness on earth, *for in these I delight*" (vv. 23-24, NIV, italics added). God likes kindness, in fact. And it's time I showed more of it.

With a deep breath and a plea to the Holy Spirit, I listen to my husband. So I hear his heart. He wants to please God and complete this fast. He also knows its restrictions. No pleasant foods, including his all-time favorite—breads. All breads. Luscious breads. A true challenge to a breadaholic like him. Thus, kindly, I sit at my computer, searching for breads we can eat. As I collect recipes for unleavened cornbread, tortillas, Indian flat bread, and more, I know I'm also delighting God. Because kindness is of God. It's what God does. So why shouldn't I? Or as my husband would answer: Let's eat. 🌿

The person who sows seeds of kindness enjoys a perpetual feast.
AUTHOR UNKNOWN

Kindness: At Our Churches

Do these things, and you will never fall away.
2 Peter 1:10

False teaching was the target of the apostle Peter's second letter to early Christians of Asia Minor. To fight it, Peter lifted up a list of strong virtues—including such "heavy hitter" life skills as knowledge, self-control, patience, and godliness.

To those, however, Peter added "brotherly kindness" (2 Peter 1:7, NIV). A surprise? It would seem so if we consider Peter was taking harsh aim at bold, arrogant, blasphemous, adulterous, lustful, greedy, seducing, corrupt leaders. (You can read his comments in 2 Peter 2.) To be sure, Peter didn't mince words in this controversial letter.

Yet as he advised the early Christians how to fight such deceptive and dangerous false teachers, he added brotherly kindness. "For if you possess these qualities . . . [and] do these things, you will never fall" (2 Peter 1:8, 10, NIV).

But why would kindness provide such godly protection—especially against ungodly leadership?

Could it be that the kindly are, by definition, thoughtful? And that thinking people are less likely to follow corrupt leaders down the slippery slope of destruction? The idea intrigues me. Kindly folks would seem to be "nice"—the most likely to allow corrupt people to infiltrate their church.

But Peter must've understood something deeper. To be kind, according to the roots of this word, is to be "cognitive"—or thinking. Such a person, while certainly nice, isn't stupid.

The blessing of being kind is related to what kindness requires of a believer: a warm heart but also a thoughtful mind. With it, we perceive corruption for what it is—something unworthy of a believer who takes the time, not just to be nice, but to think. 🌿

Don't be yourself—be someone a little nicer.
MIGNON MCLAUGHLIN

Kindness: To Be Kept by God

Continue in his kindness. Otherwise, you also will be cut off.
Romans 11:22, NIV

It's easy to gloat. Too easy. No surprise, then, that gloating Gentiles arose in the early church at Rome. These new Christians realized their special status. They were "grafted into" God's family tree while unbelieving Israelites were "broken off."

Yet the apostle Paul hands these Gentiles a strong warning: "Consider therefore the kindness and sternness of God: sternness to those who fell, but kindness to you, provided that you continue in his kindness. Otherwise, you also will be cut off" (Romans 11:22, NIV).

Sharp warning. The reminder, however, sheds light most on God and on the nature of *His* kindness. We're not asked to emulate human kindness, not with all of its many shortcomings. Rather the apostle sets a higher benchmark: continue to be kind as God is kind.

But how is God kind? And when?

He grants us grace, even when we don't deserve it. Paul, in this story, reminds the Gentiles of exactly that by making a critical point: that, yes, the unbelieving Israelites were broken off from the family tree. But he adds: "If they do not persist in unbelief, they will be grafted in, for God is able to graft them in again" (v. 23, NIV).

He then uses a provocative image to point out that if God was willing to cut us out of a wild olive tree and graft us into a "cultivated" olive tree, "how much more readily will these, the natural branches, be grafted into their own olive tree!" (v. 24, NIV).

So we shouldn't be conceited about God's adoption of us, Paul warns. Instead, we are to be kind as God is kind—to continue in His kindness, even when others don't deserve such grace. When we continue in this way, we can be assured of a marvelous blessing: we'll never be cut off from the graciousness, goodness, and power of our God. 🌱

Kind words also produce their own image on men's souls;
and a beautiful image it is.
BLAISE PASCAL

Kindness: Inside Our Families

"The LORD bless you, my daughter," he replied.
Ruth 3:10, NIV

One of my mother's life lessons still stands out—and always has. Be kind to family. Or as she reminded me, "You only have one sister. And the two of you should let nothing ever come between the two of you." Then she got to the point:

"When I die, whatever you do, the two of you should never fight over anything of mine." She was adamant about this. "You only have one sister. The two of you should always act like it."

Her lesson stuck. Since my mother passed a few years ago, my sister and I have made it our business not to argue, and certainly not over our mother's personal possessions. Why? Kindness within a family blesses and empowers that family. The Bible story of Ruth, her mother-in-law, Naomi, and their kinsman Boaz teaches it particularly well.

When Ruth's husband died and his mother was left alone, Ruth chose to stay with Naomi—returning with her mother-in-law to Israel, the two of them arriving in Bethlehem just as the barley harvest was beginning. Right away, Ruth's kindness got people talking.

Or as Boaz told her: "I've been told all about what you have done for your mother-in-law since the death of your husband. . . . May the LORD repay you for what you have done. May you be richly rewarded by the LORD, the God of Israel" (Ruth 2:11-12, NIV).

In the end, of course, Boaz took Ruth to be his wife and they had a son—Obed, the father of Jesse, who became the father of David—in a lineage that led to Joseph, the husband of Mary, "of whom was born Jesus, who is called Christ" (Matthew 1:16, NIV). A small matter being kind to family? This story, more than many, shows the lesson my own mother taught. Kindness in families matters for eternity. 🌿

Always be a little kinder than necessary.
JAMES M. BARRIE

Kindness: To Benefit Myself

Those who are kind benefit themselves.
Proverbs 11:17, TNIV

Do you celebrate your birthday? Or as my friend says: "What are you doing on your birthday—for *you*?"

She asks me that every year. Still, the question always catches me off guard. What am I doing? For myself?

In the Christian life, which focuses so often on our outreach to others, it can seem *un*-Christian to do something nice to reward ourselves. Like a dinner out. A relaxing massage. A movie date. A long nap. A short walk. A nice vacation. A new dress. Some new earrings. Or, ah, a brand-new pair of shoes.

Indeed, if I think about it hard enough, I could contrive a way to take a break from helping others—just to reward myself. The Bible lets us know such a reward is not only okay but pleasing unto God.

My favorite biblical moments of Jesus, in fact, are those times when He was doing just that—taking a nap on a boat, fixing breakfast for His friends, reclining at dinner, taking a walk in the mountains by Himself.

Restoring Himself. Renewing Himself. Rewarding Himself. Such actions remind us that it's perfectly okay with God if we value ourselves enough to give ourselves a gift. But such a gift doesn't have to cost money. Instead, the cost for such a reward can be the simple act of kindness—to ourselves.

"Those who are kind benefit themselves," says the writer of Proverbs 11. That's in contrast, according to that verse, to cruel people—who bring trouble on themselves.

The choice seems simple, to be sure.

So on this day, choose an act of kindness. Even to yourself. But don't be surprised. The benefits will flow back to the heart that birthed them. ❧

If I do not live a life that satisfies Thee, I shall not
have a life that satisfies myself.
AUTHOR UNKNOWN

Going Deeper

So he reassured them by speaking kindly to them.
Genesis 50:21

What does kindness mean to you? What kindness have you been given or shown in the past week?

To whom in your life could you show more kindness?

What can you do to develop the virtue of kindness in your heart?

If you'd like, write a prayer that reflects what God is trying to teach you about the virtue of kindness.

A simple act of kindness can change the world.
MATILDA RAFFA CUOMO

Generosity

His Promise

Give, and you will receive.
Luke 6:38

My Prayer

O Generous God, empower me with
a spirit of deep generosity,
then generously allow me to reap
in like measure.
Then I can give again.

Generosity: With Courage

One man gives freely, yet gains even more.
Proverbs 11:24, NIV

Money was on my mind when I sat down to try to reflect on generosity. But immediately I knew I was off track. To be sure, money is one component of generosity, but hardly the first or most important. Why? For one thing, God owns everything (Psalm 50:10).

The least of what He owns, however, is money. As well, God's greatest generosity is about the gift of His Son. A priceless gift, for certain.

But what about the rest of us? To be generous, what kind of people must we be? Good-hearted and loving? Or bighearted and kind? Such traits are key. But topping my list, when it comes to generosity, is Spirit-empowered courage. A lack of fear, yes, but also trust in the all-sufficiency of God—allows otherwise tightfisted people to let go and give back. When we fearlessly trust God to provide all of our needs, we demonstrate that, in giving, we are confident we won't be left not having enough.

Giving without fear. Are you giving like that?

Or are you stingy—believing that, in giving, you'll be left holding a half-empty bag? I'm aware of such people because I've been one myself. Over the years, when I was asked by pastors to tithe or by family members to lend, my first reaction was to question the request. In the end, I might give but always reluctantly. Or with limits. Or not at all.

As my prayer life keeps turning, however, and I focus not on getting things—but on getting changed—I'm surprised to discover that by seeking in prayer to know God, I end up empowered to trust God. And with trusting God comes the courage to trust Him enough to give *and let go*. Should we give wisely? Of course. Should we give prudently? Absolutely. But to give fearlessly—understanding that in giving we gain—is the best and blessed giving of all. 🌿

No one has ever become poor by giving.
ANNE FRANK

Generosity: As God Gives

For God loved the world so much that he gave.
John 3:16

Why be generous? Because God is—and so is everything God created. Charles Spurgeon, the great nineteenth-century Baptist preacher, explained this principle in his unique way: Flowers in bloom give their fragrance—and "all the rivers run into the sea."

Generously.

Spurgeon went on: "The sea feeds the clouds, the clouds empty out their treasures, the earth gives back the rain in fertility, and so it is an endless chain of giving generosity." Spurgeon further declared: "Generosity reigns supreme in nature. There is nothing in this world but lives by giving, except a covetous man, and such a man is a piece of grit in the machinery; he is out of gear with the universe."

His insight should alert any of us still hanging on to what we don't own in the first place—our time and talents, our property and purses. Such a person, says Spurgeon, "is a wheel running in the opposite direction to the wheels of God's great engine. . . . He is out of date; he is out of place; he is out of God's order altogether."

No surprise, indeed, that God rewards generosity. It reflects the nature of God. "The cheerful giver," Spurgeon adds, "is marching to the music of the spheres. He is in order with God's great natural laws, and God, therefore, loves him, since he sees his own work in him."

Many arguments could be made for withholding our gifts. God could've made such arguments Himself. Yet God so loved the world—the ungrateful, sinful, selfish, disappointing world—that He gave.

What a powerful model for anybody dealing with ungrateful, sinful, selfish, disappointing people. We should not withhold our best from others. When they're at their worst, we can give our best—and for one reason only. That's how God gave to us. 🔥

Let us learn, then, from the analogy of nature, the great lesson,
that to get, we must give.
CHARLES SPURGEON

Generosity: For the Good

The generous will prosper; those who refresh others
will themselves be refreshed.
Proverbs 11:25

What the world needs now is a bounty of . . . refreshment?

In a weary world filled with poverty, crime, despair, and all manner of evil and sin, why would the psalmist promote refreshment? I ponder this irony: the Bible's teachings on generosity often focus less on the tangible than on blessings intangible.

Like refreshment.

Like the phone call I received yesterday from a church friend. She'd missed me at the Sunday service because I stayed home with a head cold. Her call, late on Sunday afternoon, to say kind things—*I missed you, I'm praying for you*—lifted my spirits and, in fact, refreshed my soul. The next day, I felt measurably better. Refreshed, indeed.

Did it cost her anything to pick up the phone and call? It took time. But as we chatted, she shared a concern about one of her adult children—and I offered the answer she seemed to need. "Thank you!" she said as our chat drew to a close. "That's just what I needed to hear!" That is, she'd called me to offer her generous concern, but by the end of our chat, she was refreshed in return.

Theologian John Calvin explained the ironies of generosity this way: "There cannot be a surer rule, nor a stronger exhortation to the observance of it, than when we are taught that all the endowments which we possess are divine deposits entrusted to us for the very purpose of being distributed for the good of our neighbor."

Jesus said this: "Give as freely as you have received!" (Matthew 10:8).

Can we give all the time? Or give all we have?

Of course not. Yet we each can give more—more consistently and with a greater appreciation for Him who gave His all. When I give that way, somebody else will get blessed with refreshment. But often the first somebody is me. 🌿

For it is in giving that we receive.
SAINT FRANCIS OF ASSISI

Generosity: With Little

Then a poor widow came and dropped in two small coins.
Mark 12:42

Do we give God enough? Tough question. How do we measure it?

Jesus offers an answer. He says look at the poor widow and her two small coins. In fact, I think I saw her just the other night. After a program at my church, the audience was asked to leave donations for the nonprofit sponsor of the event.

I stood to attention. Serving as an usher that night, I'd help collect the offering—thinking there would be a lot because the evening program was outstanding. A renowned keynote speaker and a soaring one-hundred-voice community choir drew hundreds from across the city.

But now it was time to collect money. I noticed, however, that only a few people leaving the event were dropping in donations. Still, I held out the offering plate. Not judging. Just serving. Or so I tried. Then I noticed a middle-aged woman, slowed by heavy leg braces, making her way up the center aisle of the church. Finally stopping to face my offering plate, she greeted me with an accent that, to me, sounded African. Then, as she smiled, she opened a worn purse and dug to the bottom for what seemed like endless minutes before finally lifting out a few coins. With a look of joy and grace, she placed her few coins in the offering plate, told me thank you, and turned slowly to leave.

The widow's two coins? Here was a picture of that story in real time. Later, I read Jesus' words: "I assure you, this poor widow has given more than all the others" (v. 43). Thinking of the woman in leg braces and the effort she made to walk out of the church, stop to search her purse, then to give with thanksgiving what appeared to be a portion of her meager possessions, I realized her gift clearly totaled more than those others had so casually given.

More is a subjective measurement, of course. But when the measurer is Christ, may He help us all today to be on the blessing side of the ledger. ❧

When we come to the end of life, the question will be, "How much have you given?" not "How much have you gotten?"
GEORGE SWEETING

Generosity: With Much

*But who am I, and who are my people, that we should be able
to give as generously as this?*
1 Chronicles 29:14, NIV

Mother Teresa of Calcutta inspired millions by serving the poor. She may
have done more, however, by teaching the lessons of generosity to the rich.
In America, for example, she saw consumerism run wild—even among those
who desired to help the needy. Thus, a story is told about an obviously
wealthy woman who came to visit Mother Teresa in the slums of Calcutta.
This rich woman was known to love fancy *saris*, spending eight hundred
dollars on each—while Mother Teresa, in contrast, might spend barely eight
dollars.

Then the rich woman asked an amazing question: "How can I help the
poor?"

Draped in jewels and silks, she asked: "How can I help the poor?"

Wearing designer shoes and carrying a custom handbag, she asked:
"How can I help the poor?"

Wafting in the scent of costly perfumes and luxury cosmetics, she asked:
"How can I help the poor?"

As the story goes, Mother Teresa, with love, simply told this perplexed
rich woman: "Next time you buy a sari, buy a 700-dollar one and take 100
dollars and give it to the poor." As author David Scott, a biographer of
Mother Teresa, says: "And you watch the slow progression of the woman—
she's not consuming as much and giving more away. I think that would be
her answer: if we have to live in a consumerist society, consume the least
amount you can and give all you don't need to the poor."

Or as King David of the Bible prays to God: "But who am I, and who are
my people, that we should be able to give as generously as this? *Everything
comes from you, and we have given you only what comes from your hand*"
(1 Chronicles 29:14, italics added).

We have all that we need, that is, to help the poor. It comes from God.
And what we don't need, let's give it away. ❧

If you can't feed a hundred people, then feed just one.
MOTHER TERESA

Generosity: Without Grudging

Give freely without begrudging it, and the LORD your God will bless you in everything you do.
Deuteronomy 15:10

Big givers seem rare. Like the NFL athlete who donates half his Super Bowl winner's paycheck to charity. The never-married secretary who steadily banks her paychecks, finally—in old age—donating millions to a college. Such stories make news.

The Bible, however, teaches that giving freely—without begrudging—is the normal and blessed state of affairs. As Moses told the children of Israel, "There will always be some among you who are poor. That is why I am commanding you to share your resources freely with the poor and with other Israelites in need" (Deuteronomy 15:11). Give freely, therefore, without "a grudging heart," says the Bible. "Then because of this the LORD your God will bless you in all your work and in everything you put your hand to" (v. 10, NIV).

Ah, yes—the grudging factor.

We fall short there. Or I should speak for myself. I fall short. My husband, in fact, has just asked me to give away free copies of my latest book to yet another of his friends. Just two books. Not enough to blink. Still, I stand in line at the post office, not with joy, but with resentment—as if these two books were gold. As if I owned them. As if I inspired them and not our inspiring God.

But the next morning, while writing this reflection, I stopped. Looking to heaven, I cried to the Lord to kick out the grudge with His grace, and also gratitude. And generosity. Then I called my publisher to order more books. Not to sell but to give away freely. Without the grudge. But who gets the glory? The true Giver. May we bless Him with generosity not stained by grudge. 🕯

I have found that among its other benefits,
giving liberates the soul of the giver.
MAYA ANGELOU

Going Deeper

Freely you have received, freely give.
Matthew 10:8, NIV

Describe your giving. Is it offered freely or grudgingly?

Reflecting deeper, what is stopping you from giving generously
as the Lord requires?

Invite the Holy Spirit to show you ways to change your giving so it more
reflects Christ.

If you'd like, write a prayer that reflects what God is trying to teach you
about the virtue of generosity.

Giving back involves a certain amount of giving up.
COLIN POWELL

PEACE

His Promise

The Lord blesses his people with peace.
Psalm 29:11, NIV

My Prayer

In this world of strife, confusion, and chaos,
bless us to see not the problems—
but Your power to replace
our struggles with Your peace.

Peace: Like God

For he himself is our peace.
Ephesians 2:14, NIV

It's a sunny winter morning. I haven't read the morning's newspaper. Yet, like most of us, I can predict what's on the front page. Despair, destruction, and death—more than any one day should bear. Still, I head down to the kitchen to fix oatmeal. Before I can eat, however, I feel conflict. Brewing and bubbling. Sure enough, on this day, a group of politicians is questioning a popular children's charity about its salaries. Blogs are hopping over the charges, guns blazing. "All crooks!" shouts one blogger. "Every one of these organizations for kids. *Crooks!*"

And it's barely 8 a.m.

The day's strife, however, starts long before sunrise. Divorce. Drugs. Suicide. War. Weapons. Scandal. Hatred. And so it goes. All day. Every day. This same chaos was just as common in the early church. When the apostle Paul wrote his letter to the Ephesians, the body of Christ had withstood bloody persecutions and false teachers alike. But their besieged spirits were lacking peace. Thus, Paul warns them: "Don't let the sun go down while you are still angry." His reason is simple: "For anger gives a mighty foothold to the devil" (Ephesians 4:26-27).

But Paul offers the better way. Choose Christ. Take a deep breath, breathing in His Spirit. *For He Himself is our peace.* As Paul puts it: He "made the two one and has destroyed the barrier, the dividing wall of hostility" (Ephesians 2:14, NIV).

Paul is writing here to Christians about fights between Jews and Gentiles. But the principle fits all. Jesus is Peace. No need to look elsewhere. No need to seek love, approval, drugs, sex, power to find the peace He offers over chaos.

What will you choose today? The devil's foothold—or Christ's calm?

Bless God by choosing Christ. His peace will empower you with blessings untold. ❧

God cannot give us a happiness and peace apart from Himself,
because it is not there.
C. S. LEWIS

Peace: With God

Submit to God, and you will have peace.
Job 22:21

First she lost her house. Then she lost her job. Then a long-standing health problem flared up, leaving my friend's body weary, her bank account empty, and her spirits broken. In this storm she dared ask God an angry question: "Why *me*, Lord?" Her tears fell hard. "I mean, why *me*? And how much more am I supposed to take!" Her questions, she realized later, echoed those asked by Job when the "blameless" Old Testament man lost everything—his sons and daughters, his livestock, and his good health. In painful skin sores, head to toe, he pleaded to God: "What have I done to you?" Or as he put it: "Why have you made me your target?" (Job 7:20, NIV).

With that, Job cried his way through a tortured discourse on the nature of God and the futility of man: "How can a mortal be righteous before God? . . . Who has resisted Him and come out unscathed?" (Job 9:2, 4, NIV). Or as he added: "Who can say to him, 'What are you doing?' . . . How then can I dispute with him? How can I find words to argue with him?'" (Job 9:12, 14, TNIV). The book of Job is, indeed, a classic exploration of the questions that mere mortals dare to ask an unquestionable God. The journey, however, leads to a vital conclusion:

That despite God's love for us, God is still God. God alone. Or as the Lord said to Job: "Who has a claim against me that I must pay?" (Job 41:11, NIV). To be sure, God isn't some arbitrary, capricious dictator. Job finally repented for daring to suggest it. Instead, as he heeded the advice of his friend—to stop quarreling with God and be at peace with Him—things went well for Job.

With a renewed heart, Job even prayed for his friends. Then "the LORD restored his fortunes," giving him "twice as much as before!" (Job 42:10). My friend, as well, stopped asking, Why me? Making peace with God, she started praising Him again—not for fixing her problems, but for blessing her with the power of His Son—our peaceful Solution. 🌿

Any hurt is worth it that puts us on the path of peace.
EUGENE PETERSON

Peace: Of Mind

But the LORD said to him, "Peace! Do not be afraid."
Judges 6:23, NIV

Mighty warriors aren't wimps. We're not supposed to be, anyway. But in this story, the doubting wheat farmer Gideon is skittish, frightened, and nervous. First, the local bad guys, the Midianites, are running roughshod over his people—camping on their land, ruining their crops, racing their camels over hearth and hill and home, and scaring Gideon half out of his wits.

In the midst of it all, an angel of the Lord appears to Gideon and addresses him as "mighty warrior" (Judges 6:12, NIV).

Is Gideon honored? No. He answers with doubts. "But sir," as he puts it, "if the LORD is with us, why has all this happened to us? Where are all his wonders?" (v. 13, NIV).

The complaints are another way for Gideon to say what he truly means: *I'm a wimp—and I'm afraid.* A mighty warrior? *No way.* Or in Gideon's case, he keeps begging for proof, finally crying, "I am doomed!"

Fear sounds like that, and it's at the heart, for sure, of much of our worry. So God Himself finally cuts Gideon off with one word:

Peace.

When we heed this order—choosing peace despite feeling everything but peaceful—God responds by calming our situation. Notice the order here. God doesn't step in to calm us before our problems turn to peace. In reverse order, we first invite in God's peace. *Then* God steps in, calming our fears—easing our troubled minds.

We see that same lesson in the New Testament when the apostle Paul tells the church at Philippi to turn from worry by thinking instead about good, pure, and noble things. "Then the God of peace will be with you" (Philippians 4:6-9).

Not the other way around. Think peace first. By faith. Invite peace in. By faith. Walk in peace. By faith. Then the God of peace makes His empowered presence our blessed reward. 🔥

The war is over.
JERRY BRIDGES

Peace: In the World

Blessed are the peacemakers, for they will be called children of God.
Matthew 5:9, TNIV

Two friends on Facebook are panicked. They live in Jos, Nigeria, and as they write, their town is awash in murder, blood, and violence. "Our city was a battleground last week—and it will continue sporadically in future except a lasting solution is found." That's how the young husband, a devoted Christian, describes the situation in his Facebook entry.

A week earlier, his young pregnant wife's comments showed sheer terror. "Am losing my mind," she wrote. "Am so afraid. I need prayers. GOD PLEASE HELP US."

Her horror was justified. Thousands have died in and around Jos in religious and ethnic violence, according to Human Rights Watch, since military rule in the area ended in 1999. Then on a bloody Sunday in 2010, upwards of four hundred died in machete and gunfire attacks by Muslims against Christians—a reprisal for attacks by Christians against Muslims a few weeks before. In that firestorm, three hundred were massacred and a mosque was torched. Watching broadcasts and reading the news, I tried to make sense of a situation where neighbors were killing neighbors, even hacking and burning alive pregnant women, children, and babies. Soon I got the gist of it. In a fertile area where Christians and Muslims once worked and lived together, now poverty and discrimination—with Muslim settlers left out of opportunity—have turned Nigeria's countryside into an ethnic powder keg. Revenge and reprisal. Blame on blame. An endless cycle.

Who could change things? The Bible writes a clear prescription: a peacemaker. In praying about this situation, I decided to overlook the endless charges and countercharges, searching instead for a voice of hope. Finally, buried in one story, I found one: "We are against this crime," said one politician, a former senator. "We don't want any blood shed anymore. We want to live in peace as we used to live, both Christian and Muslims." A peacemaker, yes. So now, O God, *bless him.* 🕊

> To be of a peaceable spirit brings peace along with it.
> THOMAS WATSON

Peace: In the City

*And those who are peacemakers will plant seeds of peace
and reap a harvest of righteousness.*
James 3:18

It was called the Boston Miracle. After years of fighting and murders, two of Boston's most dangerous street gangs met in the summer of 2006 and called a truce. The meeting—moderated by pastors, social workers, and Boston police officers and held at the John F. Kennedy Presidential Library—had immediate effect. Shootings in the two gangs' neighborhoods dropped dramatically in the first six months after the meeting.

Even better, according to the *Boston Globe*, "Within days of the two gangs shaking hands on the treaty, members of other gangs began contacting clergy and youth workers to ask for similar peace summits."

Peace reaps peace, just as the Bible promises. Or as one truce organizer said of the gang members: "They were ready to lay it down. They just didn't have the mechanism in place." That mechanism—including weekly meetings with clergy and incentives such as tutoring and tickets to Celtics games—helped maintain a nearly three-year stretch without deadly violence between the rival gangs.

And, no, the peace hasn't held totally. But the effort proves what the Bible has long promised. When peacemakers plant peace, a harvest of righteousness grows.

Said one police official: "I don't think there will ever be a strategy for dealing with gangs in Boston again that doesn't involve a truce. They don't want to be afraid. They don't want to shoot each other."

Peace, that is, isn't some lightweight, everybody-hold-hands-and-be-nice response to conflict. Peace is power. Planting peace saves lives, yes. But more than that, planting peace *changes* lives. For the better. For the right. For the good. For God. 🌿

Lord, make me an instrument of Thy peace. Where there is hatred,
let me sow love; where there is injury, pardon.
SAINT FRANCIS OF ASSISI

Peace: In Our Churches

*And those who are peacemakers will plant seeds of peace
and reap a harvest of righteousness.*
James 3:18

Peace begets peace. Even between pastors. That's what happened in Boston, where rival gangs challenged rival pastors to end their "clergy wars."

In fact, prominent pastors vying for national media attention and government sponsorships for their antigang work had themselves become bitter rivals. Three key pastors, in particular, "were barely speaking to one another," reported the *Boston Globe*. Or as one of the three told the newspaper, "Youths on the street were saying to pastors, 'How can you tell us to squash things when you all can't get along?'"

To break that cycle—and renew peace in their churches and their city—some one hundred clergy gathered at a nighttime prayer meeting where the themes were repentance, forgiveness, and unity.

"Anything to bring about reconciliation between pastors who have not really been talking, have not been on the same page, needs to happen for the sake of the community," said one of the pastors. As he put it: "If pastors are willing to put their beefs away, then that gives us the authority to speak to young people who are still beefing."

After praying for nearly three hours, the pastors stayed to talk over a meal. Some, according to the *Globe*, "quietly approached others and asked forgiveness for any past slights." Planting seeds. Believing in a harvest of righteousness.

What a glorious work for a church and her members. As we plant peace within our walls—pew to pew, pastor to pastor, choir to choir, altar to altar—the harvest grows. "We live in a mirror society," said one Boston pastor. "Prayerfully," he added, "this will trickle down to our young folks to help combat the violence." A good harvest, yes.

And let God's church say amen. 🔥

The more fractured we are, the greater we become spectacles to the world.
The more we are united in love, the more the world sees Christ.
CURTIS C. THOMAS

Going Deeper

May the Lord of peace himself give you his peace at all times.
2 Thessalonians 3:16

When your life is peaceful, how do you feel?

In what area of your life do you most desire peace?

Reflecting deeper, what is stopping you from living in peace as the Lord requires?

Invite the Holy Spirit to show you ways to find more peace in Christ.

If you'd like, write a prayer that reflects what God is trying to teach you about the virtue of peace.

Peace is not merely a distant goal that we seek, but a means
by which we arrive at that goal.
MARTIN LUTHER KING JR.

PATIENCE

His Promise

I am slow to anger and filled with unfailing love.
Exodus 34:6

My Prayer

For Your forbearance, Lord, I bow before You.
Strengthen me to demonstrate great patience
as a way to honor You.

Patience: Like God

I am slow to anger.
Exodus 34:6

Is God patient? Yes, even when we don't deserve it. Or especially when we don't deserve it. That is the real truth of what it means to be patient like God. I reflect on that as I stand in a long line at the airport. I wait with my husband almost an hour, in fact, for a regional airline to send a ticket clerk to check in the passengers.

Tempers are flaring. "This is ridiculous!" one traveler complains. Others chime in. So I listen, trying to hear. But what are they really saying? That they are angry. And feeling neglected—paying customers without a server.

Imagine, then, how God must feel. He gave His all but can't find helpers to spread His gospel, to serve in His name. We could imagine that, yes.

Or we could read today's Bible story. Lots of anger marks this story, in fact. First, the children of Israel get impatient with Moses, but also with God, turning on Him by creating an idol god of gold—in the shape of a calf—to worship. In return, God gets angry with His children. *Let Me at them*, God rages. But Moses pleads for them, asking God to show Himself "so I may understand you more fully" (Exodus 33:13).

To this provocative request, God passes in front of Moses, calling out His own name. "I am the LORD, I am the LORD, the merciful and gracious God. *I am slow to anger* and rich in unfailing love and faithfulness" (Exodus 34:6, italics added). Moreover, God said He forgives "every kind of sin and rebellion" (v. 7).

But what about us? Are we as patient as God? At airports? With family? With friends? With life? When our patience isn't deserved? When we haven't called on God's Spirit to indwell us with His patience? We should ask, not to look godly patient ourselves, but to reflect God's nature. He is slow to anger. Rich in unfailing love. That's what other people need today from you and me. Not our talk about God. But our behavior. Few things show God better than patience. And few things bless others more. 🔥

The key to everything is patience.
ARNOLD GLASOW

Patience: With Church

*So accept each other just as Christ has accepted you;
then God will be glorified.*
Romans 15:7

Even in church, not all people get along. No surprise, in the fledgling church at Rome, Jews and Gentiles were tense factions. So the apostle Paul wrote them one letter. A tough letter. Tough to write. Tough to read.

Tougher to swallow.

But be patient with each other, Paul wrote.

Patient with somebody who eats the "wrong" food? Pays the "wrong" taxes? Believes the wrong kind of gospel?

Exactly, Paul wrote. So be patient. "For even Christ didn't please himself" (v. 3). Christ's self-denial, with His sacrificial love on our behalf, is our example, Paul added.

"So accept each other just as Christ has accepted you." Look at the blessing. "Then God will be glorified" (v. 7).

We think that patience is a gift we give others, period.

However, according to Paul, our patience for others in church glorifies God, reminding outsiders that God is great. Or as Paul said in verse 5, "May God, who gives this patience and encouragement, help you live in complete harmony with each other."

What a gift. *Complete harmony.* Indeed, what a promise. A church that demonstrates complete harmony is a living advertisement for the glory of God. *Look what God can do!* He can empower people who probably shouldn't get along to work together. "Each with the attitude of Christ Jesus toward the other" (v. 5).

Is patience easy? Of course not. The root of the word, the Latin *patiens*, means to suffer. In hospitals, the suffering are called just that—the patients. Yet we can pray for God to bless us with the patience to forbear others, just as Christ forbears us. Thus, let us pray for patience for one reason only—so God gets all the glory. What do we get? The blessing of harmony. 🌿

A Christian without patience is like a soldier without arms.
THOMAS WATSON

Patience: In Families

And remember, our Lord's patience gives people time to be saved.
2 Peter 3:15

She prayed. For seventeen years, she prayed. The heartbroken Monica—whose rebellious, carousing, worldly son is known as Saint Augustine—prayed with a patience that is legendary. Let my son turn, she prayed, from the sins of the world and embrace Christ. Her story remains so inspiring, in fact, that it reminds any parent of a prodigal child, sibling, or loved one that it pays to be patient.

Her example also shows, however, that patience—just like its definition—is long-suffering. For Monica, that meant suffering, not only over her son, but also over an unsaved husband with a violent temper—and an equally difficult mother-in-law. Her household was ripe for turmoil, upheaval, conflict, and pain.

With patience, however, Monica believed and prayed for a better outcome. Even when she couldn't see it. Even when she was ridiculed. Even when she was shunned. According to historical accounts, not even church leaders thought her prayers would be answered, some turning from her when she begged yet again for their prayers.

Then finally one religious leader conceded: "It is not possible that the son of so many tears should perish."

When her last tears fell, and the dust settled, everybody in Monica's household accepted Christ—yes, her husband, his mother, and all three of her children, including her most rebellious offspring, the thirty-three-year-old Augustine. In his best-known writing, his *Confessions*, he declared: "You have made us for yourself, Lord, and our hearts are restless until they rest in you." Would he have come to such certainty without the prayers of a patient mother? Perhaps. God can do anything, even save rebellious children and worrying parents. But why not show faith in God by praying for lost loved ones, not to mention praying for yourself. How? Patiently. God understands such prayers. They bless people with time to be saved. ❧

Patience is the companion of wisdom.
SAINT AUGUSTINE

Patience: By the Spirit

But when the Holy Spirit controls our lives, he will produce
this kind of fruit in us: love, joy . . . patience.
Galatians 5:22

So, you don't like suffering in patience? You're not alone. The Bible itself makes it clear—the virtue of patience doesn't come naturally.

In our natural state, instead, the apostle Paul writes, we produce all sorts of sadness. His list of that sadness is long: "Sexual immorality, impure thoughts . . . idolatry, participation in demonic activities, hostility, quarreling, jealousy, outbursts of anger, selfish ambition, divisions, the feeling that everyone is wrong except those in your own little group, envy, drunkenness, wild parties, and other kinds of sin" (vv. 19-21).

A long list, yes. Then he tacks on the consequence—"anyone living that sort of life will not inherit the Kingdom of God" (v. 21).

A stern warning. For in this case, he was writing to the churches in Galatia, a Roman province where new Christians were divided over doctrine. Were they saved by keeping all the Jewish laws, as some argued? Or, as Paul taught, by believing in Jesus Christ?

In fact, Paul taught that when the Holy Spirit controls our lives, not only are we saved for eternity, we produce a harvest of holy fruit—patience included—right now.

It's not human fruit, to be sure. Instead, patience is birthed by surrendering our lives to God's Spirit—and living by His Spirit. Day by day.

In fact, that takes the pressure off. When I stop trying to be patient and ask the Holy Spirit to control me instead, I don't create the fruit of patience—the Holy Spirit produces the harvest within me. He's our fruit cultivator. But He must be invited to the field of our hearts. So invite Him. Let Him plow, seed, water. Blast away weeds. Then bless Him with a Spirit-blessed harvest: more patience for a hungry world. 🌿

Care less for your harvest than for how it is shared.
KENT NERBURN

Patience: Under Pressure

We give great honor to those who endure under suffering.
James 5:11

Doctors called it impossible. Four weeks after a Haitian shop clerk was buried alive during a crushing earthquake, he was pulled alive from the rubble of the marketplace where he worked. His feet suffered wounds, and he was severely dehydrated and malnourished. Otherwise, he was fine. Expected to fully recover.

"This is just unbelievable," Dr. Barth Green, a Miami neurosurgeon who cofounded Project Medishare for Haiti, told reporters, "because to our knowledge, nobody has ever survived this long and the rescue efforts were called off almost two weeks ago."

What made the difference? "His family never gave up," Dr. Green said. His mother confirmed just that. "I stayed strong. I thought that I would find him."

Patience? Or a miracle? Or both? How else to explain the unidentified person "giving me water," as the man told doctors? In any case, the man kept waiting for help. Patient and believing.

It's the way we can wait. Believing God will move. Believing prayers will be answered. Letting the Holy Spirit empower our waiting with stubborn confidence, grit, and faith. Why, indeed, shouldn't we wait that way?

Patience under pressure. It is honorable, wrote James, the brother of Jesus. He was encouraging those in the early church at Jerusalem who were eager for the Lord's return.

But keep enduring, James urged, and his words still speak today. As the relief doctor in Haiti said of the patient clerk, "I think he's set a world record. . . . It'll be quite a story when fully told."

So it can be with us. Let it be said that we didn't give up on God. Not this generation. While others fainted, we failed not. Not today. Not tomorrow. Not forever.

> When a man has quietly made up his mind that there is nothing he cannot endure, his fears leave him.
> GROVE PATTERSON

Patience: In the World

But that is why God had mercy on me, so that Christ Jesus could use me as a prime example of his great patience.
1 Timothy 1:16

"You're a *Christian*?" Yes I am. That's how I answered this college student in a class I taught. Yes, I'm a Christian. She seemed amazed. But also put off. "Christians are always so *pushy*." She frowned deeper. "And *so* impatient."

"In fact, you're right," I agreed. "Some Christians *are* pushy." Impatient, too, I said.

Not easy to admit. But the pushy, impatient Christian is now a too-common fixture in every corner of the world. Eager to draw others to Christ, we push them away by our impatience.

Perhaps we'd do well to recall the apostle Paul's reminder, in his letter to Timothy, that first God was patient with each of us. True, Paul writes, Jesus came into the world to save sinners, "and I was the worst of them all" (v. 15). But that's why God had mercy on me, he adds. "So that Christ Jesus could use me as a prime example of his great patience with even the worst sinners" (v. 16).

Great patience? With even the worst?

Exactly, Paul says. Great patience is precisely what the world needs from those of us longing to offer them Christ. In my own life, to be sure, I could function as a "pushy" Christian—impatient with friends, family, students, and others who haven't accepted Christ or who, like me, love the Lord but still sometimes love the things of the world.

Yet show patience, Paul writes. Great patience. Like God's patience. "Then others will realize that they, too, can believe in him and receive eternal life" (v. 16).

In that way, patience blooms like a refreshing blessing for those who expect condemnation for bad choices, sinful lives, and lost living. Instead, when we offer Christ, we would remember to also offer what He first gave us. His patience. More than enough. 🔥

There are three indispensable requirements for a missionary.
1. Patience. 2. Patience. 3. Patience.
HUDSON TAYLOR

Going Deeper

We prove ourselves by our purity, . . . our patience, our kindness.
2 Corinthians 6:6

Are you in a hurry about something? Or for God to do something?
If so, why is it so hard for you to wait?

After reflecting on patience this week, what can you do to give God more
time to act in your life? In the lives of those you know and love?

How would more patience change your relationship with the Lord?

If you'd like, write a prayer that surrenders to God your needs concerning
the virtue of patience.

Just pray for a tough hide and a tender heart.
RUTH BELL GRAHAM

FORGIVENESS

His Promise

I have swept away your sins like the morning mists.
I have scattered your offenses like the clouds.
Isaiah 44:22

My Prayer

I am swept into glory, O God,
by Your precious forgiveness of me.
Now help me bless others with the same
golden gift.

Forgiveness: By God

I show this unfailing love . . . by forgiving every kind of sin and rebellion.
Exodus 34:7

The girls in the jail were excited but subdued. It was their GED graduation day. But as teenage felons, they weren't graduating from jail. Most still had months, and some years, left to serve for their serious crimes. As their graduation speaker, what could I possibly say that would fit the occasion but also match their reality?

After praying and asking the Holy Spirit for help—especially since public speaking is its own challenge—I was intrigued when the perfect topic for my speech came to mind. Forgiveness.

My aim? To show the power of forgiveness to heal so we can move on. So I told the Bible story about Jesus and the lame man at the healing pool at Bethesda. One day, after the man had been lying there for thirty-eight years, Jesus asked him, "Would you *like* to get well?" (John 5:6, italics added). I wanted to show, first, that seeking forgiveness is a choice—that to forgive an old hurt or to forgive oneself is also like saying to Jesus, "Yes! I *would* like to be healed." Also, however, I sought to assure the girls in lockup that God forgives sin. Every kind of sin.

As I shared about God's healing forgiveness, many in the audience—girls, parents, and administrators—wiped away tears. It seemed the Holy Spirit was blessing us all with the reminder to forgive ourselves. So I closed with a gentle dare: "Look in the mirror tonight," I said. "Then tell yourself *you are forgiven.*" God loves you, I added. It was time now to move on.

A few weeks later I got an envelope of thank-you letters from the girls. "I really needed to hear this," one girl wrote. "I even told my sister about it." Many said similar things. The whole experience reminded me that, when it comes to forgiveness, the first thing to know—whether we seek forgiveness or whether we need to forgive—is that God forgives first. Every kind of sin. My worst. Your worst. He wants to bless you and me that way today.

Will you let Him? As you answer yes, you will bless His Spirit with your love. 🌿

Your own sins, no matter how big, are not bigger
than God's pleasure in forgiveness.
EDWARD T. WELCH

Forgiveness: For My Soul

If you forgive others, you will be forgiven. If you give . . .
your gift will return to you in full measure.
Luke 6:37-38

He was standing at the foot of a mountain. Large crowds, from all over Judea and as far north as Tyre and Sidon, gathered around Him. They were waiting on Jesus. Waiting for His teaching. His touch. His healing. But Jesus wanted to give more. He wanted them to know how to give love. So He taught them His Beatitudes—His lessons on loving enemies and His teachings on being compassionate. More than anything on that day, however, Jesus taught lost people the principle of forgiveness.

When we forgive, we get back. How exactly? When we forgive, we are forgiven in return by God. Yet many Christians, when teaching this principle, teach it in the negative. If we *don't* forgive, they say, God won't forgive us. To be sure, Jesus taught forgiveness from that perspective, especially in the context of prayer. Forgive first, *then* pray (Matthew 6:15).

In the Sermon on the Mount, however, Jesus taught about forgiveness from the perspective of blessings. If you forgive, you will be forgiven. And if you give, "you will receive . . . in full measure, pressed down, shaken together to make room for more, and running over."

I try to think of it this way: Jesus said forgive. *Then I can bless you beyond measure.* But why this request from God? Perhaps our heavenly Father wants us to know how hard forgiving is, so we appreciate just how much the Lord offers when He forgives us.

The process of forgiveness takes work. Jesus went to Calvary's cruel cross so we could be forgiven. And in return may we do what He asked on the mountain—forgive others. Then may He bless us for this hard work. But not a little, O God. When we forgive wounds and hurts, bless us a lot. Blessings running over. What a wonder for us. And what empowered glory for You. 🌿

Because we are the most forgiven people in the world, we should be
the most forgiving people in the world.
C. J. MAHANEY

Forgiveness: For God

For the honor of your name, O LORD, forgive my many, many sins.
Psalm 25:11

I grew up black in the fifties—and Jim Crow was alive and well. So in the South, while visiting family, I couldn't sit in seats on the main floor of movie theaters, try on clothing and shoes in department stores, drink from water fountains with signs that shouted "Whites Only"—and I couldn't dream. Hate stops it.

So in return, I hated back. Even as a churchgoing Christian from birth, I thought all white people were bad. I tried hard to convince myself, anyway.

Years later, however, in my forties, the clogging burden of unforgiveness overwhelmed me. Desperate for healing, I sought the Lord's help in learning to forgive. It was cathartic, of course. Releasing burdens feels luxurious. We breathe better when we're forgiven. We breathe even better, however, when we forgive.

But why does God provide such an amazing gift? To mere human beings—who can remember the past with all its hurts and wrongs but can't change any of it—why would a Holy God offer this divine remedy called forgiveness? So we can feel better? In fact, yes.

But a greater reason prevails.

God forgives because it blesses and glorifies Him. The psalmist affirms it: "For the honor of your name, O LORD, forgive my many, many sins." God's reputation, that is, is elevated by the fact that He forgives. But also, when we forgive others, God is glorified—by our obedience and by our love.

A popular bumper sticker on the cars of countless Christians simply states it with one word: *Forgiven.* In my own life, forgiving racial wounds blessed and changed my life. But forgiving others, as some have told me, blessed and changed them more. Still, the healing wasn't just for us. When we forgive, it counts most for God. 🖋

Evangelism and reconciliation are two sides of the same message.
BRENDA SALTER MCNEIL

Forgiveness: For Love

Love prospers when a fault is forgiven, but dwelling on it
separates close friends.
Proverbs 17:9

They sit at long tables on folding chairs. Many are crying. As mothers of murdered children, they bear pain too deep to imagine. Living in a gang-ravaged neighborhood, they witness ongoing violence as still more children die. Moreover, at every turn, they are pressured to forgive. Some can't do it.

"It's too hard," one young mother sobs. "My *son is dead*. He'll never walk this earth again. I know the Lord says forgive, but why should I forgive *that*?"

Her question, asked in the fellowship hall of a Denver church, cuts the atmosphere like a knife. I've come to talk about forgiveness. But this is no casual discussion group. These mothers hurt. To the core. Why, indeed, should they forgive?

When it is my turn to talk, I dare to try to offer some key reasons. That forgiveness is not about the person who hurts us—not at first, anyway. That we forgive to get healed. Then, when we're ready, God offers His amazing remedy. Forgiveness. As important, however, we forgive *for* God—especially to reconnect with God. So forgiveness blesses God—showing we trust God enough to handle the injustice of the awful thing that happened. Then we move on, to serving God and blessing His Kingdom.

Oh, I prayed this was right.

I believe it is. As the late theologian Lewis Smedes wrote in his beautiful book *The Art of Forgiving*, "As we start on the miracle of forgiving, we begin to see our enemy through a cleaner lens, less smudged by hate. We begin to see a real person . . . a human being created to be a child of God."

Will we become close friends with the person who wronged us? Only God knows. But either way, with forgiveness, we *will* renew our friendship with God. And what a friend. His love is too precious for any hurt to come between His Spirit and ours. 🕯

Forgiveness brings great joy, not only to the forgiven,
but especially to the forgiver.
PHILIP GRAHAM RYKEN

Forgiveness: For Life

*Even if he wrongs you seven times a day and each time turns again
and asks forgiveness, forgive him.*
Luke 17:4

The best way to forgive? Learn the process. That's what the late Lewis
Smedes, a professor at Fuller Seminary, advised in *The Art of Forgiving*. In
fact, that's why he wrote it: "To clear up some false notions":

> Like the notion that if we forgive someone we are virtually inviting
> him to wallop us again. Or that if we forgive what he did we are
> implying that what happened was not all that bad. Or that if we
> forgive someone for doing us wrong we are exempting him from the
> demands of justice. Or that if we forgive we are expected to go back
> into the old relationship that he ruined.

As Smedes pointed out, forgiving our enemy doesn't suddenly turn him
into a close friend. Or a promising husband. Or a trustworthy partner.
Forgiveness, in other words, "does not diminish the wrongness of what he
did to us." As an example, Smedes tells of a beloved Episcopal priest who
violated his wife's trust—and his parishioners'—by sexually "comforting"
women who came to him for help. The priest, Smedes pointed out, wasn't
granted automatic forgiveness when he begged for it. That "was the business
of his victims," Smedes wrote. The vestry, in fact, welcomed him back—
"back to the pew and back to the communion rail. But not back to his old
job. Not yet." Or as they put it: "We forgive but we will not rehire."

So while forgiveness covers big hurts, it can take time. And nobody else
can judge our pace. God is patient, and we should be so with ourselves. Don't
struggle to forgive. Cry to God's Spirit to help. Faithfully, His Spirit will do
exactly that. Then, when we feel even the smallest stirrings of benevolence
toward the one who wronged us, said Smedes, "we can be sure that we are
teamed with God in a modest miracle of healing." Our own. 🌿

Don't let your wounds get in your way.
VASHTI MURPHY MCKENZIE

Forgiveness: Like God

But I do not excuse the guilty.
Exodus 34:7

Forgive the guilty? It seems unfair. Yet to become like God—that is, to forgive those who have wronged us—is exactly what we're called to do. But there's more to this matter.

As the LORD told Moses when the children of Israel turned their backs on Him to worship the golden calf, *I forgive iniquity, rebellion, and sin.* "Every kind of sin," as the first edition of the New Living Translation puts it.

But, says God, "I do not excuse the guilty."

Forgiveness is not a free pass.

In exchange for His amazing gift of forgiveness, God expects something. We are first forgiven by God in order to repair our relationship with Him. In that same way, we forgive others to repair our relationship with God. Either way, we can serve Him again. So forgiveness is much more about God than it is about the person who wronged us.

When David committed adultery with Bathsheba—another man's wife—then arranged for her husband to be killed, Nathan boldly confronted him. The king's first thoughts after being accused, however, were of God. Confessing to the prophet Nathan, he moaned: "I have sinned against the LORD."

That's right, Nathan said, "but the LORD has forgiven you, and you won't die for this sin. But you have given the enemies of the LORD great opportunity to despise and blaspheme him, so your child will die" (2 Samuel 12:13-14). Nathan also prophesied that violence would be "a constant threat" to David's family (v. 10). And it was.

As wondrous as forgiveness is, in other words, it doesn't excuse wrong. A sober truth. But it's a truth every believer should digest. Forgiveness costs. In return, may God bless us today by helping us honor the One who paid. 🌿

When we sin, therefore, our personal relationship with God
needs to be restored.
PHILIP GRAHAM RYKEN

Going Deeper

Now it is time to forgive him.
2 Corinthians 2:7

Have you ever been deeply hurt? Describe what happened and how you responded. Did you forgive?

The word *forgiveness* in the Greek—*aphiemi*—means to release, or to let go. To cancel. Or to send away. But what does forgiveness mean to you?

Be honest: is there any unforgiveness in your life? Explain how you intend to respond to it.

If you'd like, write a prayer that surrenders to God your needs concerning the virtue of forgiveness.

Our greatest need was forgiveness, so God sent us a Savior.
CHARLES SELL

MERCY

His Promise

And I will show mercy.
Exodus 33:19

My Prayer

You are so generous, O God, and we seem
to need so much.
Thank You for the priceless blessing
of Your mercy.

Mercy: All My Life

Surely goodness and mercy shall follow me all the days of my life.
Psalm 23:6, KJV

Why David? That's what I wondered. Why such mercy for him? And why such goodness for a man with appalling sins—especially that matter with Bathsheba, including the illicit sex, the murder, the whole disconcerting mess.

And yet. David, of all people in the Bible—and with astonishing certainty—states clearly that goodness and mercy will follow him. Surely. And not just for a little while. Forever.

Brazen confidence? Or knowledge that God's goodness and mercy—His "unfailing love," as the New Living Translation describes it—will pursue those who pursue God? Always it will follow them. What a strong, sweet promise for all of us broken, sinful believers. Like David, we've all fallen short. Big time. My own sins are as red as scarlet.

But God won't give up on us. On pursuing us. On chasing us down. On running after us, time and again, to pick us up and set us right while He pours His unfailing love into our broken, dirty, bruised—and sometimes stupid—hearts.

It was stupid, for sure, for David to have sex with another man's wife, then arrange for her husband to die in battle. David's twenty-third psalm reminds us, however, that not even a perverted act of adultery—with murder on the side—is too much for God to forgive, then to repair with His sweet mercy.

Do you feel guilty for past wrongs? Then pray like David. But this time, says theologian R. C. Sproul, "don't ask Him to forgive you for the sin that is haunting you. Rather, ask Him to forgive you for insulting His integrity by refusing to accept His forgiveness." His mercy is a gift—and it's in pursuit. Let us stop running today. Then the blessing of mercy will catch us. ❧

Right now counts forever.
R. C. SPROUL

Mercy: In Kind

God blesses those who are merciful, for they will be shown mercy.
Matthew 5:7

William Shakespeare tried to capture the essence of mercy in his tragic comedy *The Merchant of Venice.* "The quality of mercy is not strained," says his character Portia in the play. "It droppeth as the gentle rain from heaven. . . . It blesseth him that gives and him that takes. . . . It is an attribute to God himself."

While various scholars have debated the underlying meanings of Portia's plea to the moneylender Shylock, her "mercy speech" stands out for seeing that mercy blesses going and coming. In fact, in the Beatitudes of Jesus, from which today's Scripture is taken, mercy is the only attribute shown to reproduce itself in kind. That is, those who are merciful "will be shown mercy." Not so with the other Beatitudes—as in blessed are the poor for "the Kingdom of Heaven is given to them." Or blessed are those who mourn for "they will be comforted" (vv. 3, 4).

Mercy, however, as Shakespeare's Portia declares, "is an attribute to God himself." So mercy is a gentle gift, dropping from our spirits as "rain from heaven." Only by God's Holy Spirit, indeed, can any of us not forever hold somebody accountable for a wrong. In kind, that same person can cut us some slack when we fall short.

The nature of humanity is to mess up. Sometimes a lot. Sometimes big-time.

Mercy steps back from human frailty to grant, not a pardon, but godly understanding. So mercy acknowledges wrong. But mercy doesn't force people to stay pinned to the ground in their error. Mercy extends a hand. To lift up. To pull the fallen to their feet. We can do the same today. Just as God does for us. As we do, God promises a blessed payback for mercy. More mercy to us. 🌿

Heaven have mercy on us all—Presbyterians and pagans alike—
for we are all somehow dreadfully cracked about the head,
and sadly need mending.
HERMAN MELVILLE

Mercy: For Generations

His mercy goes on from generation to generation, to all who fear him.
Luke 1:50

I sat in the movie theater, watching while a character on the screen made fun of God. Laughing. Sneering. Joking. The movie was a thriller. But in a scene in a big airport, one character shook his hands and rolled his eyes, creating a distraction by shouting: "I got the Holy Spirit!"

All around me, people laughed.

But as I sat in the dark, listening to the sneering audience, I thought of the casual way many refer to God—and for a simple reason. They don't fear Him. Not one bit. So they miss His mercy. It's a gift "to all who fear him." Even more, unlike those of us who fear God—who bow at His name, who are awed by His power, who worship at His feet, not because we're so good but because He's so merciful—those who don't revere Him won't know His merciful abundance. From generation to generation.

That's the kind of mercy God promises to those who fearfully revere Him.

To be sure, many of us pondering this Scripture today are blessed by mercy secured decades ago by God-fearing parents and God-fearing grand-parents, long before we were conceived or born.

In today's Scripture—taken from the Magnificat, the song of praise offered by Mary, the mother of Jesus—we hear her thankfulness for God's blessed promise:

"His mercy goes on from generation to generation, to all who fear him."

Do you want to bless generations of your family? Like Mary, do you want to bless your yet-unborn child? Your grandchild? Your great-grandchildren? And *their* children? Start today. Stand in fear. Not of the world, but of the Mighty God. Then stand back. Your family's mercy is at hand. ❦

For as the heaven is high above the earth, so great is his mercy
toward them that fear him.
PSALM 103:11, KJV

Mercy: Like God

Shouldn't you have mercy on your fellow servant,
just as I had mercy on you?
Matthew 18:33

After twenty-plus years of marriage, the woman's husband confessed. Along the way in their marriage, he'd had sex with another woman. Or maybe more than one. The full truth was emerging slowly. But this truth—and the debilitating pain it caused these many years later—left her bitter, angry, hungry for revenge.

But as this woman shared the story of this deep trauma to her marriage, she revealed how she coped and how they finally healed. "I had mercy." Rather than rake her repentant husband over the coals with her hurt—then force him to grovel in the full details of the betrayals, again and again—she took her pain to God. She left it there with God. Then she offered her husband what it seemed he didn't deserve. Her mercy.

Just like God offers His mercy to us. Even when we don't deserve it.

Then the miracle. "My own healing," she said. "I could feel the pain start to lift. With ups and downs, yes. But healing nonetheless." Even more, the marriage healed too. More sooner than later, in fact.

She could've taken another path, acting like the unmerciful servant in a parable of Jesus (Matthew 18:21-35). After begging for mercy, the servant was forgiven his big debt—of millions of dollars—by the merciful king. But when a fellow servant, who owed him a few thousand dollars, begged for mercy, the unmerciful servant "grabbed him by the throat and demanded instant payment" (v. 28). Likewise, this woman, whose own sins have been forgiven by God, could've grabbed her husband by the throat and demanded emotional payback, forgetting how God had shown mercy for her flaws. But mercy prevailed. Then healing followed. Are you hurting today from a deep betrayal and driven to pay it back with reprisals? Ask the Holy Spirit to empower you to pay back the hurt with the unthinkable. With His mercy.

Then watch God make a miracle by granting you His healing and mercy too. 🌿

There is healing in the telling.
CECIL MURPHEY

Mercy: By Choice

And I will show mercy to anyone I choose.
Exodus 33:19

My church friend was worried, stressed, and dismayed. "My mother's over at the hospital. Her brother has a blood clot and gangrene in one leg." She sighed. "But that's not all. Her sister has a blood clot too. All at the same time. My mother's overwhelmed."

My friend's eyes showed concern, weariness, fear. So what else to do? I offered to pray—not sure exactly what I could ask of God. I didn't know her relatives. I don't even know all of mine. But as I wrote my prayer notes, the prayer request became clear and urgent. Pray for mercy.

So I prayed exactly that. *Mercy, O Lord.* I wrote the words in big letters in my prayer notebook. Big letters, yes, because a prayer for mercy can sometimes seem desperate, almost like begging. Among the blessings, mercy is that unlikely, lenient compassion for someone "under one's power." God is our Boss, that is, but still He grants mercy.

He decides for mercy, as He told Moses, for whom He chooses. The irony, however, is that anybody He chooses is subject to His sovereign power. No wonder pleading for mercy can feel like begging. And, yet, here's the good news.

He *will* decide for it. As He promises, "I *will* show mercy."

Now what about us? When others seek mercy from us, will we extend it, choosing to grant mercy rather than choosing against it?

If we withhold mercy, that's a choice all its own. But to be merciful as God is merciful, we must choose like God. *I will show mercy.* We each must say that. It's not an option. It's part and parcel of a godly life.

A merciful choice. May God help us offer it without making others beg. 🌿

Mercy is something we extend, not just something we intend.
GEORGE GRANT

Mercy: From God

God blesses those who are merciful, for they will be shown mercy.
Matthew 5:7

My shoulder ached again. Mercilessly. Since a surgery to remove my thyroid a year before, my left shoulder always throbbed with pain. I dislike pills—unnecessary pills, that is. So after my doctor ruled out any disease, I asked him to prescribe strengthening exercises. Great idea, he said, because, in fact, my shoulder pain actually was radiating from my neck. "During your thyroid surgery, you probably experienced some muscle or nerve damage." Exercise will help, he said.

But it didn't.

So I prayed. Not for mercy so much. I just wrote down "neck pain" in my prayer notebook. For a year, I'd never simply done that, never just asked the Lord to ease my suffering. But now I prayed. "I need Your help, O God." In effect, I was pleading for His mercy.

Then came the little pillow.

Such a silly little pillow, in fact. Yellow fake silk with flowers across the front. Something I bought on sale at a discount store. Just one of many in my growing pillow collection. My husband teased me about them. "Oh, *another* pillow?" he'd ask. Sly wink.

Then one morning, for some reason, the little pillow caught my attention. Unlike the others, which were large and cushy, this cheap one was small and misshapen. Good to support a shoulder? It seemed silly. But that night, as I curled under the covers, I propped the sad-sack little pillow under my left shoulder. I sighed in relief. Real comfort. And surprisingly solid—like a rock. I slept soundly. Comfortably. The next day my shoulder hardly ached.

And the next day. And the next. For the first time in months, in fact, I could get dressed without shoulder pain. But that's not all. In church, for the first time in months, I could lift my arms far above my head to praise the Lord for His mercy. And all I had to do was ask for the blessing. Now what about you? ❦

The only qualification for mercy is affliction.
BOB LAFORGE

Going Deeper

This is what he requires of you: to do what is right, to love mercy.
Micah 6:8

Have you ever prayed for mercy? Did God answer? Explain.

Why does He ask us to love mercy?

This week, who did the Holy Spirit show needs your mercy?

Name some ways you can show mercy to the person who needs it from you.

If you'd like, write a prayer that addresses your needs concerning the virtue of mercy.

Mercy is compassion in action.
AUTHOR UNKNOWN

Gratitude

His Promise

But giving thanks is a sacrifice that truly honors me.
Psalm 50:23

My Prayer

Stir up a spirit of gratitude within me, O God,
that I might forever honor You.

Gratitude: In Our Hearts

One of them, when he saw that he was healed, came back to Jesus.
Luke 17:15-16

Ten lepers. All healed by Jesus. Yet only one came back to say thank you. But why?

What made the one turn back to say thank you to the Healing Christ? And why not the other nine?

Scholars have written volumes on this provocative scenario.

Charles Spurgeon writes that to neglect to thank God for answered prayer "is to refuse to benefit ourselves." Gratitude to God promotes the growth of spiritual life, he adds. "It helps to remove our burdens, to excite our hope, to increase our faith." Other people get the benefit, too, when we show gratitude to God. "Weak hearts will be strengthened, and drooping saints will be revived as they listen to our 'songs of deliverance.'"

Certainly this is right. But what about those nine?

Clearly, they felt compelled to go, as Jesus instructed, to show themselves obediently to their priests. They were more worried, apparently, about getting religious approval than blessing the one who'd approved them for healing. We see this, says John Reed, about the nine lepers, when "the spiritual razzmatazz becomes more significant than the converts' ongoing relationship with Christ."

C. S. Lewis notes that the healing itself took precedence over the Healer.

With the tenth leper, however, the Healer mattered more than the cure. As self-centered as most of us are, it's quite easy to forget to say thank you, even to God. The exception is when God means more to us than anything else—church rules, other people's opinions, expected blessings, and even our own delight in answered prayer.

Far better to delight in Him. He changes hearts. That's what healed the tenth leper. A new heart. The blessing? An empowered new life. 🌿

Gratitude is when memory is stored in the heart.
LIONEL HAMPTON

Gratitude: For God's Church

And he took a cup of wine and gave thanks to God for it.
Mark 14:23

The fellowship hall at church was packed. The Sunday service was over. But an overflow crowd stayed to celebrate our pastor's birthday—and for one reason. We love our pastor. He's hardworking, productive, and passionate for all things of God.

But one particular thing sets him apart.

He's grateful.

And he means it.

Or as he says, time after time, from the pulpit: "I *love* you. And I appreciate each and every one of you. So, from the bottom of my heart, *thank* you."

Just a nice gesture? No, it's more. Because his gratitude, as we recognize, honors God—placing God at the forefront of everything.

Especially His church.

We see that as Jesus ate with His disciples in the upper room for the Feast of Unleavened Bread. He was on His way to Calvary. But as He took bread and wine, showing it to represent His body and His blood, soon to be broken and spilled, He gave thanks. So gratitude is proper, certainly. To be grateful is the right thing, to be sure.

But as Jesus shows us by example, thanksgiving to God honors God's body—for who He is, for what He is doing in His world, and for what He seeks and intends to do through each of us.

If you're struggling to find your purpose or if you've found your purpose—in the role of a good pastor or good teacher or good parent or good business owner—then bless God today by telling Him thank you. Then watch the world see God in all you do. 🌿

If God never does another thing for me, He's done enough.
TIMOTHY E. TYLER

Gratitude: Like God

While they were eating, Jesus took bread, gave thanks . . .
Mark 14:22, NIV

Some dinners are big. For me, this would be one of them. I was to meet, for the first time, my new book agents—two influential Christian women. So I was nervous. Hungry, too. I'd flown from Denver for our meeting in Michigan. After I had settled in at the hotel, they picked me up and drove us to a lovely restaurant. The ambience was cozy and the service prompt. And I was famished. So when our plates came, I grabbed my fork and dove in.

Then I noticed an awkward silence.

"Shall I say a blessing?" one of the women asked.

I grimaced. Swallowed hard. *How dare I not say thanks?* These were my new *Christian* agents—and here I sat, mouth stuffed, without muttering one word of thanks to God. For bountiful food. For this day. For safe travel. For these two women. For God's provision. If I had stopped long enough to think, first, about the goodness of God, I could've made a table-length list of things to thank God for that evening. Especially since I grew up in a family that "said grace."

Without thinking too much, in fact, my family said grace.

But in today's Scripture, here is Jesus—thoughtfully taking up bread, blessing it, and saying thanks for His own body, knowing He'd soon be crucified. Yes, broken for us. So He took that bread, gave thanks, broke it into pieces, "and gave it to the disciples, saying, 'Take it, for this is my body.'" Feast on My sacrifice, He says, inviting us to be grateful. Yet here I sat, forgetting to thank God for even a meal in a restaurant?

That's how I questioned myself later, challenging myself not to ever eat a meal or do God's ministry—or open my eyes for a new day—without stopping first to thoughtfully give God thanks. Have you thanked Him yet today? Praise God there's still time.

So thank Him now. Not just because it's right. But because He gave all. ❧

Thanks are the highest form of thought, and . . .
gratitude is happiness doubled by wonder.
G. K. CHESTERTON

Gratitude: For the Good

Enter his gates with thanksgiving.
Psalm 100:4

America's first Thanksgiving? Some say it was that December day in 1619 when a group of British settlers, led by Captain John Woodlief at Berkeley Plantation, Virginia, knelt in prayer and pledged "thanksgiving" to God for their safe arrival after a frightful voyage across the Atlantic.

Others cite that harvest meal in 1621 when the Pilgrims, after a brutal first year in the New World, celebrated a plentiful bounty—enough food to store and keep them alive through the coming winter. They were at peace, as well, with the native Indians. So Governor William Bradford, their leader, proclaimed a day of thanksgiving shared by colonists and neighboring Indians alike.

Still other ceremonies of thanks have been recorded among settlers in North America—including Native Americans who observed harvest celebrations of thanks long before colonists or anybody else arrived.

What is the common denominator? And what do these thanksgivings teach us?

God deserves to be thanked—and should be. But taking time to bless Him with our thanks blesses us, too. We gather together. We circle a table. We pause to reflect on the countless marvelous things God does and provides every minute—from our next meal to our next breath—then we take time to savor it all.

The one hundredth psalm unveils it like this: "Enter his gates with thanksgiving; go into his courts with praise. Give thanks to him and bless his name" (v. 4). Any way we say it, however, God is blessed to hear it. Just as we're blessed to say it. So open your mouth right now and shout in your spirit: *Thank You, God!* 🌿

As the Lord loveth a cheerful giver, so likewise a cheerful thanksgiver.
JOHN BOYS

Gratitude: For Others

I always thank my God when I pray for you.
Philemon 1:4

Marriages fail. Businesses fail. Prayers fail. All for the lack of a thank you. One business writer, reporting about a retail chain's high-profile failure a few years back, attributed the stores' demise to one thing: they treated their customers poorly. Not enough genuine gratitude.

Gratitude, it seems, is that important. To be sure, gratitude is notable throughout the Bible. In Psalm 50:23, in fact, God makes it clear: Gratitude honors Me.

In the New Testament, Jesus makes gratitude His signature. Before raising Lazarus from the dead, for example, "Jesus looked up to heaven and said, 'Father, *thank you* for hearing me" (John 11:41, italics added). The apostle Paul followed suit. "I always thank God," he wrote to Philemon, "when I pray for you."

Marriage expert M. Gary Neuman says spouses would do well to remember such wisdom. In a survey, he said most husbands who cheated in failed marriages said the problem wasn't sex or money—the usual suspects. "The majority said it was an emotional disconnection, specifically a sense of feeling underappreciated. Lack of thoughtful gestures." As one husband, Josh, told Neuman during a popular women's talk show, he cheated on his wife because he felt underappreciated at home and started feeling insecure. "That insecurity was really the catalyst," he says. "I didn't feel comfortable going to the one person in the world I should be going to, which is my wife."

What if you and I tried harder? By just saying thank you. What a great way to start a letter, a conversation, a business. Or a marriage. Or a prayer. Or a meal. Or a brand-new day. Gratitude blesses others, but certainly God. So why not send up a blessing today. Tell somebody thank you. Then tell God. Then show by your actions that you mean it. 🕯

Feeling gratitude and not expressing it is like
wrapping a present and not giving it.
WILLIAM ARTHUR WARD

Gratitude: For the Bad

As far as I am concerned, God turned into good what you meant for evil.
Genesis 50:20

In my twelfth year as a journalist, I hit a big bump in my career. When the dust settled, I didn't have a job. *My* job, as I saw it, was given to someone else. And I was stunned. Devastated. Shell-shocked. In less than a year, however, I realized that losing that high-profile newspaper position—the worst career downfall I'd ever experienced—turned out to be one of the best things that ever happened to me.

Instead of weeping and raging at myself and at God, I should have thanked God, in fact, that even in what looked like trouble, He was right there in the middle of it. Even better, He was ahead of it.

That low point led me to a high point—my next job, teaching newspapering on a large college campus. There I was forced to dig deep—to stir up in my soul enough humility to learn how to teach. And teach well. Because to teach well, I had to learn empathy, listening, patience, clarity, order, dignity, preparation, self-control, prudence, vision, integrity, passion—and to change lives while God changed mine. Newspaper people can stir up such gifts, I'm sure. But to be honest, I never sought such virtues, day after day, until I stood in a classroom to teach.

I thank God every day for allowing this unexpected journey—for turning what appeared to be bad into something far better than I ever imagined. I laugh to think, yes, that teaching forced me to learn public speaking—which I thought I hated—but also how to teach and facilitate workshops and seminars, all skills I routinely use in my life now as a Christian author.

I couldn't see any good, at first, in the bad. Most of us can't. But today, if you're smack in the middle of one of life's curveballs, catch it. Then bless God's Spirit by thanking Him for sending it your way. Know, like Joseph, that what life means for evil, God will turn into good—good enough for your thanks. 🌿

Gratitude is the mother of all virtues.
G. K. CHESTERTON

Going Deeper

I thank my God every time I remember you.
Philippians 1:3, NIV

You and I often forget to thank God—and thank each other—for favors, blessings, and mercies. Name three reasons you neglect to show gratitude.

Do you think gratitude honors God? Explain.

Whom did the Holy Spirit show you this week who needs your thanks?

If you'd like, write a prayer that addresses your needs concerning the virtue of gratitude.

The highest appreciation is not to utter words, but to live by them.
JOHN F. KENNEDY

HOPE

His Promise

Come back to the place of safety, all you prisoners,
for there is yet hope!
I promise this very day that I will repay you
two mercies for each of your woes!
Zechariah 9:12

My Prayer

Welcome me back, heavenly Father,
to Your cradle of safety—
and to Your bounty of hope!

Hope: From God

Return to your fortress, O prisoners of hope; even now
I announce that I will restore twice as much to you.
Zechariah 9:12, NIV

Hard to imagine. But *hope*—as a concept—wasn't always considered a good thing. In the ancient world, poets and writers dismissed hope as a cruel joke of the gods. It's a vice, they said, luring gullible people to believe for a better future, only to let them down.

Hope, that is, was just another word for disappointment—a kind of glitter, said the Greek poet Euripides, that "beckons many men to their undoing." Generations later, philosopher Friedrich Nietzsche called hope "the evil of evils" because "it prolongs man's torment."

In the Bible, however, the prophet Zechariah summons prisoners of such false thinking. "Return to your fortress, O prisoners of hope."

Rather than grovel in the lie that hope is evil—or stay bound in hopelessness against fierce enemies, as the children of Israel did—we are urged to come back to our place of safety. Return to God, that is, because He *is* our Hope. The Hope of safety. The Hope of deliverance. The Hope who promises to restore twice as much as we've lost—"two mercies for each of your woes"—in exchange for us placing our hope in Him. Then, like a warrior, God says He will stir up our hope "against the Greeks" (v. 13). Yes, take *that*, Euripides!

Strong language. The Lord intends us to know, indeed, that hope is power—especially when our hope is in Him. What better place to take our deepest longings than to Him. While we can't deliver ourselves, we hope in a God who can. As we hope, He restores *times two* all the valuables we've lost in our battles.

Go ahead and praise Him today for that promise. Two mercies for every woe. That's confirmation that hope in God hardly is a vice. It is a gift. And it's divine. 🌱

Hope is the best part of our riches.
CHRISTIAN NEVELL BOVEE

Hope: In God

Put your hope in the LORD. Travel steadily along his path.
He will honor you by giving you the land.
Psalm 37:34

We were saving money. So we said no to adding a GPS for our rental car. But soon we were lost—despite two sets of directions. One was a map from the Internet. The other was hand-drawn directions from our hotel desk clerk, showing a "better" route. "Faster," she said, even though we were only going a few miles. Yet, my husband and I still got lost, unable to figure our way through a maze of unfamiliar streets in a town we didn't know.

One hour later, after several phone calls and several wrong turns—and more than one false start—we found our destination. It was right where the map said it would be, except for one problem. We'd traveled the wrong path.

Hoping for a faraway desire can seem like that—as if we're navigating a maze, and a destination, with no end in sight.

In the Scriptures, however, the psalmist exhorts us to hope in the Lord *and* travel steadily along *His* path. Then He will honor us by giving us the territory we desire.

Hope is not an idle pursuit. While we hope in the Lord for a desired outcome, we'll shorten our wait time by sticking to God's path. By the things we do. By the way we live. By the way we walk. Day by day. Thus, hoping in God means that while I wait on Him, I'll work on elevating my life, determining to be more like Him.

Too many of us think hope is enough in itself. But godly hope means walking in a higher way. On higher ground. As Andrew Murray noted about hopes expressed in prayer, "My prayer [hopes] will depend on my life." So move today from hoping to achieving. How? Stick to God's path. God will bless your sticking by delivering the outcome that lines up with Him. ❦

If you do not hope, you will not find what is beyond your hopes.
SAINT CLEMENT OF ALEXANDRIA

Hope: In Love

Let your unfailing love surround us, LORD,
for our hope is in you alone.
Psalm 33:22

This isn't a race card. But it's a race story.

For many African Americans like me, there was intense anticipation in November 2008 when an African American candidate was elected president of the United States. Politics aside, the election of Barack Obama was a major milestone for a nation whose history is marked by the stain of slavery. Thus, at my church on the Sunday after the election, many people wore T-shirts showing images of the new president—or with photos of his best-selling book *The Audacity of Hope*.

And yet, our pastor reminded us, "As excited as many of us are, our hope is not in Barack Obama. Our hope yet remains where it should be—our hope is in God."

Great blessings await those, indeed, who hope, not in people or politics, politicians or potentates—but in the living God, whose "unfailing love surrounds" our feeble hope. When our hope seems to hang by a fraying thread, we can exchange that thread for the sturdy surety of God. As the psalmist says, "We depend on the LORD *alone* to save us. Only he can help us, protecting us like a shield" (Psalm 33:20, italics added).

It's easy, in contrast, to depend on others to save us—to try vainly to provide for our needs, and God knows they are many. We crave approval, jobs, housing. Romance, love, marriage. Healing, renewal, transformation. Friendship, financial freedom, and just plain fun. All are needs many of us "hope" are coming our way. And, in truth, such things aren't bad hopes. But, says the psalmist, "*You* are the God who saves me. All day long I put my hope in you" (Psalm 25:5, italics added). Then when we do, "May integrity and honesty protect me, for I put my hope in you" (Psalm 25:21).

So, no, hope is not a wish and a prayer. It's trust and a prayer. Not so with the godless. Their hopes evaporate, says Job (8:13). But with God, our hopes bless us all with love. 🌿

In the unlikely story that is America, there has never been
anything false about hope.
BARACK OBAMA

Hope: In God's Plans

"For I know the plans I have for you," says the LORD,
". . . to give you a future and a hope."
Jeremiah 29:11

Captive in Babylon for seventy long years, the children of Israel had every reason not to hope for good things from God. Then the prophet Jeremiah sent them the most unlikely letter of instruction. *God says relax!*

In exile?

Exactly, God says.

Settle down and get comfortable in your place of exile. But that's not all. Find a sweetheart and get married. Same for your sons and daughters. Yes—eat, drink, work, plant, and make yourself at home.

In exile?

Exactly, God says.

While we wait, that is, for a better day—and while things aren't exactly as we'd like them to be—with our family members still not saved, our finances still in disarray, our purpose still not clear, our ministry still in development—*relax*. Settle in with God, for He knows His plans for us over the long term. And they truly are wonderful plans. He plans to prosper us and not to harm us. Even more, He plans to give us—as a personal gift from Himself—a better future and the glory of His hope.

If you're dragged down by the present state of your life, feeling as if you're exiled from the best of God, Jeremiah encourages you to relax and settle in with God. Tomorrow will come, and God promises it will be better, but also blessed.

But in the meantime, start living. In vain?

No, in the blessed hope of the Lord. 🌿

I know how men in exile feed on dreams of hope.
AESCHYLUS

Hope: Despite Sin

We have been unfaithful to our God. . . . But in spite of this
there is hope for Israel.
Ezra 10:2

We cheat God. We choose wrong. We compromise. We make mistakes. We yield to carnal temptations. In short, we sin. All of us.

That is, we doubt God. We go our own way. All told, we are unfaithful to God—not trusting that God knows how to be God—and that His commandments and requirements are not just good rules, but a matter of our living and of life. Yet like the children of Israel during the reformer Ezra's day, we flat out disobey God, widening our separation from the only and great source of our help.

Even more, God isn't surprised at our failures. "For he understands how weak we are; he knows we are only dust" (Psalm 103:14). And yet, despite the dust and weakness of our failures, there is hope for us—just as the children of Israel realized there still was hope for them.

Imagine their relief, knowing full well how far they'd turned from God. In blatant defiance, they'd married against God's will, taking up with pagan wives and their wives' idol gods. So serious was the problem that it threatened the survival of the nation of Israel itself. Their sin was so great that Ezra—in repentance—tore his clothes, ripped out his hair, "weeping and throwing himself down before the house of God" (Ezra 10:1, NIV).

Such remorse drew the sinners themselves to confess, even as they rejoiced at still having hope—in their forgiving God. In their faithful God. In the source of saving, renewing, and transforming hope.

If you need such hope today—because your sin is so blatant, so troubling, so carnal, so indefensible that you feel hopeless—then repent and rejoice. The hope of God remains. Fly-by-night hope can't offer such assurance. But rejoice today in the hope that blesses our failures and empowers our repentance. Thus, despite our sins and our failures, you and I can claim hope that's not fleeting or false. Our hope in God will last. ✹

My hope is built on nothing less than Jesus' blood and righteousness.
EDWARD MOTE

Hope: Despite Gloom and Trouble

In my distress I prayed to the LORD,
and the LORD answered me and rescued me.
Psalm 118:5

The woman's mother was depressed. Clinically depressed. And it baffled her. Once the "fun" mom among her friends' mothers—the one who found fun things to do on rainy days, drove them as children to picnics and swim parties, loved silly jokes, and told funny stories—her mother now spent her days curled up in a chair. Refusing to go anywhere. Refusing to get dressed. Refusing to live her life.

But her daughter clung to hope.

After seeking God in prayer for answers—and pressing her mother's doctor for relief—a treatment plan emerged: A change in her mother's medicines. An improved diet. Exercise. Psychotherapy. Morning and evening prayer. And sunlight.

In their gloomy Midwest-winter environment, her mother was prescribed a half-hour regimen of "full-spectrum" light therapy from a lamp that simulated the sunlight her mother was missing. Over time, with the combination of treatments, her mother's depression started to lift. But none of this would have happened, this woman insists, if she had not first sought God with hope. "I was at the end of my rope," she says. "My mother was miserable, and so was I." So, like the psalmist, she prayed to the Lord, and the Lord answered. *Get up with hope—then take your mother to the doctor!*

Get up in the dark, that is. Even when you can't see any hope. Even when you can't imagine that a hopeful resolution is even possible. *Get up anyway.* In distress, get up with hope. Then, in that darkness, God sees and God hears and God answers. "We could still be sitting in the dark, feeling lost and hopeless," this woman says. Instead, she let distress stir her failing hope. She let distress force her to stand up. She let distress jump-start her feeble plea. Then the faithful God responded. Our distress doesn't scare God, in other words. Our distress softens His ear. Then as we pray, He answers. How? With the bright blessing of hope. ❧

Hope is patience with the lamp lit.
TERTULLIAN

Going Deeper

Having hope will give you courage.
You will be protected and will rest in safety.
Job 11:18

Look up the word *hope* in the dictionary. Which definition inspires
you most?

God responds to our distress, rescuing us with His hope (see Psalm 118:5).
What distress in your life have you yet to take to God?

What hope do you carry in your heart for someone else?

If you'd like, write a prayer that addresses your needs concerning
the virtue of hope.

LORD, you know the hopes of the helpless.
Surely you will hear their cries and comfort them.
PSALM 10:17

PRAISE

His Promise

Open your mouth wide,
and I will fill it with good things.
Psalm 81:10

My Prayer

Let my praise be wide open and unlimited,
Blessed Father.
Then fill up my praise
with good things from You.

Praise: That Shakes Things Up

Suddenly, there was a great earthquake.
Acts 16:26

Don't wait. Not a minute. Not a second. Instead, praise God now. If you and I wait to praise God until *after* something earthshaking and amazing happens, we've got the wrong order. Praise comes first. Doubt that?

Consider the classic praise story in the Bible—this scenario where Paul and Silas, bound in chains in the dungeon of a jail, their bodies bruised and bloodied by their jailers, still lifted their voices to praise God.

And what an odd sound. Praise in a jail. Sung by two beaten, bloodied prisoners. It's not logical. But as the book of Acts records, as they praised God, the earth shook. "And the prison was shaken to its foundations. All the doors flew open, and the chains of every prisoner fell off!" (v. 26). Praise is power, indeed. But *praise comes first.*

When we're bound up by some situation, in the midst of that mess, it's hard to remember that we should praise God first. Not after it's all cleaned up. But while it's happening. That is the proper order of praise.

In fact, the word *praise* (which in Latin means "prize") shares a root with the Latin word for preposition. As we recall from grammar lessons at school, a preposition is the word that comes *before* the main thing. Such words hold the "before" position—the *pre*position—setting up the main topic. In our spiritual lives, praise sits in that same place. It holds the *pre*position, setting up God's power so it can follow, moving in our hearts and lives.

And no prison chains can tie down that power. So don't wait for your chains to fall or your prison walls to crumble. Praise God *first.* Right now. Despite your circumstances. Praise Him for being God. For His mercy. For His deliverance. For His hope. For His blessing. For His empowering Spirit. Then stand back. Your prison walls are coming down! 🌿

Some think that worship is a response after the Holy Spirit moves upon them. However, it's the other way around.
DALE A. ROBBINS

Praise: With Power

And the chains of every prisoner fell off!
Acts 16:26

Every prisoner in the jail was freed? Does that get your attention today? *Every* prisoner freed. An amazing detail in this story of the apostle Paul's praise meeting in a grungy, bloodstained jailhouse with Silas.

Those faithful men prayed and praised God—so it's no surprise that God loosed the chains of these two. But, *in addition*, every other prisoner bound in that cold and dingy jail got freed. As their praise shook that jail, *all* the chains on *every* prisoner flat out fell off!

Maybe, like me, you'd forgotten this little detail: that our feeble but faithful praise can prompt God to loose, not just our chains, but the chains of others around us.

So, in church, get on your feet and praise the Lord! Somebody in the next pew might catch the fire and find his or her chains loosed too.

In your family, open your mouth and praise Him. Somebody sitting around your kitchen table—or in your family tree, or on your Facebook page, or in your Twitter feed—might find his or her own spiritual bindings unraveling. Why? Because God is good and *you* praised God.

It's an amazing and supernatural phenomenon. In this story, in fact, even the jailer experienced freedom. Realizing the freed prisoners had not bolted and escaped, he called out: "Sirs, what must I do to be saved?" (Acts 16:30).

"Believe on the Lord Jesus," Paul and Silas replied, "and you will be saved, *along with your entire household*" (v. 31, italics added).

Praising God is contagious! Supernaturally.

God's Spirit alone could make it so—this remarkable principle that *my* praise can cause *your* soul to be freed, blessed, and delivered. Yes, praise is an additive. Let it overflow your heart, freeing someone else's life on this God-given day. 🌿

We increase whatever we praise.
CHARLES FILLMORE

Praise: In Particular

David sang this song to the LORD on the day the LORD rescued him.
2 Samuel 22:1

In America, we gush over our children—maybe too much—for their "accomplishments." Even minor deeds prompt the all-too-common words: "Good job!"

Far better, say child psychologists, to give "descriptive" praise. "I like the way you made your bed every day this week without any reminders. What a big help!"

That descriptive pattern is clear, leaving no doubt about the sincerity of our praise.

Interesting, then, to see that same descriptive model in the praise songs of David of the Bible. Never does he trivialize God or His great accomplishments by tossing out a casual "Good job!"

Instead, David's praise songs to almighty God are specific. Sincere. Passionate. The perfect model for the praise deserved by the God of the universe. Thus, in the Second Book of Samuel, David declares with great specificity:

> *The LORD is my rock, my fortress, and my savior . . . in whom I find protection. He is my shield, the strength of my salvation, and my stronghold, my high tower, my savior, the one who saves me from violence. (vv. 2-3)*

Or as David concludes: "You give great victories to your king; you show unfailing love to your anointed, to David and all his descendants forever" (v. 51).

Now what about you—and me? Is our praise to God that particular, descriptive, and passionate? If not, let's take a cue from David. Let's name, one by one, every way God has rescued and blessed us this week. Expect to say far more than "good job." Expect instead to sing. 🌿

These are but scattered beams, but God is the sun. These are but streams.
But God is the ocean.
JONATHAN EDWARDS

Praise: Into His Presence

O thou that inhabitest the praises of Israel . . .
Psalm 22:3, KJV

A gloomy Sunday? Sometimes they hit. So I dragged myself to church and sank into my pew. Feeling empty. Feeling angry. Feeling lethargic. A family matter weighed heavy on my heart. My arms felt like lead weights. Lift them to praise? I couldn't manage it—not on my own. Not on this Sunday. That's what the enemy wanted me to think. But I clung to a Scripture verse I've heard all my life—that God inhabits, or enthrones Himself, in the praises of His people. That when we praise Him, our praise lifts us into His comforting, uplifting, empowering, strengthening, invigorating Presence.

So I opened my mouth. Wide. I started to sing along with the choir's praise song. *Thank You, Lord! Thank You, Lord! I just want to thank You, Lord!*

As the words left my mouth, I could feel my arms rise from my sides. As they rose, I thought—in particular—about the many ways the Lord has blessed me, my family members, my church, my work, my friends, my neighborhood, my nation, our world, because of who He is.

In fact, I closed my eyes, recalling my older daughter's recent acceptance into a prestigious graduate school, my younger daughter and her husband's announcement that their next baby would be a healthy little boy, my husband's recovery from a major medical crisis, the merciful pain relief from my own shoulder injury—and more. In fact, the more I praised, the more I was flooded with images of how great and good God is.

In moments, I was moved from my emotional emptiness to a celebration of rejoicing at God's goodness. Or as my pastor declared: "Can't you feel it? Feel God's presence in this house today?" I nodded—tentatively. Could I feel His presence? Not in the sanctuary, I decided. But I *could* feel His Presence in my heart, enthroned on my praise. And what a feeling. It felt comforting, strong, protective, powerful. Loving. Yes, my praise gave God a place in my heart to stand up and stay. Unmovable. 🌿

Praise is the honey of life.
CHARLES SPURGEON

Praise: That Scatters My Enemies

At the very moment they began to sing and give praise, the LORD caused the armies of Ammon, Moab, and Mount Seir to start fighting among themselves.
2 Chronicles 20:22

Life gives us enemies. People who don't like us. Coworkers who sabotage our efforts. Bosses who are toxic and intolerant. Loved ones who hurt us. But spiritual enemies too. Our own doubts and fears. Our pride and greed. Our shortcomings and sin.

Yet in the face of all this, what's our best weapon? It's praise.

To praise God, as the king's singers praised Him while leading Judah's feeble army into battle, is to unleash a direct hit against our every enemy. In this story, in fact, the people of Judah faced the wrath of not one—but three—vicious enemies.

What a fitting number, so similar to how our lives can feel when not one, but three or more messy problems swirl into our lives, threatening to drag us down to defeat.

We can give up. Or, like wise king Jehoshaphat of Judah, we can appoint ourselves as praise singers—Judah, in fact, means "praise"—going before God's army and singing praises to God. They praised Him "for his holy splendor" (v. 21).

They sang this: "Give thanks to the LORD; his faithful love endures forever!" (v. 21).

Notice they weren't singing about the battle. Or the enemies. Or the trouble. Yet as they sang, "at the very moment," the Lord caused the enemy armies to start fighting among themselves, killing off each other. In fact, when the army of Judah stopped singing and praising, finally arriving to the lookout point at the battle site, not a single one of the enemy had escaped. *They were all dead.*

What a wonderful reminder. All our enemies—real and imagined, physical and spiritual—fall before God when we praise Him. Or as God told Jehoshaphat, "The battle is not yours, but God's" (v. 15). The same is true today. So bless God today with praise. Then watch your enemies scatter, stumble, perish. Against His Spirit, no enemy stands. ❧

Where the battle rages, there the loyalty of the soldier is proved.
MARTIN LUTHER

Praise: At All Times

All who seek the LORD will praise him.
Their hearts will rejoice with everlasting joy.
Psalm 22:26

It doesn't make sense. Something bad happens, but we praise God anyway? To praise this way is to understand that, despite life's ups and downs—and even while storms rage around us—God is still good. Or perhaps more important, God is still God.

This perspective keeps us from thinking we can manipulate God with our praise. We can't.

True, God rewards praise to Him with amazing and supernatural power and peace.

But praise isn't a strategy to dislodge supernatural gifts from God.

Praise flows from a true and deep understanding of who God is *all the time*, despite what else is going on in our lives.

"All who seek the LORD," sings David in Psalm 22:26, "will praise him." Even the poor, he declares, "will eat and be satisfied."

It's a statement that understands this critical truth:

Since God is God, and since God is good, whatever He allows in His divine will, ultimately, will be perfect and right. Even when we feel poor, we will eat and be satisfied.

The process of seeking God naturally leads to praise.

Of course, we want only what's good. That's human nature. But that's the point. In our humanness, we fail to see what God knows about the circumstances of our lives—that He has a vantage point that takes in the entire spectrum of our lives, beginning to end. So no matter what happens, He still reigns.

Knowing that, and knowing Him, we can fill our days, not with worry, but with the blessing of praise. "I will praise the LORD at all times," declares David. "I will constantly speak his praises" (Psalm 34:1). Even during bad times? Especially then. 🌱

Doth not the thunder praise Him? . . . Doth not the lightning write His name
in letters of fire? . . . And shall I, can I, silent be?
CHARLES SPURGEON

Going Deeper

Let all who take refuge in you rejoice;
let them sing joyful praises forever.
Psalm 5:11

By definition, praise holds the *pre*position to God's power. Why do you think that's the proper order—praise before power?

Rather than generalized praise, what can you praise God for today that is specific and particular?

In those times when life makes it hard to praise God, how will you find ways to praise Him anyway—at all times, as David says in Psalm 34:1?

If you'd like, write a prayer that addresses your needs concerning the virtue of praise.

In petition we act like men; in praise we act like angels.
THOMAS WATSON

FAITH

His Promise

*Even if you had faith as small as a mustard seed
you could say to this mountain, "Move."*
Matthew 17:20

My Prayer

Increase my faith, O God,
empowering even me to move mountains.

Faith: That Pleases God

So, you see, it is impossible to please God without faith.
Hebrews 11:6

Ah, faith. We can't buy it. We can't borrow it. We only need a smidgen of it—as small as a mustard seed, say the Scriptures. And that little bit, in fact, is a gift from God. But on that smidgen of faith rests every aspect of our relationship with our heavenly Father. Faith is, indeed, the substance of things we hope for, the evidence of things not seen. But what exactly does *that* mean?

On a sunny Monday morning, I chew on such thoughts. But on this same morning, did I know the sun would rise? Not by my own proof. Yet I knew it by a lifetime of previous dawns—and by the sound of birds chirping while it was yet dark, and by the leaf buds at the peak of their bloom, and by the hint of brightness cresting on the eastern horizon—that the sun would rise. By such evidence, I had faith.

No, the sunlight had not yet arrived. But as I waited in the dark for it, I expected, by faith, my evidence was right and it would arrive. And it did.

These thoughts remind us of the Germanic root of the word *faith*—the odd-looking word, *bheidh*—meaning "to await trustingly" or "to expect with trust." Such a definition is the perfect explanation of why God is so pleased when we demonstrate our faith in Him. While we wait in the dark, in the midnights of our lives, for Him to shine through and act, our faith demonstrates our belief, based on His evidence, that He *will*.

So faith is not just waiting around. It is waiting with trust. We may not see the sun rising yet in our situations—in our marriages, our ministries, our families, our futures. But by faith, we trust God that it *will*. Even though we can't see it now. Thus, Hebrews 11:1 asks, "What is faith?" But the answer—"it is the confident assurance that what we hope for is going to happen"—explains why our faith blesses God. Confident assurance. Trustful waiting. Expectant trust. Our God deserves no less. So today? Believe Him. 🌿

Faith is deliberate confidence in the character of God whose ways
you may not understand at the time.
OSWALD CHAMBERS

Faith: That Glorifies God

Didn't I tell you that you would see God's glory if you believe?
John 11:40

Lazarus was dead. Stone-cold dead. In the grave four days. As dead as some of our dreams. More dead than many of our hopes. He was so dead that his sister Martha, though distressed that Jesus hadn't arrived soon enough to keep him alive, feared to open his grave. It would smell, she said. A "terrible" smell, she insisted (v. 39).

The smell of death is foul, to be sure.

When dreams die—and things don't turn out as we'd hoped, but sometimes much worse—the stench of our disappointment can befoul our entire lives. Looking back, all we see is the grungy brokenness of our upended desires.

Worse, our "friends" follow behind us, questioning our God. "This man healed a blind man. Why couldn't he keep (your dream) from dying?"

Jesus' answer presents a sharp rebuttal to such smelly circumstances.

The unraveling of a beloved dream—or a life plan or lifetime goal—may appear to be a total and irreversible disaster. Bankruptcy. Sickness. Divorce. Job loss. Theft. Murder. War. All are horrible, for certain. But they don't have to end in irreversible death.

"No, it is for the glory of God," Jesus said. "I, the Son of God, will receive glory from this" (v. 4). Or as he told Martha, "Those who believe in me, even though they die like everyone else, will live again. They are given eternal life for believing in me and will never perish" (vv. 25-26).

Lazarus was raised from death by Christ. But we who believe also are raised from the death, disillusionment, and deception of dashed dreams. We can bemoan our losses. Or we can believe that God will revive us as we walk by faith from death to new life, for His glory. Yesterday *is* dead. But today? Look with faith to God for the blessing of future life. 🌱

Never be afraid to trust an unknown future to a known God.
CORRIE TEN BOOM

Faith: That Gains Salvation

God saved you by his special favor when you believed.
Ephesians 2:8

You and I are special to God. But you don't feel it today? Consider the apostle Paul's letter to the churches at Ephesus—that for having faith in Jesus, whom we've never even seen, God gives us the priceless favor of eternal life with Him.

And we can't boast about this. "It is a gift from God," Paul writes. Or as he says: "Salvation is not a reward for the good things we have done, so none of us can boast about it" (v. 9).

Instead, salvation is a reward for having the faith that God gave us in the first place. And, yes, that's one remarkable arrangement.

It's so remarkable, in fact, that it can be hard to fathom that God loved us "so very much," as Paul writes in Ephesians 2:5, "that even while we were dead because of our sins, he gave us life when he raised Christ from the dead."

That's more love than most of us will ever experience in human terms. Such love just isn't common. Instead, most of us love with strings attached: I'll love you *if* you love me back.

But God doesn't even ask for our love in exchange for the gift of salvation—this prize of eternal life, with the extraordinary benefit of spending eternity with Him and His only Son.

Instead, He favors us for having the faith He gave us in the first place, lest any of us boast. But our faith must be nurtured, cultivated, grown, and developed. It can die without daily watering and feeding. It can atrophy from neglect and indifference. It can shrink for failure to pray and praise, obey and worship, fellowship with other believers, give back to God's Kingdom. Yes, value this gift that God has given us. Bless Him for this favor. Then rest. Your salvation is already secure. 🖋

We sometimes think we have grabbed hold of God and found Him,
but it is really the other way around.
G. K. BEALE

Faith: That Makes Miracles

Anything is possible if a person believes.
Mark 9:23

Jesus' disciples are in a quandary in this story. A sick boy's father has begged them to cast out an evil spirit from his son. But no go. They can't do it.

Then Jesus shows up. In His presence, the evil spirit goes berserk—throwing the boy into a violent convulsion, leaving the boy writhing on the ground and foaming at the mouth. A disturbing scene. A big problem. Or as the boy's father puts it: "Have mercy on us and help us. Do something if you can" (v. 22).

If He can?

Jesus is bemused. "What do you mean, 'If I can?'"

Jesus questions the extraordinary suggestion that perhaps He can't cast out the ungodly spirits in our lives. Jesus can't? It's absurd. Yet, like the boy's father, we doubt Him. So Jesus turns the tables, challenging the father: "Anything is possible if a person believes" (v. 23). Now *that's* an extraordinary suggestion. Jesus can. If *I* can.

It's a theological principle that challenges the best of us. Or as the boy's father says: "I do believe, but help me not to doubt!" (v. 24).

We need to say that today. Help, O God, my unbelief. My uncertainty. My need for proof. Help me to stop stumbling over my human obstacles and to focus, not on problems, but on Your divine ability to accomplish anything, including what looks impossible.

In this story, in fact, as a crowd gathers around, Jesus casts out the evil spirit, demanding that it never enter the boy again. By His power? Absolutely. But that power was kindled by a feeble man's faith. Like yours. Like mine. So stop struggling today with feeble faith. Confess your doubts. But count on God. His Spirit will transform that doubt into a blessing of faith. Why? Because He can. 🌿

Faith takes God without any ifs.
D. L. MOODY

Faith: That Moves Mountains

You could say to this mountain, "Move from here to there," and it would.
Matthew 17:20

In Colorado, we see our share of mountains. More than fifty Colorado peaks are ranked as fourteeners (higher than 14,000 feet). That's more fourteeners than any state in the United States, including Alaska with twenty-one four-teeners. Next comes California, with twelve peaks over that 14,000 mark.

But Colorado is the mountain-peak champ.

Yet it took life on the ground to teach me what Jesus meant when He said His followers, with even faith as small as a mustard seed, could say to a mountain: "Move from here to there, and it would move."

In fact, I see it happen every day. While driving down I-25 along the Front Range of the Rocky Mountains, mountains do move—or appear to move. But first I have to move. I've noticed this for years, that a mountain peak appearing in one place when I start driving will seem to shift its position as I keep driving. And not just a little shift.

I can turn a bend in a road and a huge mountain—a big guy like Pikes Peak or Longs Peak—can seem not just to move, but to move across the road.

Theologically, over the years, I began to understand that Jesus wasn't exaggerating when He said if we have faith—even as small as a mustard seed—we could tell a mountain to move, from here to there, and it would move, *if we move.*

As we turn, that is, from the mountain peaks in our lives and to God instead, our mountains can't help but move—because we moved closer to God. Then there, in the safety and blessing of His protection and power, our mountains don't just move. By faith they crumble. ❦

I believe that the happiest of all Christians and the truest of Christians
are those who never dare to doubt God.
CHARLES SPURGEON

Faith: That Empowers Prayer

If you believe, you will receive whatever you ask for in prayer.
Matthew 21:22

It's controversial, this promise that Jesus made—that if we just believe when we ask, we will receive what we ask. But it doesn't work, say those whose circumstances haven't changed. Perhaps they are missing the real lesson.

That odd lesson, yes, when Jesus first curses a fig tree for sprouting only leaves.

"May you never bear fruit again!" he declares (v. 19). And immediately, the Scripture reports, the fig tree withers and dies. The disciples, amazed, start questioning Jesus about why the fig tree withered so quickly.

But Jesus answers by teaching—that if we have faith and believe, we can do such things. ("You can even say to this mountain, 'May God lift you up and throw you into the sea,' and it will happen," v. 21).

Then Jesus adds: "If you believe, you will receive whatever you ask for in prayer" (v. 22).

From figs to prayer? It seems an odd way to teach a lesson on faith. So some scholars say Jesus was targeting hypocrisy—in "religious" people who put on the outer appearance of being fruitful, as fruitful as a fig tree, but aren't fruitful at all. Others say Jesus was making a point about faithless Israel, a nation professing to be faithful to God, but often failing to obey Him.

Either way, the larger point seems to be about the role of faith in our lives: that those who walk in faith can do what seems impossible. Our faith shapes our prayers, that is, but also our lives. So if we believe our answer is coming, we act like it. Even before we see it. Across the ages, legions of Christians have doubted this, based on their circumstances. But this Bible story shows that the blessing of answered prayer doesn't depend on circumstances. Answered prayer rests, instead, on blessing God with our faith. Then we watch God's Spirit bless us with a harvest. 🌿

Beware in your prayer, above everything, of limiting God.
ANDREW MURRAY

Going Deeper

Your faith is far more precious to God than mere gold.
1 Peter 1:7

We've learned that faith is confident assurance, trustful waiting, or expectant trust—but which of these definitions seems best to you? Explain.

Faith is a precious gift from God, but it must be nurtured. What will you do this week to nurture your faith in God?

Faith can move mountains, Jesus assures us. Name a mountain in your life that you will move by moving closer to God.

If you'd like, write a prayer that addresses your needs concerning the virtue of faith.

Faith sees the invisible, believes the unbelievable, and receives the impossible.
CORRIE TEN BOOM

JOY

His Promise

The joy of the LORD is your strength!
Nehemiah 8:10

My Prayer

Fill me with Your joy, O Jesus,
replacing my weakness with the great strength of You.

Joy: With Feasting

Don't be dejected and sad, for the joy of the LORD is your strength!
Nehemiah 8:10

Joy is a choice. Seems obvious. Seems downright lifesaving. But as believers, many of us get so focused on "being a good Christian" that we forget this reminder from God on what that means: To live life to the fullest. *To not* be dejected and sad. To find joy in God.

Or maybe we're dragged down by some nagging life issue, and to tell the truth, we don't feel like finding joy. Not even in God.

We're perhaps like the children of Israel in Nehemiah's day. They were weeping and wailing as Ezra the scribe read them God's Word. During their long exile in Babylon, they hadn't heard the Book of the Law. During that time, as well, they had sinned. Openly. Blatant sins. Indefensible sins. Thus, as the Levite priests read from God's law, explaining the meaning of each passage, the people wept.

But Nehemiah, their governor, showed compassion by focusing not on their sins but on their revival. "Don't mourn or weep on such a day as this! For today is a sacred day before the LORD your God" (v. 9).

In fact, said Nehemiah, go celebrate! Feast on choice food and sweet drinks, sharing with people who have nothing prepared. Or as he repeated, "This is a sacred day before our Lord" (v. 10). And the joy of the Lord is our strength.

Thus, studying God's sacred Word should make us joyous, not sad.

In a Bible study or church, if the pastor or teacher makes people feel guilty, bad, and unlovable, something is wrong. Hearing God's Word should pierce our hearts regarding sin, but not leave us dejected. Just in case, however, Nehemiah presents the right perspective. No matter what happened in our past, as we restart our journey with God, we are to throw out the weeping and wailing. God asks us to bless Him with something deeper. Hope-filled and empowered joy. 🌿

A gloomy Christian is a contradiction of terms.
WILLIAM BARCLAY

Joy: With Strength

For the joy of the LORD is your strength!
Nehemiah 8:10

She's laughing. Even though her home is a wreck. She's laughing. Even though her project looks lousy. Paint colors all wrong. Fabric choices too costly. When the kitchen cabinets finally arrive—several weeks late—both the size and wood grain completely miss the mark.

"But I'm laughing," says the TV host of the home renovation show, giggling into the camera. "It's how I deal with setbacks," she explains. "I mean, you *have* to laugh. It gets me back on track."

It's a timeless philosophy. Joy imparts strength.

For believers, however, joy in the Lord activates His strength. In our lives. In our circumstances. In our projects. Both big and small.

Speaking to His disciples, Jesus put it this way: "Here on earth you will have many trials and sorrows. But take heart"—be of good cheer—"because I have overcome the world" (John 16:33). We love that promise, indeed.

But why should joy in Him—and not courage or bravery or boldness—deliver the strength of almighty God? Could it be the illogic of the principle? That the beauty of joy is so winsome that it's disarming?

No enemy expects a foe to fight back *with joy.*

Yet there's something strangely powerful about joy. About laughing in the face of a storm. About sizing up your enemy but knowing that, compared to God, your enemy is powerless. About staring up at a mountain and assessing its peaks, crags, and valleys, but knowing—as you laugh—the mountain can't overcome God's power. Is this rationalizing? Or denial? Or is it wisdom?

"I have told you this so that you will be filled with my joy," Jesus told His disciples in the upper room (John 15:11). "Yes, your joy will overflow!" Then as His joy flows, your enemies flee. Can you laugh at that? Try it today. Your victory will follow. 🌿

Joy comes to your rescue—if you let it.
BONNIE ST. JOHN

Joy: In His Presence

In thy presence is fulness of joy; at thy right hand there are pleasures for evermore.
Psalm 16:11, KJV

The preschool choir members toddled to the church microphones. These little ones would be singing an upbeat spiritual featuring a tiny soloist—with a missing front tooth but a gigantic smile. He started singing:

"Every time I feel the Spirit—moving in my heart—I will praaaaaaay!"

Standing tall, the little boy sang at the top of his voice, clapping a little off beat but with total enthusiasm, his smile growing wider with each stanza. Soon people in the audience were on their feet, joining him in song.

But why was his singing so engaging? So infectious? So downright charming?

Then it hit me. He exuded joy. And not the fleeting gladness of "happiness."

Just a child, he seemed nevertheless to stand firm in the psalmist's truth—that in God's presence is joy in full. Thus, to reside with Him—as trusting as a child, singing His praises, right there at His right hand—is to experience His joyous pleasures forever.

And that pleasure shows. It's a visible witness. That's what we were seeing on the little boy's face—evidence, first, that this little saint had gone to Jesus, perhaps asked Him to help him sing his solo. To hit the right notes. To not be afraid. To understand the song so he could sing it right. His prayers were answered, to be sure. But the bonus for seeking the presence of God, and being received in God's presence, was joy. In full.

What an advertisement for God's Spirit. He can fill us with abundant joy. The little boy's face and singing and bright smile testified to that. Now, if a child can know and show the joy of Christ—witnessing to the greatness of God—why can't we?

Answer that question with this prayer: may our God's mighty Spirit, in whose presence we find rest and joy, fill us up with such joy. When? Now. But also forevermore. 🌿

Taste and see that the Lord is good.
Oh, the joys of those who trust in him!
PSALM 34:8

Joy: Doubled

Well done, thou good and faithful servant. . . . Enter thou into the joy of thy lord.
Matthew 25:21, KJV

Want to know what God expects from us? Not a little. Not a lot. Double. Yes, twice what God gives us in His blessings, He wants double that back. A lot to ask? Not when we consider what He longs to give us in return:

Yet more life. More blessings. More joy. *His* joy.

More than we can contain. More than we can imagine.

Not so our enemy.

"The thief's purpose is to steal and kill and destroy," Jesus says of Satan, but also of any enemy that robs us of His joy (John 10:10). But what is the purpose of Christ? "I am come that they might have life, and that they might have it more abundantly" (KJV).

He explains how in the story of the three servants. All three received money from their master, but in differing amounts. Right away, the first servant got busy investing his money—and doubled it. The second servant did the same—doubling his amount. Both earned their master's praise. "Well done!" They also both got job promotions. "I will give you many more responsibilities" (v. 21). Best of all, however, they were invited to celebrate, sharing their master's joy.

To share their master's strength, that is. Abundantly. And, yes, such a blessing comes with a price. That price can never compare, however, with the price Christ paid on the cross for our joy. Double His benefits? In truth, we should be willing to give back even more—because it all belongs to Him anyway.

The third servant learned that the hard way. Fearful, he dug a hole and hid his master's money so he wouldn't lose it. But he lost much more. He lost his master's joy. Want a different outcome? Get up and get busy for Christ, empowered by God's Spirit. Your blessing? Your Master's joy. 🔥

The most precious truth in the Bible is that God's greatest interest is
to glorify the wealth of His grace by making sinners happy in Him.
JOHN PIPER

Joy: With Obedient Love

*When you obey me . . . you will be filled with my joy. Yes, your joy will
overflow!*
John 15:10-11

The path to obeying Christ is no mystery. He highlighted only two commandments. Both focus on love. And we know the two commandments
well. Love God with all our hearts, souls, and minds. And love our neighbors
as ourselves (see Matthew 22:37-39).

Discussing such love in the upper room, however, Jesus further explained
the benefits of obeying Him in these matters. In short, we find joy.

"When you obey me, you remain in my love," Jesus said, "just as I obey
my Father and remain in his love." Then He added: "I have told you this so
that you will be filled with my joy. Yes, your joy will overflow!"

There is great blessing, Jesus is saying, in doing what God asks. And what
He asks is simple. Love Me. Love our neighbors.

We could complicate all of this—and we often do. One young man even
asked Jesus to explain, exactly, who is a "neighbor." You may recall Jesus then
told the story of the Good Samaritan, featuring so-called good people—
including a priest—who stepped around an injured man rather than get
involved to help him.

It's not the Good Samaritan that Jesus mentions, however, when He gathers with His disciples in the upper room, the night before His crucifixion—
that night before the day when everything in the universe changed. On that
night, Jesus talked not about gloomy, horrible, torturous things. Instead,
He washed His disciples' feet, encouraging them to follow His mandate to
love. Why? "So that you will be filled with my joy." Well, more than filled.
By loving, we will overflow with joy. Silly sometimes with joy. Then we will
rest with joy.

Those who make following Christ a long laundry list of dos and don'ts—
or *thou shalts* and *thou shalt nots*—might instead be refreshed by returning to
the upper room. There, Jesus offers us a simple prescription. Take His love
and give it back. In exchange, He blesses with joy. 🌿

The religion of Christ is the religion of joy.
OCTAVIUS WINSLOW

Joy: With Purity

Create in me a clean heart, O God. . . .
Restore to me again the joy of your salvation,
and make me willing to obey you.
Psalm 51:10, 12

To the world, joy comes from sin. That message floods our airwaves and Internet alike. Or as one popular pudding product tempts us in its TV commercial: "It's time to give in." Give in to what? "Sixty decadent calories." In fact, the word *Temptations* is part of the product's name.

And it's just chocolate pudding.

There's no joy, however, in decadence. At the grocery store, reading the label on the chocolate pudding, I found a list of chemical-sounding ingredients I'd hardly want to give in to—let alone eat.

The Bible offers another way to joy, however. Purity.

There is unending pleasure in doing the right thing. Choose the wrong thing, however, and the first thing to depart is joy.

King David, after committing adultery with Bathsheba—and having her husband murdered—pleads for moral restoration in Psalm 51. "Oh, give me back my joy again. . . . Don't keep looking at my sins" (vv. 8-9). Or as he intones: "Create in me a clean heart, O God. Renew a right spirit within me" (v. 10). Regarding the murder, he entreats: "Forgive me for shedding blood, O God who saves; then I will joyfully sing of your forgiveness" (v. 14).

Joyful singing? We can't attain such a godly state by making ungodly choices. "My shameful deeds," David laments, "haunt me day and night" (v. 3). In contrast, David understands that joyful choices—and motivations and actions—will spring from a clean heart that first seeks closeness with God. But even with dirt still in our hearts, when we get up from sin, turning from it—and seek God instead—He offers relief through one holy and blessed gift: joy. ❦

Only those who are obedient—who are pursuing holiness as a way of life—
will know the joy that comes from God.
JERRY BRIDGES

Going Deeper

For the Kingdom of God is not a matter of what we eat or drink, but of living a life of goodness and peace and joy in the Holy Spirit.
Romans 14:17

Joy differs from happiness—but in what ways? How would you explain the difference between having joy and being happy?

Joy in God is a gift from God, but it's also a choice. What would stop someone from choosing joy— especially during times of trouble or trials?

In your own life, what challenge still leaves you feeling gloomy? Would you be willing to accept Jesus' instruction to "be of good cheer" because He has overcome the world? What might that look like?

If you'd like, write a prayer that addresses your needs concerning the virtue of joy.

In commanding us to glorify Him, God is inviting us to enjoy Him.
C. S. LEWIS

HOSPITALITY

His Promise

Cheerfully share your home with those who need
a meal or a place to stay. . . .
Then God will be given glory in everything
through Jesus Christ.
1 Peter 4:9, 11

My Prayer

Replace my reluctance to open my home
with a cheerful will to open my heart—
especially to You.

Hospitality: To His Angels

Don't forget to show hospitality to strangers, for some who have done
this have entertained angels without realizing it!
Hebrews 13:2

The wife couldn't boil water. Not a cook, she didn't try. Her husband didn't either. So they ate at restaurants every night. But that got expensive. So after a while, one of them would grab fast food on the way home. Or not come home. Or not share a meal at all. Soon they were strangers living in the same house. Like ships passing each other in the night. Soon, in fact, the marriage was over.

Sound familiar? It's a composite scenario, to be honest. But it describes how too many couples and families live these days. Strangers existing under the same roof.

If such believers aren't hospitable to each other, how can they show hospitality to real strangers? Today's Scripture offers us a way to start. Show hospitality first, that is, to the strangers in our own families. But how?

By learning to slow down and take time. To learn to cook. (Not a crazy idea, after all. People *do* have to eat.) To swipe the dust off furniture. To care for the home God gave us in the first place. Then to surrender to the process of loving, giving, and sharing.

While hospitality among early Christians was a necessity—providing safety and sustenance in a hostile world where believers were hunted down and persecuted—today the virtue of hospitality requires a different kind of motivation.

To get up and serve God, start at home. So if family members feel like strangers, we can treat them instead like God's valued guests. What a powerful blessing to discover that, right in our own home, reside God's angels. Then when unknown strangers need a place to stay or a meal to eat, we'll know what to do. Open the door and share God. 🦋

Hospitality should have no other nature than love.
HENRIETTA MEARS

Hospitality: Without Fear

Whenever you enter a home, give it your blessing.
Luke 10:5

We're afraid. Is that why we're reluctant to open our doors to strangers, not to mention to friends? We fear our cooking is bad, our homes aren't grand, our furniture is worn, our children are unruly, and our small talk isn't big. More than that, we fear strangers themselves. In a world marked by crime, terrorism, and all manner of sin, letting in a stranger seems downright foolish. If not terrifying.

Nobody knows that better than Jesus. At His own birth, His parents couldn't find a room in crowded Bethlehem. Yet with great deliberateness, He taught His disciples the ways of Christian hospitality—both for givers and receivers.

First, get up with courage. Don't be afraid.

"Remember," He told them, "I am sending you out as lambs among wolves" (v. 3).

We'll encounter unbelievers, He said—some hostile to the cause of Christ. But enter their homes anyway, Jesus insisted. Then don't move from home to home, trying to upgrade your accommodations for a more luxurious place. Eat and drink "whatever is set before you" (v. 8). But that's not all. Heal the sick. In a few words, Jesus packed a wallop of instructions associated with traveling and its related activity—the giving and receiving of hospitality. At its heart, however, is the mandate not to fear.

Why? In the practice of hospitality, Christ goes with us.

"Anyone who accepts your message is also accepting me. And anyone who rejects you is rejecting me. And anyone who rejects me is rejecting God, who sent me" (v. 16).

We don't go alone, to be sure, into the work of hospitality.

No matter which side of the door we find ourselves on, Christ stands with us. Steadying our trembling knees. Straightening our shoulders. Dusting off our discount furniture. Setting our wobbly table. Allowing us to say what He keeps saying to our hearts. *Welcome.* 🕊

There is no hospitality like understanding.
VANNA BONTA

Hospitality: As God's Witness

Then God will be given glory in everything through Jesus Christ.
1 Peter 4:11

Christians were getting killed. By the hundreds they were getting slaughtered. So in the early life of the Christian faith, hospitality wasn't just a nice gesture—it was an urgent necessity. A matter of life and death.

Persecuted for refusing to worship Roman emperors as divine, they encountered outright hatred, torture, and death—trials that the apostle Peter insisted "are only to test your faith" (1 Peter 1:7). Even so, as persecuted believers who traveled to evangelize their faith, their first need while traveling was finding a safe place to rest and refresh.

Yet to get up to take in strangers wasn't easy. *Strangers?*

Apostle Peter understood the challenge. In his letter to early Christians in the provinces of Asia Minor, he encouraged the new believers to "see to it that you really do love each other intensely" (1:22)—or as he said, "with all your hearts."

That meant showing respect to kings and officials, and to "unbelieving neighbors" (2:12)—and to one's husband or wife, and to one's elders—but also to strangers, showing deep love. "For love covers a multitude of sins," Peter wrote (4:8).

Therefore, "Cheerfully share your home with those who need a meal or a place to stay," Peter added (4:9). Not grumbling. Loving.

In the end, sincere hospitality may impress an unbeliever, drawing that person to Christ. Or as Peter put it: "Even if they accuse you of doing wrong, they will see your honorable behavior, and they will believe and give honor to God when he comes to judge the world" (1 Peter 2:12).

A passionate plea, indeed. And a critical reminder. Welcoming believing strangers into our homes blesses and glorifies God. Any inconvenience is irrelevant. What matters is the brightness of our witness. *Other people notice.* Our courage. Our selflessness. Our trust. Our love. Then God's mighty Spirit gets the glory. ❦

Let me live in my house by the side of the road, and be a friend to man.
SAM WALTER FOSS

Hospitality: For His Glory

Then God will be given glory in everything through Jesus Christ.
1 Peter 4:11

Summer vacation in the fifties. Sound idyllic and sweet? And it was fun—a time for car trips to beaches or mountains, or fun treats at ice cream stands or pizza parlors.

Yet to some families—especially African American families like mine—a summer car trip could be a dangerous and nerve-racking journey.

For my family, car trips meant finding amusement parks that would admit us and restaurants that would serve us. Nights meant finding a place that would allow us to rent a room to sleep. My father would drive our car to the "colored" part of town. Then stopping any black stranger on a street corner, he'd ask where our family might stay. "Know anybody who rents rooms?"

During that time, when hotels and motels routinely denied lodging to African Americans—even big-deal celebrities—my humble family found ourselves on the back porches or in the living rooms of many a stranger's home. On lumpy couches and mattresses. Not always clean. Probably not always safe.

Next morning we'd sit at a stranger's kitchen table for a breakfast of varying tastes and quality. Sharing a kitchen table with a complete stranger meant for some close and sometimes awkward encounters.

Looking back, however, I see that if any glory could be found in such situations it went to God. I can't remember the names or faces of those homeowners who took my family in as we traveled. But the fact that they got up to welcome us speaks only to one sure thing: God was providing.

Too often, when it comes to hospitality, we get distracted by worrying over how others will see our homes, food, or furniture. But a weary traveler only wants one thing: the blessing of a safe haven. Or as my daddy would say as we drove to our next stop: "Thank God!" 🔥

Who practices hospitality entertains God Himself.
AUTHOR UNKNOWN

Hospitality: By Faith

So there was food every day for Elijah and for the woman and her family.
1 Kings 17:15, NIV

Feed strangers? On *my* budget? Perhaps you've struggled, as I have, with the challenge of sharing hospitality when your own cupboard feels bare. That excuse fizzles when we recall the widow of Zarephath—so poor and bereft she was gathering sticks to cook her last meal "that we may eat it—and die" (v. 12, NIV).

But the prophet Elijah shows up with a pep talk. "Don't be afraid" (v. 13, NIV). Always a good word. But he also wants food. Specifically, *her* meager food.

Still, by faith, she obeys—going to her hovel to make up a small cake of bread for Elijah from her last handful of flour and last drops of oil. But, sure enough, as Elijah promises, there is food every day for Elijah and for the woman and her family. Why?

"For the flour was not used up and the jug of oil did not run dry, in keeping with the word of the LORD spoken by Elijah" (v. 16, NIV).

That same word is spoken to us today. In short, regardless of how much—or how little—we have in our homes to share with others, we are commanded to give. And just look at the benefit. When we share by faith, as the widow at Zarephath shared, God restores and multiplies what He's blessed us with in the first place. And no, this never should be the purpose of our hospitality—to be rewarded by God with more.

Yet that's the outcome. In the book *Making Room* on reviving Christian hospitality, author Christine Pohl describes the ways hospitable Christians get blessed—from sensing God's presence to finding new friends. With more friends, it's hard to run out of resources, spiritually or practically. In fact, when the widow's son gets sick and dies, her guest Elijah prays to God, asking Him to restore to life the boy whose mother "has opened her home to me" (v. 20).

Her blessing shouldn't surprise us. Her boy lived. 🌿

Good hosts discover . . . they are themselves beloved guests of God's grace.
CHRISTINE POHL

Hospitality: Without Limits

Didn't our hearts feel strangely warm as he talked with us?
Luke 24:32

Who is this stranger? Knocking at *my* door? A reasonable question. But in the early days of Christianity, strangers weren't asked to give their names until they were welcomed inside a believer's house and given a basin of water to wash their feet and a warm meal to fill their bellies. Only at that point, writes scholar Andrew Arterbury, was a stranger asked to say who he actually was.

By faith, Christians opened their homes to other believers—strangers, in particular—not because of who the guest was, but because of who Jesus is. In hospitality, our mutual focus is *Him.* His grace and His message. His Kingdom and His joy. His life.

Even as I offer sanctuary and sustenance, my offerings are not the main item on the menu. Neither is my house. Or my decorating skills.

Hospitality, in its essence, is all about Him. Jesus is the Host, and He welcomes us daily into the wonder of His Presence—His grace, peace, and love—so we may welcome others into our homes in His name. As He said to Cleopas and the other disciples when He appeared following the Resurrection: "Why are you frightened?" Pressing them, He added: "Why do you doubt who I am?" (v. 38).

Such questions remind us not to trust in our meager cooking skills or decorating choices. It's trust in our Savior, empowered by His Spirit, that equips us to get up, stand up, and throw open the doors of our imperfect homes—and our hearts—to weary souls.

Sharing with them the warm touch of Jesus, we discover that both our guests and we ourselves are empowered for greater service. His Kingdom abounds and grows, yes, when we accept the challenge to welcome others into the intimacy of our ordinary homes for the extraordinary sake of Christ.

He *is* the Host. Let Him preside at our tables, blessing us all—without limits. 🍃

We may encounter God's presence in the midst of our hospitality.
ANDREW ARTERBURY

Going Deeper

Cheerfully share your home with those who need a meal or a place to stay.
1 Peter 4:9

What makes you feel welcome—at a church or in another person's home?

If Christian hospitality is a gift you and I give to strangers, how can you update your definition of what it means to practice hospitality in your home?

What can you do to prioritize hospitality as a virtue in your life?

If you'd like, write a prayer that addresses your needs concerning the virtue of hospitality.

And, if you give Him entrance to that very ordinary heart of yours,
it too He will transform.
A. J. GOSSIP

Reverence
and
Fear of God

His Promise

Happy are those who fear the Lord.
Psalm 112:1

My Prayer

I never imagined such happiness, Blessed Father,
that comes in fearing only You.

Reverence and Fear of God: For Our Minds

The fear of the LORD is the beginning of knowledge.
Proverbs 1:7, NIV

God is not safe. That's the terrifying and wondrous truth. And most believers fight that truth. Some for entire lifetimes. Or, in my case, I dared to ask a brave question: how could the God who is Peace, Love, and Joy be the same God who inspires my fear? It didn't add up. But I was ignorant.

And the fear of the Lord is the beginning of knowledge.

So I had to make peace, as the writer of Hebrews puts it, that it's "a terrible thing to fall into the hands of the living God" (Hebrews 10:31). He's a friend but not a buddy, another writer said.

Instead, as God Himself declares in Deuteronomy 32:39, "I am the one who kills and gives life; I am the one who wounds and heals; no one delivers from my power!"

Only as I get to look at the terrifying truth of God's real danger—danger to sin, to Satan, and to all who give in to Satan's ways—will I understand the central fact of godly knowledge: that if it's terrifying to fall into the hands of God, it's more terrifying not to fall into His hands at all.

This point was dramatized with great insight by C. S. Lewis in his classic children's book *The Lion, the Witch and the Wardrobe*. When the children in the story probe their host about Aslan the Lion, they ask: "Is he—quite safe?" The obvious answer: *no.*

He's a lion. Of course he's dangerous. The same could be said of God—who is, indeed, almighty God. With omnipotent power. With infinite might. With purifying justice. So, *yes.* He's terrifyingly dangerous. So He's absolutely not safe. Not one bit. But the children's host adds the corresponding truth:

"But he's *good.*"

Knowing this, we can rise up for the terrifying and wondrous journey of being His children. Knowing that God can't be controlled. Knowing that God won't be compromised. Knowing that God isn't safe. Then falling at His feet in the awe and blessing of being chosen for safety in Him. ❧

I fear God, and therefore I have none else to fear.
JAMES GARDINER

Reverence and Fear of God: For Our Prosperity

Who are those who fear the LORD? . . . They will live in prosperity,
and their children will inherit the land.
Psalm 25:12-13

My dad took no prisoners. He was tall and stern. A World War II veteran. Not given to foolishness. Not inclined to compromise. Not kidding around when it came to the things of family or things of God. He'd made a pact with God, as the story goes, that if he survived World War II—where he served for three years as an infantry unit commander in the South Pacific—he would serve Him all the days of his life.

Bargaining with God? I don't think so. But my dad kept his promises. So he was faithful to his wife, responsible for his children, devoted to his church, and fearful *only* of God. But something else.

My dad was prosperous. Materially, in fact, he did well—although not all who obey God succeed in this way. But as the Latin *pro spere* implies, my dad succeeded with favor, *according to his hope.* (*Spere* in Latin means "hope.") That is, Daddy feared and revered the God in whom he hoped and whom he feared.

Still, for my dad, prosperity wasn't about material success. As in the Hebrew definitions of prosperity—to journey well, to press on against great odds, to have wisdom, to enjoy peace and well-being—my dad's first goal was to prosper in his soul.

Despite a rocky road. As a young black veteran—a civil servant who worked thirty-plus years for the U.S. government, enduring the Jim Crow era and all manner of racial injustice and bias—my dad faced tough roadblocks. Surely, indeed, each of us faces our own rough challenges in life.

My dad taught me to overcome challenges, however, by fearing only God.

So he lived right. And he prospered—especially as God prospers us. Thus, instead of faltering, Daddy endured—aiming high, working hard, going far. Along the way, he taught his children about Jesus—surely our greatest inheritance, and his greatest legacy. You, too, can bless your children with such holy prosperity. How? Fear only God. 🕊

Those know enough who know how to fear God.
MATTHEW HENRY

Reverence and Fear of God: For Our Wisdom

Fear of the LORD is the foundation of wisdom.
Proverbs 9:10

Fearing God? But what exactly does it mean?

I reflect on this question on an odd day—one day, sadly, after lashing out at my daughter's good friend. And feeling *this* small for acting so petty and disrespectful.

She'd invited me to a surprise birthday party for another of their pals. After driving around lost for an hour, trying to make sense of her directions, I finally found the reception hall, jumped from my car, slammed the car door, and rushed into the party, only to berate her for "the worst directions I've seen in my life!"

The look on her face told me how wrong I was. I felt *this* small, indeed, in her eyes. Even smaller in God's eyes. Why, I kept asking myself, did I allow myself to lose control over some driving directions? Then a light turned on and I started to understand.

The fear of God, as David Hubbard so elegantly puts it, "sees each moment as the Lord's time, each relationship as the Lord's opportunity, each duty as the Lord's command, and each blessing as the Lord's gift."

Fear of the Lord, that is, stops us from seeing God's creation from our point of view. Fearing God, instead, we contemplate God's ultimate holiness, purity, power, and glory. We become aware of His greatness—and our smallness—provoking us to live in awe and honor and gratitude of Him and of everyone He created.

So we don't lash out at others. Or forget it was an honor to be invited into their hospitality in the first place. Fearing God, we shut our mouths. Fearing God, we become wise. Fearing God, we tread carefully. Fearing God, we take our proper place in the world He created. So I apologized to my daughter's friend. Humbly. And, in humble fear, I asked God to forgive me for dishonoring and offending Him. Then I thanked Him for His fearsome mercy. It pardons me. Then it sets me free. 🌿

No man more truly loves God than he that is most fearful to offend him.
THOMAS ADAMS

Reverence and Fear of God: For Our Health

*Fear the LORD and shun evil. This will bring health to your body
and nourishment to your bones.*
Proverbs 3:7-8, NIV

The health fair at my church would address the top five medical problems
affecting modern Americans—from heart disease to cancer to HIV/AIDS.

Not exactly church topics?

Perhaps not—except for one thing. Jesus cares about our bodies. As He
taught in Mark 12:30, we are to love God with all our hearts, all our souls, all
our minds, "and all [our] strength." Theologians interpret "strength" in this
verse to mean all of our energy and power. Both take good health, to be sure.

But good health, writes the author of Proverbs, first requires our fear—
fear of God.

As I listen to the workshop panelists at my church, I start to see the
connection.

When we revere and fear God, we feed and care for our bodies—not so
we can look great in next season's fashions or feel great just to feel great—but
so we can serve Him at our best. That means making good choices. Or to
paraphrase one of the panelists, good choices build a path to good health.

The apostle Paul puts it this way in his letter to the church at Rome: "If
you live according to the sinful nature, *you will die*; but if by the Spirit you
put to death the misdeeds of the body, *you will live*" (Romans 8:13, NIV,
italics added).

Or perhaps we don't want to consider such things today.

We'd rather rely on multivitamins, organic foods, and hours at the gym.
All those things are fine, our psalmist would write.

But if whole health is your aim, get up and shun evil—in fear of God.

This prescription isn't as fancy as choosing a new workout wardrobe or
hiring a high-priced personal trainer. But it works.

Fear only God. Then act like it. You'll see the empowered results in the
mirror. 🌿

Faith and prayer are the vitamins of the soul.
MAHALIA JACKSON

Reverence and Fear of God: For Our Safety

*For the angel of the LORD guards all who fear him,
and he rescues them.*
Psalm 34:7

My older daughter heard a loud pop from her left wheel tire. A blowout. On busy I-10 in Dallas, she had no choice but make for an outside lane and exit the freeway. Right away, however, she found herself on a tough block in one of that city's worst areas.

"Absolutely no place to find help, not even a McDonald's." Finally she saw a drugstore, pulled in the nearby lot, and parked. With no one around, she opened her door and checked her trunk for a lug wrench. But as she stood there, a man in a pickup truck pulled in to the lot, parked his truck next to hers, and got out. He shrugged—showing he didn't speak English. Then reaching into his truck, he retrieved a larger lug wrench.

In minutes, he removed her bad tire and replaced it with the spare. When she tried to pay him, he shook his head. Instead, he cleaned his hands, got back in his truck, and with a polite wave, drove away.

But who was he?

"An angel," my daughter said. That's how she explained it. "God sent an angel. That's the only way I can explain it. It was like he showed up to rescue me." Then, after changing her tire, he waved politely and left. Coincidence? Or a real angel? It seems ludicrous, in modern times, to claim that God sends angels who rescue. Or does He send more? His *presence.*

That, in fact, is what my daughter felt in the helpful stranger. God's presence in an unlikely place—the "worst" part of town made holy by the wondrous presence of God. Can we experience His presence in the worst part of our lives? We will if we believe what seems impossible: God sends His angel to rescue those who fear Him.

So let this be a day our reverence sends His angels to each of us who bless Him with the unexpected—our holy fear. 🔥

The LORD is like a father to his children,
tender and compassionate to those who fear him.
PSALM 103:13

Reverence and Fear of God: With Great Abundance

True humility and fear of the LORD lead to riches.
Proverbs 22:4

"Who's rich?"

The woman at the battered-women's shelter asked her question. Her good question. "It makes me smile to think about it," she said. "So I'll ask everybody here tonight—are you rich?"

None of us at this Bible study, in fact, was a wealthy fat cat—surely not in money. Of our small group, half the women were from my inner-city church. The others were residents of the shelter, all trying to find jobs, resettle with their children, and restart their lives. By our bank accounts, in truth, some could be called "poor."

Yet we all raised our hands. Or as one young woman said, "I *know* I'm rich."

She explained: "I have life in my body. Air in my lungs. Joy in my heart. Salvation in Christ. I look out at the beautiful day and I can see it. So yes—I *am* rich!"

A perfect answer. A godly answer. To be sure, the Bible sometimes speaks of riches as a blessing from God—as in Proverbs 8:18. Other Scriptures, however, warn against hoarding riches or trusting in riches instead of God. So Psalm 62:10 makes it plain: "If your wealth increases, don't make it the center of your life."

Jesus stressed the same, noting, "How hard it is for the rich to enter the Kingdom of God!" (Mark 10:23).

At this humble women's shelter, likewise, our friend's question provoked us to see with new eyes God's promise that honoring Him may lead to material wealth.

For certain, fearing God leads to spiritual wealth. Without limits.

This abundance, built fearfully and humbly, relying on God's Spirit and His incomparable mercies, doesn't just make you and me rich. It is a treasure that is priceless. ❧

The real measure of our wealth is how much we should be worth
if we lost our money.
J. H. JOWETT

Going Deeper

How great is the goodness you have stored up for those who fear you.
Psalm 31:19

After reflecting this week on reverence and the fear of God, what does fearing God mean to you?

God's Word makes numerous promises to those who fear God. Which promises excite you the most? Explain.

Which promises about fearing God challenge you the most? Explain.

If you'd like, write a prayer that addresses your needs concerning the virtue of reverence and fear of God.

The fear of the Lord tends to take away all other fears. . . .
This is the secret of Christian courage and boldness.
SINCLAIR B. FERGUSON

OBEDIENCE

His Promise

*If you fully obey the LORD your God
by keeping all the commands I am giving you today,
the LORD your God will exalt you above all
the nations of the world.*
Deuteronomy 28:1

My Prayer

For my own good, O Lord,
and for Your glory,
stir up my hunger to obey
Your commands.

Obedience: To the Father

I will send you rain in its season, and the ground will yield
its crops and the trees their fruit.
Leviticus 26:4, TNIV

A sovereign God demands obedience. No surprise. It's His right. From on high He can issue a simple decree: obey Me.

But our God sweetens the pot, so to speak. Obey Me, God says, *and* I will send rain in its season. The ground will yield its crops. The trees will yield their fruit. But that's not all. In eight more verses in this passage, God lays out a jam-packed bounty of blessings for His people who are willing to obey. Why so much bounty?

Only one thing can explain it.

God blesses because He loves. Or to make it plain, He loves *us*. "Yet the LORD set his affection on your forefathers and loved them, and he chose you, their descendants, above all the nations" (Deuteronomy 10:15, NIV). It follows that He wants the best for us. He wants the most for His people and all their descendants.

Or as Moses explained in Deuteronomy 10:13, God asks us to obey His commands and decrees "*for your own good.*"

Those are His motives, yes. But we can't expect such good without His terms. Thus, obedience, first, is about coming to terms with who God is. Sovereign and Almighty. A giver of amazing gifts. "*Then,*" God says, "you will know that I am the LORD your God" (Exodus 16:12, italics added).

I've tried to scoot around this fact. Tried to act like God is too loving to speak so plain. But here's the truth. Only we who accept our God as Sovereign *and* Lord bless Him with such obedience. As the writer of the book of Hebrews says of Christ: "Once made perfect, he became the source of eternal salvation for all who obey him" (5:9, NIV).

In the same way, God sees where we stand with Him by how we obey Him. With a grudge—or with joy? Obeying is our spiritual barometer. But why would God choose obedience as an indicator? Why not some other test? Because He alone is God. 🌿

The golden rule for understanding in spiritual matters
is not intellect, but obedience.
OSWALD CHAMBERS

Obedience: To the Son

"Follow me," Jesus said.
Luke 5:27, NIV

As commands go, these two words of Jesus are plain and clear. But for me, on a cool, cloudy springtime afternoon, the words seemed complex and deep. I'd just returned from a meeting with my pastor—where I'd asked officially to be considered as a local deacon. I'd be on the path to ordination. But was I ready? Ready to follow Jesus *there?*

Such following challenges God's servants for two key reasons. First, if we stay too far behind the Lord—not drawing near to His Spirit—we never catch up to His ways, His deeds, His truth. Second, however, we can't follow if we don't know Him. In today's Scripture, the tax collector Levi—despite his crooked lifestyle—knew precisely who Jesus was. Jesus was Levi's path to a new life. At Christ's call, Levi "got up, left everything and followed" (v. 28, NIV).

What a contrast to the people of Nazareth. "Isn't this Joseph's son?" they asked. They were amazed, reports the Gospel of Luke, "at the gracious words that came from his lips." At first, in fact, they spoke well of Him (Luke 4:22, NIV). Then the tables turned. The people got sidetracked. They wanted Jesus to perform in Nazareth the miracles He had performed in Capernaum and elsewhere. Jesus' reply—"no prophet is accepted in his hometown"—revealed the true spirit of the Nazarenes (v. 24, NIV). True, they were intrigued by Joseph's returning son. But they were "furious" that He refused to perform deeds for them (v. 28). Not seeing His divinity, they tried to throw Him off a cliff.

Levi, instead, set off on a life-changing adventure with Jesus. At the word *follow*, he would understand its Hebrew essence—*halakh,* meaning "walk," was like saying *walk with me.* It's what makes obedience to the Son such a blessing. Despite the challenge of walking with Christ—of obeying His call to go where He leads—something precious keeps us on the journey: No matter our ministry or mission, when we get up to travel with Jesus, we never walk alone. 🔥

Unless he obeys, a man cannot believe.
DIETRICH BONHOEFFER

Obedience: To the Spirit

If you love me, you will obey what I command. And I will ask the Father,
and he will give you another Counselor to be with you forever—
the Spirit of truth.
John 14:15-17, NIV

What does truth have to do with obedience? Jesus offers the answer. "If you love me, you will obey," Jesus states to a room full of disciples. Then, He says, "the Father . . . will give you another Counselor . . . the Spirit of truth."

The men are crowded into an upper room, trying to digest the uncompromising teachings of their beloved Christ—and the fact that soon He will give up His life. He will be betrayed, He tells them. Peter will deny Him. Then, standing face-to-face with His betrayer, Judas, Jesus begins to teach not about truth—but about love.

"If you love me. . . ." It's the first step to truth.

I smile at this scene. To be sure, my Savior knows my "downsitting and mine uprising," as the psalmist says (Psalm 139:2, KJV). So I can't *pretend* to love Him. Or just say I love Him. Or profess to love Him. If I love Him, I obey Him. Pure and simple. But why is truth the blessing? One key reason: truth makes us known to God's Spirit—the very Spirit of truth.

Truthful people "dwell in [the LORD's] sanctuary," David writes in Psalm 15:1-2 (NIV). Moreover, God's love "is ever before" those who walk in His truth (Psalm 26:3, NIV).

God's truth also protects (Psalm 40:11). In fact, the Lord is near "to all who call on him in truth" (Psalm 145:18). Even more, "the LORD detests lying lips, but he delights in men who are truthful" (Proverbs 12:22, NIV).

But first? Stand up and obey. Then stand firm to love. Then, promises Jesus, he will send "you a Counselor to be with you forever—the Spirit of truth." It's a priceless blessing. The Spirit of truth enables us to be discerning, shrewd, perceptive, knowledgeable, prudent. Loving and loved. For such a blessing, I bow before Him to ask for a spirit to obey. Then I see! The door to His heart swings open. 🌿

The person who wants to know God but who has no heart
to obey Him will never enter the sacred courts where God reveals
Himself to the soul of man.
SINCLAIR FERGUSON

Obedience: In Peace

If you . . . obey my commands . . . I will grant peace in the land. . . .
I will remove wild beasts from the land.
Leviticus 26:3, 6, TNIV

In recent years, my suburban Denver neighborhood has experienced its share of wildlife. Coyotes. Red foxes. Bull snakes. A few rattlesnakes. Then this spring, local officials issued a warning about raccoons. Keep small pets and children away, the officials advised, and "make noise with pots and pans" to drive them away. But if the critters take shelter in a fireplace flue, a city memo said, drive them out with "a bowl of ammonia." And set a radio next to it—tuned "to a talk program or hard rock station."

Works every time?

With raccoons, I'm not sure. But this Scripture offers a quieter, cleaner, sweeter way to rid our lives of its wild beasts: obedience to God. To be sure, life's ugly, annoying, dangerous beasts attack us from every direction—lies, doubts, guilt, condemnation, fear—both physical and emotional, material and spiritual.

We fight back with obvious weapons. Noisy outbursts. Foul-smelling attitudes. Clanging cymbals of every version, variation, and variety. Always, on our own, we fail. Yet many of us keep aiming our own weapons at every beast we battle. No matter how hard we fight, most escape to attack us another day.

But God's battle plan is best—and He fights with a curious implement. Without asking us to break a sweat, clench our fists, raise our arms, aim our guns, or turn on loud radios, He invites us to triumph over our enemies simply by giving Him our surrendered best—our obedience.

Our willingness floats up like a sweet song to the ear of our God. In exchange for our yielding, He transforms our beasts into His blessings. That's enough to make us shout with gratitude and sing with praise—*if* we're tuned to the right station. The Solid Rock.

In many ways, the attitude of obedience is much more vital than the act.
JOHN MACARTHUR

Obedience: In Plenty

I will look on you with favor and make you fruitful and increase your numbers.
Leviticus 26:9, NIV

Like all Christians, I want God's favor. I long for it, in fact. To be honest, I want not just to be loved *and* liked by God. I want to be one of His favorites—so much that He blesses me with fruitfulness for Him. *But also increases it.*

That may sound like a greedy, worldly, clawing desire. As I commit to obeying Him, however, I find my desires don't shrink—as some theologies suggest they should. Instead, my desires expand. That's how it should be. Obedient followers don't want less from God. We *should* want more.

But not for ourselves. In obedience, we should want more of God—*for* God—and for His people.

It follows that God offers, in return, exactly what obedient followers crave. A great harvest. "You will *still* be eating last year's harvest," the Lord promises the obedient, when it's time to "make room for the new" (Leviticus 26:10, NIV, italics added).

Such blessed extravagance! But as we read deeper into these verses, we are shown why. "I will look on you with favor . . . *and I will keep my covenant with you,*" declares the Lord (v. 9, italics added). As obedient followers, our favorable status and our fruitful increase both witness to the world, not our greatness, but the faithfulness of our God.

Yes, the Maker of the covenant also keeps it. Those who see will understand exactly who He is: the Promise Maker *and* the Promise Keeper.

What a great lesson for believers longing for godly favor but never seeming to find it. The solution? Obedience. It should be assuring, in fact, to learn that God isn't arbitrary with favor and increase. *If* we follow His decrees, He says, we'll realize these blessings. For God, it is the perfect arrangement. He can give much to the obedient. Why? He knows we will give it away. 🌿

A great work is made out of a combination of obedience and liberty.
NADIA BOULANGER

Obedience: In Action

Your threshing will continue until grape harvest and the grape harvest will continue until planting, and you will eat all the food you want and live in safety in your land.
Leviticus 26:5, NIV

My former pastor complained often about what he called "Christian busy-work"—from too many potluck dinners to an abundance of pancake suppers. Not bad work, certainly. But not always Kingdom work. That's how he saw it. One thing's for certain, however. Obedient followers *will* stay busy. Threshing and harvesting. Harvesting and planting. Obedience, it turns out, leads to action. We see that in the Hebrew word for "obey"—*shema*—the same word, in fact, as the Hebrew word for "listen."

Shema O Israel. . . . "Hear, O Israel," says the *Shema* prayer. It draws listeners to God, implying that listening to God is, by default, an actively obedient response.

This is a provocative concept for contemporary believers—many of us tend to live our faith in theory, not in practice. In the pew, not on the firing line.

Obeying God, however, requires that we *do* something. Jesus narrows it down: "Love the Lord your God with all your heart and with all your soul and with all your mind and with all your strength." This is the first and greatest commandment, He says. And the second is like it: "Love your neighbor as yourself" (Mark 12:30-31, NIV).

Our problem with obeying this command is that *love*, as such, has become just another word—overused, underrealized, sung about in too many songs that sound catchy but mean little. Obeying God's decree to love, however, means putting our love into action. Expect to thresh wheat and barley, oats and rice—until the grape harvest. Then expect to harvest grapes until it is time, once again, to plant grains. Is this what Jesus meant when He said to love God with our everything? Until there is a harvest?

It's an exciting challenge. Our love may not reap a harvest in our own lifetimes. In the meantime, however, obedient love gets up and gets to work anyway. But even better, our harvests for Him will be divine. 🔥

God visits industrious men with His favors.
MATTHEW HENRY

Going Deeper

We must obey God rather than any human authority.
Acts 5:29

What is your attitude toward obedience to God? Do you believe God's promises to the children of Israel apply to you today?

Read Deuteronomy 6:1-9. Regarding obedience, what one change could you make to obey God more?

What special insight has God taught you this week about obeying?

If you'd like, write a prayer that reflects the principles—or your needs— regarding the virtue of obedience.

I always stress that we are responsible to obey the will of God, but that we are dependent upon the Holy Spirit for the enabling power to do it.
JERRY BRIDGES

RIGHTEOUSNESS

His Promise

The eyes of the LORD watch over those who do right;
his ears are open to their cries for help.
Psalm 34:15

My Prayer

For Your glory, O Lord,
help me
to do the right thing.

Righteousness: In Full

Blessed are those who hunger and thirst for righteousness,
for they will be filled.
Matthew 5:6, NIV

I can walk. But on that day, I was crawling. That Daniel Fast—yes, that tough fast—left me *starving*. Or, by day four of the twenty-one-day fast with my church, that's how I felt. Flat-out hungry. From my insides out. But what was I hungry for?

Meat? Bread? Butter? Ice cream? A huge plate of fettuccine pasta topped with marinara and meat sauce and grated parmigiano-reggiano cheese? In fact, when the fast ended and I went back to regular eating, with pasta in the spotlight, I was satisfied after a hearty meal. By the next meal, though, there I was—hungry again. Thirsty, too.

But to hunger and thirst after righteousness—to hunger to do God's will as Jesus reveals it—is a longing God promises to satisfy. In full.

Jesus described it this way: "I want your will to be done, not mine" (Luke 22:42).

Likewise, real disciples hunger to see the Father's will always done in their lives—knowing, by faith, it will be better than anything we think or want. Too often, sadly, we hunger for what we see, then seek to base our thirsts on our own flawed sight.

But God's right way for our lives will, by faith, always be far better than our own plans or ways.

Don't feel such a hunger? Can't feel that thirst?

Then stand up tall to pray. Ask, that is, for God's Holy Spirit to stir up in you a hunger and thirst for His righteousness, allowing Jesus to reveal to you what the Father's righteous will is for every empty and parched corner in your life.

Pray like that, yes, to be hungry and thirsty. In a world where physical starvation is real, it may even seem to be an insensitive and frivolous prayer.

But to be hungry and thirsty for God's righteousness—for ourselves and others, too—will bless our hungry world. No other satisfaction will match it. 🌿

God has created each of us with a thirst that only He can quench.
DAN STONE

Righteousness: At Home

He blesses the home of the upright.
Proverbs 3:33

Our ragged shake-shingle roof had seen better days. Now at its worst, the roof was falling apart in tatters. With every stiff wind gust, another rotting shingle took to the skies—landing in a shattered heap in our yard. Dried and brittle, the shingles also were clearly a fire hazard. Obviously, it was past time for a new roof.

As roofing contractors came to inspect, leaving more and higher bids, my husband and I contemplated whom to hire. But as I looked over the bids yet again one night, feeling confused and frustrated over costs and decisions, I finally put down the bids to pray.

Whom, O God, should we hire to replace our crumbling roof?

And I loved this prayer.

It reminded me about the "roof story" in the Bible, where four friends brought their paralyzed friend to Jesus. But because a big crowd blocked the house where Jesus was teaching, the four friends tore off the roof to gain entrance. Laying their friend at Jesus' feet, the four showed such faith that Jesus forgave the sick man's sins—then healed him.

But would God bless my own roof story? That is, would He bless us for daring to seek His will for repairing our torn-up roof? For trying to repair it right—as He would? For an answer, my husband stood up with a simple question. "Have you called our neighbor?"

She and her husband had hired a good roofer a few years ago. Other neighbors hired the same guy. It made sense for us to do the same. But it took prayer to remind us.

So we hired him, confident it was the right choice. A few days later, as this contractor and his crew tore off our decaying roof—stomping around overhead and tearing away the old rotting shingles—I sat inside and listened to the sound. Crunching. Ripping. Pulling. Breaking. The noise of making a wrong thing right.

But what did all that noise sound like? God blessing a humble home. 🌿

The whole world could abound with the services to the Lord . . .
not only in churches but also in the home.
MARTIN LUTHER

Righteousness: In Peace

And this righteousness will bring peace.
Isaiah 32:17

During the prophet Isaiah's day, honest leaders were rare. Priests and prophets "stagger with alcohol and lose themselves in wine," the prophet wrote. "They reel when they see visions and stagger as they render decisions" (Isaiah 28:7). Fortune tellers and astrologers served as consultants (Isaiah 3:2-3). No surprise the people under such "leadership" were just as rebellious and sinful.

But, *look*, Isaiah cried: "A righteous king is coming!" And "honest princes will rule under him" (Isaiah 32:1).

He was prophesying about the Messiah, who would provide shelter from the wind and a refuge from the storm, "like streams of water in the desert and the shadow of a great rock in a parched land" (v. 2). It was a provocative promise, but also a warning to "you women who lie around in ease" acting "smug" and wearing "pretty clothes" (vv. 9, 11).

But to the poor and underserved of Isaiah's time, such a prophecy would have sounded life giving, renewing—maybe even remarkable.

Even better would have been the prophet's promise that "justice will rule in the wilderness and righteousness in the fertile field. And *this* righteousness will bring peace" (vv. 16-17, italics added).

Not the false righteousness of crooked, cruel, stingy, godless rulers. Or of fancy clothes, houses, and sprawling lawns and land. Instead, the righteousness of Christ would sweep away such brash, showy emptiness. In its place, His righteousness would "bring quietness and confidence forever" (v. 17). Thus, not only does conflict end when Christ's righteousness reigns in our homes, families, and nations, but personal wholeness and confidence reign. Light reigns over darkness. Hope reigns over despair. Knowledge reigns over ignorance. Love reigns over hate. *This* righteousness rules. So stand and walk in Christ's righteousness today. The blessing? His empowered, righteous peace. 🕯

He brings the peace of God (Philippians 4:7) to those who walk with Him.
JOHN MACARTHUR

Righteousness: In Christ

The effect of righteousness will be quietness.
Isaiah 32:17, NIV

The film clip on sexually transmitted diseases ended. And the church was silent. Pin-drop silent. This was only the second time at our church that an open discussion on HIV/AIDS was presented, and only the first time such a discussion was held in the formal sanctuary—and not in the casual fellowship hall.

Then one woman raised her hand with a comment. Something about condoms. And the floor didn't fall in or the ceiling fly off. So before long, questions rang out.

Except one. Nobody asked about sin. The word wasn't mentioned even once.

The film, in fact, implied it was wrong to judge those with sexually transmitted diseases such as HIV/AIDS. I agree. We shouldn't judge.

Medical concerns were first, my husband said later. "That's where people are." It's God's righteous mercy, that is, and not God's condemnation that stirs up in all of us a longing to get right with our loving God. Healing starts there. Not in the noise of accusations. But in the quiet confidence that God's righteousness will reign. Thus, our topic that night was HIV/AIDS.

Yet all have sinned and come short of the glory of God. And yes, it is true as the writer of 1 John declared: "If we claim we have no sin, we are only fooling ourselves and not living in the truth." Indeed, if we confess our sins, "He is faithful and just to forgive us our sins and to cleanse us from all wickedness" (1 John 1:8-9).

Therefore, the discussion at my church was timely and convicting. But wallowing in mistakes and immorality wasn't the aim. Instead, the effect of sitting in God's sanctuary—in the seat of God's righteousness—was quietness and confidence. Not in ourselves. But in Him. Our healing starts there. 🕊

Our sins are now not ours but Christ's, and Christ's righteousness
is not Christ's, but ours.
MARTIN LUTHER

Righteousness: In Friendship

He offers his friendship to the godly.
Proverbs 3:32

God wants to be our friend. An amazing truth. Too hard to believe? It could even be too hard to consider. But the Bible confirms His holy longing for friendship with His creation. Listen in Revelation 3:20 to Jesus: "Look! Here I stand at the door and knock. If you hear me calling and open the door, I will come in, and we will share a meal as friends."

Or ponder Abraham—who believed God, "so God declared him to be righteous," then he was called "the friend of God" (James 2:23).

In the upper room, meantime, Jesus told his disciples: "You are my friends if you do what I command. . . . I have called you friends, for everything that I learned from my Father I have made known to you. You did not choose me, but I chose you" (John 15:14-16, NIV).

Me? Amazing. But there is a condition to God's friendship.

We have to get up, by His grace, and act godly. By keeping in touch with God. Being trustworthy. Confiding in God. Obeying. Forgiving. Listening. Following through. Not just talking about being a friend, but acting like one. By sticking closer than a brother.

To be a real friend, in other words, requires our best. We try to take the high road. Sacrificing our own interests. And in that effort? God chooses us as His friends. Right here on earth.

Then look at the blessings. We can confide in Him. Enjoy His forgiveness. Share and listen. Sharpen our honesty, integrity, and truth. Then whatever righteousness we brought to the friendship grows even more. Are you enjoying His friendship this year? Stand up and say yes. Then let Him bless you with a priceless gift—the rightness of Him. 🌿

It is in relationships that we develop into what God wants us to be.
KENT HUGHES

Righteousness: In Abundance

He grants a treasure of good sense to the godly. He is their shield.
Proverbs 2:7

I was a church girl, but not enough. So lacking godliness in the deepest parts of my life, I lacked what I needed most: common sense.

It doesn't come easy, indeed. Common sense is developed. Often over a long lifetime, common sense may finally settle in, giving those who employ it a sense of command in life, a supply of good reasoning in decision making, and an air of favor where others experience disdain or despair.

Common sense is worth its weight in gold, to be sure. Or as the nineteenth-century American populist Josh Billings put it: "Common sense is the knack of seeing things as they are, and doing things as they ought to be done."

But what if it didn't require a lifetime of experience to acquire such good sense?

In his writings, King Solomon of the Bible shows how: follow God.

When we cry to God's Spirit, seeking to walk in His ways, God grants a treasury of good sense, Solomon promises. For godly people, that is, God's storehouse of grace and protection never runs out when it comes to common sense.

A priceless blessing, to be sure.

So, buy a piece of land near a vile swamp? Common sense says no. Marry a beautiful, rich woman with an evil, sharp tongue? Common sense says no. Wear a thin coat on a cold and bitter day? Common sense says no. Go into business with a known cheat? Common sense shouts *no*. We ignore common sense to our own peril, Solomon warns. When our desires, lusts, and egos get in the way, common sense loses out.

But trusting God enough to stand up for His ways over others' blesses us with the keys to one of God's greatest treasuries: His good sense. As you consider this priceless treasure, rise up today and choose right. Then watch blessings flow. ❧

The voice of the Lord is the voice of common sense.
SAMUEL BUTLER

Going Deeper

Plant the good seeds of righteousness, and you will harvest a crop of love.
Hosea 10:12

In matters of morality, righteousness is defined by some theologians as knowing God's will, revealed by Jesus Christ. How does this differ from what you may have thought righteousness means?

God blesses those who hunger and thirst for righteousness. But how deep is your hunger and thirst for the righteousness of God? How can you deepen it?

What special insight has God taught you this week about righteousness?

If you'd like, write a prayer that reflects the principles—or your needs— regarding the virtue of righteousness.

The way of the righteous is like the first gleam of dawn,
which shines ever brighter until the full light of day.
PROVERBS 4:18

Humility

His Promise

Those who humble themselves will be exalted.

Luke 14:11

My Prayer

Humble my heart, O God,
that I might find honor in Your sight.

Humility: Like Christ

God blesses those who are humble,
for they will inherit the whole earth.
Matthew 5:5

Wash some feet. Jesus' best example of what it means to be humble teaches us exactly that. Wash some feet. In His day, nothing was more humbling. To stoop to wash the dusty, crusty, dirt-smeared, smelly feet of somebody else was a servant's humble job. In feet washing, therefore, Jesus illustrated His most important lesson on how to be great in His Kingdom. Bow down to serve others.

Wash some feet.

Jesus said it this way in His Sermon on the Mount. "God blesses those who are humble, for they will inherit the whole earth." He was quoting from Psalm 37, which contrasts the wicked and the lowly. "Soon the wicked will disappear. Though you look for them, they will be gone" (v. 10).

But the lowly? "The lowly will possess the land" (v. 11).

We tend to believe it's just the opposite—that the shrewd, savvy, and cunning will come out on top. That the clever crooks and fat cats will own everything.

But Jesus asked the clamoring crowds to think outside of this box—to understand that it's not in clawing our way to "greatness" that we reach greatness. It's our willingness to stoop to serve others that gives us honor in God's sight.

One can imagine, indeed, the rapt attention such a sermon would evoke. The so-called important people hearing such words would have been scandalized, if not horrified. But to the lowly, Jesus' words would've offered affirmation, encouragement, comfort, and a challenge: See yourself as God sees you. Not as the least, but as the greatest. And look! Humble service comes with a bonus: a sure place in the land of God's Kingdom. Sound impossible?

We have only to look down at the one washing our feet. Our Savior is our Servant. And now He's our King. Let us bless His mighty example today. How? Wash some feet. 🔥

God's choice acquaintances are humble men.
ROBERT LEIGHTON

Humility: With Peace

*The lowly will possess the land
and will live in peace.*
Psalm 37:11

Wash some feet?

We come reluctantly to such a position of lowliness. Or let me speak for myself. The first time I washed my mother's feet, during the last months of her life, I wasn't confident I'd wash them "right." She'd traveled eighty-eight years of good and productive living—in a body no longer able to bend down low. So I sat on the floor at her feet. Willing to wash.

Then finally I understood. Humility is love. Therein lies the power of humility. It's not holding back. It's stooping down—and putting others first—then getting up to work. So I washed my beloved mother's weary feet.

She let me touch her, in other words.

After some years of tension between us—and not a few harsh words—she let me touch her aching feet and wash them. So I tried to wash like Jesus.

To wash feet right, that is, you have to go down to the floor, to kneel there. You go low. Then, looking up from the grungy sadness of the other person's bone-tired feet, what do you see? You see gratitude. You see trust.

And the fear is gone. The lies that keep people apart vanish. All the little irritations and misunderstandings and wrong words and bad feelings crumble when you do what looks hard—a humble show of love—but, in surrender, isn't so hard after all.

Once we start washing, in fact, it's easy. Even as pie. The other person can't move, for one thing. You've got their feet in your hands, just washing away, splashing water and soothing the aches. So they sit there, letting you soothe. Then the blessing happens. You're soothed too. The clawing way of ambition and competition can't compete. Humble washing, in contrast, is peaceful. Just as the Scriptures promise.

So I ask: do you need peace today? Jesus shows us how. Wash some feet. 🌿

Humility like the darkness reveals the heavenly lights.
HENRY DAVID THOREAU

Humility: With Grace

He . . . gives grace to the humble.
Proverbs 3:34, NIV

The altar call followed a powerful sermon. As our pastor preached, in fact, a sizable part of the congregation stood for half of the sermon. It was that inspiring. That moving. That on point. As he issued the invitation to come to Christ, I expected crowds of hungry seekers to step forth. Instead, on this Sunday, only one came.

A young woman. Dressed more like a man. Her hair was cornrowed roughly. A too-big, buttoned man's shirt hung loosely from her thin shoulders. A pair of men's trousers and sneakers completed her outfit. But as she was introduced, her name was a girl's. Then the pastor placed his hand on her head to pray. And something happened.

This rough-looking girl, before our eyes, was transformed into a graceful angel.

This new church member dropped to her knees at Pastor's feet, that is. Humbled to be in God's house. Humbled to stand in God's presence. So she dropped to her knees before God's servant.

"Welcome home," the pastor said. As he held out his hand to help her stand, she looked different. Turning to face the congregation, she showed a shy smile. Graceful. Delicate. Beautiful.

Whatever rough look she'd brought with her down the aisle had vanished in her show of humility. "Welcome your new member!" the pastor said.

With loud applause and a shout, the congregation greeted her.

God's daughter. Our new sister in Christ. A graceful child, captivating our attention, compassion, and acceptance. And she didn't break a sweat to get it. Instead, she fell to her knees. Humbled. With that, she inspired us to respond with godly grace. Thus remembering this moment, I pause to pray: Help me today, O God, to kneel at Your feet and bless You with this same gift—my humility. Then bless me in return, precious Christ, with the power of Your grace. 🔥

Fairest and best adorned is she whose clothing is humility.
JAMES MONTGOMERY

Humility: With Strength

For when I am weak, then I am strong.
2 Corinthians 12:10

Satan tricks us. Our enemy wants us to think humble people are losers. Thus, to us, humility can feel weak, passive, and wimpy. We're conditioned by our culture, in fact, to see meekness and mildness as nerdy and negative.

God's Word repeatedly tells us, however, how the Lord honors our honest nothingness. With His peace. With His inheritance. With His wisdom. With "riches, honor, and long life" (Proverbs 22:4).

Thus, John the Baptist's urgent longing that "He must become greater and greater, and I must become less and less" (John 3:30) only begins to capture the divine rewards in choosing lowly humility over self-preening pride.

To make it plain, God cares for the humble.

Why? The humble allow God to be God.

The apostle Paul—perhaps the most influential Christian in the history of the faith—reflected on the surrendering power of such humility. In Paul's second letter to the Corinthians, he described being given a "thorn in my flesh . . . to torment me" and "keep me from becoming proud." Three times, in fact, he begged the Lord to take this thorn away. But each time, the Lord told Paul: "My grace is all you need." Why?

"My power works best in weakness."

As Paul observed: "That's why I take pleasure in my weaknesses. . . . For when I am weak, then I am strong."

Will you let the deep truth of this promise sink into your soul today? Perhaps you're not top dog in your circle. Or perhaps you were top dog, but you're laying down such vain ambition to walk humbly with God. Will you bless Him by trusting His promise—that He honors, cares for, and empowers the humble? If you will, get ready to experience more strength than you can ask for or imagine. For when you are meek and lowly and humble and weak, *He* is stronger. 🕯

God created the world out of nothing, and so long as we are nothing,
He can make something out of us.
MARTIN LUTHER

Humility: With Wisdom

With humility comes wisdom.
Proverbs 11:2

I was a hotshot writer, or so I thought. Since grade school, awards and plaques covered my bedroom walls—largely due to strong scores in English and composition. Then I went to college.

My first papers earned only average grades. Lots of Cs. Far too many Cs, in fact. Then on a cloudy fall day, I held a paper in my hand with an F.

I stared at it. Holding back tears. Trying to listen to the professor. Forcing myself not to cry. Or scream. An *F*? For *me*? The high school honor student? It was all I could do not to crumple the paper in shreds and storm out of the classroom. Then I read the professor's note. The writing was fine, she wrote, but I'd made an error of fact. Result? An automatic F.

So I dried my eyes. I swallowed hard. Humility doesn't go down easy.

I approached the professor after class, thanking her for pointing out the mistake and vowing not to let it happen again. The next day, I visited another professor—asked him to review my mistakes. I asked to see some A-quality papers, to get a better idea of his standards. I swallowed hard as he shared "better" papers than mine. Then I listened hard as he explained why mine fell short. Then he showed me how to improve.

Humbling? Humbling beyond words.

But owning my mistakes and shortcomings, and asking for help to improve a skill I thought I'd already mastered, proved to be one of the wisest choices of my college years. Before long, I was earning As in both those classes. But even if I hadn't worked to raise my grades, the wisdom required to try came only after swallowing the hard pill of humility.

Do you lack wisdom in certain areas of your life? Can you swallow a hard pill? Ask the Holy Spirit to grant you a spirit of humility. God promises wisdom will follow. 🍃

Humility is the mother of all virtues.
STEPHEN COVEY

Humility: With Long Life

True humility . . . lead[s] to riches, honor, and long life.
Proverbs 22:4

At ninety-six, she is the oldest living member of our church. Joining the congregation in 1927, she can count eighty-plus years of service in one of the oldest churches in our state. So this charming and still vibrant woman of God has seen much. But how does she do it? What's the secret, at almost one hundred, of staying so vibrant, mentally sharp, and active?

On a recent afternoon, she offered a humble and wise answer.

"I pace myself."

In other words, this beautiful almost-centenarian knows that she's not the center of the universe. "And never tried to be." She lets others get the spotlight and, in the end, seems so often to stand in the spotlight herself. Recently she was honored by her college alma mater with an honorary doctorate of letters degree. The biggest school district in the state recently named an elementary school in her honor.

Yet a more humble person would be hard to find.

When I picked her up one evening for a ride to a church book club, she wanted to leave early "so I'm not late. I never want to keep other people waiting."

At the meeting, when she was asked about her long life as a schoolteacher, she prefaced her remarks by describing not what she knows—but what she doesn't know. "I don't know everything about teaching," she began, then finished with many humble but sharply astute and wise observations.

She is relaxed, in other words. Humility, for all its virtues, is also a practical way to live with low stress. Not trying to be "the star," humble people are content to let others scramble, compete, climb, and wear themselves out trying to be on top. But an almost-centenarian shows there's a wiser way to move through the years—and be rewarded with a long life.

Be humble. Then quietly bless God for the powerful years that roll along. 🖋

Life is a long lesson in humility.
JAMES M. BARRIE

Going Deeper

Humility precedes honor.
Proverbs 15:33

Humility gets a bad rap. It's seen as weakness or as false meekness. How have you defined humility—and how has your study of humility changed your definition of what it truly is?

Think of a time in your life when you showed humility, or when you should've shown humility. What did you learn in that situation?

What special insight has God taught you this week about humility?

If you'd like, write a prayer that reflects the principles—or your needs—regarding the virtue of humility.

In the school of the Spirit man learns wisdom through humility.
JOHANNES TAULER

PURITY

His Promise

God blesses those whose hearts are pure,
for they will see God.
Matthew 5:8

My Prayer

Oh to see You, O God!
Create in me a pure heart.

Purity: By Heart

God blesses those whose hearts are pure, for they will see God.
Matthew 5:8

Imagine life with a clear view. No confusion or distraction. No fog or clouds. No muddied missions or misguided motives. Imagine, indeed, a single-focused life with a single goal: to glorify God, in order to see God. That's the life Jesus invites us to today. As he taught: those whose hearts are pure—whose single motive is only to seek, know, and glorify God—will experience the incomparable blessing of seeing God.

Our spiritual eyes, that is, will see above the distractions of this world, locking in on His perspective. With a pure focus, we can see who God is and what God is doing in this world. When we're distracted by self-serving motives, our spiritual path is so crooked and corrupted we can't possibly see clearly to God.

So I ask today: What is my motive? In trying to walk for God? To work for God? If I dare ask, such questions lift my eyes above the foggy distractions of life. Then an amazing thing happens. *I can see.* See God's hand. God's power. God's love.

Now what about you? Is your spiritual eyesight cloudy and blinded?

Dare to ask the Holy Spirit to purify your heart. To scrub every deceit, ulterior motive, immoral behavior, and shameful lie clouding your path. To scour the dirt from your eyes and your heart. To redirect your gaze—from yourself and from the lures and lusts that would distract you—and to direct your eyes toward Christ.

Then, as you look, bless God by praying King David's prayer of Psalm 51:10. "Create in me a clean heart, O God." Then get up and see. Fog all gone. 🌿

How to be pure? By steadfast longing for the one good, that is, God.
MEISTER ECKHART

Purity: In Friendship

Everything is pure to those whose hearts are pure. But nothing is pure to those who are corrupt and unbelieving.
Titus 1:15

Show me your friends. I'll show you your future. The prison supervisor shared that pronouncement at a GED graduation at a lockup facility in my city. She spoke truth—so she said it again. "Show me your friends. I'll show you your future."

The truth of her words rang out in the prison auditorium, sinking into hearts. Surely, I could feel it sink into mine. Our peers and acquaintances are that influential, in other words.

That's the same truth the apostle Paul tried to impress on Titus, his young church delegate on the Greek island of Crete. In that era, Crete was considered a morally corrupt place, so much so that Paul quotes a Greek leader who himself lamented: "The people of Crete are all liars, cruel animals, and lazy gluttons" (Titus 1:12).

Therefore, as Paul noted, "They must be silenced, because they are turning whole families away from the truth by their false teaching" (v. 11).

Show me your friends? I'll show you your future.

To believers who seek a life of purity, impure friends will sabotage our every commitment and effort. By definition, corrupt friends and acquaintances and even family members sow corruption. In fact, to such people, Paul states, nothing is pure. They're like the *Peanuts* cartoon character Pig-Pen. They spread dirt everywhere they go—but not just outside dirt. Open the door of your heart to such people and prepare to get dirty through and through.

As Christians, we seek to help fallen people—and well we should. If we take on aspects of their fallen life, however, that impurity will rub off. Nothing is pure to the corrupt and the unbelieving. Help the fallen, for sure. But watch whom you befriend. The purity of your future depends on it. ❦

Cleanse the fountain if you would purify the streams.
AMOS BRONSON ALCOTT

Purity: Inside Out

If you keep yourself pure, you will be a special utensil for honorable use.
2 Timothy 2:21

Springtime. Time to clean house. So at our house, I started with my own closet. A jumble of clothes, shoes, purses, coats, and enough wire hangers to outfit a local dry cleaner, my closet was one tangled mess. Every time I pushed back the sliding doors, I felt frustrated. In fact, one door had slipped off its runner and wouldn't open all the way. With each push, it groaned.

So did I. The carpet on the closet floor was dusty and dirty. Getting dressed was a long exercise in frustration and condemnation. *Nothing* is right about a dirty closet, and with mine, everything was wrong. Time to clean, indeed.

And God is merciful. Because my best friend in all the world is a neat freak. Her closets are clutter free and magazine-picture perfect. Over the years, however, she's taught me one key thing about cleaning away impurity and clutter.

"Take *everything* out," she says. "Then wash everything. Then sort. Throw away. Give away. *That's* how you clean a closet." Or a cupboard. Or a cabinet. Or a heart?

Take everything out? Down to the dust. That's how I cleaned my closet that day. Or actually three days. It took that long to get down to the dust—to sort through the rubble of junk and wire hangers. Then the washing started, leaving me with six oversized plastic bags of giveaways to donate. Next came the vacuum—including the little squiggly attachment. Indeed, I confess: The dust I vacuumed went back years. So did the piles of wire hangers, now returned to our local dry cleaner. Then I sewed on missing buttons. Emptied purses. Buffed shoes. My husband fixed the lopsided door. I washed the door mirrors. Then I took stock.

I had fewer clothes. But they were clean, simple, and easy to find. Getting dressed became a blessing—and quick. I marvel, in fact, how a clean closet equips us for honorable use. Is it the same with our hearts? Test it today with your closet. You'll find a clean heart. 🖋

By two wings a man is lifted up from things earthly: by simplicity and purity.
THOMAS À KEMPIS

Purity: By the Blood of Christ

But if we are living in the light of God's presence . . . the blood of Jesus,
his Son, cleanses us from every sin.
1 John 1:7

A clean heart shines. But a dirty heart? It's downright grimy. Jesus tells us why: "Out of a person's heart, come evil thoughts, sexual immorality, theft, murder, adultery, greed, wickedness, deceit, lustful desires, envy, slander, pride, and foolishness."

That's a load of dirt. And all from the heart. In fact, Jesus confirms that "all these vile things come from within; they are what defile you" (Mark 7:21-23).

Is there any hope for us, then, if our hearts are so vile and corrupt?

In fact, there is Good News for our hearts.

First, as believers, we alone don't have to scrub dirt and impurities. Instead, the blood of Christ is the cleansing agent that, at our invitation, cleanses us from unrighteousness. Sound too churchy to you? Or will you just accept the promise: "If we confess our sins to him, he is faithful and just to forgive us our sins and to cleanse us from all wickedness" (1 John 1:9).

Our part of the bargain is confessing our sins—a tough thing for some of us, especially when we convince ourselves we're "not that bad" or "not that wrong" or "we can't help ourselves" in what we think or do.

Instead, the way to come clean with God is to come clean with ourselves. Don't know how to do that? Get up and say this: *God, I'm a sinner.* Start there, yes. Then add: *I failed You. And my sin separates me from You. So clean my heart.*

Then rest. That's a big prayer, indeed. So God blesses it with the light of His presence.

"God is light," writes John, "and there is no darkness in him at all" (v. 5). Standing in that light, we come clean with Him and with each other. Then He outshines every sin that might lure us. Even better, as He washes, He shows us the work He's appointed us to do. So think of God's light as solar power. It's enough heat to clean—but enough warmth to love. 🔥

Confess your sins, not your neighbor's.
AUTHOR UNKNOWN

Purity: In Body

*So stay away from all sexual sin. Then each of you will control
his own body and live in holiness and honor.*
1 Thessalonians 4:3-4

The woman's husband was hooked on Internet porn. The wife, flirting with
a man at work, was no picture of innocence herself. To save their marriage,
however, the husband took the first step. Realizing the damage his habit had
caused his marriage, he yanked his computer plug out of its wall socket and
hurled the monitor out a window. Storming out to the yard, he grabbed a
baseball bat and beat the computer screen to smithereens. To seal the deal,
he replaced his computer with a vase of roses and a card to his wife: *I love
you more.*

This scene, from the Christian film *Fireproof,* is the movie version of how
one man dealt with his pornography habit. (The Greek word *porneia* refers
to any sexual union outside marriage.)

A drastic example? Yes. But it illustrates at least three key ways to confront
sexual impurity and the havoc it wreaks in families and our relationship
with God. First, tell the truth. Confront head-on the losing battle with sin.
Second, eliminate the temptation. Throwing a computer monitor out a window is drastic. But it showed the husband's determination to rid his life of his
method for feeding his addiction to porn. Finally, the husband took the most
powerful step of all: he opened his Bible and began to study God's Word.

He perhaps read this passage from Paul's letter to the early Christians at
Thessalonica. There in the Mediterranean region, as Paul noted in many
epistles, sexual immorality, including prostitution, was rampant. But among
Christians, all sexual involvement outside of marriage is prohibited because
porn and lustful passion defile the soul and dishonor God's ways. (See, for
example, Ephesians 4:17-19 and Ephesians 5:3-9.)

The remedy? Knowing God's Word and applying it to our hearts. The
benefit? We clean up. Then we live in holiness and honor. Sound too simple?
Read God's Word today, determined to see its light. The blessing? A holy
marriage—and an empowered soul. ❧

Use God's Word, not what people around you are willing to accept,
to set the standards for what is right or wrong.
BRUCE BARTON

Purity: With Christ

And everyone who has this hope in Him purifies himself,
just as He is pure.
1 John 3:3, NKJV

We want to be like Christ. As believers, that is our hope. So we go to church. We study God's Word. We seek to do God's will. Or to put it plainly, we are trying to clean up. Down to the dirt.

In every church, in every pew, countless Christians are pursuing this hope: to be more like Jesus.

A big task? Monumental! But this pursuit, and the hope that fuels it, purifies us. Look at your own life. Surely your hope to become more like Christ has led you to know more about Christ—then to try to become more like Christ. The effort, over time, is transforming, healing, refining. Purifying.

This isn't a statement of superiority. It's a simple fact. Our hope in Christ makes us more like Him. And the more we become like Jesus, the more we become pure. Ironic, yes—because we're not perfect. Any perfection we might claim is based on the work Christ did on the cross at Calvary. But our hope in Him—and in the power of what He accomplished for us—purifies us. Down to the dirt.

I thought of that as I read an article in my morning newspaper. It featured a popular local hairstylist who competed on a national reality TV show. In a Q & A, the man was asked to name an overrated virtue. He answered: "Cleanliness."

But as I read that answer, I reacted. Because cleanliness—yes, purity in spirit, mind, and body—*is* a virtue. Overrated? Hardly. Our pursuit of Christ, and our hope in Him, convicts us of that.

We know the Standard Bearer, that is. Christ is the Benchmark for purity. The Cornerstone. The Plumb Line. Our hope in Him—and the journey we take while we hope—alerts us along the way when we fall from His standard. Purity is a high hurdle, no doubt. But we keep pursuing. Keep seeking. Keep believing. Keep hoping. Keep blessing. Of such hope is built our road to the destination of purity. 🌱

If you do not hope, you will not find what is beyond your hopes.
CLEMENT OF ALEXANDRIA

Going Deeper

Purify your hearts, for your loyalty is divided between God and the world.
James 4:8

The journey to purity forces believers to choose between sin and holiness. In what areas of your life have you made this choice?

How does pursuing purity change your relationship with God? With your family? Your church? Your job? Our world?

What distractions will you eliminate to show God your commitment to a pure heart?

If you'd like, write a prayer that reflects the principles—or your needs—regarding the virtue of purity.

Purity is the fruit of prayer.
MOTHER TERESA

Trust

His Promise

Those who trust in the Lord are as secure as Mount Zion;
they will not be defeated but will endure forever.

Psalm 125:1

My Prayer

You are my Solid Rock, O God!
Remind me to stand always on You.

Trust: In the Lord

You will keep in perfect peace all who trust in you,
all whose thoughts are fixed on you!
Isaiah 26:3

If only we could know God. Maybe you're saying that today. But how do
we know the unknowable? How do we trace the untraceable? As the scholar
Pauline Matarasso says, when it comes to giving in to God in trust: "There is
no map." Or as she adds: "There is only surrender." Yes, only trust. But *how?*

The prophet Isaiah explains—even though he's facing a tough crowd.
God's people in Judah were standing down a huge enemy, that is. The empire
of Assyria, sweeping down from the north, sought to wipe them off the face
of the earth. For a while, their good king Uzziah and his strong army seemed
tough enough to withstand the coming onslaught.

But when King Uzziah died, and ungodly rulers followed him, Isaiah the
prophet—along with everybody else in Judah—wondered what to do. *Who
can we trust?*

God responded by giving Isaiah a vision that convinced the prophet what
every believer should know: God is totally and absolutely dependable. In
fact, we're certain to go down in defeat if we trust anything or anybody *but*
God.

Such trust only comes, however, in knowing God. God lamented in Isaiah
1:3: "Even an ox knows its owner, and a donkey recognizes its master's care—
but Israel doesn't know its master." Likewise, believers who don't know their
Master God—who fix their sights on people, piffles, and problems—will
perish if they don't turn their sights on Him and *fix them there*. To learn His
character. His ways. His laws. His promises. In this learning, then, we come
to know Him. He is the God who keeps in perfect peace all those who stop
depending on themselves, surrendering in trust to Him.

How can we surrender our worries? Stand up to know Him. Or as a
beloved family member advised me many years ago: "Go back to your Bible."
Of all places, the God we can trust blesses us right there. 🔥

Trust that God is enough for you.
HENRI NOUWEN

Trust: In His Word

So Noah did everything exactly as God had commanded him. . . .
Then God blessed Noah.
Genesis 6:22; 9:1

Is God *really* right? Did he *really* mean we should not marry unbelievers? Or should *not* commit adultery? Or should *not* steal? Or should heed all the priceless godly wisdom recorded for us in the five wisdom books of the Bible (Job, Psalms, Proverbs, Ecclesiastes, Song of Solomon)? In other words, can we *really* trust God?

The question troubles only those who don't know God.

That's why Noah didn't second-guess God's instructions to build an ark, a large rectangular barge, and fill it with pairs of every kind of animal—and enough food to feed the animals and the eight members of Noah's family, for forty days and forty nights.

And that sounds downright crazy.

But not to a righteous man, who "walked in close fellowship with God" (Genesis 6:9). Noah knew God well enough to trust Him. So when God told Noah to do something—or *not* to do something—Noah trusted the Source. Even when that instruction didn't make sense. Or especially when it didn't make sense.

So Noah built that crazy ark. Thus, Noah and his family were the only humans spared when God sent a flood to destroy everyone else on the earth because "all living creatures" were so corrupt (Genesis 6:12-13).

True, God spoke directly to Noah, the Bible says. But God speaks directly to us, too. Unlike Noah, we have His Word. We don't have to trust our own thinking. We can trust God to be right, even as He blesses us for believing Him.

But build an ark? Noah says do it. Then don't be surprised when the ship of your life lands—blessed, dry, and on holy ground. 🌿

We must learn to trust God when He doesn't tell us why.
JERRY BRIDGES

Trust: In His Name

Those who know your name trust in you, for you, O LORD,
do not abandon those who search for you.
Psalm 9:10

Names are important. The Bible says so (Proverbs 22:1, NIV). But so does modern psychology. Among recent studies, for example, a project at Yale University determined that students with names that began with a C or D earned lower grade point averages than those whose names started with an A or a B.

But what about God's names? Theologians teach us that God reveals His character in the more than two dozen Hebrew names ascribed to Him in the Old Testament. That's what happened after God parted the Red Sea for the children of Israel. After traveling for three days, they found themselves in the wilderness with only bitter water to drink at a place called Marah. As they complained against Moses, their leader cried out to the Lord for help, and God showed Moses a piece of wood whose touch turned the waters sweet. Then God made a point about His name:

"If you will listen carefully to the voice of the LORD your God and do what is right in his sight, obeying his commands and keeping all his decrees, then I will not make you suffer any of the diseases I sent on the Egyptians; for *I am the LORD who heals you*" (Exodus 15:26, italics added).

Now, neither Moses nor the people were looking for a healer at that moment. They just wanted water. But by looking to God to resolve their water problem, they discovered so much more about God. They discovered His healing Name and, in His Name, a reason to trust Him to do precisely that: to heal.

In fact, as the Hebrew people trusted God enough to follow His dietary laws, they survived diseases that wiped out other ancient peoples. But first, they had to seek Him.

Just as you will. By His Spirit, yes, get up and look for your needs today in His Holy Word. Then trust the Name that He reveals, even when you aren't looking for it. 🔥

God is who His name is because He does what his name says.
PHILIP GRAHAM RYKEN

Trust: In His Way

*Trust in the LORD and do good. Then you will live safely
in the land and prosper.*
Psalm 37:3

Over his lifetime, King David stood up to plenty of people doing bad. The giant Goliath, of course. And King Saul, who tried to kill this boy musician-turned-warrior. Then, after doing bad himself—by fathering a baby with another man's wife and having her husband killed—David repented before God, but he and his family still suffered the consequences. His son Amnon raped David's daughter Tamar, who was Amnon's own half sister. Tamar's brother Absalom murdered Amnon. Later, Absalom waged war against David, seeking to steal the throne while David was still alive.

Talk about doing bad and paying for it.

More than anybody in the Bible, indeed, David had authority to write in Psalm 37 what he'd learned the hard way: "Trust in the LORD." Not in yourself.

Not in your emotions. Not in your lusts. Not in your shrewdness. One wonders, in fact: did David actually think having sex with a woman who wasn't his wife and murdering her husband would make things *good*?

Finally, he figured it out.

Trust in the LORD. But that's not all. *Do good.*

That's another way of saying, do what God wills. That is, do what God commands. Do what God teaches. Do what God requires.

Don't know what *good* is? Or what God commands? Then let's spend time with God. Fellowship with God. Study God's Word. Quiet our own interests. Instead, let's seek God to learn His way. Then what happens?

David explains clearly. "Then you will live safely in the land." But that's not all. Those who trust in the Lord—*and* do good—live safely in the land *and they prosper.*

Is there any reason to doubt it? Trust Him today and see. 🔥

If God has said it, it will be so.
CHARLES SPURGEON

Trust: And Prosper

*Trust in the LORD and do good. Then you will live safely
in the land and prosper.*
Psalm 37:3

Businessman Truett Cathy wasn't a billionaire when he opened the first
Chick-fil-A restaurant in 1967. But he trusted God. So he dared to keep the
restaurant closed on Sundays. His reason? To give employees and customers
a day to rest, spend time with family and friends, and worship where they
chose.

The company's corporate purpose, in fact, is "to glorify God by being a
faithful steward to all that is entrusted to us. To have a positive influence on
all who come in contact with Chick-fil-A."

Bad for business? Not so. In 2007, Chick-fil-A surpassed $2.6 billion
in sales—its fortieth consecutive year of sales growth. That same year, the
Chick-fil-A Bowl surpassed all other sports bowls in charitable giving. Today,
according to a recent company annual report, the more than 1,600 Chick-
fil-A restaurants contribute about 10 percent of their profits to charity. And
every one of their restaurants is still closed on Sundays.

It's a corporate story that shows in real terms the promise of Psalm 37:3.

To trust God enough to defy conventional wisdom—by keeping a restaurant chain closed on busy Sundays so employees and customers can worship
where and how they choose—speaks volumes about trust. Like most of you,
I don't personally know Truett Cathy or anyone in his family or restaurant
chain. Mentioning him here isn't meant to endorse his business.

But I know about the chain's "Sundays closed" policy and about its charitable outreach. Like you, I can see for myself what these policies teach us
about people who trust God with their businesses, their lives, and their
revenues. In short, trusting God *and* doing good reaps real blessings. Doubt
that? Just ask a billionaire who trusts. 🌱

Faith expects from God what is beyond all expectation.
ANDREW MURRAY

Trust: In Full

*Even strong young lions sometimes go hungry, but those
who trust in the LORD will lack no good thing.*
Psalm 34:10

Among the cat family, lions are the only social breed. Living in large groups called prides, these families of about fifteen lions are made up mostly of related females and their young. The male lion doesn't hang around long. Within prides, as such, the female lions are affectionate, showing lots of touching, head rubbing, licking, and purring. Hunting mostly at night, the females work in teams to stalk and ambush their prey, bringing down food for their young.

Thus, it's *very* unusual for a young lion in a pride to go hungry.

But even a strong, beloved lion might miss a meal sometimes.

As a shepherd boy, David—the author of this psalm—would know that well. He fought off bears and lions, learning their ways and habits in order to protect his sheep.

But he also learned the ways of God, in whom David trusted. So he learned that, with God, he never lacked good things. Courage. Skill. Wisdom. God provided enough, always.

Young lions couldn't claim that. As pampered and well fed and petted as they were, they'd go hungry sometimes. Their mothers failed to find food sometimes. They had to scramble among themselves to get the best morsel sometimes. And they themselves sometimes became food for a bigger enemy.

But with God, as David learned, all of his needs—spiritual, physical, and emotional—were met. Always. "Oh, the joys of those who take refuge in him!" David sang in this psalm. Even strong, young lions go hungry. But as he declared, "Those who fear [God] will have all they need" (vv. 8-9).

In our spiritual imaginations, we can picture David singing this psalm—composed to celebrate the time he outsmarted Abimelech. Perhaps he recalled his years shepherding sheep and fending off wild animals. So those lions sometimes went away hungry, David recalled. But when we trust in God, His blessing of grace, love, and power provides for all. 🌿

The God of the Bible is the kind of God whose greatest delight comes not
from making demands but from meeting needs.
SAM STORMS

Going Deeper

Unfailing love surrounds those who trust the LORD.
Psalm 32:10

To trust God is to know God. After this week's study, what do you know about God that builds your trust in Him?

Think of a time you trusted God for what you couldn't see. How did God reward you?

Name an area of your life that could benefit from your increased trust in God. Explain.

If you'd like, write a prayer that reflects the principles—or your needs—regarding the virtue of trust.

Trust God or worry.
JAMES BLANCHARD CISNEROS

KNOWLEDGE

His Promise

The people who know their God will be strong.
Daniel 11:32

My Prayer

As I seek to know You, O God,
strengthen my learning
for Your glory.

Knowledge: Of Christ

May God give you more and more grace and peace as you grow
in your knowledge of God and Jesus our Lord.
2 Peter 1:2

Are you a know-it-all? Knowing all the answers in Bible study? Answering every question about the gospel? Finding every Scripture before most people can open their Bibles? I know you because I was a know-it-all too. The worst kind. My hand always up, waving at the teacher. My mouth always set to show off how much I knew.

But this isn't knowledge. Not godly knowledge. The apostle Peter stressed that in his letter to early Christians at Rome. In that prideful city, the fledgling communities of Christ were struggling, under persecution, to convince doubters who Christ really is and what it means to follow Him.

As their own knowledge of Christ grew, however, Peter urged them: "May God give you more and more grace and peace." Not quick answers from a know-it-all. Simply, more grace and peace. Those things show a lost world who Jesus is.

Not a know-it-all.

Or as Peter said: "The more you grow like this, the more productive and useful you will be in your knowledge of our Lord Jesus Christ" (v. 8).

We learn about Christ, that is, to show Him to a world desperate to know Him. Bible answers may leap to our quick tongues. But grace and peace are true evidence of real knowledge. Is your witness for Christ ineffective and useless? Aim to learn more of who Christ is. Then let that knowledge flow from your brain to your heart. That path will transform show-offs into productive, useful, graceful servants—blessing the Christ who knew us first, so we can walk like Him now. ❧

We will not become more like Christ if we don't know more
of what Christ is like.
DONALD WHITNEY

Knowledge: Of God

Knowledge of the Holy One results in good judgment.
Proverbs 9:10

Let me teach you.
Matthew 11:29

Remember the smartest kid in your class? The real "brain"? The guy or gal everybody envied for his or her book smarts? Maybe that person was you. Or maybe you were the street-smart kid—smart enough to survive on life's mean streets, but not much for books. Both kinds of knowledge have value.

But the best knowledge for life—for making the best decisions throughout life, to navigate the many twists and turns of life and to give the best back to life—is to know the Holy God.

The holiness of God as a subject of study is so life changing, says the writer of this ninth chapter of Proverbs, that it multiplies our days and adds years to our lives.

To know God as holy expands and completes everything else we need to learn for life. As the Holy One, God is sacred and set apart, above everything and everyone.

But as we expand our thinking about what it means that God is holy, we realize God isn't just sacred and set apart. As holy, God also is whole and complete. Wholesome. Healthy. Hearty. *And* holy.

To know this about God—and to personally know Him as holy—impacts every judgment call and decision we will make in life, big or small, with the hearty and healthy holiness of the God we serve. The blessing?

Good judgment. Not silly judgment. Or stupid or frivolous or immoral or amoral or biased or dumb or ditzy or depressive judgment. Instead, seek to know God as holy. Then watch something remarkable happen to your decision making. In a hearty and healthy, whole and holy way, your judgment will be transformed. 🌿

A true love of God must begin with a delight in his holiness.
JONATHAN EDWARDS

Knowledge: From God

From his mouth come knowledge and understanding.
Proverbs 2:6

Money didn't buy them knowledge—not in this sweat lodge in Sedona, Arizona, where more than sixty followers of a self-help guru paid nearly $10,000 for a weeklong spiritual retreat. Because something went wrong. In the dark, crowded, steam-filled "purification" ceremony, three people died. Some nineteen became ill.

Later, several Native Americans criticized "sweat lodge" practitioners who lack true knowledge of their cultural ceremony. Said one: "I would like to clarify that this lodge and many others are not our ceremonial way of life, because of the way they are being conducted."

Sadly, indeed, more than sixty people apparently were seeking spiritual knowledge and insight from a source that couldn't provide it. The source of true knowledge is almighty God. "From his mouth," says the writer of the second chapter of Proverbs, "come knowledge and understanding."

We can seek enlightenment from various paths—and countless people do. "Self-help" is a multibillion-dollar industry. Human beings will pay through the nose to discover "enlightenment" or "knowledge" for life.

All true knowledge, however, is of God. "In him lie hidden all the treasures of wisdom and knowledge," Paul writes in Colossians 2:3. Daniel declares the same: "He gives wisdom to the wise and knowledge to the scholars," revealing "deep and mysterious things." Only God, Daniel adds, "knows what lies hidden in darkness" (Daniel 2:21-22). Thus, God may direct us to other outlets for knowledge—books and retreats, colleges and universities, travels and experiences. But seeking Him lights this path. "You will grow as you learn to know God better and better" (Colossians 1:10).

Tired of ignorance? Of stumbling in darkness? Of trying unreliable sources? Cry to Him who is Knowledge, Understanding, and Light. If we but ask, He enlightens. How? He is the Source of all. ❦

The end of all learning is to know God.
JOHN MILTON

Knowledge: Of Self

We ask God to give you complete knowledge.
Colossians 1:9

Know thyself. Since ancient times, philosophers have urged our inner knowledge. But the Bible encourages us to approach it differently. "Commune with your own heart upon your bed," says Psalm 4:4 (KJV). Take some good time, that is, to know how God wired you. Then marvel at how He made you and use His unique creation to glorify and bless Him. Complete knowledge of ourselves, yes, glorifies Him.

A lot of work, in fact—this knowing ourselves.

But when it comes to looking inward completely, what exactly should we know?

First, know your gifts. Your strengths. That special anointing placed in each of us by God's Spirit. "Each person has a special gift from God" (1 Corinthians 7:7). What's yours? Can't figure it out? Ask God to show you. Then as you seek God for this self-awareness and discover it, you'll see how to best give back to God's Kingdom. Even if it looks unusual. In fact, the more unusual it looks, the more correct it probably is.

So also know your weaknesses. Your temptations. Your shortcomings. And what evangelist Arthur Pink called our "constitutional sins"—that "particular turn or cast of mind" by which we are most in danger of sinning against God and our neighbor. Examine it thoroughly, Pink says. "Every man has his weak side, and every wise man knows where it is, and will be sure to keep a double guard there."

At the same time, know your needs—those things that matter most to you—so you can explain yourself to others close to you. We can't read minds. So know your priorities, then bless others by telling them—so they can address those needs if they can.

Most important, know who you are in Christ. Victorious. Triumphant. A new creature in Him. Able to do all things through Christ who strengthens you beyond any weakness because He shines brighter.

And that's not just a slogan. That's the blessing of complete knowledge of Him. 🔥

The man is what his heart is.
ARTHUR PINK

Knowledge: For Life

A person with understanding is even-tempered.
Proverbs 17:27

The boss was a fireball. Driven, demanding, reactive, angry. On his good days. On his bad days, he spit four-letter words and threw furniture. In the office, employees walked on eggshells. Except one calm, savvy woman.

"He's actually afraid," she told me. "I know his type." She didn't lose sleep over our hot-tempered manager. No eggshell-walking for her either. "I understand these people. I'll outlast him." And she did. Years after he was gone, she still had her job. How?

She understood people. Her people skills were well honed and time tested. Long before pop-culture authors wrote about "management styles," she'd figured out the emotional terrain of our office and traveled over it without problem or panic.

Maybe she'd studied the Four Temperaments. First identified by the Greek physician Hippocrates, the four types are now commonly called: Drivers. Expressives. Analyticals. Amiables. Or maybe she'd examined the personality theories put forth by psychologists, physicians, theologians, and philosophers.

Or perhaps she'd read the book of Proverbs, with its deeply perceptive and commonsense wisdom for life. If so, she'd learned that "a person with understanding is even-tempered" (v. 27). Indeed, fools "bring grief to their father" and bitterness to their mother (v. 25)—and maybe to their job sites. But knowledgeable, sensible people are a blessing to all.

Knowledge is power, for certain.

But understanding people takes focused attention—and godly direction. Are you feeling confused about the people you work or live with, or people you know socially? Cry to the Holy Spirit for understanding. For insight. For the blessing of knowledge. Then watch the choppy climate around you unravel and smooth. As smooth as your even temper.

The light of understanding has shone upon my little pupil's mind,
and behold, all things are changed.
ANNE SULLIVAN

Knowledge: With Long Life

The LORD preserves those with knowledge.
Proverbs 22:12

Smart people live longer. Science has said that for years, and apparently that science is true. Some say old "smart" people just make better decisions throughout life, so they live longer. Other scientists point to a gene, known as SSADH, that slows aging in brains but that also makes those people who have it smarter.

This Scripture makes a deeper point, however.

It cautions the wise that *God* is in control of their intellect—and is not only the inspiration for and the giver of knowledge, but also the preserver of those who seek it.

As the entire passage points out: "The Lord preserves those with knowledge, but he ruins the plans of the treacherous." An interesting pair of ideas. It seems to mean that those schemers who would use their "knowledge" for ill gain might think twice. They may feel smart, thinking their "insider info" gives them an advantage.

But those with complete knowledge—God inspired and God given—are preserved by God's power and love. In fact, to use godly knowledge for selfish reasons is sure to come back and bite those "treacherous" plans.

Let us instead bless God by using knowledge as God intended it to be used—for His glory and to benefit others. So let us share knowledge with others. Let's develop our minds vigorously, deepening our intelligence about God's ways and about the godly gifts He has given us. Let's support Christian education programs in our churches, improved programs in our local schools, and continuing education programs for all believers, young and old.

As for those smart old people? God help us to listen and learn from those He has preserved. 🌿

If we do not use the mind that God has given us, we condemn ourselves
to spiritual superficiality and cut ourselves off from many
of the riches of God's grace.
JOHN STOTT

Going Deeper

Knowledge will rescue the righteous.
Proverbs 11:9

Do you know enough about God? If you don't, what would it take for you to learn more? Explain.

What do you know about yourself? Your strengths? Your weaknesses? Your temptations?

Name a situation in your life in which you could use more knowledge. How might you pray for knowledge in this situation?

If you'd like, write a prayer that reflects what God is trying to teach you about the virtue of knowledge.

Our joy is the fruit of what we know and believe to be true of God.
SAM STORMS

PRUDENCE

His Promise

The prudent understand where they are going.
Proverbs 14:8

My Prayer

Bless You, Precious Savior, for showing me what's ahead—
and how to prudently get there Your way.

Prudence: For Life

The prudent understand where they are going.
Proverbs 14:8

On the road of life, we sometimes get lost. But we don't have to stay lost. We have a guide, and He tells us exactly where we are going—to His glory, being transformed to His likeness (2 Corinthians 3:18). Then He tells us how to get there.

Be prudent.

But I laughed at this word. It sounded prudish and proper. But then I sat down and read. And the joke was on me. Because a prudent person, according to any good dictionary, is a planner—wisely avoiding mistakes or faults—by looking down the road at what's to come. So prudent people aren't "prudes." They're cautious and circumspect, looking at all sides of a situation and, therefore, careful in their conduct.

This deep power in being prudent is seen in its Latin origin, *prudens*, meaning "to foresee." In fact, it's a contraction of the Latin word *providens*, or provident, meaning "to see ahead." Seeing ahead those things that could possibly trip us up or bring us down or that pose a danger, prudent people act accordingly.

Thus, seeing ahead, prudent people plan for retirement.

Thus, seeing ahead, prudent people repair the roof when the sun is shining—instead of waiting until it falls apart in the rain.

Thus, seeing ahead, prudent people seek out strong, honest friends who can lift them up in life—they do not fool around with lazy, dishonest ne'er-do-wells wrangling for a free ride.

"Fools deceive themselves," says Proverbs 14:8. But "the prudent understand where they are going." With eyes wide open, they look down the road of life and plan as God advises. Then they live accordingly, expecting an outcome that God can bless.

Can you see your blessed life? Look down the road today. Ask your loved ones to do the same. Then with understanding, respond together with the visionary blessing and grace of empowered prudence. 🌿

God's providence is not blind, but full of eyes.
JOHN GREENLEAF WHITTIER

Prudence: For Family

A prudent person foresees danger and takes precautions.
Proverbs 22:3

Nobody likes to think about the worst. Not even Christians. So some believers argue that preparing ahead for emergencies shows a lack of faith. But while we can respect each other's convictions on such matters, we might consider how one notable Bible hero was blessed by looking ahead. Yes, prudently.

I'm talking here of Joseph in the book of Genesis.

Known as an interpreter of dreams, Joseph was saved from a prison cell in Egypt when only he, with God's help, could interpret the pharaoh's dreams. As Joseph explained to Pharaoh, the leader's dream meant that seven years of prosperity in Egypt would be followed by seven years of famine. Famine "so severe that even the memory of the good years will be erased" (Genesis 41:31).

But Joseph wasn't finished. Appoint a good adviser to manage the crisis, saving back food from good years to use during bad years, he counseled Pharaoh.

Impressed with Joseph's foresight, Pharaoh put the ex-prisoner Joseph in charge of all of Egypt. His job included overseeing a national plan to collect, in the fat years, the surplus crops. Then in lean years, enough food would be on hand to save the people.

And sure enough, prosperity came to Egypt for seven years. Followed by seven years of famine. But thanks to prudent Joseph, when famine struck, he "opened up the storehouses and distributed grain to the Egyptians." But that's not all. "People from all around came to Egypt to buy grain" (Genesis 41:56-57). Among them were the brothers who'd betrayed him long before.

In fact, Joseph's prudent planning saved not only Egypt, but also the people of Israel and the lineage of Christ. Prudent planning, for certain. God blesses it.

Still fearful to plan? Stand up and be prudent, like Joseph—looking ahead to God for your long-range provision. Then watch with joy as He blesses you for the long haul. 🌿

The best preparation for tomorrow is doing your best today.
H. JACKSON BROWN JR.

Prudence: At Work

*So those who are smart keep their mouths shut,
for it is an evil time.*
Amos 5:13

At his job, where the pay was low—painfully low—my friend's son decided to look for another job. He considered his tactics. He could call people. He could send around résumés. He could tell everybody he knew he was hunting for employment.

But something stopped him.

"When I thought about it, I could see the danger of talking too much." Somebody in his office might hear he was scouting out a new job. As a new employee of only a few months, he thought it prudent to keep quiet.

To be sure, in a recession—"an evil time," as the Bible would put it—the young man decided it wouldn't be smart to offend his employer. But, as he thought more about his situation, something else held his tongue.

He *liked* his job. "I love it, in fact," he said. "I love the work. Enjoy my coworkers. Feel I'm making a difference. Plus, they're flexible with my schedule." The only problem was the low pay.

Prudently, however, he prayed. Looking ahead, he decided to stay another year at this job he loved. Despite the pay. "God will provide," he declared.

During the next months, meantime, he threw himself into his job—making it a point to do his best, joyfully, despite desiring to earn more. Leaving his dilemma with God, he just worked harder and smarter. And kept his mouth shut.

"Those who are smart keep their mouths shut," declared the prophet Amos, "for it is an evil time." Good advice still?

My friend's son would say yes. Hold your tongue. Trust God. Wait for the Lord to speak and act on your behalf. The blessing for my friend's son? Peace. Clarity. Assurance. And, eventually, a pay raise. 🕊

> The true test of a man's spirituality is not his ability to speak, as we are apt to think, but rather his ability to bridle his tongue.
> KENT HUGHES

Prudence: At Church

Only simpletons believe everything they're told!
The prudent carefully consider their steps.
Proverbs 14:15

He wore jeans, a worn shirt, and sneakers. His eyes, meanwhile, looked weary and hard. After the young man sat down in the Sunday school room at our church, he introduced himself and told a story about his car breaking down during a cross-country trip. Immediately, our teacher "passed the hat"—taking up a collection for the young man and his family.

Soon, however, we learned we were wrong, not in wanting to help—but by jumping ahead of God's way.

"We're a compassionate church," our Sunday school teacher told us the following week, "but we're also prudent. We don't give money to anybody who walks in and asks. We have a process for helping people, that is—and I apologize—I didn't follow it."

A good lesson?

I pondered it deeply. As Christians, most of us are eager to help "the least of these." No questions asked. Interesting, however, that Jesus often first questioned those who cried to Him for help. He sought relationships, yes. But also information. So he asked carefully considered questions.

"Who touched me?" Jesus asked the woman with the issue of blood (Luke 8:45).

"What do you want me to do for you?" Jesus asked blind Bartimaeus (Mark 10:51).

"Would you like to get well?" Jesus asked the man at the Pool of Bethesda (John 5:6).

Then to the demon-possessed man at the Gerasenes, he asked the most basic question of all: "What is your name?" (Luke 8:30).

If we follow that model of Jesus', we won't step out to act until we first ask some basic, prudent questions. Whether helping or healing, we'll first consider who and what is involved. We'll test the facts, then test the waters—with the blessing of prudence. Is this path speaking to you today? Then answer. Then let God bless you for following it. 🌿

The skeptic does not mean him who doubts, but him who investigates.
MIGUEL DE UNAMUNO

Prudence: In Selecting a Mate

Only the LORD can give an understanding wife.
Proverbs 19:14

The perfect wife? Is she out there? Online dating services promise they hold the key to lasting romance—and millions apparently agree. The online dating industry was projected in 2010 to generate 834 million dollars in revenue, according to IBISWorld. All this from an industry not required to do background checks on its members—so even a convicted murderer, as one Texas newspaper discovered, can join a site and set up a Friday night date.

Some men turn to matchmakers. Or best friends. Or neighbors. Or somebody at work. Or at church. But these ways yield mixed results. Christian men and women still get divorced, sometimes at rates higher than nonbelievers.

But the Bible offers another way. The best way. The trusting way. Only the Lord, that is, can give a born-again man an understanding wife. Or in the words of Proverbs 19:14 (KJV): "House and riches are the inheritance of fathers: and a prudent wife is from the LORD."

And what a gift. Surely, the best mate is prudent and forward thinking, discerning, discreet, understanding, and wise. True, a man may look first for other traits in a woman—beauty, charm, wealth, and a long list of other "wants" in a wife. And that man may find such things in the woman he marries. All good.

A prudent and understanding wife, however, is a gift from God. A Christian man praying for a wife would do well to pray, in particular, for God to lead him to that understanding wife.

Will she be beautiful? Perhaps. Charming? Perhaps. Above all, however, if she is understanding and prudent, that man will know one thing for certain. His blessed wife is from God. 🌿

In marriage, being the right person is as important
as finding the right person.
WILBERT DONALD GOUGH

Prudence: Forever

Simpletons are clothed with foolishness,
but the prudent are crowned with knowledge.
Proverbs 14:18

The human brain. It lets us dream. Allows us to remember. Provokes us to laugh. And when we laugh, three parts of the brain are involved—the part that helps us get the joke, the part that stimulates muscles to grin, and the emotional section that analyzes the humor.

Amazing, this seat of our knowledge—this little organ inside the skull delivers the power for us to think, compute, speak, plan, and imagine, all while controlling body temperature, blood pressure, heart rate, breathing, plus our walking, standing, sitting, and other physical movements.

It's worth our effort, in other words, to protect this unique and precious part of our body. But how? Let God crown us with knowledge. Pray to be prudent, that is. Pray, yes, to have foresight, discernment, discretion, and understanding. To follow that path, according to the writer of the book of Proverbs, will grant us that crown. Of diamonds and gold? No.

Prudence earns us a crown of knowledge.

Unlike the foolish, who are clothed in foolishness—sometimes literally—the prudent understand that the best protection for our bodies, head to toe, is a crown of good sense.

Asking for more prudence, in fact, is a perfectly reasonable prayer request. Imagine God's delight when, instead of our begging for earthly pleasures, we come to Him crying for more godly foresight for our lives.

Imagine, indeed, God pausing in the business of being God to look with joy on one of His children seeking to see better what may be ahead. When blind Bartimaeus prayed for sight, his whole life changed. Instantly, the man could see. Then he followed Jesus down the road, his eyes wide open (Mark 10:51-52). His head was crowned with the knowledge of salvation. Prudence blessed his life. Dare to let it bless yours right now. 🕊

There are better things ahead than any we leave behind.
C. S. LEWIS

Going Deeper

The prudent understand where they are going.
Proverbs 14:8

Are you a planner? Or do you act on impulse? Either way, explain the impact of planning—or not planning—on your life.

If you are married, are you a prudent spouse? In what ways?

Think of a situation in your life where you need to ask more questions in order to consider your steps prudently. If you'd like, write down some of the questions here:

If you'd like, write a prayer that reflects what God is trying to teach you about the virtue of prudence.

He that takes truth for his guide, and duty for his end, may safely trust
to God's providence to lead him aright.
BLAISE PASCAL

Self-Control

His Promise

*Supplement your faith with a generous
provision of moral excellence, and moral excellence with
knowledge, and knowledge with self-control. . . .
Then God will give you a grand entrance
into the eternal Kingdom.*

2 Peter 1:5-6, 11

My Prayer

Show me, Blessed Jesus, the secrets of self-control.
Then I can walk with grandeur into Your eternal Kingdom.

Self-Control: By His Spirit

But the Holy Spirit produces this kind of fruit in our lives.
Galatians 5:22

So now, here comes the hard spiritual fruit. Self-control.

But self-control isn't gritting our teeth. Instead, as theologian Richard Foster might say, self-control is falling in love.

Especially with God's Spirit. Then it's inviting God's Spirit to dwell in our hearts, minds, souls, and bodies—each day. Every hour.

I need to think about that today. A day when I need the blessed assurance that God loves me and His Spirit longs to dwell in me. So I need to stop trying so hard to control myself. In fact, when I consider self-control, I might want to stand down and be quiet. The human idea of self-control, that is, can seem so hard. Who's *that* perfect? That disciplined? Great questions, it would seem.

But the Bible helps us find the best answer—that self-control isn't forcing ourselves not to indulge in our human lusts. It's not gritting our teeth and screaming, "*I will not* gamble, cheat, smoke, overeat, worship idols, sexually sin, get drunk, act jealous, show envy, fight, do drugs, throw wild parties—or anything else." In fact, self-control doesn't shout at all.

Self-control whispers. *I surrender*. Yes, quiet words.

Come in, Holy Spirit.

Talk about a great prayer to whisper each day! *Come in*. Then all the fruits of the Spirit—love, joy, peace, patience, kindness, goodness, faithfulness, gentleness, *and* self-control—become evident. Or as Jesus said so beautifully: "You will receive power when the Holy Spirit comes upon you. And you will be my witnesses" (Acts 1:8).

"Supergood" people may act good. But they miss out on the relationship. Self-control is about falling in love. *So come in, Holy Spirit.*

Have you issued that invitation to the Lord? Draw near and whisper those words today. The fruit of self-control will hear, bless, and follow. 🌿

Jesus shows us a more excellent way. The way of helplessness.
RICHARD FOSTER

Self-Control: In Thought

Better to have self-control than to conquer a city.
Proverbs 16:32

Want more self-control? Watch what you think. Science proves it, in fact.

In a 2010 study at the University of Georgia, researchers found that just thinking about someone with good self-control made people practice self-control themselves.

But here's a warning: the same correlation applies to thinking about people with bad self-control. Among hundreds of volunteers in the study, this "thinking" effect was so powerful that just seeing the name of someone with good or bad self-control flashing on a screen for ten milliseconds changed the behavior of volunteers.

"The take-home message of this study," said Michelle vanDellen, a visiting assistant professor in the UGA department of psychology, "is that picking social influences that are positive can improve your self-control—and by exhibiting self-control, you're helping others around you do the same."

The Bible, of course, shines God's light on this same idea. "As iron sharpens iron," says Proverbs 27:17, "so a friend sharpens a friend."

Paul's letter to the Romans puts it this way: "So letting your sinful nature control your mind leads to death. But letting the Spirit control your mind leads to life and peace" (Romans 8:6). In fact, in the study, volunteers who thought about a friend with good self-control persisted longer on a hand-grip task commonly used to measure self-control, while the opposite held true for those who were asked to think about a friend with bad self-control.

Think of the irony. Brute force may, or may not, conquer a city. But sitting quietly and thinking about a friend who displays the virtue of self-control enhances our own excellence. And what a friend we have in Jesus, whose yoke is easy and whose burden is light. So stop struggling to wrestle more self-control into your life. Instead? Just think of Him. 🌿

The thought life, then, is our first line of defense in the
battle of self-control.
JERRY BRIDGES

Self-Control: In Knowledge

Supplement your . . . knowledge with self-control. . . .
Then God will give you a grand entrance into the eternal Kingdom.
2 Peter 1:5-6, 11

A key step to self-control? Learn more about God.

I consider that as I sit at my desk, trying to do just that. I look up Scriptures on self-control. I reflect. I pray. I ask the Holy Spirit to teach me today.

Then I find myself picking up an old dictionary. It's heavy and worn. But I go to the entry for *control* and find an odd reminder. I see that the amazing Latin meaning of *control* is actually a phrase: against the wheel.

God, as the center of our lives, is that standard against which we test our own lives, showing us when something is off or wrong.

I stare at the dictionary, thinking hard to hear what God wants me to know about this. Finally, I think I see: self-control is never forcing myself to surrender a lust. Instead, self-control is making God my standard. My counterweight. My wheel in the middle of my own turning. In the science experiment of my life, if I make God my standard—my control—*and* I commit to knowing more about God, I gain an accurate measurement for testing my own actions.

It's a critical test. Because the Bible issues a clear warning against ignoring God's standards and following "the desires of your sinful nature" (Galatians 5:19). Declares verse 21: "Anyone living that sort of life will not inherit the Kingdom of God." But look at the reward for making God our measure, and testing ourselves to stay on track. "Then God will give you a grand entrance into the eternal Kingdom."

Self-control is that important to God. It shows that we're pursuing God—and the things of God—and not pursuing the things of the world.

We trust God, that is, to be far more satisfying than anything the world tries to offer. More than giving up something, we gain when we trust God to bless us more.

Want self-control? Stop trying so hard. Instead, study God. Then invite Him in. He is the Door. 🌿

No conflict is so severe as his who labors to subdue himself.
THOMAS À KEMPIS

Self-Control: In Deed

Don't be drunk with wine. . . . Instead, be filled with the Holy Spirit.
Ephesians 5:18

Imagine a love letter. A beautiful letter. A letter filled with hope, encouragement, grace, and wisdom. A letter filled with the secrets to living a life that reflects the light of Jesus—for Jesus.

Then open the book of Ephesians. There, in its gorgeous pages, we hear such words—first sent to early churches in Ephesus and other Roman provinces. Yet they speak to us today, praising God—"the Father of our Lord Jesus Christ, who has blessed us with every spiritual blessing in the heavenly realms because we are united with Christ" (Ephesians 1:3).

Then the letter tells us how to live like Christ. Despite being surrounded by sin. And pursued by sin. And tempted by ungodly living. And living amidst a culture that not only tolerates sin but also celebrates sin. So this letter spells out dos and don'ts. "I beg you," as Paul says, "to lead a life worthy of your calling, for you have been called by God" (4:1). Ah, yes. A self-controlled life.

So be humble, gentle, patient, united. (It's a long list.) It goes on, exhorting us to throw off our old nature—and "let the Spirit renew your thoughts and attitudes" (4:23). Yes, the Spirit, again, is our key to self-control. So stop telling lies, Paul writes. "If you are a thief, quit stealing" (4:28). If you curse, stop cursing. If you're angry, "don't let the sun go down while you are still angry" (4:26).

And be careful about it! "Don't live like fools, but like those who are wise" (5:15). Or as Paul adds: "Don't be drunk with wine, because that will ruin your life. *Instead, be filled with the Holy Spirit*" (5:18, emphasis added).

Filled to the brim. Otherwise this list will seem too hard to keep. But by God's Spirit, Paul's long to-do list won't also seem impossible. It will feel exciting. Spirit-filled living always is. 🖊

All change that pleases God is the fruit of the Spirit.
JAY E. ADAMS

Self-Control: Through Christ

It is no longer I who live, but Christ lives in me.
Galatians 2:20

Not even Paul could control himself—all by himself. "For when I tried to keep the law, it condemned me" (Galatians 2:19). Sound familiar?

Trying on our own to fight our sins by keeping God's laws always leads—ironically—to more sin. "So I died to the law," Paul wrote. He explains it this way: "I stopped trying to meet all its requirements."

Instead, he invited Christ's Spirit to live in Him.

Sound too theological? In plain English, what are the signs that we have invited Christ's Spirit to live in us? First, we've stopped trying so hard.

Instead, we let Christ control our actions, feelings, desires, and words. We don't fly off the handle at every situation. We can count to ten when something angers us—then, after counting down, we can count up as our anger dies down.

Thus, we let Him delay our gratification. Instead of going in debt to buy that dress or house or car or shoes right now—and instead of ramping up our ministries right now—we can wait. Wait on God's direction, guidance, wisdom, and power.

So we let Him conquer our temptations. Then, we lose our taste for them. Wisely, also, we don't hang around old temptations. It's our old life, and we've chosen Christ. Prudently. So we've moved on.

Then we can laugh with life. Be positive and cheerful, too. Trusting God, we face life's challenges—the good and the bad—with a good heart.

We ask the best from ourselves—even when others aren't asking anything. When others are slacking, we give ourselves a swift kick and get moving. For the good.

And the good is Christ—the Good Shepherd—who wants the very best for His children. But without struggle. Now what about you? Are you making self-control too hard? Bless yourself today and take a break. Give your struggle to Christ. As you relax, He'll lead you back to Himself. 🌿

Come, let us rise with Christ our Head and seek the things above.
CHARLES WESLEY

Self-Control: With Strength

A person without self-control is like a city with broken-down walls.
Proverbs 25:28

Even in young children, self-control pays off. In a famous experiment from the sixties called the Marshmallow Test, psychologists at Stanford University determined that kids who could say no to eating a marshmallow did better in school and in life.

The kids were just four years old.

Each was given a marshmallow, then promised another one—but only if they could wait fifteen minutes before eating the first one. Some children managed to wait. Others could not. The research team then followed the progress of each child into their teen years. What did they find? The children with greater self-control as four-year-olds tested higher as teens on key life variables—such as happiness, psychological adjustment, and dependability. They also scored significantly higher on the SAT.

To lack self-control is to end up just as the Bible predicts. We're left weak and vulnerable, with holes in our armor and weak spots in our defenses—"like a city with broken-down walls." But there's good news. We can improve our self-control—building up and strengthening our life's walls. How?

Make self-denial a lifestyle. Trying to lose weight? Take a nutrition class to learn how to eat right. Trying to cut down on your computer time? Plan time instead to help others or to learn a new skill. Struggling to stop smoking? Don't go it alone. Join others in a stop-smoking program.

Then practice self-control as a lifestyle. Dirty dishes in the sink? Wash them. Piles of clothes on the stairs? Pick them up. Missing a button on a blouse? Sew it on. Soon you'll see how your attention to one area positively influences your actions in all areas. Remind yourself today that self-control matters to God. He wants His children to enjoy strong lives—not broken down by weakness. So on this day, invite His Spirit in to bless and empower this journey. With every step, you'll find more strength. Not yours. His. 🌿

When you surrender your will to God, you discover the resources
to do what God requires.
ERWIN LUTZER

Going Deeper

The more you grow like this, the more productive and useful you will be.
2 Peter 1:8

Have you struggled with self-control? In what area of your life are you weakest? Explain.

Rather than trying so hard to control yourself, what are some ways discussed in this week's devotions that you might try instead? Explain.

As you invite the Holy Spirit to control your life, your actions, and your emotions today, what happens? How will your day be changed?

If you'd like, write a prayer that reflects what God is trying to teach you about the virtue of self-control.

When His people are without strength, without resources,
without hope, without human gimmicks—then He loves to stretch
forth His hand from heaven.
DALE RALPH DAVIS

CONTENTMENT

His Promise

True godliness with contentment is itself great wealth.
1 Timothy 6:6

My Prayer

Enrich my heart with contentment in You!

Contentment: From God

True godliness with contentment is itself great wealth.
1 Timothy 6:6

Great wealth. Can you imagine what it would feel like? Taste like? Sound like? Ponder what it would look like if you could experience it for just one day. How about this?

No desire to buy anything.
No panic to achieve anything.
No worry to stop anything.
No pressure to start anything.
No envy of other people.
No comparing with other people—or anger at other people.
No hunger for money.
No worry about money.
No longing for more of anything—except more of God.

Just contentment with God. And with His delight in His world—and your part in it. And with His promises for you. About His love for you. About an awareness that He sees you and is caring for you. In His wonderful time. In His wonderful way.

Your wealthy and contented day, therefore, would be a quiet day. Walking with God. Resting in His power as He opened some doors—and closed others. Stilled some waters—and stirred others around. Sowed some seeds—and harvested others. Lit some fires—and put others out. Quieted some storms—and shook others up. Opened some hearts—and mended some others. Dried some tears—and let others fall. Closed some work—and let other work begin. Deepened some hope—and silenced some worry.

An assured day, yes. Not worried or hurried. Not grasping or clasping. Not coveting or stealing or murdering or lying or gossiping or pushing or prying or pulling.

Just resting. Trusting. Rejoicing. Relying. Triumphing.
In Him. 🌿

God is most glorified in us, when we are most satisfied in Him.
JOHN PIPER

Contentment: With Godliness

True godliness with contentment is itself great wealth.
1 Timothy 6:6

They were church people in Ephesus, but they craved great wealth. Grasped for it. Schemed for it. Then they took the lowest of the low roads to obtain their wealth. They taught that God would give rich people even more wealth—a prosperity gospel of some sort—if they'd pay up yet more money to the church. Then they'd all be rolling in dough—all enjoying fat-cat cash.

A lie. That's what the apostle Paul warns Timothy about this scheme.

"These people always cause trouble. Their minds are corrupt, and they have turned their backs on the truth" (v. 5).

Wealth to them, that is, was all about money—and their hopes of feeding some deep spiritual discontentment with the false satisfaction of money.

Great wealth, however, is about godly well-being, Paul writes.

It's a teaching that should sink deep daily into every believer's heart. As it does, we understand, as Paul says, that "if we have enough food and clothing" (v. 8), we can be content. So instead of pursuing monetary wealth—a path that traps people with temptations and "many foolish and harmful desires" (v. 9)—let's reach for godly wealth.

Indeed, "pursue righteousness," Paul wrote, "and a godly life, along with faith, love, perseverance, and gentleness" (v. 11). In these simple and beautiful things we find spiritual wealth, yes—in fact, *great* spiritual wealth.

No denying, surely, that monetary wealth can buy pretty things. But great wealth buys "the eternal life to which God has called you" (v. 12), Paul writes. So don't spend your life pursuing earthly wealth, which in the end can stir up foolish desires, plunging us "into ruin and destruction" (v. 9), Paul warns. Instead ask God today to replace your craving for "wealth" with a craving for *great* wealth. The sweet contentment that results will bless you now—but even better, it will bless you forever. 🌱

Contentment comes from trusting God.
JOHN MACARTHUR

Contentment: Without Envy

*Their trust should be in God, who richly gives us
all we need for our enjoyment.*
1 Timothy 6:17

What stirs up our discontent? How about envy? It tops the list. In fact, in the apostle Paul's laundry list of depravity—those soul-killing sins listed by name in his letter to the church at Rome—the sin of envy beats out even murder.

Yes, envy is that bad. As bad as "every kind of wickedness, sin, greed, hate, envy, murder, quarreling, deception, malicious behavior, and gossip" (Romans 1:29). It's all foolish thinking, Paul writes, the result of worshiping idols instead of worshiping God.

God's great displeasure with envy—and its first cousin, coveting—is seen first in the Ten Commandments. *Thou shalt not covet* is set down as a basic mandate for life. Thus, you should not "covet your neighbor's house. You must not covet your neighbor's wife, male or female servant, ox or donkey, or anything else that belongs to your neighbor" (Exodus 20:17). *The Message* concludes the matter this way: "Don't set your heart on anything that is your neighbor's."

Envious people look with malice, greed, and even hate on somebody else for who they are or for what they have. (The Latin word for envy, *invidia*, comes from *invidere*, meaning "to look at with malice.") So envy doesn't just cause discontent. Envy can lead to lust, theft, and even murder.

Some theologians say the deeper problem is pride. "For the world offers only a craving for physical pleasure, a craving for everything we see, and pride in our achievements and possessions" (1 John 2:16).

The remedy? Rest in God, trusting Him completely for how much—or how little—He has given you. Step back and look hard at His gifts to you. Open your eyes, not with malice, but with gratitude. See today that what He has given you is great. It's beautiful. It's enough. He blesses richly, in fact, "for our enjoyment." See *that*. Now enjoy it all.

I make the most of all that comes, and the least of all that goes.
SARA TEASDALE

Contentment: For God

Then others began coming—men who were in trouble or in debt or who were just discontented—until David was the captain of about 400 men.
1 Samuel 22:2

Is all discontent bad? Not always. That's important to know. In church, when we talk about contentment, we often act like discontent can be only bad.

Good discontent, however, provides the perfect warning. It says something deep in our lives is wrong, wrong, wrong. That the only right thing—and the only way to find that right thing—is to come to God.

The psalmist of Psalm 42 captures that feeling perfectly: "As the deer longs for streams of water, so I long for you, O God. I thirst for God, the living God. When can I go and stand before him?" (v. 1-2).

Thirst. Longing. This is the cry of someone who has tried everything, been everywhere, bought everything, been everything. But now discontent—a holy discontent—finally cries out for the only One who can give lasting satisfaction.

As you read about contentment today, are you *dis*contented? With yourself? Your career? Your spouse? Your kids? Your home? Your finances? Your lot in life? Pay attention to this longing and point it to God. Then as you pray, acknowledge your discontent.

That's what the men in the twenty-second chapter of 1 Samuel did. Many were in debt, in trouble—worn down, rung out, and just flat-out disheartened. They came to David, forming an army of some four hundred. Scholars of the Bible say this incident foreshadows Jesus, who would attract to Himself the down-and-out, the hurting, the outcast, the lost, the burdened—then transform them into His army, the body of Christ. Sound like you?

Are you discontented today? In a good way? Praise God for His holy signal that He's calling you. Run to Him, discontent and all. As you sink into His presence, rejoice that you've taken your thirst and hunger to the right place. Then rest. The blessing of godly contentment is at hand. 🌿

Contentment comes only from God, and the sooner we start
seeking it in Him, the better off we will be.
RICHARD D. AND SHARON L. PHILLIPS

Contentment: With Yourself

*For God is working in you, giving you the desire and the power
to do what pleases him.*
Philippians 2:13

Looked in the mirror lately? If you're like most adults, you're discontented enough with your looks that you would choose cosmetic surgery—such as teeth whitening, tummy tucks, and liposuction—if money wasn't an issue.

In fact, more than half (54 percent) of all US adults in a 2009 Harris Interactive study—including 67 percent of women and 40 percent of men in the survey—would have cosmetic work done if money were not a problem.

That's a lot of wishful brightening and tightening.

How can we be happier with ourselves? With our bodies—and our minds and lives? Look instead at Christ. Then shine for Christ.

Then have the mind of Christ.

That's what the apostle Paul desired for the believers in the Roman colony of Philippi. As they faced persecution and trials—and all the human tensions such problems create—he urged them: "Have the same attitude that Christ Jesus had" (Philippians 2:5).

Though He was God, He humbled himself in obedience to His Heavenly Father. Then God "elevated him to the place of highest honor" (v. 9). Likewise, when we look to Christ as our model, humbling ourselves before God—and not trying to impress others—God elevates us, brightening us more than any teeth whitener or skin peel ever could.

"For God is working in you, giving you the desire and the power to do what pleases him." This is irony, indeed. By not worrying so much about what we're wearing or what we look like—but by wearing Christ's humility—we will be seen as beautiful, "shining like bright lights in a world full of crooked and perverse people" (v. 15).

So put down your mirror. Instead, gaze on Him. Then model His humble beauty, peace, and grace. As you do, your contentment in Him will shine in you. 🌿

For I have learned how to be content. . . . I can do everything
through Christ, who gives me strength.
PHILIPPIANS 4:11, 13

Contentment: With Others

If one part is honored, all the parts are glad.
1 Corinthians 12:26

Somebody else always has more. Not just in things. But in spiritual gifts, too. In our churches, therefore, when different people have vastly different gifts—and some appear to be more spiritually gifted than others—the ugly green monster called jealousy can rear its discontented head. Just like in the world.

In the church, however, such discontent can leave us deceived and disheartened. For in comparing ourselves with others, we'll find ourselves overestimating somebody else's talents—or underestimating our own.

As Paul told the Christians in Galatia, "Pay careful attention to your own work, for then you will get the satisfaction of a job well done, and you won't need to compare yourself to anyone else. For we are each responsible for our own conduct" (Galatians 6:4-5).

In short, we all have gifts. It doesn't matter, therefore, if somebody else's gift appears more important. Or if they get more attention. Or more credit. Or if they use their gifts in big or small ways. In fact, judging others for how they use their gifts is not our business. So here's a reminder for us all.

Love each other—and each other's gifts. Then *relax.*

In our churches, says Paul, there will be apostles, prophets, teachers, healers, and more—all with our quirks, hiccups, complexities, and kooky, sometimes maddening ways. But if we appreciate each other's gifts, then lay down, as theologian Richard Foster says, "the everlasting burden of always needing to manage others," we'll be blessed with contentment. But not just with others. We'll be content with ourselves.

Is that your challenge today? Find somebody in your church who's hard for you to love—because his or her gift seems greater. Then love that person anyway. You'll be overjoyed at how much, in turn, you love God and yourself. 🌿

Love the body of Christ—our true brothers and sisters—in such a way that the world and spiritual powers are stunned by our oneness.
EDWARD T. WELCH

Going Deeper

True godliness with contentment is itself great wealth.
1 Timothy 6:6

Are you content with your life? With yourself? With your talents or your gifts? Or are you not content? Explain.

If you're not content with yourself—or with some aspect of your life—what have you learned this week that would develop and deepen your contentment?

As you look at Christ, what aspects of His character would increase your contentment with yourself and with your life?

If you'd like, write a prayer that reflects what God is trying to teach you about the virtue of contentment.

We pass violets looking for roses.
UNKNOWN

DIGNITY AND MODESTY

His Promise

A gracious woman gains respect.
Proverbs 11:16

My Prayer

Teach me the principles of modesty,
planting them deep in my heart
as self-respect.

Dignity and Modesty: Inside Out

She is clothed with strength and dignity.
Proverbs 31:25

What would Jesus wear? An odd question perhaps. But in a room full of stylish Christian women, I find myself asking exactly that. What would Jesus wear? Because in this gathering of fashion-forward believers, only one truly reminds me of Jesus. Why? She isn't stylish. In her plain cotton skirt and simple blouse, she seems a bit out of place. Then she speaks. And I hear gold. Every time this modest woman comments at this meeting, she's on target. Thoughtful and challenging. Not distracted by fashion, she seems clothed by Christ—dressed in strength and dignity.

Back home, I ponder this challenge of fashion versus faith. But I wonder: is it your challenge too? Loving the beauty of this world—including the clothes, jewelry, and shoes we sashay around in—we can be motivated by ego. Dressing to be seen and admired. Even in church. Or am I preaching to myself? More motivated for fashion some Sundays when I get dressed for church than motivated for worship?

These are timely and urgent questions. They challenge our social culture—where entire families go into debt buying fancy, expensive fashions. They convict us as believers to take a hard look in our mirrors. What do we see? Followers of Christ? Or followers of Christ whose need to stand out and get noticed has compromised our modesty?

To answer today, let us ask the Holy Spirit to show us what to wear. "You should clothe yourselves . . . with the beauty that comes from within, the unfading beauty of a gentle and quiet spirit, which is so precious to God" (1 Peter 3:4). Yes, our fashion tastes start in the heart. Not at the mall. In fact, when shopping for our clothing, let's not leave home without God—and a prayer: Give me a clean heart, O God. Then our appearance, from hat to hemline, will bless and glorify our God. Our maker. Our keeper. Our dresser. 🌿

So dress and conduct yourself so that people who have been
in your company will not recall what you had on.
JOHN NEWTON

Dignity and Modesty: In Behavior

*When you bow down before the Lord and admit your dependence on him,
he will lift you up and give you honor.*
James 4:10

Thousands watched in the rain while the pop singer—"the most popular living person on Facebook"—belted out songs at an outdoor concert. To fuel the public's fixation with her celebrity persona, she wore look-at-me outfits—gyrating provocatively in front of a chorus line of equally provocative backup dancers.

Still I didn't watch. Turning the channel, I thought about what psychologists say about the public's fascination with celebrities, celebrity fashions, and celebrity behavior. "Celebrities are fascinating because they live in a parallel universe—one that looks and feels just like ours yet is light-years beyond our reach." So says Carlin Flora, features editor at *Psychology Today* magazine. Compared to our dull and safe lives, their lives seem exciting, important, and enviable. That's what we tell ourselves, anyway. "Stars summon our most human yearnings: to love, admire, copy and, of course, to gossip and to jeer," Flora adds.

Then comes James. The brother of Jesus reminds us of the dangers of worshiping the brazen immodesty of pop-culture icons. "Don't you realize that friendship with this world makes you an enemy of God?" (v. 4).

Does that mean God hates pop singers and Hollywood celebrities? I feel certain He does not. In fact, I'd argue God loves these pop icons as much as He loves the least celebrated among us. He sent His Son to die for us all.

But when we return His love by fawning over the immodesty and indignity of certain cultural idols, we cozy up to the devil—pushing God away. Our gossip on Facebook about stars and their coarse displays can feel fun. But stop laughing, says James. Instead "let there be sorrow and deep grief. Let there be sadness instead of laughter, and gloom instead of joy" (v. 9). Turn from false fun. Instead, uplift the wholesome. Then bow down before the Lord, showing your dependence on Him. As you bow, He will lift you up—blessing you with honor. Not like a pop star. But like His own Son. 🌿

Remember that God's approval is infinitely more important than the world's.
BRUCE BARTON

Dignity and Modesty: In Our Speech

And if you don't brag about the good you do, then you will be truly wise!
James 3:13

The college student was smart. Bragged about it a lot. Bragged so much, in fact, that other students complained—to his face.

"You're such a know-it-all."

"You won't let anybody else talk."

"Don't you care about what other people think?"

"Just shut up already!"

But the bragging student couldn't shut up. It's as if the switch in his head that said "enough" didn't work. And no wonder. Bragging isn't just annoying. As James wrote to rich church leaders who bragged about their charity, "Such things are earthly, unspiritual, and motivated by the Devil" (3:15). Strong words.

That's because bragging isn't a problem of the tongue. It's a problem of the heart. Or as James said in his letter to the early church, the tongue is set on fire "by hell itself" (v. 6). Bragging, to be sure, can seem just annoying or even "harmless." But like other problems of an untamed tongue, it sparks jealousy and selfishness and is "not God's kind of wisdom" (v. 15).

Modesty in our speech, in contrast, reflects a heart generating words that demonstrate wisdom—a transformed heart, producing "a life of steady goodness so that only good deeds will pour forth" (v. 13). Bragging words, however, reflect Satan. They say: I don't trust God. He won't honor me. So I'd better show off myself for myself.

It seems shocking, indeed, to think of bragging as a product of hell. But James asks us to carefully consider what such an immodest tongue reveals. To be modest in our speech, however, reveals God's Spirit residing in our hearts, producing peace, gentleness, and a "willing[ness] to yield" that follows. God in the heart. That's what the college student needed. And you? If you can't control bragging, don't bite your tongue. Instead, quiet your heart. How? Let God in. He'll bless your tongue with the true wisdom of a humble heart. ❦

Conceit spoils the finest genius.
LOUISA MAY ALCOTT

Dignity and Modesty: In Our Struggles

Don't copy the behavior and customs of this world.
Romans 12:2

How did young Wangari Maathai of Kenya fight political persecution, environmental threats, and antiwoman put-downs? She planted trees. Without fanfare. Or self-promotion. Or showing off. Instead, the bright young biologist and college professor heard complaints by rural women in Kenya that they lacked enough firewood and clean water.

Her modest response: "Why not plant trees?"

A dignified and simple plan. "And so they just started—very, very small. And before long they started showing each other." Soon, all across Kenya, women inspired by Maathai began "empowering each other to plant trees."

End of story? Of course not. A modest woman doesn't make big noise. But she can make big change. Soon, indeed, Kenyan political leaders—fearing Maathai's organizing efforts—targeted her endeavors and independence, suggesting she was "crazy" and a "mad woman" and a "threat to the order and security of the country."

With dignity, however, Maathai stood up to such charges, spending time in jails and prisons, using hunger strikes and protests in efforts to fight for democracy in Kenya—but also quietly fighting, without fanfare, to heal environmental damage in Kenya and across the world by planting trees of hope. Maathai's One Billion Trees campaign—a project of the Green Belt Movement she founded—earned her the 2004 Nobel Peace Prize, and, in 2005, *Time* magazine named her one of the one hundred most influential people in the world and *Forbes* magazine called her one of the one hundred most powerful women in the world.

But you don't know her name? That's because she hasn't sought fame.

Dignity doesn't work that way. Perhaps that is why God has blessed her efforts—just as He will bless ours, too, as we modestly work with dignified strength to bless His world. 🍂

It's the little things citizens do. That's what will make the difference.
My little thing is planting trees.
WANGARI MAATHAI

Dignity and Modesty: Head to Toe

This is how the holy women of old made themselves beautiful.
1 Peter 3:5

Modesty matters to God—and it's clear why. If we're modest, we don't glorify ourselves. That was the problem facing one young woman's heart—and her closet. "When choosing what to wear," said this woman, "I thought only of what would flatter me, what would bring more attention my way, and what most resembles the clothes I saw on models or other stylish women." As quoted in C. J. Mahaney's book *Worldliness: Resisting the Seduction of a Fallen World*, the young woman said, "I wanted to be admired for what I wore." Or as she confessed: "I enjoyed my attire, the undue attention I received."

She had no clue about the concept of modesty, or what the word *modest* means (*modestus* in Latin or "keeping due measure," not overdoing our behavior or appearance). As well, she didn't know what the Bible teaches about modesty. As the apostle Paul wrote to the young preacher Timothy, "I want women to be modest in their appearance. They should wear decent and appropriate clothing and not draw attention to themselves by the way they fix their hair or by wearing gold or pearls or expensive clothes" (1 Timothy 2:9). Rich women could help the church, in fact, by focusing less on fashion and more on Christ.

As women of Christ, in other words, we should measure our clothing by what is appropriate to worship God. "Exalting God and not ourselves," as Mahaney says, we show the character of our hearts but also the character of Christ. And, no, being a Christian woman doesn't mean being out of style. It means dressing to praise God and not to be praised ourselves.

As Mahaney says: "Modesty is humility expressed in dress."

"This is how the holy women of old made themselves beautiful." By foregoing fancy clothes and jewelry—or anything akin to the popular fashion we see today. Still, they grew beautiful in spirit. Humbly beautiful. Gracious in dress and demeanor, they gained respect. Even better, their gracious beauty showed off the beauty of God. Will we bless others with such beauty today? It's a choice God will celebrate. ❧

Modesty is a product of pure thinking.
MICHELLE BROCK

Dignity and Modesty: For All

So God created people in his own image.
Genesis 1:27

At nine months pregnant, the young woman holds her belly up as she walks. The parking lot must feel endless. The grocery store must seem far. The July sun must feel hot. But as she picks her way across the blacktop, the neatly groomed young mother doesn't look defeated. She looks determined.

No summer heat will stop her. Not from grocery shopping. Not from walking. But most of all, not from carrying her baby to its highest moment of dignified destiny: birth. Then from that moment, I want to believe, she will cherish and treasure and guide her child through the twists and turns of life as carefully as she steps with caution and determination across the potholes in the steaming pavement.

Why? Dignity matters.

I want to promote that today. On a day when, as I write, the number of abortions worldwide will reach approximately 125,000 before the sun goes down—or 40 million to 50 million abortions in the year 2010, according to the World Health Organization—I want to remember. Dignity matters.

I want to ponder that today. On a day when, as I write, the news features grim accounts of political prisons so defiled by rats, vermin, and disease that some inmates try to kill themselves, I want to remember. Dignity matters.

I want to publicize that today. On a day when, as I write, a worldwide church still faces the ongoing problem of church leaders sexually molesting the mentally disabled as well as children, I want to remember. Dignity matters.

For every person. Every child. Every woman. Every man. God created people in His own image. His very own. So on this day, dignity is my right. But also yours. God made it so. Amen. 🔥

> The dignity of human life is unbreakably linked to the existence
> of the personal-infinite God.
> FRANCIS SCHAEFFER

Going Deeper

So God created human beings in his own image.
Genesis 1:27

When you think of dignity and modesty, what characteristics come to mind? What could these words mean in your own life?

How do women and men who dress modestly serve others?

What can you do to help promote human dignity in the world?

If you'd like, write a prayer that reflects what God is trying to teach you about the virtues of dignity and modesty.

And so, dear brothers and sisters, I plead with you to give your bodies to God because of all he has done for you. Let them be a living and holy sacrifice—the kind he will find acceptable. This is truly the way to worship him.
ROMANS 12:1

Silence and Solitude

His Promise

In quietness and confidence is your strength.
Isaiah 30:15

My Prayer

Quiet my spirit, O God.
Then in confidence and solitude,
bless me as I silently seek You.

Silence and Solitude: To Hear God's Voice

After the fire there was the sound of a gentle whisper.
1 Kings 19:12

The wall-to-wall sound system was a monster. And my husband was in love. "*Wow*." He stood in the appliance store, awestruck, facing the fancy amplifiers as they pounded out a movie soundtrack. "Can you *feel* that?" He was mesmerized.

I nodded, smiling, impressed but secretly praying: *Please, don't let him buy that!*

Of course, to hear sound is a blessed gift. I understand that. But later, I thought about the sound of God.

The prophet Elijah hears this sound only by God's mercy. In fact, God is chastising Elijah for running away in fear from the evil and godless Queen Jezebel—and hiding in a cave. "What are you doing here, Elijah?" (v. 9).

It's a question most of us have heard. Heard in our hearts.

As we've stood in the storms, earthquakes, and fires in our lives, then tried to run, weren't we surprised to learn that God didn't speak in upheavals? Yet *after* them, when we finally stopped swirling and worrying and shaking in our boots, the gentle stillness of God—always there—could finally be heard.

So it is with Elijah. Humbled and duly aware of the quiet whisper of God's power, he yanks off his cloak and wraps it around his face—his reverence raw and awestruck. Can you *feel* that? He might, as my husband in the appliance store, want to ask such a question about the sound of God. It is so intense yet so soft. Yet we won't hear or feel it if we don't quiet our storms and seek His face. Not running from God, but running to Him.

God's still voice? To hear it, turn off the loud sounds of life. Open His Word and listen. Unlock your spirit and hear. Turn from your storms, your fires, your earthquakes. And feel. What will you hear? The empowered blessing of His answer. 🌿

Listen to the inward Voice 'til you learn to recognize it.
A. W. TOZER

Silence and Solitude: In Worship to God

Be silent before the LORD, all humanity, for he is springing into action.
Zechariah 2:13

O Lord, my God. Did A. W. Tozer, the self-taught theologian, pray like this? I suspect he did. A word or two. Then silence. Or as Tozer put it: "Retire from the world each day to some private spot, even if it be only the bedroom." Or for Tozer, the furnace room "for want of a better place."

Now that's a provocative picture. Imagine Tozer, one of the most well-loved Bible teachers and speakers of his time, alone in the basement with himself and with his God next to the furnace. Or perhaps that makes perfect sense. In that humble place, this man Tozer—who spoke before crowds of hundreds and thousands—would've felt his real humanity. There, in the steam heat of winter and the cold darkness of summer, he would best understand: When we worship God in our own still silence, we finally hear. That God *isn't* silent. In fact, God is springing into action.

Like Tozer, the prophet Zechariah in today's Scripture understood that. Worshiping God in silence, the prophet was able to hear this message: don't stay trapped in exile or captivity—whatever your personal Babylon might be.

"The LORD says, 'Shout and rejoice, O beautiful Jerusalem, for I am coming to live among you. . . . I will live among you, and you will know that the LORD of Heaven's Armies sent me to you" (vv. 10-11).

What blessed assurance—to be reminded that Jesus our Christ is already moving on our circumstances, springing into action, even before we speak a word about it. Our tendency is to bend God's ears with our worries, thereby staying trapped with them—in a Babylon of our own making. But both Zechariah and the self-taught preacher Tozer urge us to consider silence. As we quiet our panic, God springs into action for those who dare, in silence, to believe. 🔥

Stay in the secret place till the surrounding noises begin to fade out of your heart and a sense of God's presence envelops you.
A. W. TOZER

Silence and Solitude: With Prayerful Hope

I wait quietly before God, for my salvation comes from him.
Psalm 62:1

The fireworks vendors in my town set up weeks before Independence Day. Vacant lots on every corner, it seems, get transformed into mom-and-pop firecracker stores. By July 4 itself, enough noisemaking explosives have been sold in my suburb to light up the night *and* split a few eardrums.

It's that way by design. As John Adams, the second US president, wrote in a letter to his wife dated July 3, 1776, Independence Day "ought to be commemorated, as the Day of Deliverance, by solemn acts of devotion to God Almighty. It ought to be solemnized with pomp and parade, with shows, games, sports, guns, bells, bonfires and illuminations, from one end of this continent to the other, from this time forward forever."

Such noise fits that occasion.

When we wait on God, however, the psalmist says it's fitting to wait in silence.

What a contrast. A big national party should be joyous and loud. The more noise the better. Likewise, our praise of God is joyous. *Make a joyful noise unto the Lord.*

To wait quietly for Him at other times, however, displays the depth of our faith.

By faith, we don't badger the Lord with our worries. Or rage at God. Or worry whether God even sees us. By faith, we believe. He sees. He knows. He understands. And He is springing into action. Not because of our noise—but despite our silence, He reaches out with salvation and hope. Do you believe that? Then on this noisiest of days, show God the depth of your faith. Not with noisy demands, but with the explosive blessing of your assured quiet. 🌾

There are some things you learn best in calm, and some in storm.
WILLA CATHER

Silence and Solitude: To Hear like Christ

Then Jesus . . . was led by the Spirit to go out into the wilderness.
Luke 4:1

Was Jesus an introvert? Is that a crazy question? Or one open for debate? I consider the question today, in fact—reading blogs and Internet chat forums and magazine commentaries on just that subject. Jesus, an introvert? Arguments run the gamut. One theory even implies that Jesus advised His followers "to pray to the Father in secret" because the Savior was an introvert.

That view I don't buy. Clearly, however, Jesus honored the two-tiered disciplines of silence and solitude. As an introvert? I wouldn't even guess. From the Word of God, however, we see many clear benefits of Jesus' time alone—away from crowds—with His Father. The most important benefit? Sheer power.

It's an example all believers should closely study. In today's Scripture, for example, Jesus—"full of the Holy Spirit" (v. 1)—is led by the Spirit into the wilderness where He is tempted by the devil for forty long days. Still, when He returns to Galilee, He is "filled with the Holy Spirit's power." Then, He "became well known throughout the surrounding country . . . and was praised by everyone" (vv. 14-15).

Throughout the Gospels, Jesus displays this same pattern.

After feeding the clamoring crowd of five thousand, "he went up into the hills by himself to pray" (Matthew 14:23). Night fell while He was alone. Yes, for a long time, He sat or lay or stood in silence and solitude. Then what came next for Jesus? He walked on water.

Such power is rendered by solitary silence with God. Not your style? Are you a classic extrovert, energized by big doses of other people and lots of talking? Dare to bless yourself with a break. Not by yourself, but with God. Empowered, Jesus set that standard. May He inspire us all today, introverts and extroverts, to follow. 🌿

The worship of God does not always require words.
DONALD WHITNEY

Silence and Solitude: To Gain God's Perspective

It is good to wait quietly.
Lamentations 3:26

What's the best way to open our minds? Close our mouths.

Dare I try it? Or will I have to learn like Zechariah, the husband of Elizabeth?

I study his story with close attention. If you recall it, Zechariah in old age was told he and his aged and barren wife would have a son. This child would become John the Baptist. But Zechariah doubted. He asked God's messenger Gabriel for proof. "How can I know this will happen?" (Luke 1:18).

Wrong question. It lacked faith.

Therefore, said Gabriel, "since you didn't believe what I said, you won't be able to speak until the child is born" (v. 20). Nine months of silence. Lots of time to think. Silent time. In fact, when the child finally was born and Elizabeth said his name would be John—a name never before used in their family's priestly line—Zechariah finally understood God's plan. The child would be John the Baptist, indeed. Asking for a writing tablet, Zechariah scratched out: "His name is John!" (v. 63).

Instantly, Zechariah could speak again.

"And he began praising God" (v. 64).

Few of us would want to gain godly perspective from such an imposed silence. The story, however, illustrates how purposeful silence can open our minds to God. The prophet Jeremiah made this same case in the book of Lamentations. During the darkest period of his life, he came to understand that, as bad as things were, God's mercy saved him from even worse. "It is good to wait quietly for salvation from the LORD."

Is this a perspective you can use today? Not just that holy silence yields fresh understanding—but that God is faithful through all of it. His love is unfailing, resulting in salvation and deliverance. Now that's understanding worth waiting for. How can you and I test it today? Silently. 🌿

God speaks in the silence of the heart.
MOTHER TERESA

Silence and Solitude: To Seek God's Will

He prayed to God all night.
Luke 6:12

Everybody wants to know God's will. But few of us have the discipline to seek God alone and wait for His answer. So let us look to Jesus.

What did He do when making perhaps the greatest administrative decision of His ministry—selecting His top twelve disciples? He went alone to God.

The Gospel writer Luke explains. Jesus had healed a man's deformed hand on the Sabbath—and the enemies of Christ were enraged. So they started plotting what to do with Him. But did Jesus start plotting in return? No.

Instead, He "went to a mountain to pray, and he prayed to God all night" (v. 12). Yes, the solitary pursuit of God takes time—and discipline and patience. But also it takes faith and confidence that God will see our solitary silence and will answer.

Thus at daybreak, after pursuing God alone all night long, Jesus "called together all of his disciples and chose twelve of them to be apostles" (v. 13). Talk about acting on a clear answer.

Seeking God silently also inspired missionary Hudson Taylor. Serving in the mid-1800s, he determined to expand his outreach into central China—where no missionary had dared to go. Exhausted but fervent, he took his burden to God in solitary prayer. Walking along the beach at Brighton, England, almost paralyzed by fear of the responsibility of expanding his mission, he could discern God's answer to his solitary prayer: "Why, if we are obeying the Lord, the responsibility rests *with Him,* not with us! *Thou, Lord, Thou* shalt have all the burden! At Thy bidding, as Thy servant I go forward, leaving results with Thee."

Describing the moment to a friend, he reflected: "How restfully I turned away from the sands. The conflict ended, all was joy and peace."

Solitude with God works. Why? With Him, we are never alone. 🌿

Whatever is your best time in the day, give that to communion with God.
HUDSON TAYLOR

Going Deeper

A truly wise person uses few words.
Proverbs 17:27

Do you talk too much? What is "too much" when it comes to talking to God? Explain.

Think of a time when your silence would have helped a situation. What role does silence play in the life of faith?

Jesus prayed all night in solitude before making a big decision—the naming of His twelve apostles. What decision in your life deserves all-night solitary prayer? What would it take for you to pursue God alone for that long?

If you'd like, write a prayer that reflects what God is trying to teach you about the companion virtues of silence and solitude.

I listen and give input only if somebody asks.
BARBARA BUSH

TEMPERANCE

His Promise

Do you like honey? Don't eat too much of it.
Proverbs 25:16

My Prayer

Restrain me, O God,
so I can moderate my energy—and my words—
while blessing You.

Temperance: In All Things

Do you like honey? Don't eat too much of it.
Proverbs 25:16

Just a little bit. That's how much garlic pepper I sprinkled on the zucchini I'd cut up for dinner. With high blood pressure a factor in my family, I've cut back—way back—on my sodium intake. Unlike table salt, my garlic pepper blend has a fraction of salt. But would I miss that bright snap that salt adds to flavors? I tasted the vegetables, now roasted and browned on the edges. I licked my lips. Not salty but still delicious. Moderation didn't hurt this dish one bit.

It's a good thing, in fact—moderation. Or temperance, to use an old-fashioned-sounding word. That's what temperance asks of us. Moderation.

In fact, the Latin word *temperare* means to adjust or to modify by "adding some moderating agent." So temperance is not just about "teetotaling" abstinence, say from alcohol.

Temperance, instead, is about restraint. How? By adding what we need.

More of the Holy Spirit—that is, a deeper relationship with the Holy Spirit—helps me temper the lie that I need to salt my food to make it taste good. And helps my husband, who's watching his cholesterol, cut out his nightly bowl of butterfat ice cream. Instead, he now tempers that craving with smoothies he makes from frozen fresh fruit, orange juice, and a splash of low-fat milk. A pretty easy switch, he says. But our blessed Holy Spirit, as I see it, assists him in sticking with it.

A tougher challenge for him was giving up cigarettes about fifteen years ago—cold turkey. A spiritual journey? "In all honesty, I don't think so," he tells me. "But after smoking for forty years, and after trying so many times to stop, I remember thanking God when I did." Tempered with a little bit of thanks, he hasn't picked up a cigarette since.

What little change do you need to make today? Start small. Your temperate try will seem meager. Humbling, too. So add Christ. He'll temper and bless your meager with His might. 🔥

Get out of the way; let God take over.
NANCY LEIGH DEMOSS

Temperance: In Our Work Lives

One day as Jesus was walking along the shore . . .
Matthew 4:18

Jesus was not a workaholic. Or a perfectionist. Or an obsessive-compulsive. We know He worked hard. But, with divine wisdom, He tempered His work with exercise and rest.

As we are told in Matthew 4:18, "One day as Jesus was walking along the shore . . ."—and that small portion of Scripture paints a deep portrait of the temperate nature of Jesus' work life. But what do we see? We see Him slowing down His day, shaking off tensions, turning His attention from the grind of needs to the freshness of nature. We see that if taking time out from work for a walk was good enough for Christ, surely it's good enough for us.

This break provided needed relaxation. But pay close attention. Because as Jesus walked along the beach, His walk inspired His work. That is, He noticed two brothers—"Simon, also called Peter, and Andrew—fishing with a net" (v. 18). So Jesus called to them. "Come, be my disciples, and I will show you how to fish for people!" (v. 19).

That's job recruitment Jesus-style.

While resting, in other words, He recruited two key workers. No hard sell. No heavy pressure. No cajoling. No arm twisting. Just an amiable, gentle invitation to learn from Jesus, then share Him with others. In contrast to the fast-paced, hectic, feverish frenzy that describes many work lives today, the workdays of Jesus were busy but balanced. In taking a break to walk, He encountered a man—Simon Peter—whom Christ later declared the Rock on whom He'd build His entire church.

And what about us? Taking breaks from work to walk is advised by any number of experts—doctors, psychologists, life coaches, artists—as one of the most effective, temperate habits any of us can practice. Have you taken a walk today? Stop now and take your break, knowing with each temperate and blessed step, Jesus is walking with you. 🌱

Rest time is not waste time.
CHARLES SPURGEON

Temperance: In Our Lifestyles

Enjoy what you have rather than desiring what you don't have.
Ecclesiastes 6:9

We can't shop our way to happiness. So why do people keep trying? In fact, psychologists insist that having more, buying more, and experiencing more don't make people happier. Experts even have a fancy name to explain the problem—"hedonic adaptation." It means that when things improve in our lives (we get more money, fancy cars, bigger houses, success in work or missions), we soon become used to such things.

After a brief boost in happiness, our happiness levels sink back to "normal."

So those who chase bigger payoffs soon find they need yet more payoff to feel better. (Psychologists call this the "hedonic treadmill.")

It's as King Solomon wrote: "Those who love pleasure become poor; wine and luxury are not the way to riches" (Proverbs 21:17). Tempering our consumption, instead, enriches our happiness. Instinctively, it seems, we all understand that less *is* more.

So tempering our lusts for luxuries—in whatever form—grants the peace and pleasure we were seeking all along. To know, for example, that drug use in the United States is higher than in any other nation tells us something about this hedonistic paradox. (Americans have the highest levels of lifetime illegal cocaine and marijuana use and the highest rate of lifetime tobacco use in the world.)

We can be absolutely confident, however, in the Bible's reminder that "it is better to have little with fear for the LORD than to have great treasure with turmoil" (Proverbs 15:16).

In fact, the best things in life—loving relationships, good health, purpose, the beauty of nature—are free. So let us temper our craving for more. The blessing? The empowered surprise of joy in Him. 🔥

God is always better than gold.
JOHN PIPER

Temperance: At the Table

If you are a big eater, put a knife to your throat.
Proverbs 23:2

It's our biggest big problem. Obesity rates are growing—literally—all over the world. But why is eating so out of balance?

Globally, for example, more than one billion overweight adults, at least 300 million of them obese, account for a threefold or more increase in the problem since 1980, according to the World Health Organization. Most obesity is in the United States, with 68 percent of adults, according to the Centers for Disease Control, deemed overweight, and 34 percent of those obese.

Are we that hungry?

Or are we hungry for more—to know God?

And to be known by Him? As Jesus, in the wilderness, quoting the Scriptures, declared: "People do not live by bread alone, but by every word that comes from the mouth of God" (Matthew 4:4).

So the solution for our hunger—both physical and spiritual? A little temperance. A little more knowledge about who God is. A little more knowledge about how to eat right. A little more physical activity. A little more forgiveness. (Stop berating yourself.) A little more desire to honor God's gift of life. The result: a better body for God.

Starting our days with God's Word, that is, tempers our hunger for emotional fat—and for sugar-laden, fat-clogged breakfasts and snacks. I'm humbled to think back that my own decision to add morning devotions, some thirty years ago, seemed to lead to my switch from drinking soda to water. A small change, yes. But cutting out sugary sodas still helps me hold off extra pounds—while the morning devotions still enrich my soul.

Trying to lose weight? Eat God's Word. He'll bless you with a bonus—more love for yourself and others, and more hunger just for Him. ✇

There is more hunger for love and appreciation
in this world than for bread.
MOTHER TERESA

Temperance: In Our Morals

Let us follow the Holy Spirit's leading in every part of our lives.
Galatians 5:25

Where does temperance draw an absolute line? We know the answer.

Temperance draws a line with sin. Some human appetites should be curbed, that is, but others never should be tested. But which ones?

The apostle Paul spells out those appetites in his letter to the churches in the Roman province of Galatia—naming in 5:19-21 everything from adultery and fornication to wild parties and drunkenness. (He repeats a similar list in Ephesians 5:3-7.)

"Let me tell you again, as I have before," Paul writes, "that anyone living that sort of life will not inherit the Kingdom of God" (Galatians 5:21).

Of course, we can look also to the Ten Commandments, the book of Proverbs, and even the Seven Deadly Sins outlined for Roman Catholics by Pope Gregory I (from gluttony to pride) for lists of don'ts.

Abstinence from such things moves our temperance from moderation to self-denial.

It's for our own good. But not by our own effort.

Instead, "when the Holy Spirit controls our lives," Paul writes, "*he* will produce this kind of fruit in us: love, joy, peace, patience, kindness, goodness, faithfulness, gentleness, and self-control" (vv. 22-23, italics added).

This Spirit-produced fruit nails the passions and desires of our sinful nature to Christ's cross, Paul writes, and crucifies them there. Trusting God's fruit to satisfy us far more than our own carnal desires, we can "follow the Holy Spirit's leading in every part of our lives" (v. 25).

In our eating and drinking, behavior, dress, work, and speech, we'll show the tempering effects of living "by the Holy Spirit." This is for our benefit, but not for our glory. So "let us not become conceited," Paul concludes (v. 26). Instead, now tempered, let us bless Christ by displaying the fruit of His moral harvest as a blessing for others—but through Him. 🌿

Fruit is borne not by trying, but by abiding.
JOHN MACARTHUR

Temperance: In Our Ambitions

He must become greater and greater, and I must become less and less.
John 3:30

Delicious gourmet chocolate doesn't start out that way. Neither does strong steel. Nor beautiful gold. Nor durable glass. All have to be tempered. Modified, that is. Yes, cooled off. Then reheated at the right but low temperature until the substance is "tempered." The end result? A stronger, more beautiful object that's also more durable.

Tempering, ironically, yes, decreases brittle hardness. But it increases inner toughness. So tempered objects are less likely to break. More likely to endure. Less likely to crack. More likely to last. And they look better.

What, then, if we tempered our ambitions? Moderated them, as John the Baptist did, so we decrease as Christ increases. The end result? A more beautiful and stronger, as well as a more durable, ministry.

In today's church, everybody, it seems, wants to be a star. "The bigger the better," as some see it. So some ministries burn bright for a time. Then they flame out.

But what if we moderated our ambitions?

John the Baptist did precisely that. While he was baptizing people at Aenon near Salim, his disciples complained that everybody was going to Jesus to be baptized "instead of coming to us." But John replied: "It is the bridegroom who marries the bride, and the best man is simply glad to stand with him" (John 3:26, 29). A tempered man, John turned away glory from himself, working instead for Jesus' success.

Tempering his own ambition helped grow the Kingdom of Christ, *for* Christ. So must our ministerial ambitions be tempered—decreasing so Christ increases. That way, as with the best chocolate, the strongest steel, and the most durable glass, our tempered ministries won't crack under duress. They'll endure while Christ gains. Above all. 🖊

We are not the center of it; Christ is.
DAN STONE

Going Deeper

Don't weary yourself.
Proverbs 23:4

Temperance is not always abstinence. It also means to adjust or modify "by adding some moderating agent." How then would allowing the Holy Spirit into your daily behaviors and decisions temper you? Explain.

Tempering takes trust. Why is that so?

What needs tempering in your life? How exactly do you intend to display more temperance?

If you'd like, write a prayer that reflects what God is trying to teach you about the virtue of temperance.

Temperate temperance is best.
MARK TWAIN

SACRIFICE

His Promise

Obedience is far better than sacrifice.
1 Samuel 15:22

My Prayer

Equip me, blessed God, with the excellent
sacrifice of obedience.

Sacrifice: To Our Holy God

Because you have obeyed me . . . I will certainly bless you.
Genesis 22:16-17

Sacrifice is self-denial? That's what I once thought. But I was wrong.

Sacrifice is giving up something to appease God? That's what I once thought. But I was wrong.

Sacrifice is making a show of my giving, bribing God into giving something I want in return? That's what I once thought. But I was wrong.

Dead wrong.

I was shocked, finally to learn the true nature of sacrifice—that to sacrifice means to "make holy" or "make sacred." That this Latin word—*sacrificium* ("sacred") with *facere* ("to make")—has nothing whatever to do with giving up what's important to me to impress God.

Do you think Abraham knew that? When he obeyed God, by offering the life of his only son to God, he wasn't denying himself. Abraham was preparing and purifying himself. He was making himself holy—in sacrifice—to serve our holy God.

I like thinking about that today. It helps me understand why God provided a ram to stand in for Abraham's son. Why? Because of Abraham's obedience. That obedience, and not Abraham's sacrifice, established forever his relationship with God. Then his obedience changed the history of mankind.

God promised him: "I will multiply your descendants beyond number . . . and through your descendants all the nations of the earth will be blessed—all because you have obeyed me" (vv. 17-18). Yes, obedience is far better than sacrifice. And giving a holy God our best shows how much we, His people, understand that.

Thankfully, because of Jesus, we no longer have to sacrifice burnt offerings of bulls or rams or birds or grain to purify ourselves for God. Jesus paid that price.

But as Abraham was willing to offer his only son's life to God, we should offer God our lives in Christ. And why not? Christ is life. When we give Him ours, we always gain. 🦋

Obedience is the road to freedom.
C. S. LEWIS

Sacrifice: Of Our Prayers

Ask me.
Jeremiah 33:3

God is waiting. He wants to hear from us today. To hear from me. To hear from you. To connect up in that amazing communion between mortality and immortality—whereby the Sovereign Power of the universe hears our personal, private requests and answers.

Yet daily prayer, unlike five other faith habits, has not seen an increase among those who practice it, according to experts. In a study, The Barna Group examined seven religious faith habits—including Bible reading, church attendance, church volunteerism, and Sunday school attendance. While prayer is the most practiced faith behavior, the percentage of respondents who say they pray daily has not changed since 1993. The only other behavior that showed no increased practice by believers? Evangelizing, or telling someone about Jesus. We get cold feet, apparently, when it comes to sharing Christ.

But, first, back to prayer.

We know it blesses us. We know it blesses God. In fact, we know God desires our prayers—and that, indeed, He rewards those who diligently seek Him.

"Ask me," He told the prophet Jeremiah, "and I will tell you some remarkable secrets about what is going to happen here." But should God have had to plead with Jeremiah to stop long enough to commune with Him? Should He have to plead with us?

Have we forgotten that prayer is how God works in His world? That, as the psalmist was told by God, "When they call on me, I will answer" (Psalm 91:15).

To be sure, when Jesus arose very early in the morning—"long before daybreak"—and went alone into the wilderness to pray (Mark 1:35), He *always* returned with fresh answers. With renewed energy. With a revived spirit. To be certain, He returned with power. Then why not you? Will you sacrifice prayer to God? Right now? He is waiting for your offering. Mine, too. Let us bless Him by sacrificing our praises and our requests, then watch with wonder as He blesses us with love—empowering us to tell others He lives. 🌿

God expects to hear from you, before you can expect to hear from Him.
WILLIAM GURNALL

Sacrifice: Of Righteous Living

Give your bodies to God.
Romans 12:1

Is my body righteous and holy? Holy enough to worship God, but also to serve Him?

I dare to savor such questions today. I like what they ask of me, to answer in a new way. I could rush, that is, to volunteer more service to my church and to His Kingdom. But what if I sacrificed a tendency to judge? Or a heart that criticizes? Or eyes that covet? Or a spirit that lacks gratitude—or that won't trust God?

When the apostle Paul issued this mandate, to give our bodies to God, many new believers among the Roman provinces kept thinking about animal sacrifice—their old way of atoning for sin.

In "the Lord's presence," young bulls were slaughtered. The animal's blood was presented by "splattering it against all sides of the altar" (Leviticus 1:5). A bloody body sacrifice.

Then the bull was skinned, cut into pieces, and all but the hide burned on the altar before God (Leviticus 1:6-9).

What a contrast to what Paul asked of the believers. Not to kill animals, or to die themselves on a bloody altar—but to die to their own interests, living holy and sanctified in the light of Christ's love. Not offering things to God, but offering themselves—renewed and righteous.

He asks that still of us today.

"Let [your bodies] be a living and holy sacrifice," Paul wrote, "the kind he will find acceptable. This is truly the way to worship him" (Romans 12:1). Not the old way. Not the bloody sacrifice, which many had abused anyway, offering diseased and feeble animals to God. And not the newfangled way, copying "the behavior and customs of this world" (v. 2). Instead, offer to God the life He paid for on the cross. It's precious to Him. My life. Your life. But is it acceptable? In fact, it's priceless.

The dedicated life is worth living.
ANNIE DILLARD

Sacrifice: Of Our Continual Praise

These are the sacrifices that please God.
Hebrews 13:16

Ah, the illogic of God. So marvelous. So challenging. So downright discomforting and tough. Like His desire for us to praise Him, in advance, for all He's going to do in our lives. Yes, before we can even see it.

Advance praise. Tough, yes. But it's not hard to see why it pleases God. Praise displays faith. So praise doesn't follow a blessing. We praise God *before*. Believing Him for deliverance *before*. Expecting His healing *before*.

Knowing who God is, we "offer through Jesus a continual sacrifice of praise to God, proclaiming our allegiance to his name" (Hebrews 13:15). Before.

But why? But how? The answers to advance praise are in God's names. Jehovah Jireh—God our provider. Jehovah Rapha—God our healer. Jehovah Shalom—God our peace. Just a few of God's names, of course. But every name of God gets dishonored if we don't praise Him, in allegiance to His names and their promises, even before He acts. And that feels illogical. But that's the point!

Try praising God today for something He *hasn't* done yet. Maybe for children who *will* be saved. A marriage that *will* be restored. Income that *will* be produced—and debts that *will* be retired. Praise God with faith, that is. Yes, for souls who will be saved. For churches that will be revived. For being God, whether He blesses us or not.

We have Jesus to thank for such audacious praise. His ultimate sacrifice allows it. His perfect sacrifice, yes, makes the praise from our lips a precious offering to God—holy and acceptable and empowering and pleasing. "You have broken me," David writes. "Now let me rejoice" (Psalm 51:8). Our praise can burst forth at hard times, indeed. But such sacrificial praise pleases God—especially praise offered in faith. 🌿

The only path to pleasure is in pleasing God.
RICHARD OWEN ROBERTS

Sacrifice: Of Our Talents

My ambition has always been to preach the Good News.
Romans 15:20

Your talent is awesome. That's why God wants it back. He created it. Made it unique. Set it apart from everybody else's. But you doubt it's useful. Comparing yourself with others, you may have buried your talent—rarely using it, not even for the glory of God.

Or you could choose to be confident about your God-given talent, as confident as the apostle Paul—both about his talent and who created it. "For I am, by God's grace, a special messenger from Christ Jesus to you Gentiles" (Romans 15:15-16). Talk about self-confidence.

Normally modest in Christ, Paul doesn't hold back, however, when explaining how he has given himself to the Lord. "I dare not boast of anything else. I have brought the Gentiles to God by my message and by the way I lived before them" (v. 18). Living right, then, "I have fully presented the Good News of Christ all the way from Jerusalem clear over into Illyricum" (v. 19).

As far as it takes? Can we sacrifice that much to tell somebody about Christ?

If not, think today of Paul, born of a branch of the tribe of Benjamin— circumcised when he was eight days old, a Pharisee, and a "real Hebrew if there ever was one!" (Philippians 3:5). Yet he gave all that up, then gave himself to Christ, *for* Christ. Jailed, mocked, and whipped, never complaining or questioning, Paul never stopped giving all he was back to God.

Then he changed the world. It was Paul who wrote almost one-quarter of the New Testament. His thirteen letters of the Bible—to churches, elders, and pastors—influenced the growth of Christianity, as some see it, more than any one person other than Jesus Himself.

But what about us? What talent will we offer to God for the cause of Christ? Think your talent isn't good enough? Or special enough? Think today of Paul. With all his credentials, he gave to Christ by only one way. "By God's grace." Knowing this, throw away what matters to the world and give yourself to God. Then trust Him to bless what's left. 🌿

He cannot bless us unless He has us.
C. S. LEWIS

Sacrifice: Of Our Broken Hearts

The sacrifice you desire is a broken spirit. You will not reject
a broken and repentant heart, O God.
Psalm 51:17

King David couldn't believe he'd done wrong. His sin had so poisoned his spirit that he couldn't see the audacity and horror of all he'd dared to do.

But when his adviser confronted him—looked him in the eye and challenged him for adultery and murder, for duplicity and deception—then David could see. *He had sinned.* Sinned against God. "Against you, and you alone, have I sinned," he confessed to God. "I have done what is evil in your sight" (v. 4).

So no ritual sacrifice would be enough to atone.

No burnt offering. No extra tithe. No volunteering to paint the church kitchen or to take food to the poor or to plant some flowers around the church parking lot.

Those are all good things. To do good and share with those in need pleases God.

When we sin, however, God wants our hearts. Broken.

Only then can He rebuild our lives—start the work of putting us back together again in His way. It's quite beautiful to see, in fact, as David finally saw, that a broken spirit excites God.

It shows we trust Him to do what we can't do ourselves—make ourselves right.

So I dare today to think, not about my sins, but about my heart.

I imagine it broken. Gathered up in a simple cardboard box.

It's not fancy enough to offer to God. Yet I can imagine Him reaching down to receive it.

He accepts it. It's a treasure to God. A priceless gift to God. Thus, with love, He takes a cracked and bruised piece. Holds it. Loves it. Mends it. Heals it. Your heart, too. He is taking it up and renewing—not rejecting—this sacrifice of a broken heart. True, we have sinned. But He redeems. The place to start? In the blessing of our broken hearts. 🔥

What is the first thing we need, in order to be Christians? A new heart.

J. C. RYLE

Going Deeper

I want all of you to share that joy.
Philippians 2:17

To sacrifice, to "make sacred" or "make holy," isn't about self-denial as much as self-renewal. Do you agree? Explain why your sacrifice matters so much to God.

The Bible illuminates many types of sacrifices that please God— a broken heart, obedience, holy living, service, praise, prayer. Of these (among others), what could you offer more of to God? What would that look like?

How would a sacrificial life change you? How would it change God's Kingdom?

If you'd like, write a prayer that reflects what God is trying to teach you about the virtue of sacrifice.

Those who give much without sacrifice are reckoned as having given little.
ERWIN LUTZER

REST

His Promise

God gives rest to his loved ones.
Psalm 127:2

My Prayer

Bless You, Precious Father,
for pouring into our weary souls Your loving rest.

Rest: In His Promises

He makes me lie down in green pastures.
Psalm 23:2, NIV

Even Jesus rested. He took walks on the beach. He took breaks from crowds. He sat down when He got weary. He prayed when He needed wisdom. He took His disciples on vacations. Both God and man, He cared for His humanness by pulling back from the crush of life and taking rest. On a regular basis.

Thank God for a Bible that shows us this human side of Christ.

In Him, we see what real rest looks like.

It's intentional.

"He *makes* me lie down in green pastures," David writes in Psalm 23:2 (NIV, italics added). In that way, our heavenly Father restores our souls—guiding us in the paths of righteousness, to bring "honor to his name" (v. 3). When we rest ourselves and our souls, we get back on track, which honors God, glorifying who He is. Ever noticed how a restful day at a park, lake, or even on your own porch provides time to notice the beauty of God's creation?

Or is your busy life too hectic for a day in the park? It is? So plan for it. Make yourself lie down. Yes, rest is regular.

"On the seventh day, having finished his task, God rested from all his work" (Genesis 2:2). So rest follows our work. By design. So pull out your calendar and schedule rest for the remainder of this year. It's that important. A good rest revives energy, say health experts, cutting chemical wastes that pile up in the body from fatigue.

Ironic, then, that rest also is holy. "And God blessed the seventh day and declared it holy, because it was the day when he rested from his work of creation" (Genesis 2:3).

If you're storing up vacation days for a two-week trip, aiming to restore a year's worth of fatigue in a short holiday, you'll come home tired. Instead, follow Jesus' path. Work hard as usual. But when the week ends, rest. You'll feel restored. And you'll also look divine. 🌿

We shall do more by sometimes doing less.
CHARLES SPURGEON

Rest: In His Invitation

Come to me, all of you who are weary and carry heavy burdens,
and I will give you rest.
Matthew 11:28

She couldn't sleep. Bone tired. But she couldn't rest. "Family trouble," this woman explained. Her mental turmoil, that is, was taking a big toll on her body. Feeling worn-out and stressed, her mind racing with anxiety, she couldn't calm herself enough to sleep right or rest well.

That's perhaps how Jesus' new followers were feeling.

Torn between their old beliefs, with heavy legal requirements set by the Pharisees and religious leaders—and a new life and family in Christ—they were worn out with worried stress. But Jesus offered spiritual refreshment.

"Come to me," He invited them. "All of you."

He issues the same invitation to us today. Yes, to all of us.

Come.

It's the perfect invitation. An offer from Jesus Himself. He alone knows how spiritual turmoil feels, and He alone can do something about it.

We are weary, and He knows. We are burdened, and He knows. We are carrying more worry than any of us should try to carry, thinking foolishly that carrying around our emotional or spiritual burdens—like martyrs—will somehow enable us to fix them.

Knowing better, Jesus offers not an answer to our problems—but an invitation to simply leave them with Him, then to rest *while He works them out.*

Rest equals trust, that is. We rest in Christ, not because He offers His rest, but because He delivers on the invitation. His invitation still stands today.

Come to Me and rest. We'll hear no better words today or ever. Stand up and bless Him with your yes. Then sit down. He wants to bless you with rest. 🌿

God is calling us from others to him.
DALE HANSON BURKE

Rest: In His Sufficiency

Let my soul be at rest again, for the LORD has been good to me.
Psalm 116:7

Jesus is enough. So stop striving.

Afraid to stop? Ditch the fear and stop striving, even if you're scared. In today's Scripture, the psalmist is pausing to remind himself of exactly that. Sure, he could panic. Then he remembers:

How kind the Lord is! How good He is! Or as he adds: "I was facing death, and he saved me" (v. 6). *So let my soul be at rest.* Again.

What's his point? That the well of God never runs dry. It refreshes us, again and again. And that's as it should be. A onetime rest with God, just like a once-a-year vacation, isn't enough.

Instead, we go back to the Lord—over and over—for yet more of His rest. He is, as He Himself declared, Lord of the Sabbath. In Him, we can cease from our own work, and struggling over our own work, we can rest in His.

Don't you need that?

I do. I've worked hard so far this year, as I'm sure you have.

I've thrown back my feeble shoulders, toiled and labored, struggled and strained, aiming to give my best to the Lord. Or trying to. But all my labor is in vain if I don't trust the Lord to transform the least of my human efforts into His divine all.

So on this day, Jesus, let me know it's okay to take a break every now and then from this toiling. But especially, remind me that You are good.

That's enough for all of us to know today. And to rest in today.

Then, sweet Jesus, as we rejoice in Your goodness, and in Your sufficiency, we're reminded to put down our plans and tools, turn off our devices, lie in the sunshine, and indulge ourselves in the complete and wondrous All-ness of You. 🌿

God is both the water and the hose, the Supply and the Supplier.
KIRBYJON CALDWELL

Rest: In His Safety

*Those who live in the shelter of the Most High
will find rest in the shadow of the Almighty.*
Psalm 91:1

At the airport, the "upgraded" passengers for a national airline relaxed in a roomy, comfortable guest lounge. They had a pass. Whenever they traveled, their pass was welcomed at any guest lounge serving the airline.

Swipe the pass. The door opens. Entry gained.

Likewise, in the Old Testament world, only priests could gain entry into the shelter of the Most High—the Holy of Holies—where they found rest and refuge in the covering of His Almighty shadow.

As Psalm 90:1 declares: "You have been our home!"

But under our new covenant with Christ, all who believe in Him—even ordinary people like you and me—can gain entry into His holy shelter. There, we find safety and rest, now and forever, in His mighty shadow.

Dare we believe such a thing? Walking through life, joyful and restful, believing that no "terrors of the night" (Psalm 91:5)—from disturbed sleep to disturbed people—can throw us off guard? In fact, we can dare to believe it. God shows how in gentle but bold terms:

"If you make the LORD your refuge, if you make the Most High your shelter, no evil will conquer you." Just rest, in other words. Assured and loved. Then: "No plague will come near your home" (vv. 9-10).

An audacious and wonderful promise. But the ancients had a word for what engages it. *Silencio.* Or the stilling, says prayer scholar Richard Foster, of all "creaturely activity"—with all our "grasping, manipulative control of people and situations."

Don't know how to stop your grasping? Enter the Door. Faith is the passkey. Swipe it and rest. Then relax in the shadow of your upgrade. 🌿

Rest is not idleness.
JOHN LUBBOCK

Rest: In His Peace

In peace I will lie down and sleep.
Psalm 4:8

Lack of sleep won't kill you. Not in one day.

But over time, lack of sleep wreaks havoc on the body. From feeling cranky and tired, to acting dull and somber, to looking down and out—lack of sleep takes a devastating emotional and physical toll, sleep experts say.

But what about sleep-deprived Christians? As children of a God we trust, what would keep us up all night, tossing and turning in our beds, mulling over mistakes and messes or worries and wonderings?

Could it be that, unlike David, up-all-night Christians need to learn more about God? As David declared, even in the face of murderous enemies: "I lay down and slept, yet I woke up in safety, for the LORD was watching over me" (Psalm 3:5). He sleeps in peace, adds David, "for you alone, O LORD, will keep me safe" (Psalm 4:8). Talk about blessed assurance.

Here was a man in great distress—a classic risk profile for sleeplessness, according to the American Sleep Association. (ASA says primary insomnia typically has four causes: stress, distress or depression, nighttime work, or long-distance travel with jet lag.)

David hit three of these four. But "I will . . . sleep," he insists.

Thus, sleeping soundly is about trusting in God. But also: "He grants sleep to those he loves," writes Solomon (Psalm 127:2, NIV). Ah, yes, intimacy. Of course, to sleep well it doesn't hurt to have a good day of real labor under our belts. "The sleep of a laborer is sweet, whether he eats little or much," says the "Teacher" of Ecclesiastes in 5:12 (NIV). Maybe that's why on sleepless nights, I've finally learned to get up. I turn on the light. I grab paper and pen. Then I make my list: Things to give to God. Then I turn off the light, lie back down, and go to sleep. Maybe I'm just dreaming. But after a good eight hours of slumber, sleep does feel like love. 🕊

We are all geniuses when we dream.
EMILE CIORAN

Rest: In His Love

God gives rest to his loved ones.
Psalm 127:2

Life isn't a competition. It doesn't have to be, that is. But yours still is?

Then why not drop out of your rat race? Indeed, the race to win and always be on top is the wrong long-distance battle if ever there was one. We want others to like us, to admire us. But also we want God to love us.

Many of us still think we must do a lot to convince Him to grant His love. But it's the opposite. King Solomon explains:

"It is useless for you to work so hard from early morning until late at night, anxiously working for food to eat." Why? "For God gives rest to his loved ones."

But will we accept that gift?

Will we own less, and have less to take care of? Will we eat less, and have fewer things to buy and cook? Will we worry less? Trust more? Stop comparing other people's blessings with ours? Even if they seem to have more? And not envying feels hard?

A restful life is noncompetitive, indeed, because it's a trusting life. We believe what we're doing for God is pleasing to Him and what He gives to us is enough.

But how to arrive at such trust? Let's take a cue from Lynne Baab, author of *Sabbath Keeping: Finding Freedom in the Rhythms of Rest.* In it, she describes how she and her husband, while living in Israel, learned to accept God's rest because, from sunset Friday to sunset Saturday, everything around them was closed. Buses didn't run. Theaters, stores, and restaurants closed. So they read books. Walked. Talked. Her husband went bird-watching. Or they napped. Prayed together. Describing the practice to Kyria.com, she explains: "We rested in God's love and experienced his grace." Away from the rat race.

But here's the great secret about such rest. If we learn not to strive on Sunday, we learn to live in God's rest every day. We work hard and well. But without envy, doubt, or competing. Then we rest. It's a gift. Let's start now and open it. 🌿

Help me, Lord, to work resting and to pray resting.
RICHARD FOSTER

Going Deeper

*My people will live in peaceful dwelling places, in secure homes,
in undisturbed places of rest.*
Isaiah 32:18, NIV

What's the hardest thing about slowing down? About doing less?

How would cutting back on scheduled activities at home, work, or
church impact your family? How would it impact your relationship
with the Lord?

Make a list of things you'd plan to do—and not do— if you observed
the Sabbath.

If you'd like, write a prayer that reflects what God is trying to teach you
about the virtue of rest.

You have made us for Yourself, O Lord, and our heart is restless
until it rests in You.
SAINT AUGUSTINE

VISION

His Promise

*We will see everything
with perfect clarity.*
1 Corinthians 13:12

My Prayer

Open my spiritual eyes, Blessed Teacher.
Then show me what it takes
to see and follow only You.

Vision: That Sees like Christ

I want to see!
Mark 10:51

The blind man cried to Jesus.

But you know the story. It's a Sunday school classic, this blind beggar crying out to Jesus on the Jericho Road. A steep, dusty, rocky, treacherous byway—hot beyond words, crowded with pilgrims climbing the route up to Jerusalem for the Passover—it seemed a good spot for a beggar to beg for money.

So why did Jesus ask the blind man:

What do you want?

Wasn't it obvious? Dirty and down and out, the man needed an infusion of cold, hard cash. But the beggar needed something much greater. He needed the Messiah. Only one thing stopped him.

So reaching for Jesus, the blind man cried out the best answer ever: "I want to see!"

To see Christ, but to see like Christ. We understand, indeed, as blind Bartimaeus understood, that Jesus isn't just another pilgrim on the road of life. He's not just a kind gentleman who can drop a few coins into a blind man's grimy, outstretched hand. He isn't just a prophet delivering a challenging message from the heavens.

Jesus, in fact, *is* the Messiah.

Do we see that today? Our Jesus is King over all—bringing God's Kingdom, healing, and liberty to all who are crippled, maimed, and confused by spiritual blindness. Not every believer, even today, yet believes that. To Jesus' question, "What do you want me to do for you?" (v. 51) we ask for minor trifles: success, financial freedom, romance and love, a better job, a growing ministry.

But it took a blind man to ask, in faith, for the blessing that can deliver all these things. *Sight.* Yes, holy perspective. Let us see *You*, Jesus. To see who You are. To know what You know. It's a request Jesus still honors. How? With a gentle answer: *Follow Me.* 🖑

A vision gives life.
HARRIS W. LEE

Vision: That Sees New Life

For they will see God.
Matthew 5:8

Was blind, but now I see.

John Newton put words on feelings we've all experienced. As we sing his haunting refrain in "Amazing Grace," we understand: to have been blind about something, then finally to find our eyes wide open with sight, is to see God Himself. And to see all the things God wants us to know, do, think, and understand.

So we feel grateful. We've moved from darkness into light. Whatever confusion or delusion locked us down before has been conquered. Now, finally, we see salvation.

Aren't you ready for that kind of vision—spiritual sight so twenty-twenty sharp that you see God? Then stand up today and receive it.

Just look at John Newton. A seafaring captain of slave ships—and a profane heavy drinker and gambler—he could've drowned in his sins, blindly, when a ferocious storm almost capsized the ship carrying him back to England. Calling out to God as the ship filled with water, Newton was so grateful to survive, he gave his life to Christ. From that point on, he gave up drinking, gambling, and profanity—the beginning of a spiritual conversion that, literally, would change the world.

Years would pass, in fact, before Newton actually renounced the slave trade. Late in life, after being ordained as an Anglican priest, he apologized for trading in human lives, declaring "a confession, which . . . comes too late . . . that I was once an active instrument in a business at which my heart now shudders." *Was blind, but now I see.*

Working with abolitionist William Wilberforce, Newton helped wage a successful fight to abolish the slave trade in England, finally seeing the Slave Trade Act passed in 1807, the year of his death. His hard-wrought slave ban changed the destiny of millions, but also changed history. Does God open eyes? Should we pray that He opens ours and those of others we love? John Newton's story sings God's blessed answer: pray today and see. 🌿

How precious did that grace appear, the hour I first believed!
JOHN NEWTON

Vision: That Sees God's Will

Instantly . . . scales fell from Saul's eyes, and he regained his sight.
Acts 9:18

Will the Lord use you today? He will, indeed—if you can see. See as clearly as Saul.

Once blinded by his passion for persecuting Christians, he was on his way to Damascus to arrest yet more men and women "of the Way"—intent on bringing them to Jerusalem in chains—when his dark path ran headlong into light.

Light from heaven "suddenly shone down around him" (Acts 9:3). Falling to the ground, Saul heard the clear power of the Lord's voice, asking a penetrating question: "Saul! Saul! Why are you persecuting me?" (v. 4).

Hard question. Especially for a man who thought his harsh passion was on target. But in fact, when Saul picked himself up off the ground and opened his eyes, he discovered his path was all wrong, but so was his sight (v. 8). He was blind, physically and spiritually.

Have you ever found yourself in such a fix? Boldly following your own vision for your life, but stumbling in the dark as a result? Longing to know God's will for your life, but unable to see it?

You don't have to stay in such a pit. This story of Saul's conversion to faith in Christ proves how dramatically our situations can change for the better—but also change for God's glory. Just three days later, indeed, Saul's sight was renewed (v. 18). Baptized, and revived by food and a few days' rest, Saul "immediately" began preaching about Jesus in synagogues, declaring, "He is indeed the Son of God!" (v. 20).

New sight changed Saul's work, words, and ways. Then new sight changed his name. Thus this Saul, "also known as Paul, was filled with the Holy Spirit" (Acts 13:9). With a new non-Jewish name, Paul was still passionate. Still challenging unbelievers. Still traveling from town to town to make his case, but making it now—led by the Spirit—for Christ.

The same sight is possible for you. So ask for it today. Then dare to open your eyes with Christ to see it. 🔥

We need a baptism of clear seeing.
A. W. TOZER

Vision: That Sees God's Strength

I see very clearly that God shows no favoritism.
Acts 10:34

Godly vision had to start somewhere. But with prayer?

I wasn't looking for that answer.

I always assumed that a vision from God—yes, a clear message, showing us God's clear will—arrived spontaneously, unexplained. Then I stumbled on the Bible character Cornelius and immediately I could see:

Visions from God result from prayer. Prayers steeped in life. Life steeped in prayer.

That's how the Gentile leader Cornelius lived. A captain of the Italian regiment, he didn't bend over backward to get a vision from God. He just lived right, devout and God fearing, "as was everyone in his household" (v. 2).

So he gave generously to the poor. Even more, he prayed "regularly" to God. He wasn't seeking blessing or favor, only to be acceptable to the one the new believers called almighty God.

Then, suddenly, an angel came to his house. *An angel?* He was terrified.

But the encounter led to the answer that Cornelius sought—and an answer that forever changed the church: God loved him, and Gentiles like him are part of God's family. "Your prayers and gifts to the poor have been received by God as an offering!" the angel exclaimed. Then the angel added: "Now send some men to Joppa, and summon a man named Simon Peter" (vv. 4-5).

What followed was a life-changing experience for Cornelius, Peter, and all of Christianity. First, there was that famous vision where God showed Peter a sheet bearing "unclean" Gentile food. But Peter "saw" God's message: that when God declares food or people clean, they are clean, indeed. "I see very clearly," Peter put it, "that God shows no favoritism." The Jews on site saw this same truth and "were amazed" that the gift of the Holy Spirit had been poured on Gentiles, too (v. 45).

Not a small point. But whom did God use and bless to see it? A man who prayed. 🌿

Give us clear vision that we may know where to stand and what to stand for.
PETER MARSHALL

Vision: That Sees God's People

Can you see anything now?
Mark 8:23

If we matter to somebody, we feel it. Because they see us. They "get" us. They look, not through us, but at us.

That was the look of the preacher at a small church in a big Texas town. My husband and I were visiting, planning to spend a Sunday morning in church.

So we followed our hearts to a little church in a modest part of town. We'd met the pastors before. They greeted us by name, in fact. Then after church, after they greeted and hugged their parishioners, they spent time talking leisurely to us, inviting us back. Or as they both added: "It's *so* good to see you!" We basked in their warmth, in fact. To be seen completely feels wondrous. Like being touched by God.

That's how Jesus wanted the blind man to see people in today's Scripture.

So Jesus took the man by the hand, led him outside of the huge city—away from fancy distractions. Then He spit on the man's eyes. Getting his attention? Certainly. But Jesus also laid His hands on the man, asking a simple question: "Can you see anything?"

Truthfully, the man answered, he could see people. But barely. "They look like trees walking around" (v. 24). In his spiritual blindness, he couldn't see any deeper. Not their needs or hurts. Not their individual wants or problems. Not that all people are loved by God.

So Jesus placed His hands on the man's eyes again. A second touch. Every believer needs that. After the excitement of coming to Jesus, we need another touch—on our eyes.

So ask for it. Boldly. Then look at God's world. You'll see a world of people looking back. 🌿

We ought to see the face of God every morning before we see the face of man.
DWIGHT L. MOODY

Vision: That Sees God's Plans

This vision is for a future time.
Habakkuk 2:3

What's God's vision for *your* life? Tough question.

When a Facebook friend asked her large following this question, only a handful of people responded. The vision for our lives? For many, it seemed too hard a question to answer. But it doesn't have to be.

"I know the plans I have for you," the Lord has promised, and we in Christ are famous for quoting God on exactly that (Jeremiah 29:11).

Still, like the prophet Habakkuk, many of us are frustrated with God's pace and our ability to see His vision. If God knows so much about my plans, why won't He reveal them? That's how Habakkuk saw it. So Habakkuk did what more of us should. He challenged God to get moving.

"How long?" Habakkuk cried to God. "How long, O Lord, must I call for help? But you do not listen!" (Habakkuk 1:2).

Do you know God well enough to ask such a question? To finally, like Habakkuk, climb above the emotional noise of your life, so you can hear God—and see His vision for your future?

It's above that noise, the fears, and the fray, Habakkuk says, that "I will wait to see what the Lord says and how he will answer" (2:1).

It takes time and distance from noise, in other words, to know God enough to see His vision for our lives—then to do something about it. I was surprised by such an insight a few years ago. Frustrated that others were "succeeding" for God, while I dragged my feet, I cried, *how long*? What about me? *Show me, God!* And what a surprise.

God showed me the obvious. That "successful" servants see how God made them, then they give themselves back to Him. Then they work hard. Pray longer. Trust more. Serve with joy. Don't give up. Work not for their glory but for God's. He sees down the road what we can't. So bless Him by following. He wrote your plan. Go see and live it. 🔥

In his light we see light.
ANN SPANGLER

Going Deeper

Taste and see that the LORD is good.
Psalm 34:8

Spiritual blindness is addressed, time and again, in God's Word, especially in the healing stories of Jesus. What spiritual blindness in you has the Lord sought to heal?

What's God's vision for your life? Can you see it? Have you acted on it? Explain.

Name a person in your life whom you need to start seeing with God's eyes. Explain.

If you'd like, write a prayer that reflects what God is trying to teach you about the virtue of vision.

You see things; and say "Why?" But I dream things that never were; and I say "Why not?"
GEORGE BERNARD SHAW

Justice

His Promise

He loves whatever is just and good.
Psalm 33:5

My Prayer

As I stand up to seek justice for
the poor,
love me with strength to walk in goodness.

Justice: That Speaks for God

For the LORD loves justice, and he will never abandon the godly.
Psalm 37:28

What do we want? *JUSTICE!*

When do we want it? *NOW!*

Not when it's convenient. Not when it's safe. Not when it's quiet or neat or nice.

That's what I finally understood, yelling at the top of my lungs, standing with other protesters in front of the downtown jail in my town, demanding justice. *NOW.*

A homeless preacher had died in this jail. After a roughing up by city jail officers, he'd stopped breathing and died. The coroner ruled his death a homicide. Now, at the urging of my pastor, I stood with scores of fellow church members, crying out for justice for a man who no longer could cry out for himself.

I felt outraged, in fact, that he couldn't cry. As angry as God? "Prepare to meet your God in judgment!" (Amos 4:12), the prophet Amos thundered at God's people. An angry God? Amos and the other prophets and Jesus, indeed, all shout yes. So I will think today only of that. That when God's people lie around, failing to seek and do justice for the poor and the oppressed, God seethes.

Gary Haugen describes his sharp awareness of God's righteous anger in his book *Good News about Injustice.* "Standing with my boots knee deep in the reeking muck of a Rwandan mass grave where thousands of innocent people have been horribly slaughtered, I have no words, no meaning, no life, no hope if there is not a God of history and time who is absolutely outraged, absolutely furious, absolutely burning with anger towards those who took it in their own hands to commit such acts."

He saw what the rest of us should consider today. At injustice, God gets angry. At you? At me? Let's not give Him a reason by not seeking justice for those who wait for it. 🌿

> The hottest place in Hell is reserved for those who remain
> neutral in times of great moral conflict.
> MARTIN LUTHER KING JR.

Justice: That Represents God

Everything he does is just and fair.
Deuteronomy 32:4

It's no secret why God blesses justice. God *is* Justice. Just take a look at all the verses below, italicized for emphasis.

"His *justice* is seen throughout the land" (1 Chronicles 16:14).

"He will judge the world with *justice*" (Psalm 9:8).

"Righteousness and *justice* are the foundation of his throne" (Psalm 97:2).

He rules "with a scepter of *justice*" (Psalm 45:6).

"He gives *justice* to the oppressed" (Psalm 146:7).

He gives "*justice* to those with honest hearts" (Psalm 36:10).

He gives "*justice* to all who are treated unfairly" (Psalm 103:6).

He gives "*justice* to his people" and has "compassion on his servants" (Psalm 135:14).

"The heavens proclaim his *justice*" (Psalm 50:6).

"The LORD of Heaven's Armies will be exalted by his *justice*" (Isaiah 5:16).

In fact, every single thing God does is just and fair.

Yet we often forget or are misled on matters of justice, forgetting what the apostle Paul declares in Galatians 6:7: "You cannot mock the justice of God." Because God is perfectly just. While we are likely to judge with malice, God judges with mercy. While we are likely to judge with bitterness and resentment, God judges with blessing and redemption. While we are likely to find pleasure in a sinner's downfall, especially if it vindicates us in some way, God finds pleasure in a sinner's repentance. "The righteous LORD loves justice," the psalmist declares in Psalm 11:7.

But what about us? Do we understand that God blesses justice because it represents Who He is? "The LORD is known for his *justice*" (Psalm 9:16, italics added).

Knowing this, stand up today to seek justice for those who can't fight for themselves. Don't know anybody like that? Ask the Lord to show you. Then don't be surprised when He opens your eyes. ❧

Justice is the sum of all moral duty.
WILLIAM GODWIN

Justice: That's Holy and Heals

The LORD is close to the brokenhearted;
he rescues those whose spirits are crushed.
Psalm 34:18

You were wronged. Maybe by a friend. A family member. A wife. A husband. A coworker. A boss. By life itself.

If so, you're in good company. Who among us hasn't been hurt deeply, sometimes by people we love—but sometimes by complete strangers? Or sometimes by the vagaries and whims of life. No matter how our hurt happened, however, hurt still hurts. Pain is still pain. To be betrayed, misused, defamed, wrongly accused, lied about, or harmed in any way—emotionally or physically—leaves us reeling. Ready for revenge. Ready to aim and fire and blast to smithereens the one who did us wrong.

But we must not be deceived. Revenge is not our work. We can't judge our hurts right. We're sinners too. And God knows this. So He specifically cautioned against avenging our own pain. He'll handle it Himself. Perfectly just, His justice is perfect.

"I will take revenge; I will pay them back," He says in Deuteronomy 32:35. "In due time their feet will slip. Their day of disaster will arrive, and their destiny will overtake them."

God talks tough here. It's tough talk, indeed, to a generation of Israelites who defied and disobeyed Him. But to today's Christians, the apostle Paul lifts the exact same promise in his letter called Romans. "Never pay back evil with more evil. . . . Never take revenge. Leave that to the righteous anger of God. For the Scriptures say, *'I will take revenge; I will pay them back,' says the* LORD'" (Romans 12:17, 19, italics added).

But you're still hurting? If so, start trusting.

Trust that if you release your hurt to God—in effect, forgiving the wrongdoer—God will handle the injustice of it. Then comes the bonus. He rescues those broken, crushed wounds in your spirit, making you whole again. That's justice done right. That's justice done holy. Bless God today and trust Him enough to let it happen. ❧

The place of justice is a hallowed place.
FRANCIS BACON

Justice: That Obeys God

Be sure never to charge anyone falsely.
Exodus 23:7

The hit TV show *Law & Order*, airing on NBC for twenty seasons, was, at the time of its cancellation, the longest-running crime drama on American prime-time television. In fact, it's tied with *Gunsmoke* for the longest-running American drama series of all time.

Even more, the hit series inspired yet more popular TV crime dramas. You know their names: *Homicide: Life on the Street; Law & Order: Special Victims Unit; Law & Order: Criminal Intent; Law & Order: Trial by Jury; Law & Order: UK; New York Undercover; Conviction;* and *Law & Order: Los Angeles.*

During its heyday it seemed nothing was airing on TV but *Law & Order.* Why was the franchise so popular?

Experts offer various reasons. First, these shows calmed us—assuring us the criminal justice system works. They also indulged our desire to see right conquer wrong. So the series satisfied our need for law and order.

The Bible, however, offers the best reason. Justice is God's command. One could say it's in our spiritual DNA. Regardless of how we act, we can't question God's mandate to seek and walk in justice. We are commanded, indeed, to treat others in fair, honest, nonoppressive, and nonprejudicial ways. Justice is our golden rule.

So when Jesus says do unto others what we'd like them to do unto us, we can't argue. "This," He says, "is the essence of all that is taught in the law and the prophets" (Matthew 7:12).

But what does it take to walk in justice? Obey God.

"You must not pass along false rumors," God says in Exodus 23:1. "Never sentence an innocent or blameless person to death," God says soon after, in verse 7. So we must obey. Does God work through the criminal justice system? Or by our obedience to His commandment? As we trust Him, He will.

Meantime, some watch *Law & Order.* But the wise look to God. He wrote the book on justice. Let's wake up today, in our courts and communities, inspired to live by it. 🖋

If we refuse mercy here, we shall have justice in eternity.
JEREMY TAYLOR

Justice: That Builds God's Community

Then the LORD your God will bless you in all you do.
Deuteronomy 24:19

The children of Israel knew exactly what kind of justice God wanted. They also knew why—to remind them, who had once been enslaved, that God had enacted justice for them. Because you were slaves in Egypt, Moses exhorted them, and "the LORD your God redeemed you from your slavery. That is why I have given you this command" (v. 18).

Seek justice for the poor and foreigners. *Then I will bless all you do.*

A commandment with a blessing. So how could they forget?

Yet they did. We all forget, in fact. God's commandments to do right and seek justice seem, somehow, to just slip our minds. Or we get busy. Or other people's problems with poverty and injustice seem like just another segment on the nightly news. Or, to be honest, we don't care too much. We've got better things to do. Like making ourselves comfortable, not to mention making ourselves rich.

That's what happened with the Israelites. Their upper-crust wives oppressed the poor and crushed the needy. Although peasants lived in mud brick, these women begged their dishonest husbands to build them fancy houses of cut stone. Lounging in luxury, their judges took bribes, depriving the poor of justice, trampling the poor through taxes and unfair rents. Then to add insult to injury, they made a big show of worshiping God.

But enough of your religious festivals and "solemn" prayer meetings, God said (Amos 5:21).

Instead, God sought from them true justice—"a mighty flood of justice, an endless river of righteous living" (v. 24).

God, whose justice is "like the ocean depths," David says in Psalm 36:6, now demands a river. Not a trickle. God wants justice to flow. Endlessly. *Give justice to the least.* If we do, His blessings will pour back down to us. Then all of us get renewed, together. That's what a flow of justice creates—community. Many parts, one body. Sealed together with justice and love. So let's bless Him today by blessing the least, all for Him. 🔥

Charity begins at home, and justice begins next door.
CHARLES DICKENS

Justice: That Protects the Innocent

You must not deny justice to the poor.
Exodus 23:6

Charles Chatman spent twenty-seven years in a state prison for a 1981 rape he didn't commit. With DNA evidence, and the help of the Dallas district attorney's office and the nonprofit Innocence Project, his conviction was overturned in 2008.

But despite entering prison at age twenty and leaving at age forty-seven—and never backing down on his claim that he was innocent—he vowed to put prison behind him. How? By helping others. As he told the Associated Press, "I believe that there are hundreds, and I know of two or three personally, that very well could be sitting in this seat if they had the support and they had the backing that I have."

In fact, if just one percent of America's inmates were innocent—and studies suggest the percentage "may be much higher," says the Innocence Project—that means at least twenty thousand men and women may be serving time for crimes they didn't commit.

But twenty-seven years locked in prison? For Chatman, whose original conviction called for ninety-nine years in prison, he faced essentially a life sentence. But do we care? Isn't that, indeed, the core issue of injustice for God's people?

I ask the question with mixed emotions. While it's easy to point the finger at injustice occurring in countries halfway around the globe, to look at injustice in our own backyard takes a strong stomach.

But God says look. "He is the great God, the mighty and awesome God," says Moses, "who shows no partiality and cannot be bribed. He ensures that orphans and widows receive justice. He shows love to the foreigners living among you and gives them food and clothing. So you, too, must show love" (Deuteronomy 10:17-19).

And then? "If you obey, you will enjoy a long life in the land" (11:9). But so will others. Then let us bless the least by standing up to act. 🌿

The administration of justice is the firmest pillar of government.
GEORGE WASHINGTON

Going Deeper

He guards the paths of the just and protects those who are faithful to him.
Proverbs 2:8

Were you ever wronged? By whom? What happened and how did it make you feel?

How do you react to God's promise that He will avenge any injustice done to you? What will you do while waiting for Him to enact justice on your behalf?

According to good evidence, injustice occurs every day in criminal justice systems all over the world. As a Christian, how can you work with God to fight against injustice toward innocent people?

If you'd like, write a prayer that reflects what God is trying to teach you about the virtue of justice.

Charity is no substitute for justice withheld.
SAINT AUGUSTINE

TRUTH

His Promise

And you will know the truth,
and the truth will set you free.
John 8:32

My Prayer

Give me courage, precious Christ,
to seek Your whole truth—especially the whole
truth about You.

Truth: Of Who Christ Is

I am the Alpha and the Omega, the First and the Last,
the Beginning and the End.
Revelation 22:13

What is the real truth of your life?

No question may be harder to answer. Are you a driver or an easygoing follower? Analytical or emotional?

Experts offer personality tests to help us answer such questions, especially the big one: *Who am I?*

Our answers, in fact, can open eyes—but also open doors.

With Jesus, however, the truth of who He is, is never in question. He knows precisely who He is, and the Scriptures confirm it. "I am the way, the truth, and the life," He says. "No one can come to the Father except through me" (John 14:6).

"I am the gate," He declares. "Those who come in through me will be saved. They will come and go freely and will find good pastures" (John 10:9).

With clarity and exactness, Jesus confirms for any who might question His identity and authority absolutely who He is.

But what does it mean for us to know that He is the True Vine, the Resurrection and the Life, the Light of the World, the Living Bread, the Son of God, and that the Father and He are one? To know, indeed, that He is God?

On this day, no matter what situation you are facing, knowing the truth of Christ—and what He says about who He is—means you can trust what He says about you. So He is more than a good teacher. More than a prophet. More than a strong leader, mentor, or healer. He is the Creator of the universe, the author and the finisher—and the beginning and the end—of all faith. In Him all things are made and all things hold together (Colossians 1:17). Those who understand this truth don't just know something important. They stand at the Door of all their answers. Do you want to know Him—and who you are in Him? He says, just ask—an invitation that sounds too good to be true. But it's more than true. Your answer is Jesus Himself. 🖊

Christ is not valued at all unless he be valued above all.
SAINT AUGUSTINE

Truth: That Transforms Our Churches

*We will speak the truth in love, growing in every way
more and more like Christ.*
Ephesians 4:15

It's easy for doubters outside the church to lie about Jesus.

His resurrection seems impossible and fanciful. His gospel challenges logic. *Love your enemies?* Many can't imagine it.

However, untruths about Jesus can even creep into our churches. That happened around Ephesus. False teaching ran wild. From doctrine to disciplines, the gospel of Christ faced falsehood and factions. (Sound familiar?) Always under spiritual attack, both from lies and tensions—plus power struggles and personality clashes—the young churches in Ephesus and beyond could easily implode, damaging the cause of Christ.

So Paul wrote the churches a letter. Pleading, he explained the basics: "Now these are the gifts Christ gave to the church: the apostles, the prophets, the evangelists, and the pastors and teachers" (v. 11).

Simple and clear. It's the best way to speak the gospel truth. To family members, coworkers, neighbors, friends—be simple and clear.

"Their responsibility is to equip God's people to do his work" (v. 12).

Simple and clear. It's the best way to share God's plans and God's gospel. At church meetings, to committee members, to ourselves, be simple and clear.

Clear truth, said Paul, is how we in churches come to unity in our faith and knowledge of God's Son. "That we will be mature in the Lord, measuring up to the full and complete standard of Christ" (v. 13). And then? "We won't be tossed and blown about by every wind of new teaching," Paul wrote (v. 14). "Instead we will speak the truth in love, growing in every way more and more like Christ" (v. 15).

That's what the world needs from believers. Less harsh, false, divisive talk—and more mature, knowledgeable, unified, loving truth. A high standard? Absolutely. But if we seek it today, we will bless the world with more of Whom it needs most—yes, more of the Savior. More of His truth. More of His power. More of His true love. More of ours. 🔥

Unless we love the truth, we cannot know it.
BLAISE PASCAL

Truth: Of Whom Christ Saves

And now you Gentiles have also heard the truth. . . . And when you
believed in Christ, he identified you as his own.
Ephesians 1:13

My cousin was on the phone. *My cousin?* Days ago, I didn't even know he existed. But after talking to kin, exchanging photos, double-checking gene-alogy, trading e-mails, and finally chatting for one revealing hour, I hung up knowing the truth. This was my cousin—second cousin, actually. But through him, I'd uncovered a link to scores of other long-lost relations.

To dig this far into family roots, however, I also dug up long-buried truth. So a few skeletons came tumbling out. But there is no denying. We are fam-ily. And I'm ecstatic. What a precious connection.

It matters more to me, however, to belong to Christ.

Me—a little girl from two hardworking and humble parents—yes, even me. I am deemed worthy enough to be known by Christ. You are too.

Before, only Jewish people should have had this privilege. Important Jews at that.

But now you Gentiles, writes the apostle Paul, "have also heard the truth, the Good News that God saves you. And when you believed in Christ, he identified you as his own" (v. 13).

And look at how He made us official family members: "By giving you the Holy Spirit, whom he promised long ago" (v. 13). In a world where some people don't even know their neighbors, God saw our trust in Him and gave us His greatest gift, His own Spirit.

As Christ's family members, that is, we are His. And that's gospel truth.

So let that truth sink root-deep into your soul. We're members of God's family circle, grafted deep into His spiritual tree—where He'll always keep, protect, provide, and love us. Still not feeling too special today? Give Him every doubt you may still harbor about your worth—yes, every lie you've ever believed about what you haven't yet become. Celebrate instead Whose you are. The truth of His ownership makes you matter. How long? Forever. 🌾

His is not a creed, a mere doctrine, but it is He Himself we have.
DWIGHT L. MOODY

Truth: That Builds New Character

Don't lie to each other. . . . Put on your new nature, and be renewed.
Colossians 3:9-10

You can't handle the truth!

The actor Jack Nicholson spoke that famous line to Tom Cruise in the movie *A Few Good Men*, written by screenwriter Aaron Sorkin. A movie-fan favorite, it marks a showdown between two tough men struggling over different views of truth—both for soldiers guarding the walls of our freedom and for citizens who benefit from our soldiers' bravery. "Because deep down, in places you don't talk about at parties," says Nicholson's character, "you want me on that wall. You need me on that wall."

As his character, Col. Jessep, adds: "I have neither the time nor the inclination to explain myself to a man who rises and sleeps under the blanket of the very freedom I provide, then questions the manner in which I provide it! I'd rather you just said thank you and went on your way."

A compelling argument. And one of the most dramatic movie-courtroom speeches ever. Except for its obvious flaw. Not even freedom justifies murder, especially the "code-red" murder that Jessep sanctions, leading to the killing of a fellow marine. Jessep, in the end, faces justice for his crime.

But what about us? Whose truth will we believe? Our own or God's?

The apostle Paul, writing from jail, made this same challenge to the new Christians in the city of Colosse. "Don't lie to each other," he pleaded. Especially about who is good enough for Christ. Jew or Gentile? Slave or free? Circumcised or not?

"Christ is all that matters," Paul wrote, "and he lives in all of us" (Colossians 3:11).

Can we handle that truth? With everything it means for our families, churches, neighborhoods, and lives? With enough trust to set us free? There's only one way to find out. Put on Christ. Then let what comes out of our mouths show whose truth we follow. 🌿

Truth is powerful and it prevails.
SOJOURNER TRUTH

Truth: That Builds Our Prayers

Then when you swear by my name . . . you could do so with truth.
Jeremiah 4:2

Why do people lie? Because they can.

That's what psychologists say anyway. Deeper reasons are at play, of course. People lie to impress. Avoid trouble. Gain advantage. Get out of obligations. Save time. Or just to be polite. Like the pastor whose cat-loving church member left him a cake strewn with cat hair—which he promptly threw in his garbage can.

"How'd you like my cake, Pastor?" she asked the next Sunday.

"Sister," he told her, "cakes like that don't last long around my house."

As told in a reader's comment to a *New York Times* blog post titled "Why Do You Lie?," this story was just one of many from people admitting to lying—about how much they weighed, how low they golfed, or what books they read. Some confessed lying just to make a bland story better. One woman lies all the time, saying she's Jewish so Christians ringing her doorbell to give her Bible tracts will leave her alone. Which they do.

There's one place, however, where lies especially hurt. That place is prayer.

To pray with power takes truth. Why? Deception, and the wickedness that prompts it, hinders our relationship with our heavenly Father.

Liars show they don't trust God, so even their prayers aren't truthful. The words they speak don't match what's in their hearts. That's what the prophet Jeremiah preached to the children of Israel, saying: "'O Israel,' says the Lord, 'if you wanted to return to me, you could. . . . Then when you swear by my name, saying, "As surely as the Lord lives," you could do so with truth'" (Jeremiah 4:1-2).

Does your prayer life need a big dose of truth? A big dose of power? Does mine? Let's examine our hearts today. And our words. Then in faith bless God with trust—knowing God will hear our truthful pleas, then answer with His righteous power. 🌿

When in doubt, tell the truth.
MARK TWAIN

Truth: That Uses God's Power

Carefully guard the precious truth that has been entrusted to you.
2 Timothy 1:14

My tongue has a life of its own. Not glib, I stumble through conversations. Not witty, I aim for humor and fall flat. Still, I ponder the Scriptures and their warnings about the tongue—that it's "a flame of fire . . . full of wickedness that can ruin your whole life . . . an uncontrollable evil, full of deadly poison" (James 3:6, 8). Hot and cold. Sharp and weak. My tongue can be all of these things.

Until I tell the truth. There's something about putting away pretense, not trying to impress, and just telling it like it is—my own truth, God's own truth—that sets my tongue free.

So, on this day, I step to the microphone.

I'm giving a talk at a church program. Me—the awkward one at parties and social settings. I face a room full of people, who are waiting for me to speak. So I follow Paul's reminder in his letter to Timothy: "Carefully guard the precious truth." How? "Through the power of the Holy Spirit who lives within us" (2 Timothy 1:14).

Ah, yes. That's how I'll give this talk. Just tell the truth. Then I give my tongue over to God.

It's how we say what needs to be said, but say it in love. It's how we dig down to the truth of our stories, and of God's story, so we can share it in ways that heal and make us and others whole. It's how we "carefully guard the precious truth that has been entrusted" to us. Not by our own power. Or by our own clever words. Or by our own wit or wisdom. Or by biting our tongues to control our mouths.

Instead, we let go and speak truth.

The power of the Holy Spirit who lives within us gives us the right words, making us clear. Confident. Generous. Kind. The Lord's power is never pushy. We just have to open our hearts. Then when we open our mouths, even before a microphone, His truth speaks. 🌿

Truth is proper and beautiful at all times and in all places.
FREDERICK DOUGLASS

Going Deeper

Truthful words stand the test of time.
Proverbs 12:19

Jesus says He is the truth. What does that mean for you and for your life?

Nevertheless, do you tell lies? About what? Explain why.

How would being more truthful make a difference in your life?

If you'd like, write a prayer that reflects what God is trying to teach you about the virtue of truth.

If any man seeks for greatness, let him forget greatness and ask for truth,
and he will find both.
HORACE MANN

HONESTY
AND
INTEGRITY

His Promise

Joyful are people of integrity,
who follow the instructions of the LORD.
Psalm 119:1

My Prayer

Keep me, O Banner God,
on Your high road
as I follow the straight path
to honest joy.

Honesty and Integrity: In Our Prayer Lives

Honesty guides good people.
Proverbs 11:3

God can handle our honesty. So tell Him today. Your whole truth. Your gut feelings. Real frustrations. Candid fears. Everything. All the stuff He knows already. That you get worn out. Fed up. Frightened. Confused. Tell Him that, by now, you thought all your problems would be resolved—that you'd have everything figured out. That you've had enough drama, disappointments, deceit. Not to mention *delays*.

His prayer answers can take *so long*.

Say all of that. Then you'll be like King David.

He held his tongue. Or tried to. "But please stop striking me!" David pleaded honestly to God. "I am exhausted by the blows from your hand" (Psalm 39:10).

Not pretty words. Just the truth. Even after David had just praised God. "And so, Lord, where do I put my hope? My only hope is in you" (Psalm 39:7).

God can handle it all. Unlike so many places where truth seems risky or wrong, prayer is the place where the honest truth is always right.

Andrew Murray, the nineteenth-century theologian and prayer warrior, said honesty in prayer is appropriate because the Holy Spirit is the Spirit of Truth, and Jesus, full of grace and truth, is "the reality, *the substance*" of everything honestly hoped for.

So *only* truth is right for our prayers. But it's more than our sincerity at issue, Murray added—"not only a thing of times and seasons, but the outflowing of a life in Thee." As he put it: honest truth shows "actual living fellowship with God, a real correspondence and harmony between the Father, who is a Spirit, and the child praying in the spirit." No more rote prayers, in other words. And no more just praying in church.

It's time, instead, to tell God the honest truth all the time. Just like David—a man after God's own heart. He told the honest truth in prayer, allowing God's Spirit to speak. Today, God's Spirit invites us to do the same. But be prepared to be blessed by His honest answers.

I can be led continually by the Spirit only as I continually
give myself to prayer.
ANDREW MURRAY

Honesty and Integrity: In Our Everyday Lives

Joyful are people of integrity.
Psalm 119:1

Cheaters never prosper? This old joke reminds us why.

You know the story. It's about the two college students who decide to party the night before their chemistry final exam. Worn-out, they both over-sleep, missing the test. So they cook up a story for their professor—that their car had a flat tire, they didn't have a spare, and help showed up so late they missed the exam.

"Can we make up the test tomorrow?" they ask.

The professor thinks it over and agrees.

So the two show up the next day, well rested and prepared for the exam. The professor hands them each a test booklet and places them in separate rooms.

They look at the first question, worth five points. Cool, they each think. This will be easy.

They do that problem, then turn the page. Question number two says: "Which tire?" (95 points).

As told all over the Internet, including FunnyPart.com, the story illus-trates better than many the truth of the timeless platitude about cheaters. They *never* prosper. The Bible, however, provides the reason cheaters fail: God hates cheating. And honesty lives only with integrity.

Ponder, indeed, the words of Deuteronomy 25:16:

"For the LORD your God detests anyone who does these things, anyone who deals dishonestly" (NIV).

Cheating shows we don't trust God to provide. Jesus, in Luke 16:10, explained the result: "If you are faithful in little things, you will be faithful in large ones. But if you are dishonest in little things, you won't be honest with greater responsibilities."

Little cheats grow into corruption. Little lies grow into fraud. But honesty in any measure blesses our God—and our hearts—with a simple surprise: holy joy. ✿

They hurt us in that lies deceive us, not just other people.
EDWARD T. WELCH

Honesty and Integrity: In Our Work Lives

People with integrity walk safely.
Proverbs 10:9

The children of Israel were waiting at Mount Sinai.

Next stop?

The Promised Land.

But they needed instruction, especially about walking and living with a holy God, and also with each other.

The family life of Israel depended on it. That meant rules. So God's rules, from what the Israelites ate to how they worshiped to how they did business, were recorded by Moses in what we call the book of Leviticus. Even a merchant could find rules in this book.

"Do not use dishonest standards when measuring length, weight, or volume" (Leviticus 19:35).

Crooked merchants hurt the entire community with their dishonesty. Their scales were too heavy on one side and too light on the other. Sneaky, they finagled more loot that way. In the end, however, their dishonesty weakened the nation.

But "people with integrity walk safely" (Proverbs 10:9).

We all have to walk, for certain. It's the only way to move forward. To reach the next destination, and to travel to our dreams, goals, and hopes, we have to strike out on the path of life.

Then oops! Obstacles wait to trip us up. Tough decisions must be made. Partners must be identified. Strategies must be planned. In life, as well, there is land to buy. Inventory to stockpile. Houses to be bought. Crops to be planted.

Cheat while walking over these challenges and you are certain to fall. The Bible promises it. But deal honestly, our same Bible declares, and you walk in safety. Let's trust that today. Start it at home, of course. But at work, stay honest. In all things today, stay honest. The walk back home will be divinely easy. 🌿

Honesty has a beautiful and refreshing simplicity about it.
CHUCK SWINDOLL

Honesty and Integrity: In Our Money Matters

Better to be poor and honest than to be dishonest and rich.
Proverbs 28:6

Better to be poor? Not many would believe that. Poor, as we see it, isn't the goal we seek. Poor? We know too well what it means: Lacking. Inferior. Inadequate. Inefficient.

The words for poor in a dictionary go from bad . . . *undernourished . . . pitiable* . . . to worse . . . *trivial.*

Not one thing about being poor, some might say, bodes for the good. Such a point is up for debate. But add *honest* to poor? Then everything changes.

Honest poor people are joyful. They walk safely through life, kept and protected by God. So the honest have peace. By living right—and with a clear conscience—the honest poor sleep at night. Snoozing like babies. Trustworthy and true, the honest poor are respected and well liked. Delightful, in fact, in God's eyes.

As delightful as an eleven-year-old North Carolina Boy Scout who found and returned a stolen purse with nearly two thousand dollars inside, then gave forty dollars of his one hundred dollars reward money to his mom. As delightful as the Florida girl who returned a wallet to an out-of-work handyman, deciding the money inside wasn't hers but should go to its rightful owner. Liking how this is sounding?

That's because this rich-poor dichotomy isn't, in fact, about riches or poverty. Instead, in the scenario from the book of Proverbs, the big spotlight shines on honesty. That's what counts most here. Sure, poverty can grind—and wealth enrich.

On either side of the coin, however, honesty is the benchmark.

Should we not aspire then to wealth? Not the point.

Aspire to trust God. With our honesty, then, we show we believe He will provide enough—"pressed down, shaken together to make room for more, running over, and poured into your lap," as Luke 6:38 declares.

So bless God with honesty today, especially in money matters, but in all. God will bless you back with every good gift from above. A generous blessing? Actually, more. God's blessing for honesty is priceless. 🌿

Honesty is the best policy.
BENJAMIN FRANKLIN

Honesty and Integrity: In Family Matters

Blessed are their children who follow them.
Proverbs 20:7

My elder daughter, an accountant with a spanking new CPA license, has heard every tax sob story around. But she never wavers. "The rules are the rules. The law is the law." As she helps others prepare tax returns, she bends no rules and takes no prisoners.

Just like her granddad.

My late daddy, a tax accountant in his early career, heard his share of sob stories at tax time too. But he bent no rules and took no prisoners. "The rules are the rules. The law is the law."

That may not be a word-for-word quote from my late father. But, word for word, it's how he lived. Was he perfect? Of course not. But I'd dare anybody who knew him to challenge the claim that he walked a high road—led by the Holy Spirit and following the Christ he loved—with honesty and integrity.

Have you jumped on that road yet? Feel too goody goody? Too church-ladyish? Too holier than thou?

That's because it should. Honesty and integrity raise the bar, asking more from us. So get up, stand tall, and walk firm on the promise of Proverbs 20:7: "The godly walk with integrity; *blessed are their children who follow them*" (italics added).

But your children are prodigals? Even on drugs? In jail? Unrepentant and unredeemed? Or just "in progress"?

Get up anyway! Why not believe God's extravagant promise, that as you upgrade your own walk—crying out to God's Spirit to empower you to walk with honesty before your family—your children *will* follow and be blessed?

Even the prodigals. Focusing on honesty and handing over their rebellion to God will show them a new family value system that will bless and empower your entire clan. Still doubtful? Get up with honesty anyway. What you gain will keep giving for generations. 🌿

Man's character is his fate.
HERACLITUS

Honesty and Integrity: In Spiritual Warfare

He is a shield to those who walk with integrity.
Proverbs 2:7

We're in a fight. A nasty battle. Spiritual warfare, with every scary image you can think of, is real. Our enemy, Satan, has already lost. But he won't give up. So he keeps firing, nonstop, with every possible lie and deceit, whispered temptation and noisy distraction, and evil thought and despicable lure to block, burden, and keep us in his bondage.

But you already know that. You suffer from his attacks every day. We all do, feeling sometimes like the battle will never be won, nor will we ever prevail.

And we won't—not without a shield.

Jesus the Christ.

He is our Shield. In His strong Name, and empowered by His Spirit, we take on our enemy and triumph. But how exactly?

Turn back to Him. With honesty, surrender today every single part of your life—yes, every aspect. Your emotions, health, career, marriage, family, finances, feelings, temptations, thoughts, memories, goals, hopes, fears, and anything else you can think of. Then give it *all* to Christ.

With every new day, renew this relationship in prayer. Honestly. Then the rest of the day, walk with Him—letting Him shield and empower you to love.

Love, in fact, is how God fights Satan's war. Unlike those who say we fight spiritual warfare by throwing a spiritual fit ourselves, we fight instead by giving the Lord every jot of our lives. Then let Him send us back out into the world to love like Him.

Get up to love like that today, shielded by Christ. Bless God today, indeed, with surrendering love. Satan can't stand it. Or stop it. But you can launch a river of love flowing from every corner and cranny of your life, blessing others honestly—and letting the Lord bless you—as He shields. Because you love. 🌿

No hatred.
CORRIE TEN BOOM

Going Deeper

The godly walk with integrity.
Proverbs 20:7

Honesty blesses for generations. So how honest is your family? How has your family's honesty profile impacted you and your children? Explain.

The Lord detests dishonesty. Why do you think this is so?

In what ways are you honest on purpose? In what ways are you dishonest? What will change in your life if you start walking and living with honesty and integrity?

If you'd like, write a prayer that reflects what God is trying to teach you about the virtues of honesty and integrity.

Honesty is the cornerstone of all success.
MARY KAY ASH

REPENTANCE

His Promise

The pain caused you to repent and change your ways.
2 Corinthians 7:9

My Prayer

Through my pain and sorrow over my sin,
help me to change—my ways, my words, my will—
as I yield to You and Yours.

Repentance: To Gain a New Walk

The pain caused you to repent and change your ways.
2 Corinthians 7:9

Broken. Oh, I don't want to go there. To bear the breakage. To feel the pain of dropping my heart to the ground. To see the truth of real repentance—that before we turn back to God, we have to throw our hearts to the floor, falling on our faces, spilling out our truth before our God.

With guilt and grief, we collapse before God—acknowledging our sin, our offense, and how it sorrows God. Dishonors God. Misrepresents God. Then, broken with guilt and sorrowful with grief, we offer Him a heart bent to the pavement.

In mud. On dirt. Through burning sand.

Why else would the words *repentance* and *reptile* share the same root?

On the ground, our sinful hearts crawl back to God. A painful trip.

But don't neglect to take it today. Run today, in fact, not first to blessing—but to brokenness. For courage to see sin. For a longing to be rid of it.

"Bend *down* to listen," David cries out in Psalm 102:2 (italics added). "Lean *down* and listen," Daniel cries also in Daniel 9:18 (italics added), and we all understand. This road of repentance starts low. But humbling and painful as it is, this path comes with extraordinary blessings. Our painful turning lets God lift, purge, save, sanctify, heal, empower, and change us too.

That's what the apostle Paul observed in the church at Corinth. His piercing letter of 1 Corinthians so convicted wrongdoers that, after repenting before God, they changed. At first, Paul wrote he was sorry for "that severe letter" (2 Corinthians 7:8) to a sinning church. It hurt. But it hit home. Thus, he rejoiced that he sent it, "not because it hurt you, but because the pain caused you to repent and change your ways" (v. 9).

The pain of sin? The pain of truth about sin? Brutal, indeed.

But don't fear such truth. Instead, fall to the ground and crawl. It's there that God's gentle hand points us to a new way. Then He lifts us, standing, graceful, grateful, blessed, returned to Him. By His Spirit, changed. 🍃

A heart is never at the best till it be broken.
RICHARD BAKER

Repentance: To Gain Holy Vision

As I was praying, Gabriel . . . came swiftly to me.
Daniel 9:21

You long to repent. Even to be broken. But of exactly what? I see that question on faces at a women's ministry meeting. So I see pain, longing, sorrow, even embarrassment. But the leader offers encouragement, asking them to tell the truth—to lay their sins before God.

Still, their confessions surprise me. They repent of: Doubt. Lack of trust. Worry. Doubt again. Fear. Financial strain. More doubt.

These Christian women's leaders? If they are worried about life and doubtful about God, what sins must rank-and-file women struggle with on this day?

So these women's leaders prayed, repenting before God, pleading to be broken, seeking to bless God with their broken repentance—even believing such brokenness would grant them the key blessing of repentance: a clear vision from God.

Did you know of such a blessing? That God will bless you with a vision for your life when you bring Him, not your hopes and plans, but your sins and weaknesses?

Daniel's story proves it.

As he looked at the children of Israel, realizing their seventy years of exile were due to end, he "prayed to the LORD my God and confessed" (Daniel 9:4).

We have sinned against You. Rebelled against You. Scorned Your commands.

But Daniel was interrupted. God's angel Gabriel suddenly appeared, telling him to stop—because "the moment you began praying, a command was given." *Give Daniel My vision.*

"And now I am here to tell you what it was, for you are very precious to God" (v. 23).

Well, today, you are precious to God too. So repent today—blessing God. Then open your heart. It's time to see. 🔥

How else but through a broken heart may Lord Christ enter in?
OSCAR WILDE

Repentance: To Gain Holy Joy

You have broken me—now let me rejoice.
Psalm 51:8

David's sin with Bathsheba was down and dirty. We know that. But we keep studying it, wondering about it—amazed at it—asking ourselves, in our Bible study meetings and Sunday school classes, *how could he?*

But he did. Adultery, murder, lying, denial—the whole nine yards.

Just as we've fallen short, David surely fell low.

So his cry to God sounds so much like our own:

Have mercy on me, O God (v. 1). Wash me. Purify me.

Have you cried to God like that? Saying like David: "For I recognize my rebellion; it haunts me day and night" (v. 3). We understand that exactly. Down and dirty sin *is* haunting.

But what if we're not yet haunted? Not yet repentant? Most of us, in fact, probably haven't committed adultery *and* murder—surely not in one sweep.

So it's easy not to be haunted by our sin. Not to see that our sins, especially sins of omission—the justice we didn't seek, the mercy we didn't give, the humility we didn't walk in—break God's heart.

Yet we want joy? In fact, we can have it. But first?

Fall down. Drop to our faces, like David, understanding—like David—that God doesn't want our sacrifices or our worthless burnt offerings. God wants broken spirits.

"You will not reject a broken and repentant heart, O God" (v. 17).

So here is mine.

Break it, precious Christ. Then put back the pieces—scar tissue and all—in a pattern that shows Your beauty. Empowered beauty. Clean, whole, rejoicing. 🕊

Of all acts of man, repentance is the most divine.
THOMAS CARLYLE

Repentance: To Gain Holy and Peaceful Strength

I suddenly felt stronger.
Daniel 10:19

How do we spell repentance? R-e-l-e-a-s-e. That's the sweet spot of repentance.

Rather than feel worse when we acknowledge sin, we feel better. Rather than feel grungy and awful, we feel clean and blessed. Rather than feel tied in knots and burdened, we feel strong. Peaceful and strong.

Daniel described the wonder of this release. "I suddenly felt stronger."

Indeed, after confessing the sins of his people to God, fasting from rich foods (meats and wine)—and even from fragrant lotions for his skin—he was blessed with a vision. Anguished and weak from such a sight, he could barely breathe from his feelings. But the vision, of a man, encouraged him:

"Don't be afraid," he said, "for you are very precious to God" (v. 19).

Then a sweet spot.

"Peace!" the man said.

But there was more:

"Be encouraged!" the man added. "Be strong!" (v. 19).

Wonderful words, aren't they? Surely God knows our struggle with sin, and our bigger struggle to confess it. Disclosing our cover-ups, denials, blinders, and lies exhausts even the best of us. Yet when we acknowledge our faults to Him, shining the light of truth on them—with courage and honesty—He blesses us with peaceful strength.

Whatever emotional effort it took to open our mouths and confess our offenses, He blesses with His grace.

Awesome God. In fact: "There is no condemnation," the apostle Paul wrote, "for those who belong to Christ Jesus. And because you belong to him, the power of the life-giving Spirit has freed you from the power of sin that leads to death" (Romans 8:1-2).

That's release. Repent today and receive this precious and blessed gift. His Name is Jesus. 🌱

When we deal seriously with our sins, God will deal gently with us.
CHARLES SPURGEON

Repentance: To Gain Holy Zeal

Just see what this godly sorrow produced in you!
2 Corinthians 7:11

Weren't we supposed to feel lousy? Not at all. After this week of repentance and godly sorrow, we feel—ironically—our very best, not our worst. *But who knew?*

That's what I'm asking myself today. Sounding a bit like Paul. Sounding a lot like Daniel, David, Ezra, and Nehemiah. Indeed the apostle Paul, after hearing from the church at Corinth, sounded surprised at the effects of genuine sorrow and repentance.

Wow. That's what Paul seemed to say.

"Just see what this godly sorrow produced in you! Such earnestness, such concern to clear yourselves, such indignation, such alarm, such longing to see me, such zeal, and such a readiness to punish wrong" (2 Corinthians 7:11).

Such a miracle.

And who doesn't need that?

Breaking ourselves on the anvil of God's heart sharpens our souls. Bringing out gold. Yielding up fire. Raising up zeal. Waking up the dead.

In sin, yes, we are dead. Even if we're not practicing an old sin, without repenting we're dead. Maybe deader than dead. Hypocritical, too. "And you will perish . . . ," Jesus said, "unless you repent of your sins and turn to God" (Luke 13:3).

Indeed, to repent of all of it, crawling to God—so we may be purged of our old ways and filled with His Spirit and His way—leaves us clean, alive, but also *fired up for life.*

And God's Kingdom needs that from us.

Paul put it this way: "You showed that you have done everything necessary to make things right" (2 Corinthians 7:11). With zeal, this sinning and lackluster church turned the corner—walking with strength in God's goodness. Repentance will do that. It blesses us with power—so we can bless God's world with holy fire. Ready to burn? Fall on the floor. Then light the world with God. 🌿

Spend and be spent.
JOHN WESLEY

Repentance: To Gain Holy Rest

Then times of refreshment will come.
Acts 3:20

It gets better. Still better. For all the blessings of repentance—salvation, vision, joy, peace, strength, zeal, life, and more—God tops it off with rest. Holy refreshment.

But that doesn't quite capture the power of this promise.

Spoken by the apostle Peter to the same people who helped convict the Messiah Jesus and send Him to the Cross, this promise of redemption is not offered lightly.

Peter even addresses them kindly, calling them "friends"—even with forgiveness.

"Friends," he says, "I realize that what you and your leaders did to Jesus was done in ignorance" (v. 17).

In fact, God was just fulfilling what "all the prophets had foretold" about the Messiah, Peter points out—"that he must suffer these things" (v. 18). And now?

Repent.

No surprise that he would say that. Repent, so your sins may be wiped clean (see v. 19). We expect that promise. We've heard it ourselves. Peter's surprise, however, is how such repentance would bless those who schemed to kill Christ.

Then times of refreshment will come. But how?

By the presence of the Lord. Think of it, yes. To the ones who killed Him, Christ offers Himself.

Jesus Himself still makes this promise: *Come to me, all of you who are weary and carry heavy burdens, and I will give you rest* (Matthew 11:28).

His yoke is easy. His burden is light. In contrast to the heavy yoke of the Pharisees and the burden of their traditions, Christ offers His disciples a demanding life—but one lightened by the power of the Holy Spirit.

Peter sought to share such glorious refreshment. Will you accept the empowered life of Christ today? Repent. Then breathe. Your refreshment is at hand. ❧

God never takes away anything that He doesn't replace with Himself.
JACQUELYN K. HEASLEY

Going Deeper

*The kind of sorrow God wants . . . leads us away from sin
and results in salvation.*
2 Corinthians 7:10

If repentance, according to God's Word, is for sinners—what does repentance mean for you?

What sins do you no longer practice, but still require your repentance?

As you studied repentance this week, then repented, what blessing did you experience from God?

If you'd like, write a prayer that reflects what God is trying to teach you about the virtue of repentance.

When God promises to forgive His people when they repent,
He is not playing games.
R. C. SPROUL

Passion and Zeal

His Promise

For he satisfies the thirsty.
Psalm 107:9

My Prayer

Fire up my passion for You, O God of Hosts!

Passion and Zeal: For Who God Is

Moses immediately threw himself to the ground and worshiped.
Exodus 34:8

It comes from Him. This passion we feel. This zeal we ride. The word *enthusiasm*—*in theos* in Latin or "inspired by God"—says it all. So shouldn't it make sense that the first passion we pursue *is* God?

We know the right answer.

But distractions trip us up, unless we turn with passion to our Helper. So cry today to the Holy Spirit, asking His strength to put aside all else, to equip us only to seek and know Him. Really know Him. With passion and zeal, to know Him.

With such passion, Moses threw himself to the ground in the face of such knowledge on Mount Sinai.

The children of Israel had broken their covenant with God by worshiping, not the Lord, but a golden calf. In anger, Moses smashed the tablets containing the Ten Commandments. But at God's command, Moses climbed a second time up Mount Sinai into the Lord's presence, carrying two new tablets for God to inscribe.

But this time, God made sure Moses knew exactly who He was. So He "came down in a cloud and stood there" with Moses—passing in front of Moses and calling out His own name: "Yahweh!" (Exodus 34:5).

Inviting us: know Me. God calls out His name before us today, crying out for us to redirect our zeal to who He is. "Yahweh! The Lord! The God of compassion and mercy! I am slow to anger and filled with unfailing love and faithfulness" (v. 6).

Even when we expend our passion on worthless junk, golden calves, He calls. "I lavish unfailing love to a thousand generations. I forgive iniquity, rebellion, and sin" (v. 7).

On hearing God's passion for Himself, God's servant Moses "immediately" threw himself to the ground and worshiped. *Then he prayed for others,* acting as a prefigurement of Christ Himself!

Let's join Moses on that holy ground today. Our passion for God will bless Him. But it will bless us and others even more. 🔥

Be hot and earnest still.
CHARLES SPURGEON

Passion and Zeal: For Righteous Prayer

The earnest prayer of a righteous person has great power.
James 5:16

Cold church. Hateful church. Gossiping church. The church in Jerusalem was a hot mess. Barely hanging on, the church elders got a letter from James, the brother of Jesus, on how to rise above the mess, to survive and thrive for Christ.

So it's a frank letter. Not too nice. Not too gentle. Filled with zeal and passion, James cuts to the chase, in fact, right from the start. "This letter is from James, a slave of God and of the Lord Jesus Christ" (1:1). A *slave?* That got their attention. Count on it.

So the letter challenges. It preaches. Then it chastises, exhorts—taking to task every weakness in this new Christian congregation. Then it orders them to climb higher.

James's punch list is long and practical, to be sure. He urges them to endure, listen more, talk less, love the poor, stop boasting, stop quarreling, stop judging, stop committing adultery. In other words, live right! That is, live each day for *Him.*

Does his warning catch your attention today?

If so, you'll also see what fuels James's zeal: when we live right for God, we pray with passion. Even more, our fervent, passionate, earnest prayer "has great power." But that's still not all. It "produces wonderful results" (5:16).

Be passionate, that is, for being right. *Then*, says James, your earnest prayers will capture God's ear, as well as God's hand.

To be certain, it's easy to be passionate for God's answer, period. (Then to be frustrated when He doesn't seem to respond.) But to have passion to be righteous—then to cry out, in righteousness, to God in prayer—turns ho-hum praying into power.

So make me right, O God. Bless the Lord by praying that today. Turn your passion for living well to a passion for living right. Then watch your prayers ignite. 🌿

Our walk counts far more than our talk.
GEORGE MÜLLER

Passion and Zeal: For Spiritual Gifts

As they listen . . . they will fall to their knees and worship God.
1 Corinthians 14:25

Love your job—or hate it? Love your life—or filled with regrets? Passion for your life, ideals, vocation—and also faith—fuels a heart that makes a difference.

But the apostle Paul urges believers to be passionate, not just for jobs or lives, but first for "the special abilities" the Spirit gives us, especially the gift of prophecy (12:1).

Prophecy? But wait.

What about passion for our artistry? For our carpentry or baking or software engineering or designing or doctoring or for any other God-given gift we may enjoy? What, indeed, about the idea that passion "makes all things alive," as poet Ralph Waldo Emerson said? All good, Paul would say. But the apostle brings us back to ground with this reminder: be passionate first for the gifts of the Holy Spirit, in whatever form they take. Why? They build up the church and encourage the love of God.

But what kind of church, and what kind of people, would need such a reminder? The lukewarm church at Laodicea needed it (Revelation 3:15). Same for the church at Corinth. But neither church was that much different from many today.

So Paul taught this: Love is better. Prophecy is better. When people come into our churches—feeling our love and hearing our revelation of God's Word—"their secret thoughts will be exposed, and they will fall to their knees and worship God, declaring, 'God is truly here among you'" (1 Corinthians 14:25).

But you don't hunger for love or prophecy? Pray for it. Not sure you've been bestowed with a spiritual gift? Pray for it to be revealed. Then use what the Holy Spirit gives you. Not to make yourself look good—but to point another hungry person to the Cross. 🍃

God requires that His gifts should be sought for.
ARTHUR PINK

Passion and Zeal: For Helping Others

A spiritual gift is given to each of us so we can help each other.
1 Corinthians 12:7

In Max Lucado's book *Cure for the Common Life*, he offers a time-tested path for finding our "sweet spot"—that is, our passionate special calling.

With reminders that each person is given a unique gift from God, he blazes a trail on how to find it. Read your life backward, as he puts it—seeing where you've found success and what you're good at. Then stand at "the intersection" of these successes, Lucado writes, "and find your uniqueness."

The book's true drumbeat, however, explains why finding our special passions and talents is so important: it *makes a big deal out of God.*

Talk about curing the common life.

Typically, we're urged to discover our uniqueness to celebrate ourselves. Or to be happy, gain riches, build our reputations, or put ourselves in the spotlight.

But Lucado, in the spirit of the apostle Paul, reminds us to take on the struggle to discover our true selves *for God.* But why? So we can help each other.

Are you seeing this passion business with new eyes yet?

Many of us know precisely what our gifts are. But we're using them for the wrong purpose.

No wonder we're frustrated. Primed to reach for the stars so we can shine, we may end up "successful"—but miserable. Or frustrated by others' success, we waste energy envying their gifts instead of using ours. Isn't it time to turn around that picture?

Bless God today by using your God-given gifts for somebody else. Then that somebody will see God. But first, ask God's Holy Spirit to show you your gift. Big or small, unpack it and share—passing on your passion for Christ as only you can. 🕯

Heed that inner music. No one else hears it the way you do.
MAX LUCADO

Passion and Zeal: For Giving Offerings

God loves a person who gives cheerfully.
2 Corinthians 9:7

The offering basket passes by and you cringe. Or you dig deep in your wallet and pour in generously. Either way, wrote Paul, giving in church isn't so much about the money. Instead, giving money for Christian ministry reflects how much you and I have given ourselves to Christ.

But money is the test.

Paul knew that. So in his second letter to the church at Corinth, he wrote two whole chapters about giving—including a piercing reminder:

Dragging our feet to give won't bless anybody.

"I want it to be a willing gift, not one given grudgingly" (9:5).

Paul gently said that, reminding them that poverty-stricken believers in Jerusalem needed their help. But church members in Corinth, after starting to give, had slacked off. (Sound familiar?) Even a "poorer" church in Macedonia had given beyond their share, Paul wrote.

Now what about you?

Paul's question rings down through history right to your pew. Is your ministry of giving so generous and cheerful, trusting and passionate—so based, not on what you have, but on who God is—that others are blessed by your passion to give?

Put down your checkbook when you answer such a question. Look, instead, at the Macedonian believers. Despite dire poverty, they dug deep. Giving beyond their own ability, they trusted God to bless *and* restore their gifts.

Can you give with such zeal, believing, as Paul wrote, that "you will be enriched in every way so that you can always be generous" (v. 11)? You'll give like that if your giving is fueled not by money—but by trust.

What does it look like? Audacious love. 🌱

Passion will move men beyond themselves.
JOE CAMPBELL

Passion and Zeal: For God's House of Prayer

My Temple will be called a house of prayer.
Isaiah 56:7

Jesus our Savior was angry. It was Passover, and pilgrims and salesmen, money changers and hangers-on had turned the Temple in Jerusalem into a "den of thieves" (Matthew 21:13).

Making a whip of rope, Jesus chased them all out. Peddlers hawking cattle, sheep, and doves. Money changers making profit from exchanging currency.

Their worship was a farce, in other words. So Jesus drove them away from His Presence.

But what about us? When we enter our churches, is our passion for worship and praise—or for gossip and glamour? We could debate the question.

Or we could come to church to pray—with passion and reverence and zeal.

Jim Cymbala of the Brooklyn Tabernacle made prayer the "barometer" of his church. What happens at Tuesday night prayer meetings "will be the gauge by which we will judge success or failure," Cymbala wrote in *Fresh Wind, Fresh Fire*, "because that will be the measure by which God blesses us."

In his church, from the time it started with a few members in a broken-down building to its thriving ministry today, prayer has always come first. Over preaching. Over teaching. Over singing. Over praising. Prayer is number one.

"This is the engine that will drive the church," Cymbala told the congregation. "Yes, I want you to keep coming on Sundays—but Tuesday night is what it's really all about."

A praying church? We've all heard that phrase. But Cymbala decided to walk the talk. His prayer-band members are scheduled around the clock, every day—"24-7" as the phrase goes. Prayer at Brooklyn Tabernacle never stops. Is God blessed by such passion? Ask the thousands who press into the church every week. Lacking in passion? Bless God today. Show up at His house and start praying. 🌿

In every place of worship, I want men to pray with holy hands
lifted up to God.
1 TIMOTHY 2:8

Going Deeper

It was your enthusiasm that stirred up many of the Macedonian believers.
2 Corinthians 9:2

Lukewarm Christians and lukewarm churches actually disgust God. As Jesus said of such halfhearted faith, "I will spit you out of my mouth!" (Revelation 3:16). So what's your spiritual temperature?

Among your passions, what's your first priority? What's next? Explain.

How hungry and passionate are you for the things of God?

If you'd like, write a prayer that reflects what God is trying to teach you about the virtues of passion and zeal.

Catch on fire with enthusiasm and people will come for miles
to watch you burn!
JOHN WESLEY

STRENGTH AND VIGOR

His Promise

*He gives power to the weak
and strength to the powerless.*
Isaiah 40:29

My Prayer

Bless You, Living God,
for gracing and girding our weakness
with Your strengthening power.

Strength and Vigor: From the Inside Out

As soon as I pray, you answer me;
you encourage me by giving me strength.
Psalm 138:3

It's a battle. So let us stop acting surprised at life.

It's a battle. So it tests us day by day.

It's a battle. But God tells us how to fight.

"This is My command—be strong!"

That's what He told Joshua. David. Solomon. Daniel. That's what He is telling us today. *Be strong.*

And it *is* a command. So let's get up and obey it. If we couldn't obey, He wouldn't order it. So today?

Be strong. Right now. All day. Next day. Always. *Be strong.*

But how do we bless God and toughen up our spirits? Get moving and pray.

Not flex our muscles. Or talk tough. Or organize a committee. Or ball up fists.

Instead, first pray.

The process of building spiritual muscle is no different from the process of building physical strength. During rest, worked muscle builds. Likewise, during prayer, spiritual muscle strengthens. In prayer, the Holy Spirit encourages, comforts, inspires, assures, sharpens, deepens, *and* toughens.

So bless God today by leaving the battlefield *to pray.* And skip the fancy prayers. Skip the babbling, too. God knows all anyway. Instead, pray—praising Him just like David. "I will give you thanks, O LORD, with all my heart; I will sing your praises" (v. 1). For Your unfailing love. Your faithfulness. Your promises, "backed by all the honor of your name" (v. 2).

Then as soon as you pray, He answers—not with fixes but by giving strength. Lack inner strength today? Bless God so He can bless you with power. So today? Stop fighting. Start praying. 🌿

There is a strength beyond our strength, giving strength to our strength.
HOWARD THURMAN

Strength and Vigor: In Moral Battles

You have taught children and infants to tell of your strength,
silencing your enemies.
Psalm 8:2

A hurting day sneaks up on us. So we pause today. But we don't stand still.

On this anniversary of the September 11 attacks, we don't fall, falter, or faint. Instead, we get up first to praise God. *O LORD, our Lord!* His majestic name fills the earth—strengthening our hearts, girding our spirits.

On this day, therefore, millions of us will fight evil with love. So we will do community service. Clean streets. Empty alleys. Paint houses. Cook meals. Clear weeds. Plant trees. Cheer the sick. Clothe the naked. Visit prisons. Read to children.

As today's Scripture says: "You have taught children and infants to tell of your strength, silencing your enemies and all who oppose you."

If little children, even infants, can by their trust tell of God's power to strengthen hearts for goodness over evil, can't the rest of us follow?

Our moral choice today, not to hate but to love by serving, wields more power than any man-made weapon. Such strength allows us even to obey Jesus' hard command:

Love your enemies.

Today, especially, we will pray for those who seek to harm.

Not easy? Things that take strength never are.

But as we let go of anger and pain, replacing them with the power of trust in our sovereign God, He graces us with good strength. Moral strength. That's how we fight evil—standing up to scorn with trust, to lies with truth, to hate with love.

On our own? Never. God's Holy Spirit helps us. We bless Him back by allowing it. Then at the end of this day—a day we give, by faith, back to Christ—we discover another strengthening blessing. His empowering peace. ❦

The strong man is the man who can stand up for his rights and not hit back.
MARTIN LUTHER KING JR.

Strength and Vigor: In Physical Battles

Daniel and his three friends looked healthier.
Daniel 1:15

Astronauts go strong into outer space. But after months on the International Space Station, they come back weakened. With bones and muscles rarely used in microgravity, they come home with less strength and power. The result? Weaker bodies, including huge losses in bone density.

To stay strong, we actually need pressure, that is. That's true for our spirits, minds, and bodies. But something else. Our pressures are more than spiritual. Our bodies, too, war daily. Many of us want to forget that some days. When it's time to walk a mile—when two miles would be even better—we'd love to beg off and back down. When it's time to eat spinach, an ice cream sundae and fries tempt us away.

Or we could think about the Bible hero Daniel.

A captive in exile, he faced a training regimen designed to break his dependence on God and build his loyalty to his ruler, King Nebuchadnezzar.

A rich diet, plus a name change, along with a program of intense study were ordered. The king's goal? To make Daniel and the other young captives "suited to serve in the royal palace" (v. 4) by forgetting their God. A spiritual problem? Absolutely.

But Daniel fought back in his flesh.

With three friends, he asked permission not to consume the king's food and wine. His choice? Vegetables and water. Too harsh? Too austere?

In fact, at the end of ten days, Daniel and his friends "looked healthier and better nourished" (v. 15). Stronger and more vigorous. God also gave them "an unusual aptitude for understanding every aspect of literature and wisdom" (v. 17). Daniel was also graced with a special ability to interpret visions and dreams. The king, meanwhile, found Daniel and his friends "ten times more capable" (v. 20) than any of his royal assistants.

A great story? But a bigger lesson. Spiritual strength matters. But so does physical discipline. The Lord blesses both, especially when we seek them for Him. 🌿

You will not stroll into Christlikeness with your hands in your pockets.
A. J. GOSSIP

Strength and Vigor: From God Alone

*Power and might are in your hand, and at your discretion people
are made great and given strength.*
1 Chronicles 29:12

As a child, I loved Popeye cartoons. Those spinach-eating scenes, where a can
of the green stuff morphed into big biceps, always made me giggle. Nothing
is funny, however, about the health risk of muscle-building steroids. From
liver damage and high blood pressure, to infertility and mood shifts, clear
dangers face abusers of such drugs.

So why would anybody use them?

To look better? Feel stronger? Gain confidence?

Or could the problem be spiritual?

When any of us seek strength from any source other than God, aren't
we giving in to the myth that strength can be bought, consumed, or
manipulated?

King David understood this. At the coronation of his son Solomon, he
praised God alone for being the source of our strength. More amazing, however, David didn't ask God to grant His strength to God's people.

Instead, David prayed for obedience. "Make your people always want to
obey you" (v. 18). Strength will come from God, as He chooses to give it.
But obedience blesses us first.

That's still true today. Bulking up with drugs to get strong won't help
us. Begging God for strength won't empower us. We bless God, instead, by
seeking to obey Him. As we obey, we'll find ourselves empowered with the
Spirit of His love. 🌿

We are a long time in learning that all our strength and salvation is in God.
DAVID BRAINERD

Strength and Vigor: Through Trust in Christ

For I can do everything through Christ, who gives me strength.
Philippians 4:13

At a weak moment, Paul saw strength. At a weak hour, Paul spoke strength. At a weak season, Paul breathed strength. At a weak time, Paul welcomed strength.

So what are we waiting for?

Paul was in jail when he wrote these words. *For I can do everything through Christ.* Our own prisons—emotional, physical, spiritual—are no different from his.

So it was with the Philippians. Persecuted and opposed, scorned and questioned, they could give up and fall down. At a bad moment in time, they could throw up their hands and make their circumstances even worse.

But don't you dare throw in the towel.

See life with Paul's eyes.

It doesn't matter, that is, what's happening in life. Those are details. Own a lot? Or nothing. Eat a lot? Or little. Earn much? Or peanuts. Life, Paul says, isn't about measurements. It's about who God is and what He's doing in His world.

Will we get up to join Him? Can we stop wasting time worrying over our part of the details, expending our own strength when His grace is sufficient?

Too much to ask?

Or we could trust Paul's claim about Christ. Then we'd take a deep breath. Knowing we aren't enough on our own, we'd accept Paul's "secret of living in every situation" (v. 12).

I can do everything through Christ, who gives me strength.

The measure, indeed, isn't perfection. It isn't quantity. It's whether we bless Christ by trusting Him with the impossible. Then we flex our muscles. How do they look? Lean. Ripped. Whole. 🌿

We must do that which we think we cannot.
ELEANOR ROOSEVELT

Strength and Vigor: To Reveal Strong Character

For when I am weak, then I am strong.
2 Corinthians 12:10

Diamonds. Oak. Granite. Nature's strongest elements get our respect.

Their strength, durability, and beauty enchant us. We also value strong character in people. Regardless of age.

So we were drawn to the story of the eleven-year-old boy in Findlay, Ohio—a cheerleader at his school—whose left arm was broken when he was attacked by bullies. But he stuck with his sport.

"People are threatening to break my other arm because I told on them," Tyler Wilson told ABC's *Good Morning America*. But as a fan of tumbling, his sport of choice is cheerleading.

"It feels horrible that they can't accept me for who I am," Tyler told ABC News affiliate WTVG. "It's my choice. If I want to be a cheerleader, I'm going to be a cheerleader."

Where does such character come from?

By living a life for Christ, the apostle Paul found an answer.

Tormented by a "thorn in [the] flesh"—or as Paul also called it, "a messenger from Satan" (v. 7)—he sought the Lord to provide the strength to overcome. Instead, the Lord taught Paul a key power lesson:

My grace is all you need. My power works best in weakness (v. 9).

So no need to boast, Paul learned.

I want to bless God today by learning the lesson too. To stand strong, full of spunk and grit—making tough decisions, acting holy, and quoting Scripture—can turn the spotlight on me. But to stand strong in Christ in my weakness makes room for Him.

Our bully Satan will toss us around. Or try to.

Fight back? No, I'm cheering for God. Forever. 🕊

I'm not giving up.
TYLER WILSON

Going Deeper

He will keep you strong to the end.
1 Corinthians 1:8

In everyday life, what kind of strength is most important to you? Moral? Physical? Spiritual? Explain your answer.

In what areas of your life do you need more strength from God?

What special insight has God taught you this week about the virtues of strength and vigor?

If you'd like, write a prayer that reflects your needs regarding the virtues of strength and vigor.

Deny your weakness, and you will never realize God's strength in you.
JONI EARECKSON TADA

CREATIVITY

His Promise

*For we are God's masterpiece. He has created
us anew in Christ Jesus,
so we can do the good things he planned
for us long ago.*
Ephesians 2:10

My Prayer

As Your masterpiece, I ask You, O God,
to create in me the wisdom to do all the good things
planned for me
since the beginning of time.

Creativity: Inspired by God

The LORD is the everlasting God,
the Creator of all the earth.
Isaiah 40:28

Songwriter Michael Card, whose praise song "El Shaddai" was named one of the 365 songs of the century by the Recording Industry Association of America and the National Endowment for the Arts, could boast of sales of more than four million records and four hundred thousand books. But he doesn't boast.

His creativity, says Card in his book *Scribbling in the Sand: Christ and Creativity*, is inspired by the creativity embodied in Christ.

What does that look like? Look at Christ, Card says, when He interrupts a howling mob of Pharisees eager to stone to death an adulterous woman—by stooping down and scribbling in the sand. Twice.

To this day, Card writes, "we have not the slightest idea what it was Jesus twice scribbled in the sand." He explains: "It was not the content that mattered but why he did it. Unexpected. Irritating. Creative."

And *that* is art, Card says. Whatever stops the world is art. Whatever makes the world pause and pay attention to something greater. Whatever shows the world's busy people—so self-absorbed and angry with their selfness—that their world is "not the only world that existed. And so they were liberated. And that, too, is art."

Only Christ can inspire it.

So for all of us artists who are biting our nails and losing sleep and pulling our hair out trying to find the right word, design, color, song, or poem—look instead to Christ. Worship Him creatively today. Gawk at the sunrise. Cook a meal. Send a card. Call a friend. Dance under the stars. Write down a sentence that expresses it all. Inspired by Christ, let's bless Him and others by turning from ourselves today to scribble. ✎

Imagine the possibilities!
MICHAEL CARD

Creativity: Through Obedience to God

Build a large boat from cypress wood.
Genesis 6:14

The great myth about creativity? That it's free flowing, over the top, out of the box.

But as all effective artists and performers know, creativity follows obedience. That's true for painters, sculptors, chefs, writers, tailors, carpenters, web designers—any creative type. Breaking rules doesn't happen with much success until basic rules are learned and followed.

Thus, Noah could've built any old kind of boat.

But as a righteous man, when God provided *His* blueprint, Noah obeyed.

"Construct decks and stalls throughout its interior," the Lord told Moses. "Make the boat 450 feet long, 75 feet wide, and 45 feet high. Leave an 18-inch opening below the roof all the way around the boat. Put the door on the side, and build three decks inside the boat—lower, middle, and upper" (vv. 14-16).

Talk about exact directions.

Noah never even questioned God about the boat or the building of it. That's true even though such a boat—a long, rectangular barge, says the *NLT Study Bible*—was "for survival, not for navigation." The eighteen-inch opening below the roof "provid[ed] light and air." With no sail or rudder, the boat would be navigated by God, its true captain.

Closely attuned to God, Noah simply listened to the Creator's plan and followed, reflecting Psalm 19:7: "The instructions of the Lord are perfect. . . . the decrees of the Lord are trustworthy."

If your creativity suffers, try aiming for more obedience to God—in your art, but first in your life. Sure, you may not be building a big boat. But obey God. He is the Creator. The thumbprint of His Word will anoint your creative efforts with blessed grace. Because you're talented? No, because you obey. 🔥

Biblically speaking, the making of art is not an option but a command.
HAROLD BEST

Creativity: In Worship of God

I have given special skill to all the gifted craftsmen.
Exodus 31:6

Who wants to write a bestseller?

Everybody, if today's popular writers' conferences are evidence. Teaching at one recently, I saw what I always see: hundreds of people trudging from class to class, trying to learn the best technique for writing the next best-selling novel or screenplay.

Everybody, it seems, longs to be the next literary star. To write the next *Harry Potter, Left Behind, Redeeming Love,* or *The Shack*. Or to write the next hit song, script the next box-office smash, paint the next *Mona Lisa*, or launch the next popular blog.

But what if we created for God?

With God? Just to worship God? But on His terms?

Chew hard with me on these questions today.

As a published author, I confess to writing many things I hoped would sell—and never anything I hoped *wouldn't* sell. All artists hope for acceptance. Don't we?

But the Word of God teaches us such surprising truths about this God-given impulse to cocreate with God.

Foremost, there's the necessary reminder that God alone is the Creator. The rest of us, as music scholar Harold Best puts it, "are merely creative."

God Himself, speaking to Moses about a craftsman for the Ark of the Covenant, declared: "*I* have filled him with the Spirit of God, giving him great wisdom, ability, and expertise in all kinds of crafts." Moreover, "*I* have given special skill to all the gifted craftsmen so they can make all the things *I* have commanded" (Exodus 31:3, 6, emphasis added).

By God's Spirit alone do any of us create anything at all. From our first crayon drawing to our last crocheted blanket, God creates. Why not go along for the ride by worshiping Him? With our songs, poems, quilts, crayon drawings, and other artistry given to Him, we wash others' feet, as Michael Card says. Yes, creativity is washing. Not seeking bestseller status. Instead today, worship God in His way. Look for feet. 🔥

Never cease praying that you will not become a star or celebrity.
MICHAEL CARD

Creativity: In Partnership with God

He has given me a new song to sing.
Psalm 40:3

Sing about God today. Sing before Him. Sing because of Him?

I've been trying to do that this morning. So I dared to write a psalm—or tried to.

That was my assignment from last week's Sunday school class. "Write a poem or prayer declaring the excellence of God." That means "write a psalm," said our smiling teacher.

But I was frowning. I felt self-conscious. What would people think? That was my first thought. Then I thought more deeply about creativity—about the assurances of Michael Card and Harold Best and other creativity experts who keep telling us: God has already written it. If we just listen to Him speaking, we can join Him and create. So I started:

My soul sings forever to You, O God.
And I'm not a singer!

I twisted my mouth, not liking it. But still trying to hear. Trying to remember that this psalm isn't about me. So I started again.

My soul sings forever to You, O God.
God of my hope and help, God of my refuge and my redemption.
When I behold You, and when I consider all You are,
When I see how Your universe trembles at Your Name,
My heart expands
To offer songs of praise only to You.
Yes, my heart sings with awe
At Your excellent, sovereign power and grace.
Then my soul sings forever to You.

So that was it. A baby step of a psalm. But this time I didn't question: Was it too lame? Too long? Not enough? All wrong questions. The right one is easy. Did I sing today? Will you? 🌿

To draw, you must close your eyes and sing.
PABLO PICASSO

Creativity: That Fights Our Battles

Suddenly, the walls of Jericho collapsed, and the Israelites charged straight into the town and captured it.
Joshua 6:20

Your book changed my life.

Authors should love to hear that. But on those surprising times that I do, I feel shocked, embarrassed, amazed that words I struggled to write changed somebody's life.

Then I learned.

God uses creativity to win tough battles. Why? To show that He, and He alone, won the war. All over the Bible, in fact, God works through ordinary artists of all stripes and types to fight and win wars.

So it was with the Israelites at Jericho. With a well-armed enemy at their backs and the walled fortress city standing before them, what did God do? He promised victory to Joshua. "I have given you Jericho" (v. 2). How? With ram horns.

Ram horns?

That's *all*? Anybody but Joshua would have turned and run. *Ram horns*? What, O God, about swords? Spears? A couple of arrows? A few slingshots?

But you know the story. Joshua, after falling to his face in the presence of this divinity, followed the instructions—joining his fighting men to march silently around the town once a day for six days, together with seven priests carrying ram horns. Not hitting anybody with the horns, just carrying them.

But the seventh day? In holy perfection, with seven priests blowing seven horns, the priests gave one final, long blast on those horns and God's warriors shouted!

And the walls fell down. "And the Israelites charged straight into the town and captured it." Did the shout bring down the walls? No. The shout rang out first—a cry of victory. But whom did God use to inspire it? Horn blowers.

The lesson for you today? Pick up your craft. It's time to fight. 🌿

Those who plant in tears will harvest with shouts of joy.
PSALM 126:5

Creativity: That Prophesies for God

Take a large clay brick. . . . Then draw.
Ezekiel 4:1

Francine Rivers, bestselling author of *Redeeming Love* and dozens of other popular Christian novels, has this golden advice for aspiring writers.

"Commit your work to the Lord," Rivers told Christian writer C. J. Darlington in a blog interview. "Stay in Scripture every day so you're being formed by it," Rivers added. "That formation will come through in your writing in a natural way."

Great advice from a great writer. Still, I struggled to live it.

Then I read about Criste Reimer. She loved a book I wrote on forgiveness. She was also the seriously ill Kansas woman whose husband murdered her—kissing her, then throwing her off their fourth-floor apartment balcony to her death because he couldn't afford her medical bills.

He is serving a life sentence in prison.

The forty-seven-year-old Criste "had been in poor health for several years," reported the Associated Press. Partially blind with neurological problems, she weighed only seventy-five pounds, and her medical bills, with no insurance, ranged "from $700 to $800 a week."

But she read my book on forgiveness, *My First White Friend*, and gave it a five-star review on an Internet bookselling site, signing her Internet name "cuddlypoo."

That's how I learned of her. A website that advocates for the disabled quoted from Criste's review of my book, noting the irony in her loving comments, considering that soon after she was horribly murdered.

"I only hope that others will read this book with an OPEN MIND as well and realize that we are all on this earth together and that we can all be friends," Criste wrote.

It is the most important endorsement for a book I will ever receive.

It helped me believe Francine Rivers. Even more, because of it, I will never doubt my creative worth to God. On my life of clay, He draws so I can give back. The same goes for you. Get up and give Him your craft. Somebody important needs it now. 🌿

You have to write to please God.
FRANCINE RIVERS

Going Deeper

And David danced before the LORD with all his might,
wearing a priestly garment.
2 Samuel 6:14

Would you describe yourself as creative? Why or why not? What does "being creative" mean to you? Explain.

When you look at God's creation, what does it say to you about God?

In the Bible, God used people's creative talents to win battles, speak prophecy, and glorify Himself. In what ways could God use your creative talents?

What special insight has God taught you this week about the virtue of creativity?

If you'd like, write a prayer that reflects your needs regarding the virtue of creativity.

An artist's true work is to enjoy God.
MAKOTO FUJIMURA

Unity

His Promise

How wonderful and pleasant it is when brothers
live together in harmony! . . .
And there the Lord has pronounced his blessing,
even life everlasting.

Psalm 133:1, 3

My Prayer

Bless Your people, Holy Shepherd,
with Your bond of unity.
Then grant us everlasting life in You.

Unity: With Christ

I pray that they will all be one, just as you and I are one.
John 17:21

Jesus prayed. Not asking the impossible. Not asking the ridiculous. He simply prayed that His people would become one. Yes, it's a beautiful, good, and perfect prayer.

So why are Christians on TV yelling at each other? Calling each other hateful names? Demonizing each other on blogs because of our differences? Fighting within our families? Forgetting that Satan rejoices in our disunity—and worse—that our schisms, factions, nastiness grieve our precious Holy Spirit.

Apparently we forget: We're not battling each other. We're battling Satan. Our enemy comes from "the unseen world" of spiritual evil, says the apostle Paul—yes, "mighty powers in this dark world . . . evil spirits in the heavenly places" (Ephesians 6:12). Stirring up a mess.

Therefore, unity isn't just nice behavior. Unity is how we fight back. So *fight*.

Just think of the victory for Christ when we see, in every Christian, not an enemy but a brother, related by His blood. We wouldn't then be separated by doctrine.

Or by gender.

Or by color.

Or by age.

Or by language.

Or by politics.

Or by race.

Or by any other way that I'm not like you and you're not like me.

Be *one*! Jesus prayed this. If we obey, then we can rejoice, as Andrew Murray urges, that we can "love the brethren, the most trying and unlovable, with love that is not your own, but the love of Christ in you." Does this bless God, this trust that we can love like Christ if we abide in Christ? Let's bless God all year by obeying—as one. 🌿

> And the command about your love to the brethren is changed
> from a burden into a joy.
> ANDREW MURRAY

Unity: In Harmony with Other Believers

Then all of you can join together with one voice.
Romans 15:6

I sing second alto. On good days, I sing second alto. On great days, however, I follow the choirmaster. Yet here I was on this day, singing the wrong note—harmonizing on my own, but not following the music with the others.

"That's a C-*flat*," the experienced first alto said to me. It was my first rehearsal in a renowned community choir, so I was singing by ear. The first alto smiled, but I could see her displeasure. Sing it *right*, her look was saying.

I shifted in my chair, feeling her disapproval.

Later, however, thinking about her reaction, I understood. If every choir member sang a wrong note, the choir's sound would be noisy chaos.

But there was more to this matter of harmony.

After a few rehearsals, I finally saw: even if every member sings the right notes, the sound is a mess if we don't follow the choir director in unity.

She stood before us. Waiting for us to put down our music and *watch her*. If you learn your notes at home, she was saying, when we sing together "you can follow me."

So I went home and learned my music. Back at rehearsal, I could put down the paper and raise my eyes to look. Trying to follow the director. Trying to hear Paul's lesson to the various early churches all over Rome's provinces: "May God . . . help you live in complete harmony with each other, as is fitting for followers of Christ Jesus" (Romans 15:5). Then?

"Then all of you can join together with one voice, giving praise and glory to God, the Father of our Lord Jesus Christ" (v. 6).

We could ignore Paul. Or not look at Christ. Or we could work on our unity. We'll look better. We'll get more done. More than anything, we'll sound better. Then what will our unity sound like to the world's listeners? A praise song to the choirmaster. 🌾

I feel a part of the congregation.
AMY GRANT

Unity: In Cooperation for the Kingdom

Two people are better off than one.
Ecclesiastes 4:9

For lone rangers like me (and like you?), working with others can seem more trouble than it's worth. *I can do it faster, smarter, and better all by myself.* That's how we see life—and sometimes it may be true.

But most times, the doing-it-all-by-myself part is the problem. It's not what blesses a relational God. Doing it *all* alone? Can God get the glory if I, alone, do all the work? But what happens when we cooperate?

We concentrate resources and energy. We avoid duplicating efforts. We witness for Christ by our unity. Sure, we may argue. In the end, however, we find cooperation fun.

It also feels better—even *warmer*. "Two people lying close together can keep each other warm," says Ecclesiastes 4:11. "But how can one be warm alone?"

Consider, indeed, the Many Hands organization in Washington, DC.

Started by one woman, the group now numbers one hundred, each contributing one thousand dollars a year, collectively giving a hundred thousand dollars to a local charity. The group's first gift went to Our Place, DC, which offers resources to women who have been in jail or prison as they transition back into their communities.

Or consider the Mennonite church in a Pennsylvania town whose pastor didn't complain about a neighboring church's lawn signs, placed all over town, advertising an upcoming sermon series. Instead, the Mennonite pastor wrote the other pastor, inviting his church to use the Mennonite property on a busy road to post *more* signs.

"While some may see this as a conflict of interest, I do not," that pastor wrote. He added: "I support your work and ministry and pray that it will be successful in touching lives for Jesus Christ."

As I reflect on such examples, I see their truth: You and I don't compete for God when we unite for God. We bless Him by working together to grow His Kingdom. So warm up your faith today, uniting to work with others. After all, even the Lone Ranger had help. 🌱

A one-man band never gets very big.
CHARLES A. GARFIELD

Unity: Within Our Local Church

He makes the whole body fit together perfectly.
Ephesians 4:16

What's the sign of disunity in a church? It's not pretty.

"Quarreling, jealousy, anger, selfishness, slander, gossip, arrogance, and disorderly behavior."

That is Paul's list from 2 Corinthians 12:20. Paul's concern, when he arrived at the church at Corinth, was that he'd find this hornets' nest of trouble and more. "And I will be grieved," he wrote, "because many of you have not given up your old sins. You have not repented of your impurity, sexual immorality, and eagerness for lustful pleasure" (v. 21).

Talk about a church mess.

A church in disunity has lost its center.

Jesus is pushed to the corners.

Paul warned of this danger to yet another church, at Ephesus. Paul's tactic was to name, one by one, the different gifts given by Christ to the church: apostles, prophets, evangelists, pastors, and teachers (Ephesians 4:11).

Their job? To equip God's people to do His work and build up the church.

A big job, indeed. "This will continue until we all come to such unity in our faith and knowledge of God's Son that we will be mature in the Lord, measuring up to the full and complete standard of Christ" (v. 13).

But in the meantime? Disunity runs rampant in some churches as Jesus is pushed to the corners—and sometimes right out the door.

In such settings, however, the way back to unity is through the one who "makes the whole body fit together perfectly" (v. 16). In Christ, ugly turns to grace and ashes turn to beauty; the broken no longer divided but unified. Will we let Him do this work in our hearts today? If so, we'll see the blessing and evidence in church. And the world?

The world will see the one. 🌿

He is the Peace that is above every estrangement
and cleavage and faction.
KARL BARTH

Unity: Within Our Nation

May they experience such perfect unity that the world will know that you sent me and that you love them as much as you love me.
John 17:23

One nation. Under God? Not yet. True, we give voice in America to respecting and tolerating differences, to living together by shared national values. And yet? We fail.

Red states. Blue states. Purple states. Rainbow coalitions. We're all over the map.

But who's at fault? Could it be the church—the body of Christ? Might we present such a divisive witness to nonbelievers that we fail to heal the rifts in our land, adding to disunity in our nation?

I think on such questions while driving home today from a church meeting. Our annual planning meeting went off without a hitch. No arguments. No dissension. No put-downs. All in favor say aye. A great meeting, in fact.

Was there talk, however, about working with other churches? Did I or others suggest that, in our African American church, we move beyond our racial identity, not just across town, but across the street? That we partner with churches, not just in our denomination, but in our city and state? That we take a stand against churches known by skin color, but not by creed?

To answer, I challenge myself to reflect on Jesus' precious, final prayer in John 17. His priestly prayer, as it's often called, shows a portrait of His heart. *May they experience such perfect unity . . .*

On His way to be betrayed by Judas and face death by crucifixion, Jesus prayed not for Himself—but for His disciples and "also for all who will ever believe in me through their message" (v. 20). Then the world will know Him. By our unity, they will know Him—seeing that He's their Savior too.

At my beloved church, our meeting agenda was dispatched smoothly. But, in truth, all of us skipped a line item called unity. And your church? Are you skipping the unity process too? Let's bring it back to the table, then bless our nation—and bless our Lord, and His world—by living it. 🖋

Cultivate peace and harmony with all.
GEORGE WASHINGTON

Unity: In Our Families

May God, who gives this patience and encouragement, help you live in complete harmony with each other, as is fitting for followers of Christ Jesus.
Romans 15:5

Where's the best place to practice unity?

In a broken family.

It's why Jesus, from Calvary's cross, makes sure his mother, Mary, will be cared for upon His own return to glory. It's why Paul pleads with husbands to love their wives and urges fathers not to provoke their children to anger.

It's why the story of the Bible is God's never-ceasing call to His people to return home to Him.

It's there, inside the family, that we learn the ways of unity. Forgiveness and love. Joy and peace. Patience and kindness. Goodness and faithfulness. Gentleness and, last but not least, self-control. Learn this in the family and we can see all people as kin.

How else did thirty-three miners in Chile endure—with harmony—two months trapped in a mine half a mile underground? (And while, above ground, some of their relatives bickered?) Living as brothers, the miners followed a routine designed not only to keep them mentally and physically fit, psychologists told the Associated Press, "but working together."

"Togetherness," the article noted, "is what saved the miners when an estimated 700,000 tons of rock collapsed . . . and sealed off the mine shaft above them." An elaborate rescue protocol—including hot meals, movies, and laundry service—was eventually put in place. But while a team of psychologists talked with the miners twice a day or more, the men knew "their survival ultimately depends on each other."

So they prayed. Twice daily they prayed. Calling on the Holy Trinity—the perfect One-in-Three who can keep kin safe, but also keep kin unified—they prayed.

Struggling in your family to come together? Turn from your troubles and turn in prayer, together, to the Perfect Unity. What you can't fix, the Trinity already has sealed, then healed. 🌿

Of unity, of teamwork, of faith.
SEBASTIAN PINERA

Going Deeper

God places the lonely in families.
Psalm 68:6

Is your family "at one" with each other? If not, what issues keep your family members apart?

In your local church, what issues keep the membership divided? In what matters is there unity?

What new behaviors could your blood family, and your church family, put in practice to honor Christ's prayer that His followers may all be one?

What special insight has God taught you this week about the virtue of unity?

If you'd like, write a prayer that reflects your needs regarding the virtue of unity.

If you worry about who is going to get credit, you don't get much work done.
DOROTHY HEIGHT

WISDOM

His Promise

For the LORD grants wisdom!
From his mouth come knowledge and understanding.
Proverbs 2:6

My Prayer

Your wisdom, our Everlasting God,
blesses me with understanding.
As I seek Your will,
light my path so I can
light the way also for others—
as they light my path too.

Wisdom: For a Long and Satisfying Life

*If you do this, you will live many years,
and your life will be satisfying.*
Proverbs 3:2

It's another ninetieth birthday celebration at my church. But the honoree isn't feeble. She's *running*, bounding up the center aisle of the sanctuary. Grabbing her bouquet of balloons and a basket of birthday cards, she barely takes time to receive the pastor's hug before bounding back to her seat. Energy to spare.

"Is there something in the water at this church?" the pastor asks, and everybody laughs.

Great question. In fact, in churches everywhere—where ninety-plus birthdays seem the norm, not the exception—one has to wonder. Why so much vibrancy? So much energy? So much life satisfaction?

Not a few research studies in recent years have shown, indeed, that attending weekly religious services can improve life expectancy. Religious attendance, said a 2006 study at the University of Pittsburgh Medical Center, also might be more cost effective than taking the heart medicines called statins.

So what's happening in church? More social connection? Greater meaning in life? Reduced stress through prayer? Better coping? Better support networks during life crises?

All may be factors.

But the Bible suggests a deeper reason. "My child," says the writer of the third chapter of Proverbs, "never forget the things I have taught you. Store my commands in your heart. If you do this, you will live many years, and your life will be satisfying" (vv. 1-2).

Does this mean that believers who don't live to ninety or more didn't follow God's commands? None can say. But ask a ninety-year-old church member why she can still run for balloons at ninety and she shouts her confident answer: "God!" ❦

Life is what you make of it. Always has been, always will be.
GRANDMA MOSES

Wisdom: For a Blessed Life

Getting wisdom is the wisest thing you can do!
And whatever else you do, develop good judgment.
Proverbs 4:7

At eighty-five, my uncle had notched many years on the belt called life. So he didn't panic while I ranted on about my then-favorite topic—the problem of race relations in America.

We were sitting in my mother's kitchen and I was raging—hurting from a past filled with too many put-downs and slights, too much name-calling and nay-saying. Even in Colorado, where I grew up, the ugly stamp of racism had tainted my fifties childhood enough to make me, thirtysomething at that point, not just feel hate, but nurture it. So, as I saw it, I had plenty to gripe about when it came to race.

But my uncle, who was born and reared in the South—and still lived there at that visit—looked across my mother's kitchen table and gave me a patient smile.

"You can't hate people, Patricia," he said.

A voice of wisdom. Hard-earned wisdom.

I looked at him, searching his eyes. They were aging but resolved.

"If you hate," he went on, "the only person it will hurt will be you."

I sat tight lipped, agitated but listening. Considering. Hearing. Knowing he was right, and needing somebody to finally say what he was telling me: love never fails.

My uncle's words, in fact, saved my life. In a few years, I would take his words to heart and strike out on a journey that would lead me to write a book on racial forgiveness, *My First White Friend*, then travel across the nation promoting forgiveness. Even better, that journey taught me that to love others, I could start with myself. His wise words changed my life, that is.

When I consider, indeed, the power of wisdom, I think of this moment in my late mother's kitchen when a beloved uncle cared enough about his niece to share what a lifetime had taught him: love is better than hate. A pearl of wisdom. Its value? Priceless. 🍃

I've decided to stick with love. Hate is too great a burden to bear.
MARTIN LUTHER KING JR.

Wisdom: By Asking for It

If you need wisdom, ask our generous God, and he will give it to you.
James 1:5

Smart people are smart.

But they aren't wise—not unless their wisdom comes from God. His wisdom is divine. So godly wisdom isn't knowing how to play the stock market or which car to buy or which job to pursue or the best city to live in or the best college to attend.

Godly wisdom, says James in his letter to Jewish Christians, is "first of all pure" (3:17).

In this way, it is recognizable. It sounds like God. So when my beloved uncle told me love is better than hate, I instantly knew his wisdom was divine.

As James notes, wisdom from above is "peace loving, gentle at all times, and willing to yield to others" (v. 17). A high mark, yes.

So stand up and seek it today. Enough of chasing after the world's wisdom—with its false strategies and schemes for achieving success, reaching goals, and making it in life.

Instead, says James, ask for godly wisdom, "full of mercy and good deeds" (v. 17).

Feeling the challenge? If not, here's more from the same verse:

"It shows no favoritism and is always sincere."

Not what you expected? Godly wisdom is unique, to be sure. That's why you're encouraged to ask for it. But have you ever fallen to your knees, confessing to God your frustration over not being wise in a situation?

Your confession won't surprise Him. *In fact*, He calls out to you and me today, *ask Me for wisdom*. What He teaches us will make itself known, not by its cunning, but by our peace.

God knows, to be sure, that life can be confusing. But we don't have to get lost in life's mazes. Instead, ask God for His wisdom. When? Ask Him now.

What you learn will bless His world with the surprising gift of His peace. 🌿

A prudent question is one half of wisdom.
FRANCIS BACON

Wisdom: For Safety

Wise choices will watch over you. Understanding will keep you safe.
Proverbs 2:11

What is the best wisdom you've ever heard? Priceless, perfect, and on time?

For me, the words are stamped on my heart.

You need to open your Bible.

My daddy said these words. I was just twenty-three, but I was divorcing a husband. I was a young mother with a two-year-old child. I was jobless, despite a new college degree. And I was broke, a prodigal daughter come home for atonement and renewal in my good parents' home.

Come on back, they said. So I went.

Then they did the remarkable. They never once said "we told you so." They just put up a crib in my old bedroom, bought baby food and diapers, ordered nursery books and toys. Then my daddy, a tall brown man with strong arms and quiet ways, spoke in his true voice the words that would change my life. "You need to open your Bible."

Nothing more. No fancy words. No fussing or lectures. On that morning, Daddy just quietly left me in his living room, giving me a choice. So I lifted the big Bible from its place on my parents' coffee table and I opened it, surprised that the words of my recovery had been underlined years before with my daddy's black-ink fountain pen.

There is therefore now no condemnation to those who are in Christ Jesus (Romans 8:1, NKJV).

I saw my daddy's past, linked up with my mother's dreams, all tied together with my future and underscored in ink years before by my father's hopeful hand.

And we know that all things work together for good to them that love God.

Through fresh tears, I dared then to ask God to work good in me. Looking back, I can say that He answered. But first came wise words. Just a few. 🌿

Wisdom is not wordy.
GARY AMIRAULT

Wisdom: With Great Joy

Joyful is the person who finds wisdom.
Proverbs 3:13

Joy and wisdom. A pair of soul mates? Could that be right?

In fact, we find in our Bibles promise after promise linking the two together. *Joyful is the person who finds wisdom.*

Even a onetime mention would have caught my attention. But I look closer and there it is again (italics added to each verse below):

"For wisdom will enter your heart, and knowledge will fill you with *joy*" (Proverbs 2:10).

Then again:

"The man who loves wisdom brings *joy* to his father" (Proverbs 29:3).

Then again:

"God gives wisdom, knowledge, and *joy* to those who please him" (Ecclesiastes 2:26).

This last reference is especially compelling. The book of Ecclesiastes, filled as it is with sorrow and melancholy and joy, eventually settles on the importance of balance in life. As the *NLT Study Bible* puts it: "It is exactly this balance of joy and sorrow that characterizes the wise person who reflects on all of life and understands its complexities in a fallen world."

Life is tough, indeed. At its worst, it can feel unbearable.

But those who pursue the wisdom of God will arrive, despite troubles, at joy.

Do we see the extraordinary lesson?

In the midst of troubles, we do not pursue their solution—but we pursue wisdom in the midst of the trials. Then what do we experience? God's joy.

Seems illogical. But our wisdom pursuit blesses God. Then He blesses us with joy. 🌿

Joy is the serious business of Heaven.
C. S. LEWIS

Wisdom: In the Person of Christ

Christ is the power of God and the wisdom of God. This foolish plan
of God is wiser than the wisest of human plans.
1 Corinthians 1:24-25

Still failing at wisdom? Jesus knows. He understands our frustration with messing up, making wrong choices, trying hard to live wisely but too often missing the mark. That's why He came—not just to save us from sin but, in part, to deliver us from our own fumbling stupidity.

Sound crazy? In fact, Christ *is* the wisdom of God.

This "foolish plan of God," as Paul describes the message of salvation through Christ, seems to some downright ridiculous. Yet it is "wiser than the wisest of human plans, and God's weakness is stronger than the greatest of human strength" (1 Corinthians 1:25).

So that idea, that all of God's wisdom resides in Christ, confounds "the philosophers, the scholars, and the world's brilliant debaters," but also the Jews "who ask for signs from heaven" and the Greeks "who seek human wisdom" (vv. 20, 22).

So it is with us.

We look to our own understanding, our own intelligence, our own degrees and certificates, licenses and credentials as proof we can solve our problems—including the biggest problem, our sin.

Instead, when such wisdom fails, we do best to pursue Jesus. "For our benefit," Paul writes, "God made him to be wisdom itself" (v. 30).

This was good news to Corinthian believers, these new Christians whose congregation was diverse but not wealthy or important. Now came Paul with a reassuring message: Christ is all. With Him, wisdom starts and ends.

Pursue Him today, confounding those who see Christ's message as wrong and the Cross as weak. His wisdom will not only prove you right, it will bless you and His Kingdom with divine understanding and unspeakable joy. ❧

The wonder of a single snowflake outweighs the
wisdom of a million meteorologists.
FRANCIS BACON

Going Deeper

If you listen to constructive criticism, you will be at home among the wise.
Proverbs 15:31

Wisdom may come with old age, as many say. But what are ways you can acquire wisdom now, regardless of your age?

In what ways would wisdom make a difference in your personal life? Your professional life?

What gems of wisdom have you been taught by family or associates? What wisdom have you sought to pass down to others?

What special insight has God taught you this week about the virtue of unity?

If you'd like, write a prayer that reflects your needs regarding the virtue of wisdom.

If you have knowledge, let others light their candles in it.
MARGARET FULLER

COURAGE

His Promise

Be strong and courageous. . . . I will be with you.
Deuteronomy 31:23

My Prayer

Inspire me, O Mighty Rock,
to seek true strength and courage
in You.

Courage: To Face the Formidable

So Esther approached and touched the tip of the scepter.
Esther 5:2, NIV

"Who knows," said Mordecai to Queen Esther, his adopted daughter, "if perhaps you were made queen for just such a time as this?" (4:14).

Who knows? What if perhaps you were made—a teacher, preacher, missionary, doctor, writer, artist, singer, composer, leader, parent, coach—for such a time as this?

Who knows?

God knows.

So even though God isn't mentioned by name even once in the book of Esther, His character informs every plot point of that story, culminating in Esther's famous words.

"If I must die, I must die" (v. 16).

If she met the challenge, Queen Esther would thwart a plot to wipe out the Jewish population of her time. Yet Esther risked everything to warn the king of the plot, revealing that she was Jewish too.

Yet how many times have we failed to speak out against lies in our households, workplaces, communities, and nations? How often have we turned a deaf ear to injustice?

Esther could've turned away too. But after preparing her heart, fasting for three days, she rose to the challenge. Did the fasting give her courage? Or, as some have said, did the fasting put her into communion with the Spirit of the one who inspires and defines our courage?

Who knows? God knows.

Just as God knows what you're capable of doing, if you will but walk like Him.

Esther met her challenge. Now what about you? Stand up today with courage, blessing God and His Kingdom with fortitude and strength, reaching with courage to the King of Glory—knowing that as you face the formidable, God is already going ahead before you. 🔥

You must do the thing you think you cannot do.
ELEANOR ROOSEVELT

Courage: To Face the Fearsome

God is our refuge and strength, always ready to help in times of trouble.
Psalm 46:1

Trapped under seven hundred thousand tons of solid rock, half a mile underground for sixty-nine days, thirty-three miners in Chile endure their weeks' long ordeal in the summer of 2010 with real courage? But how?

I ask this question while watching on TV, along with millions around the world, as rescuers lift the miners, one by one, to safety. Afterward, days will go by before the miners meet TV cameras or give interviews or write books to shed light on their ordeal.

But as I watch, gaping with awe at the fuzzy TV picture of the solid rock that entrapped them, I believe I find my answer for their courage.

Those miners must've realized that the solid rock wasn't their tomb. It was their fortress. (Rock in Hebrew means "fortress.") So while they waited for rescue, the solid rock surrounding them wasn't their enemy, but their strength.

Indeed, this solid rock was Jesus—their defense and shelter, their refuge and keeping-power deliverance.

Jesus' tomb, indeed, wasn't His grave, but our door—our Door to abundant life.

Psalm 46 reveals this perspective. So if you're feeling trapped today, encased in what feels like a solid tomb of trouble, let the words of this powerful psalm turn your entrapment into courage. How? By knowing this:

God *is* our refuge and strength. "The God of Israel is our fortress" (v. 11).

Shielded by His strong arms of safety, get up and wait for His rescue with confidence, and even with joy. Losing hope? Think of thirty-three miners, waiting under solid rock and singing—Elvis Presley songs and hymns—for their deliverance.

Then sing Psalm 46, letting its words of assurance bless you to the core with rock-solid courage. 🕯

> Rock of Ages, cleft for me,
> Let me hide myself in thee.
> AUGUSTUS M. TOPLADY

Courage: To Witness for Christ

For God has not given us a spirit of fear and timidity,
but of power, love, and self-discipline.
2 Timothy 1:7

In a Roman prison, Paul looked at the end of his life and sat down to write a letter. Addressing it to his delegate Timothy, he used sweet words, calling him: "My dear son" (v. 2).

A warm letter, yes. It would have to be. Paul was passing the torch of ministry to Timothy, asking the young gospel preacher to return to Rome, where, almost certainly, he would face his own persecution, quite likely unto death.

Have you ever received such a summons? "Come take over my ministry, but you'll probably die doing it."

A bold and audacious request. But Paul urged Timothy to respond just as boldly.

Fan those flames, he said, beseeching Timothy to use the spiritual gift— namely, preaching the gospel—that God gave him.

Our own spiritual gifts, likewise, are valuable to God's Kingdom. But do they sit cold and unused or untested? Or will we get up today and speak life? Will we, indeed, breathe life into our gifts, nurturing and cultivating them as we're inspired by the Holy Spirit, until they burst into roaring flames— warming the body of Christ and the world?

It's no time to be modest, in other words. As Paul wrote: "For God has not given us a spirit of fear and timidity."

As small and nervous and insignificant and frightened as we can feel sometimes about our ministries and spiritual gifts, courage is our marching order.

So get up! Stand tall. Go fight. Throw back your shoulders today. Then sing your songs. Preach your sermons. Teach that gospel. Write those poems. Build that church. Plant your gardens. Bake your down-home potluck tuna casseroles. With fear? Bless God today instead with a ministry of power. ❦

Christianity is a battle—not a dream.
WENDELL PHILLIPS

Courage: That Claims Christ

The LORD is my light and my salvation—so why should I be afraid?
Psalm 27:1

She was just seventeen. Too young to be a hero. Too young to suffer multiple gunshots to the head, chest, arm, and leg.

But at Columbine High School in Littleton, Colorado, on April 20, 1999, a cute teenager named Rachel Scott was gunned down by two classmates, tragically cutting short her promising life. Rachel's assailant and his classmate gunned down eleven more students and one teacher. Another twenty-one students were injured, with three others hurt escaping the massacre that killed Rachel.

Too young. All of them.

The story of Rachel Scott, however—and those of the other victims and survivors—has become not one of unredeemed tragedy, but of awe-inspiring courage.

"God is using Rachel as a vehicle," her father Darrell Scott told *Time* magazine. "If I believed for one second that God had forsaken my daughter or that he had gone to sleep or that he wasn't aware, I would be one of the angriest men in America."

Instead, Darrell Scott helped launch Rachel's Challenge, a national campaign promoting kindness and compassion—one person at a time—in "a chain reaction" of positive cultural change in schools, businesses, and communities.

Your own response to life's hurts, wounds, and pain? Anger or courage?

Let us learn from Rachel Scott, Darrell Scott, and others who face tragedy with courage. How? Let God win. Let the power of hate crumble under the brave message of love. Then God wins. 🕊

I am not going to apologize for speaking the name of Jesus. . . .
If I have to sacrifice everything . . . I will.
RACHEL SCOTT

Courage: To Believe and Serve God

As she listened to us, the Lord opened her heart.
Acts 16:14

What makes a fireman run into a burning building?

What makes a soldier face enemy fire to rescue a fallen soldier?

What makes a schoolkid stand up for a child facing bullies on a playground?

We see the answer in the Bible story of Lydia. A wealthy merchant of purple cloth, rich enough to own a nice home, she is mentioned in only two short passages in the Bible.

As she listened with other women to Paul and Silas talk about Jesus, the Lord "opened her heart" and she accepted what Paul was saying. Then she took a risk.

Without any recorded hesitation, she invited Paul and Silas to stay in her home.

Despite the risk of harboring a controversial religious apostle.

Despite the potential costs to her business.

Despite the possible physical threats she may have faced.

What made her open her home despite it all?

She believed in the Lord—yes, in the Cross of Christ and its power to redeem.

Such belief undergirds every moral stand and physical risk ever taken by a believer. Thus, belief is why Queen Esther risked all to speak to the king on behalf of her Jewish people. It's why Lydia opened her home. Why Harriet Tubman risked capture to free slaves and why Rosa Parks refused to sit at the back of a segregated bus. Why Jim Elliot and four other missionaries risked their lives in the jungles of Ecuador to witness to a primitive tribe that killed them. It's why, indeed, Elliot's wife, Elisabeth, returned to the jungle, later living with the same tribe that killed her husband.

Standing on belief, these courageous believers served. Now in what do we believe? We can answer the question by blessing God with a clear, firm answer. Then God help us to stand up and live our answers. ❦

There is nothing worth living for, unless it is worth dying for.
ELISABETH ELLIOT

Courage: To Move in God's Character

The LORD of Heaven's Armies is here among us;
the God of Israel is our fortress.
Psalm 46:7

"The Little Engine That Could," the popular children's story about bravery, optimism, and hard work, appeared under the title "Thinking One Can" in a 1906 Sunday school publication, *Wellspring for Young People.*

Yet the church-related version of the classic story isn't surprising.

In the story, a stranded train of cars needs help from an engine to pull it up and over a mountain to its destination. After other engines refuse to try, a little engine rises to the task. As it says, puffing along, "I think I can, I think I can, I think I can." We know the story well.

But I reflected all week on real people who, like the little engine, took on seemingly impossible odds and won. Still, I wondered: How did they do it?

What gave Queen Esther and Rachel Scott, Rosa Parks and Jim Elliot, Lydia of the Bible and the thirty-three miners in Chile, and countless known and unknown servants and saints of God the courage to hitch themselves to big jobs and rise to the top with courage?

I found my answer in my own Sunday school publication. In an issue of *Precepts for Living*, the uniform lesson guide used at my church, I pondered this comment about why we need not fear "when earthquakes come and the mountains crumble into the sea" (Psalm 46:2).

Our courage over fear, said the lesson, is not based on our own ability to solve our problems. "But our courage is based on the character of God." He is with us, living with us, in us, through us—giving us the moral and physical resolve to look impossibility in the eye and say without wavering: "I—think—I—can. I—think—I—can."

Then, like the little engine, we will get up and bless God today with the words His character inspires: *I thought I could.* And I did. 🦋

Live your beliefs and you can turn the world around.
HENRY DAVID THOREAU

Going Deeper

Wait patiently for the LORD. Be brave and courageous.
Yes, wait patiently for the LORD.
Psalm 27:14

What or whom do you fear?

If courage reflects the character of God, what are ways you can deepen God's character in your own heart, allowing you to face life with more courage?

Describe the most courageous thing you've ever done. What remains in your life demanding greater courage from you? Explain.

What special insight has God taught you this week about the virtue of courage?

If you'd like, write a prayer that reflects your needs regarding the virtue of courage.

Courage is being scared to death . . . and saddling up anyway.
JOHN WAYNE

PERSISTENCE

His Promise

Everyone who endures to the end will be saved.
Matthew 10:22

My Prayer

When I falter, Holy King,
revive my faith,
blessing me to endure always in You.

Persistence: To Hold On to Faith

But the one who endures to the end will be saved.
Matthew 24:13

Don't give up. So easy to say. Just three little words. So Jesus, to be sure, knew it was easier said than done. He even warned His disciples about what was coming: wars and rumors of wars. Nations warring against nations. Famine and earthquakes all over the world. Even more, "you will be arrested, persecuted, and killed" (v. 9).

Could it get any worse for these fledgling followers?

Or for us?

Some days we feel defeated, as if we're hanging by a thread, swinging by a sliver of lint on a proverbial rope. Other days every anti-Christian power in the world seems to scream in our faces, with a rage that reminds us of what Jesus predicted:

We will be hated. Sin will be rampant. Love will turn cold. False prophets will preach and self-promote. That and worse can be expected for those who profess Christ.

When our faith walk seems at its lowest, however, and when it feels senseless to profess a faith that the whole world seems to ridicule, question, and attack, *don't give up.*

When prayers seem to go unanswered and problems seem to get worse not better, *don't give up.*

When obstacles grow higher and land mines explode louder, *don't give up.*

Those three little words would seem not enough to keep us going.

But Jesus Himself spoke this sentiment—and He still speaks: "The one who endures to the end will be saved." Saved from what? From every enemy. Every attack. Every disappointment. Every challenge. Every battle, burden, and betrayal.

So let's open our hearts today to the blessing of His promise: faith in Christ still saves the lost, but first the faithful. 🌱

A little hail and wind can't run me off.
WILLIAM NOTTER

Persistence: In Living Right

*So let's not get tired of doing what is good. At just the right time we will
reap a harvest of blessing if we don't give up.*

Galatians 6:9

In our spiritual liberty, Christians can be tempted to justify sin.

I'll be forgiven anyway.

My salvation is safe.

I harvest so much fruit, any sin I commit isn't that big a deal.

We can justify all day and all night. We can twist our freedom in Christ
so far we're able to qualify almost any act, arguing that we're "covered" by
the blood and by faith . . . and, well, we know how such arguments can go.

Especially if others are sinning. And especially if those others are sitting right there in church—sitting in the next pew—or even sinning in
the next pew.

But don't be misled. Paul writes in Galatians 6:7, "You will always harvest
what you plant." Sin, that is, only reaps "decay and death" (v. 8).

Sure, we in Christ are forgiven. Sure, we're saved by faith and not works.
Sure, we're covered by the blood. But sin always kills—our hopes and dreams.
Families and friendships. Bodies and minds. Churches and neighborhoods.
Communities and nations.

Sin always kills.

So don't get tired of doing what is good.

Seems obvious, doesn't it? As people of faith and followers of Christ, our
commitment to righteous living should be a given. But Paul cautions us.
Don't take right living for granted. Deliberately, instead, stick with right.

When we get tired, stick with right. When sin is easier, stick with right.
Let the Holy Spirit lead the way, but stick with right. Then, at the right
time, Paul writes, we'll reap a harvest of blessing, grown in the soil of His
persistent grace. 🌿

The best way to fight against sin is to fight it on our knees.

PHILIP HENRY

Persistence: In Seeking God

Search for the LORD and for his strength;
continually seek him.
1 Chronicles 16:11

Whom did King Saul seek when he needed guidance? The troubled leader of Israel turned to a medium for wisdom. That means Saul sought a soothsayer who claimed to talk to spirits communicating with the dead.

No kidding.

The first king of Israel, who could have persistently sought God Almighty Himself for divine guidance on every aspect of his life, instead "consulted a medium instead of asking the LORD for guidance" (1 Chronicles 10:13-14).

So he died in shame, the chronicler says, falling on his own sword.

Then came King David. A man after God's own heart, David exhorted the Israelites to search, not for mediums, but "for the LORD." Continually.

Or in the words of the King James translation of the Holy Bible: "Seek the LORD and his strength, seek his face continually." Persistently, indeed.

This isn't idle advice. Not then. Not now.

David knew personally how Saul turned from seeking God to seeking other sources of help. The result? Saul's life went from good to bad to worse. A promising leader with greater potential, Saul ended up a miserable, despised, dead failure.

His mistake? Talking to spirits. Thus disobeying God.

Are you hearing this today? Embracing the Bible promise—that those who seek God continually *lack no good thing*? Are you seeking continually, not psychic spirits, but God's Holy Spirit—your Comforter and your Help? Seeking the Lord continually, indeed, for the best reason ever—because He may be found? How?

Continually. Persistently. So don't give up. Then as we keep seeking, He will bless. 🌿

> The art of love is largely the art of persistence.
> ALBERT ELLIS

Persistence: While Waiting on God

Blessed are those who wait for his help.
Isaiah 30:18

If you're sitting down, waiting on God to move, *get up*. Then get moving.

Waiting on God, as the Bible presents it, isn't about sitting around, twirling our thumbs, whistling a tune until God acts.

At least four ways to "wait" on God deserve our attention, in fact, especially when it comes to the concept of persistence. Consider first, however, the Hebrew word *qavah*, meaning "to bind together two things"—hope and patience—like "a twisted rope." These two, hope and patience, should be so entwined, that as we wait we live patiently in hope. A beautiful concept.

But hold on, you say. I'm patient and hoping. But what should I be *doing*? Consider four things:

First, serve. That's what we waiters do. We attend to God, just as Old Testament priests attended. So while we wait, likewise, let's go serve. In church. At work. In our communities. While we wait for God's help, serve God and God's Kingdom. Then while we serve, God will move.

Second, learn. "Study this Book of Instruction continually. Meditate on it day and night" (Joshua 1:8). If Joshua, Moses' successor, needed to study God's Word while waiting for God to fight and win battles, we certainly need to do the same.

Third, love. Ah, yes. The hard thing.

But loving is what you and I are called to do anyway. So waiting on God to move in your marriage? Love your spouse. Waiting on God to move on your job? Love your coworkers. Waiting on God to move in your world? Love His. But also love Him.

So, fourth, stand. *Be still, and know that I am God!* (Psalm 46:10). Rest in His presence and enjoy Him as you wait. Worship Him. Adore Him. Then don't be surprised: God will bless your waiting with His power. 🕊

While I wait, I am standing on the rock.
J. C. RYLE

Persistence: For Power in Prayer

The earnest prayer of a righteous person has great power.
James 5:16

Great power. Not measly power. That's what the world needs. That's what we crave to give. But while we're working overtime to acquire great power for the world, the book of James offers the clear, pure way to experience it.

Pray. Persistently.

Not begging prayer. Not fingers-crossed prayer. Pray persistently instead, seeking God's Holy Spirit, to live right. Or as prayer warriors across centuries remind us, living right persistently *is* prayer. Andrew Murray said it as well as anybody: "My prayer will depend on my life." That is, "If I do what God says, God will do what I say."

Does it get any clearer? Live right. Keep praying. Persistently. That's the way.

Jesus taught this beautiful truth in His great lesson on prayer. It's in the eleventh chapter of Luke, where the disciples—aware that Jesus prayed with power while they often didn't—pleaded: "Lord, teach *us* to pray" (v. 1, italics added).

Of course, Jesus then taught the Lord's Prayer—which most of us know by rote.

But what followed? Jesus tells a story, the parable of the importunate friend. That's the shameless friend who knocks at midnight at his neighbor's door, pleading to borrow bread for an unexpected houseguest. How much bread? Three loaves. This guy is shameless, for sure. He wants *more* than he needs. In fact, he wants it all.

But Jesus shines a spotlight on him. With exactly such persistence, He says, we should pray. In fact, keep on asking "and you will receive what you ask for." Even more, "keep on seeking, and you will find." In addition, "keep on knocking, and the door will be opened to you" (v. 9).

Does that mean praying the same prayer over and over? Of course not. Instead, pray persistently until *you* change. As you bless God with your changed prayer, He will answer with power. 🌿

Asking nothing of tomorrow except "Thy will be done."
HELEN STEINER RICE

Persistence: In Finishing the Race

*So, my dear brothers and sisters, be strong and immovable . . . for you
know that nothing you do for the Lord is ever useless.*
1 Corinthians 15:58

How do you write a long book? One page at a time.

How do you paint a picture? Sew a dress? Bake a cake? Paint a room?
Build a building? Start a business? Raise a child? Save a soul?

One persistent step at a time.

I watched this principle at work when my husband and I renovated our
aging house, making room for my beloved mother—by God's grace—to
move in with us.

The contractor listened. Our project was big and messy. One aspect meant
raising a "sunken" living room, its outdated step-down design a hazard for
my eighty-six-year-old mother. But raising a living room? How would the
contractor do *that*?

He smiled. Then he showed me his punch list. His step-by-step list.

"That's how I work," he explained. "Take one step. Then the next step.
Then the next step. One at a time—until I finish the whole job."

Just like writing a book. The first time I tried, I sat—staring at my computer—for one long, hot, fruitless, frustrating, hair-pulling summer. Then
around August, it hit me. I'm not writing a book. I'm writing one page at
a time. By God's grace. One page a day. My new goal. So I sat down and
wrote. One page. Then the next. Soon, I saw progress.

Then after a long year, I saw a finished book.

My contractor, likewise, showed up that first day. With workers, he ham-
mered a two-by-four frame into the living room floor, not raising the floor—
but building a higher new one. Not distracted by struggling to reach the
finish line, he enjoyed every step. Finished on time, too. If that sounds like
a useful life in Christ, it's because it is. Daily persistence. One step at a time.
Bless God with me today for His persistent, wondrous path. 🕯

Persistence is the twin sister of excellence.
MARABEL MORGAN

Going Deeper

He endured the cross, disregarding its shame. Now he is seated
in the place of honor beside God's throne.
Hebrews 12:2

What, if anything, makes you give up?

When you consider the promise of Jesus, that those who endure through
challenges, disappointments, temptations, and fears will be saved, how do
you respond when you're tempted to give up?

In your life, what deserves more persistence on your part?

What special insight has God taught you this week about the virtue
of persistence?

If you'd like, write a prayer that reflects your needs regarding the virtue
of persistence.

Never, never, never, never give up.
WINSTON CHURCHILL

HARD WORK

His Promise

Good planning and hard work lead to prosperity.
Proverbs 21:5

My Prayer

Bless You, Living God,
for the provision of work
and for the path of light
that leads to godly planning and prosperity.

Hard Work: As God Calls You

And the LORD said, "This is the one; anoint him."
1 Samuel 16:12

We're all supposed to work. Always were. Even if we don't like to work—or don't like our jobs. Or can't find a job. Still, we're all supposed to work. Work, in fact, is why God placed Adam in the Garden of Eden—"to tend and watch over it" (Genesis 2:15), sanctifying the dignity of work from then to now.

Yet most Americans don't like their jobs. "About a million people a day phone in sick—and it's not the bird flu," *Forbes* magazine reported in 2005.

The problem? Some workers feel disrespected, not liked, or micro-managed. Others are in the wrong jobs. Others work for a wrong reason. But joyous workers? They feel called to their work. Bad boss or not. They feel called—*and* they answer.

Like David.

As one of the seven sons of Jesse, he was overlooked when Samuel showed up to anoint Israel's next king. And no surprise. Out in the fields, tending sheep in a smelly pasture, David didn't compare to Jesse's dressed-up, strapping other sons. Outwardly, those others looked right for the job. But God looks at the heart (1 Samuel 16:7). Indeed, as each of Jesse's first six sons passed by Samuel, the prophet recognized that God had not chosen any of them.

Perplexed, Samuel asked: "Are these all the sons you have?" (v. 11).

Jesse's older sons were healthy and work-ready, good to go as they saw it. But they weren't called by God to be king. What does that mean for you? Wait for God's true call—but keep working. Work in the field, that is—not for prestige or riches, commute times or location, or all the other reasons people seek a job. Work, instead, as a believer, to get ready for God's true call. In fact, ask Him: *What are You calling me to do?*

Bless God today with that plea. Bless Him with your field work. Then wait for His call. Even when it surprises you. Even when it shocks others. Whatever the job, if He calls, He will anoint and empower you with the heart and job that gives Him the glory. 🔥

I haven't been waiting for stardom. I've been working.
MORGAN FREEMAN

Hard Work: That Blesses Others

*Use your hands for good hard work, and then give generously
to others in need.*
Ephesians 4:28

The "worst" jobs in America are beyond description in a G-rated book. Poultry processor? High "ick" factor. Forensic entomologist? Maggots and blood. Garbage worker? More maggots—and maybe blood, too.

You get the picture.

Yet poultry processing, for example, remains one of the fastest-growing jobs in the country. People who need to work line up to apply for such jobs, putting to shame any of us who ever complained about a job in an office.

Yet *any* good, hard work, says the apostle Paul, should be judged, not by its salary or ambience—but on whether it enables us to "give generously to others in need."

Puts a whole new spin on working, doesn't it?

Working to give back to others transforms our work lives, but especially our prayer lives—taking us from "bless me so I can earn" to "bless me so I can give."

The entire verse of Ephesians 4:28 turns, indeed, on a provocative point, not about work—but about theft. "If you are a thief, quit stealing. Instead, use your hands for good hard work, and then give generously to others in need."

The matter-of-fact instruction reflects the matter-of-fact sin that non-believers practiced when Paul wrote this letter. From lying to cursing to thieving, pagans were bound by sin. But don't live like these Gentiles, Paul says, for "their minds are full of darkness; they wander far from the life God gives" (v. 18).

So stop telling lies. Don't hate. Stop cursing. And thieves, *start working*.

Are you stealing from God today? Work hard at an honest job. Then bless others. Your generous gifts will bless God and you, far more than your job. 🔥

We must work every day, whether we feel like it or not, otherwise when it
comes time to . . . listen to the work, we will not be able to heed it.
MADELEINE L'ENGLE

Hard Work: That's Empowered and Inspired by God

*And the Spirit of the LORD came powerfully upon David
from that day on.*
1 Samuel 16:13

Why do some people succeed on the job? And others fail? Do such questions stir up nagging, uncomfortable emotions?

In fact, four of five people are in the wrong job, some experts say. Others manage to love their work and thrive in it. Says film communications expert Ted Baehr in his book, *So You Want to Be in Pictures*: "These findings . . . are nothing more than an affirmation of the fact that God has designed each of us for a particular purpose."

In fact, says Baehr, God "wants us to be joyous and enjoy our work."

And if you don't? Go on a prayer journey with God to find out why.

As you examine your life in prayer, you are likely to see clear evidence of the special gifts and talents granted to you by God. For "all authority comes from God," says Romans 13:1, and "a spiritual gift is given to each of us so we can help each other" (1 Corinthians 12:7).

A Spirit-filled life, in other words, dignifies whatever honest work we do. But will we work hard and stick to godly values—despite delays and discouragement—until God inspires a Spirit-filled breakthrough? And so we can help each other?

To be sure, hard work is exactly that. Hard. Work. But God's blessed Holy Spirit empowers us to keep going, during downturns and more. That's what happened to David. Life after his anointing as king was hardly smooth sailing. The current king, Saul, kept trying to kill him. After Saul's death, everybody from David's wife to his son conspired to bring him down.

But empowered by God's Spirit, David overcame every obstacle that confronted him at work—including his own sin. Are you overwhelmed by work, by being in the wrong job, or by not having a job? Pray for God's Spirit to direct your job journey. Then work hard to help others. It's a combination that God will grace with His power. 🌿

When love and skill work together, expect a masterpiece.
JOHN RUSKIN

Hard Work: To Live with Independence

*A hard worker has plenty of food, but a person who chases
fantasies has no sense.*
Proverbs 12:11

Jesus worked most of His life as a carpenter.

The apostle Paul worked as a tentmaker.

Simple and honest work, yes. This self-employment, using humble but practical skills, was described by Paul this way: "We worked hard day and night so we would not be a burden to any of you" (2 Thessalonians 3:8).

Yet in Thessalonica, many new believers sat around all day, waiting for Jesus to return and demanding support from the church to meet their living expenses—or living off the patronage of non-Christians who paid them as "clients." In return for their financial and social support, these non-Christians expected their clients to support their causes and obligations—some of which would have been at odds with the beliefs of the Thessalonian believers.

Bad system? In fact, it was dysfunctional, demoralizing, and a drain on the soul of the people and the church. Such attitudes still hurt people and churches. As Paul put it:

"We command such people and urge them in the name of the Lord Jesus Christ to settle down and work to earn their own living" (v. 12).

Not a fancy idea. If you work, you will eat. But in this era of reality TV and overnight stardom—with people fantasizing about celebrity status and fame—the simple value of doing ordinary, humble, day-to-day work gets forgotten. Even among Christians, some see the simple, unglamorous jobs as too lowly. Others seek to work as little as manageable for as much gain as possible while working to become ministry "stars."

Avoid such a life, Paul urged. And stay away from such people, he added.

Far better to get up every day and do good hard work. The benefits?

Money for food, says Proverbs 12:11. But also the food of heaven—joy and peace, respect and honor, provision and promise. Your work isn't fancy? All the better. From house painting to tile laying, hairstyling to hammering, cake baking to street sweeping, hard work counts in the Kingdom. So work hard today. Then get ready to feast. 🌿

Learn to do common things uncommonly well.
GEORGE WASHINGTON CARVER

Hard Work: For Body, Mind, and Soul

People who work hard sleep well.
Ecclesiastes 5:12

Lack inspiration for hard work? Just look outdoors. That's what I do every Friday when I see our hardworking landscaper, a Vietnamese immigrant named Nguyen, show up like clockwork all summer to cut our little plot of grass. Rain or shine. Year after year. With a smile.

That's how Nguyen works, growing his business from a one-man venture to a citywide operation employing a host of other hardworking relatives.

In that way, Nguyen has put his children through college, purchased a home, maintained his business, and learned to speak English. I suspect he sleeps real well, too.

Maybe, as he works, he's noticed nature's hard workers—little ants, lifting loads ten to fifty times their own weight. Or honeybees toiling ten hours a day every six days, each gathering nectar for only a thimbleful of honey. For sure, Nguyen seems to thrive at his work—body and soul. As years pass, he seems stronger, happier, better.

Promoting hard work in his *Poor Richard's Almanac*, Benjamin Franklin coined this delightful phrase: "The used key is always bright."

As Franklin put it: "Sloth, like rust, consumes faster than labor wears." Still drumming home his point, he concluded: "God gives all things to industry."

Franklin credited his own success in so many areas—as author and printer, politician and postmaster, scientist, inventor, civic activist, states-man, diplomat, and more—to his lifetime devotion to work. In contrast, sloth, "by bringing on diseases," shortens life "absolutely," Franklin wrote. Or as he famously said: "Early to bed and early to rise makes a man healthy, wealthy, and wise."

Long before Franklin, however, the Bible promised hard work's many blessings, plus a bonus: good sleep. Are you convinced yet of this virtue's value? If not, bless God by getting up today, for God's glory, empowered by His Spirit, just to work hard.

Then let your body bless you tonight with sweet dreams. ❦

A well-spent day brings happy sleep.
LEONARDO DA VINCI

Hard Work: As unto the Lord

Remember that the Lord will give you an inheritance as your reward.
Colossians 3:24

I needed a tile layer. A good tile layer. A trustworthy tile layer. I wasn't afraid, in fact, to pray for exactly that for our old-school bathroom.

So there he was. A young man. A fellow church member. He posted on Facebook photos of tile work he'd just completed. He bragged, in fact, about one job he'd done, noting "how level and flat this 300 square feet of tile is. We pride ourselves on good work!"

Praise the Lord. Good work. That's precisely what I needed.

Good work. It seems so hard to find these days. A worker who shows up on time. A worker who finishes on time. Who doesn't steal—like the subcontractor we hired once who didn't pay his workers, so they came back for more money, forcing us to pay twice.

Good work. *Please, God.* I prayed hard.

Then the young man from church showed up, ready to work. And on time.

As I told him, "I just want it done right."

He smiled, showing me that "done right" was his watchword.

Still, I joked. Or tried to. "It'll be right because you'll see me at church every Sunday." He smiled again. "Nope," he said.

He looked me in the eye. "It will be right because I have to answer to Him."

He pointed upward, showing me what I needed to see. *I'm working for Him.*

As unto the Lord.

Paul taught this principle to new believers—that we work willingly and sincerely, "at whatever [we] do," in reverent fear of the Lord, "as though [we] were working for the Lord rather than for people" (v. 23). Our young tile worker did exactly that. May God bless him, but also us, to work this same perfect way on this day. The reward? An inheritance of life in Him. 🔥

The work done by a worshiper will have eternity in it.
A. W. TOZER

Going Deeper

Work hard so you can present yourself to God and receive his approval.
2 Timothy 2:15

What kind of work do you do? Do you feel called by God to do it? Explain.

"Lazy people are soon poor," the Bible says, but "hard workers get rich" (Proverbs 10:4). Do you think the word *rich* when described as a reward for work refers to money? Explain.

Retirement isn't a practice in the Bible, yet it's part of modern culture. So what do you think of retirement? Will you still work after you retire? If so, doing what?

What special insight has God taught you this week about the virtue of hard work?

If you'd like, write a prayer that reflects your needs regarding the virtue of hard work.

This is our work—to wake people up.
CATHERINE BOOTH

ORDER AND DISCIPLINE

His Promise

*Physical training is good, but training
for godliness is much better,
promising benefits in this life
and in the life to come.*
1 Timothy 4:8

My Prayer

When I get weak and undisciplined, Lord,
draw me back to You, O Christ,
for Your promised benefits are eternal.

Order and Discipline: By God's Example

Then God looked over all he had made, and he saw that it was
excellent in every way. This all happened on the sixth day.
Genesis 1:31

Looking for order in your life? Just open a Bible. But don't just open it. Read it and marvel. That's what I finally did. After so much disorder in my disorderly life, I turned to the first page of a *One Year Bible*. There, in the story of God in the first chapter of Genesis, was His orderly hand, creating everything by design. By plan. By one disciplined day after another.

Then God looked over all He had made and God saw it was excellent. "This all happened on the sixth day."

Nothing random, that is, happened during Creation—as God ordained it.

And I marveled: God *is* Order. And I wasn't. So from page one, I sat down humbled to read the story of God's order, surprised I hadn't seen His order or His story quite that way before. And I marveled.

Because everything God did in that story was planned, ordained, anointed, and right. Or as Proverbs 1:2 declared on day one of my *One Year* reading: "The purpose of these proverbs is to teach people wisdom and discipline."

Discipline with wisdom. Such a godly concept. So we talk about it. Then we give it pretty good lip service. But if we're looking for its pattern and type, we should look to God.

I'd once thought, instead, that "order" meant stifling creativity. But on the most creative day ever in the universe, God luxuriated in order. So why wouldn't you and I? Indeed, I hadn't recognized His order until I set out to seek Him anew, reading His Word all the way through—starting from the first page—then following an orderly journey to the last. Will you read it that way too? Consider my humble suggestion. Then bless God by learning from His Word as you study the gorgeous order of His will.

Then bless us, O God, to follow. 🌿

The study of God's Word, for the purpose of discovering God's will, is the
secret discipline which has formed the greatest characters.
JAMES WADDEL ALEXANDER

Order and Discipline: In All Things

Do all for the glory of God.
1 Corinthians 10:31

The disciplined life? Not for sissies.

Benjamin Franklin was just a boy when he realized that. So, at age twenty and making a living on his own as a printer, he made a list of Thirteen Virtues to guide his way. Then he sought to follow them during a long, distinguished life that ended, in 1790, at age eighty-four.

How did he stick to those famous thirteen? Consider the list:

1. Temperance	8. Justice
2. Silence	9. Moderation
3. Order	10. Cleanliness
4. Resolution	11. Tranquility
5. Frugality	12. Chastity
6. Industry	13. Humility
7. Sincerity	

Keeping such disciplined rigor would challenge anybody. So Franklin settled on a plan: He focused on one virtue per week, writing down his progress in a notebook. Then like a gardener, "who having a garden to weed, does not attempt to eradicate all the bad herbs at once . . . but works on one of the beds . . . proceeds to the second, so I should."

I studied these words in Franklin's autobiography, along with his prayer for success: "O powerful Goodness! Bountiful Father! Merciful Guide! Increase in me that wisdom which discovers my truest interest." Thus, I also read his daily schedule, including morning prayer and an evening question: "What good have I done today?"

Did Franklin succeed? Not always. But he believed the effort made him a better man on balance. He aimed high. Would that we try as well to bless God with a prayer for such discipline. 🕯

The morning prayer determines the day.
DIETRICH BONHOEFFER

Order and Discipline: Starting with Small Things

If you are faithful in little things, you will be faithful in large ones.
Luke 16:10

Fold the laundry. Wash the dishes. Make the bed. Clean the desk. Wax the car. Say thank you. Smile. Open a door. Say you're welcome. Little things.

Writing about such matters in *The Pillars of Christian Character*, John MacArthur makes this solid point: "Learning self-discipline in the little things of life prepares the way for big successes."

That's quite a promise. But as this author argues: "Those who are undisciplined in small matters will likely be undisciplined in more important issues."

Jesus understood this perfectly. Teaching His disciples this principle, He told a curious story about a shrewd manager who earns favors for life by dishonestly rewarding his friends. An odd story from Jesus, yes—until we reflect on the rich truth of His point:

If even a dishonest man knows to plan for the long length of his life, we who are promised eternal life must start planning for it in even small things.

For "if you are faithful in little things, you will be faithful in large ones." As Jesus adds: "If you are untrustworthy about worldly wealth, who will trust you with the true riches of heaven?" (v. 11).

So I made a list. Small things. Things I'd let pass that needed regular attention.

Hug my husband. Call my neighbor. Balance checkbook. Floss. Walk. Stay on top of those dishes! Then a curious thing happened. The more little things I gave regular attention to, thanking God for the privilege, the better I got at handling bigger things.

At seeing what other people needed—and providing it. At going to weekly Bible study—and learning from it. At valuing other people's time—and acting like it. Takes effort? Yes. But the effort lets God trust me with true riches. That's the glory, indeed, of such a path. Everybody can start such a journey. Why not bless God today by taking the small first step? 🔥

True freedom in any area of life is the consequence of regular discipline.
SINCLAIR B. FERGUSON

Order and Discipline: In All Thoughts

Think about things that are excellent and worthy of praise. . . .
Then the God of peace will be with you.
Philippians 4:8-9

A church friend was in the hospital. So I decided to visit to pray. But immediately the doubts rose to attack. What would I say? How would I pray? I thought hard on the matter, deciding to go in faith, but also in confidence. So praying boldly, I turned off the light and went to sleep, prepared to meet my friend the next day.

Then the attack. About 3 a.m., an hour when I'm typically fast asleep, I woke with an awful dream. It dredged up an old family issue. I sighed, tossing about for a few anxious moments, almost waking my husband. Then I stopped.

Think about things that are excellent and worthy of praise.

I'd copied that Scripture that same day while writing about order and discipline in our spiritual lives. So I recalled Paul's reminder to the church at Philippi, hearing as I lay in the dark the old King James wording: "Finally, brethren, whatsoever things are true, whatsoever things are honest, whatsoever things are just, whatsoever things are pure, whatsoever things are lovely, whatsoever things are of good report; if there be any virtue, and if there be any praise, *think on these things*" (italics added).

So that's what I did. *O true and honest God*, I spoke in my spirit, *if this dream is not of You, remove it from my mind right now.*

I didn't wait for an answer. With confident discipline, I started instead right then to think about God—and His truth, goodness, honesty, justice, purity, loveliness, and power. In seconds, the dream and its disturbing images faded, then vanished. Soon I slept in peace.

Some trick of the mind? Or did I bless God by obeying His order to discipline our minds to think of good? To answer, let's bless Him today by turning our thinking to His good. What will follow? His disciplined goodness. His ordered love. His blessed confidence. His powerful peace. 🌿

With complete consecration comes perfect peace.
WATCHMAN NEE

Order and Discipline: In All Speech

Those who control their tongue will have a long life.
Proverbs 13:3

If you can't say anything nice . . . Don't we all know the rest of *that* classic adage?

Don't say anything at all.

We've all heard this. Mostly from parents. Often from Sunday school teachers. From friends. From loved ones. Surely from the Word of God itself.

But, oh, that tongue. Talk about *un*disciplined. James was so right. It's "a flame of fire. It is a whole world of wickedness, corrupting your entire body. It can set your whole life on fire, for it is set on fire by hell itself" (James 3:6).

In fact, no one can tame it, James declares. "It is restless and evil, full of deadly poison"—pouring forth both praises of our Lord and Father, but also curses toward "those who have been made in the image of God" (James 3:8-9). Does that describe our tongues? Full of conflicting noise—both praises *and* curses?

The habit isn't just unpleasant. It shortens our lives, says God's Word. Stirring up heat and hate. Injuring others, but also ourselves. Revealing a cold heart—or making it colder.

Kind words, in contrast, "are like honey—sweet to the soul and healthy for the body" (Proverbs 16:24). For all the effort modern humans give to eating right and exercising, we'd all do ourselves more good by taming our tongues. But how?

Give our tongues to God's Spirit. Let's bless God, that is, by using our tongues today to ask for what they need most—the power of God's Spirit for control.

"Each of you," says the apostle Peter in Acts 2:38, "must repent of your sins and turn to God, and be baptized in the name of Jesus Christ for the forgiveness of your sins. *Then you will receive the gift of the Holy Spirit*" (emphasis added), to be used, in part, to control our tongues. It's the gift of life, indeed—this gift of a Spirit-led tongue. Let's bless God today and ask for it. 🌿

Focus on your mouth. . . . The rest will be subdued.
JOHN MACARTHUR

Order and Discipline: In Our Finances

For God loves a person who gives cheerfully.
2 Corinthians 9:7

Living paycheck to paycheck, I spent thirty working years frustrated by money. With every paycheck, money flew in one door and out the next. So I prayed. Finally. The right prayer? I asked God to show me the secrets of personal money management. Pretty good prayer? Apparently, because while talking about my crisis to my-daughter-the-accountant, she spoke the word that changed my financial life: budget.

"Budget?"

"Make a budget, Mom," she said. "For every year, month, day. Decide what you have to spend, what you need to spend—then budget accordingly."

She made it sound so simple. "Simple accounting, yes," she agreed. So I tried it.

And my life changed.

Not just my financial life. My *life* changed. Money management is that important. I finally appreciated my frugal dad's commitment to live beneath his income—save and invest the difference—then give back to God generously. So while others bought fancy cars and houses, Daddy and Mama bought plain. He went to glory without debt. So did my mama.

So, while living, they gave to God generously, cheerfully. And God *loves* a person who gives cheerfully. Oh, it took me so long to see this truth.

Discipline in financial matters allows us, not to hoard up money, but to steward it so wisely we always have enough to give back to God. Cheerfully.

And God loves that. Those who give back to Him trust Him. "It is more blessed to give," Jesus said, "than to receive" (Acts 20:35). But what allows such blessed giving? Knowing and loving God enough to discipline our stewardship.

Does it matter how much money is involved? Never. One penny managed well for God is a fortune. What matters is our disciplined honor of God's provision so we can give it back cheerfully. Oh, how this blesses God—not to mention empowering us. 🌾

We are not cisterns made for hoarding; we are channels made for sharing.
BILLY GRAHAM

Going Deeper

So be careful how you live. Don't live like fools, but like those who are wise.
Ephesians 5:15

What is out of order in your life? Foolishly out of order? Explain.

Describe your attitude toward discipline. Over your life, have you accepted or rejected discipline and order? Explain.

What special insight has God taught you this week about the companion virtues of discipline and order?

If you'd like, write a prayer that reflects your needs regarding the virtues of discipline and order.

Discipline is the soul of an army.
GEORGE WASHINGTON

PREPARATION

His Promise

Prepare the way for the LORD's coming! . . .
And then all people will see the salvation sent from God.
Luke 3:4, 6

My Prayer

As I prepare for the days of my life,
remind me, O returning Christ,
that my most important preparation is
preparing to meet You.

Preparation: To Meet the King

Do not eat or drink for three days, night or day.
Esther 4:16

Esther was young and beautiful—and nobody's fool. So before going to meet the king, she prepared. Seems logical. But how many of us believers stumble through our lives—without setting goals or making preparations—but expecting to succeed at life, then to meet the King of glory, then live with Him forever, all without getting ready?

In Esther's story, where the mighty name of God is never even mentioned, we still infer this important lesson: preparation matters. In life, it's critical. Even for one night with the king, Esther was prescribed "twelve months of beauty treatments—six months with oil of myrrh, followed by six months with special perfumes and ointments" (2:12).

Beauty treatments? Seems superficial perhaps. The point for us, however, is that to meet the king, she *prepared*. That word, which shares a root with such words as *parent*, *apparel*, and *repair*, honors the wise business of getting ready in advance.

Meeting her king especially required Esther's readiness in all aspects. No wonder she "accepted the advice of Hegai," the eunuch in charge of the king's harem—never asking for anything "except what he suggested" (2:15).

Do you accept advice in this way as you prepare? Do you allow time to plan for a key meeting or a strategic move? Have you prepared even for this day?

Consider that before Esther's biggest meeting yet with the king, she fasted for three days and nights, ordering all other Jews across the land to fast with her—reflecting, praying, planning. At stake were their lives. "If I must die, I must die," Esther declared (4:16). But she prepared to live.

And so should we. Starting today—in our living, seeking, serving, and praying—prepare intentionally now for eternal life with our King. Leave that life to chance? Never. Prepare to meet the King forever, but bless God today by getting ready now. 🌿

The best preparation for the future is the present well seen to.
GEORGE MACDONALD

Preparation: To Win at Battles

*But David persisted. "I have been taking care of my father's sheep
and goats," he said. . . . "The LORD who rescued me from the claws
of the lion and the bear will rescue me from this Philistine!"*
1 Samuel 17:34, 37

Poor little David. Not a single person thought he could defeat the Philistine
giant Goliath. "You're only a boy," King Saul warned him (1 Samuel 17:33).
Eliab, David's brother, mocked him. "What about those few sheep you're supposed to be taking care of?" (v. 28). Goliath sneered too: "Am I a dog . . . that
you come at me with a stick?" (v. 43). Nasty foes, indeed.

But David had prepared his whole life for this moment. As a shepherd,
tending those sheep his brother mocked, he'd fought off lions and bears
countless times.

"If the animal turns on me, I catch it by the jaw and club it to death. I
have done this to both lions and bears, and I'll do it to this pagan Philistine,
too" (vv. 35-36).

So physically he'd faced tough enemies and triumphed. Spiritually, however, David had prepared for Goliath by trusting God to protect him in
every tough fight. Thus, he knew what neither Saul nor Goliath understood:
Those who trust God always win.

It's neither the battle nor the opponent that matters.

We prepare for big battles first by counting on God's power in life's small
challenges. David would've learned that on his first night alone tending those
sheep. Just a small boy, singing praises in the dark to his God—calming the
sheep and his fears—David would learn the strategy for winning a big war.

Bless God by trusting Him. No better preparation readies a believer for triumph.

"The LORD who rescued me from the claws of the lion and the bear *will*
rescue me from this Philistine!" David insisted (italics mine). This affirmation is one we'd do well to remember. Or as David declared to his giant: "The
LORD will conquer you" (v. 46).

Challenge yourself to say and believe these same words today. Then, as
others marvel, receive the Lord's empowered blessing of knowing you've
already won. ❦

Greatness is in the preparation, not in the performance.
JACK HYLES

Preparation: For a Blessed Future

They labor hard all summer, gathering food for the winter.
Proverbs 6:8

Isn't faith enough? Do believers have to *do* something to prepare for the future?

My husband, Dan, and I were discussing such questions today. I'd written the day before about David and his battle with Goliath, so I reflected: "Look how he prepared for battle—by learning as a child to fight off lions and bears attacking his sheep."

My husband thought a minute. "But what about faith? To be prepared, isn't faith enough?"

Great question. But as I see it, David had plenty of faith to fight Goliath. But faith isn't about throwing up a prayer and winging it.

Not in the Bible anyway. For all the faith stories in the Bible, in fact, our Holy Book is filled with people who believed *but prepared*. Indeed, the Bible's preparation stories often include marching orders from God.

Noah built an ark by faith—but with God's instructions on proper measurements. Gideon fought the Midianites by faith—but with God's battle plan for his army. Joshua took Jericho by faith—but with God's directions for seizing it. Solomon built the Temple by faith—but with God's elaborate building and supply plans for erecting it.

In his business-planning book *Business by the Book*, the late Larry Burkett put it this way: "The bottom line on planning is that it is both biblical and necessary to be a good steward, and this usually involves looking ahead—with caution."

Too much planning, Burkett wrote, "can lead to self-reliance." And too little? Can lead to "unnecessary crisis."

That brings you and me to the ant in Proverbs 6:7-8. "Though they have no prince or governor or ruler to make them work, they labor hard all summer, gathering food for the winter." That is, they prepare. Short term and long term. Not hoarding. Not panicked. Preparing. Then in faith, they step wisely into the future. Now will you? 🌿

Life requires thorough preparation—veneer isn't worth anything.
GEORGE WASHINGTON CARVER

Preparation: As the Lord Prepares

I am going to prepare a place for you. . . . When everything is ready,
I will come and get you.
John 14:2-3

Still doubting that preparation matters? Then look to Jesus.

In the upper room, on the night before He was crucified—but also throughout the time we call Holy Week—He took particular steps to prepare His disciples for His suffering, death, and resurrection to eternal life.

That is, once His disciples realized He was the Messiah, He revealed "plainly" that He had to go to Jerusalem to suffer and be killed, but He would rise on the third day (Matthew 16:21-28). Very plain, indeed.

Next, in this same way, He taught them about discipleship (Mark 8:34), that to save our lives, we *lose them* for Him. An unusual lesson, to be sure. So Jesus prepared them for this kind of life—teaching and readying them.

In the upper room, then, He taught them a wondrous story about servant leadership by washing their dirty feet (John 13). Yet another unusual perspective.

So don't be troubled, He comforted them. "I am going to prepare a place for you." More plain words. "When everything is ready," Jesus added, "I will come and get you, so that you will always be with me where I am." Preparation is love, in other words.

Consider that today as you reflect on your own life. Have you asked the Lord to teach you to "number your days" as Psalm 90:12 (TNIV) says—that is, "to realize the brevity of life, so that we may grow in wisdom"?

For inspiration, look to Jesus. As sovereign Lord, Jesus could have gone straight to glory without explaining His actions to anybody. But as the Loving Christ—indeed, the Living Christ—He prepared us to live eternally with Him by preparing us to follow the Way. Let us bless Him today by making choices—and making plans—that honor the empowered gift of His preparation. 🔥

This life is preparation for the next.
RICK WARREN

Preparation: For Defeating Our Spiritual Enemies

Then the Spirit of the LORD took possession of Gideon.
He blew a ram's horn as a call to arms.
Judges 6:34

Say what you will about Gideon. But when the frightened farmer was found hiding by God's angel—who then addressed him as a "mighty hero"—Gideon prepared for battle by asking for proof. Lots of proof.

After questioning God on several points, and obeying God's order to tear down his father's altar to the idol Baal—then building up an altar to almighty God and sacrificing a bull on it—finally Gideon stepped to the task: to follow God's order and lead the children of Israel into battle against their archenemies, the powerful Midianites.

After preparation, *then* the Spirit of the Lord took possession of Gideon.

The battle was won, in fact, at that point. As believers, in this same way, we overcome our spiritual enemies, not by power or might, but inspired and prepared by God's Spirit. Even when we, like Gideon, have doubts.

Gideon kept asking for more and more proof—right up to the moment of battle. (Talk about double-checking!) He didn't raise a weapon until testing God again and again—then letting God guide him in organizing his army for the big fight.

For Gideon, that meant paring down his fighting force from thirty-two thousand to three hundred. A few brave men, who lapped water "with their tongues like dogs" (Judges 7:5), would fight a horde of camel-riding Midianites, so many they looked like "grains of sand on the seashore" (v. 12).

Yet at God's word, Gideon's troops only carried two physical weapons—a ram's horn and a clay jar with a lit torch inside. Hardly big firepower. The victory, however, was launched through divine preparation. Our lesson? Prepare today to fight God's way. Then, today, go and win. 🔥

You can be meticulous in your preparation; but without the
unction of the Holy Spirit you will have no power.
MARTIN LLOYD-JONES

Preparation: For Christ's Return

Those who were ready went in with him.
Matthew 25:10

Jesus is coming back. But are you and I prepared? It's a fair question. The most important question, indeed, for believers. To be sure, the Bible alerts us of Jesus' coming, encouraging us to get ready. The only problem? We don't know exactly when He will return.

As Paul writes in 1 Thessalonians 5:2-3, "For you know quite well that the day of the Lord's return will come unexpectedly, like a thief in the night. When people are saying, 'Everything is peaceful and secure,' then disaster will fall on them as suddenly as a pregnant woman's labor pains begin. And there will be no escape."

The five foolish virgins learned that the hard way. In the New Testament's most piercing story of why preparation for Christ is important, the unprepared women of this parable found themselves locked out of the bridegroom's wedding feast.

Indeed, I'm reading the story today thinking about myself. Am I ready? And am I carrying within my heart and soul not only the right oil but also enough of it?

Am I honest, that is, and loving? Faithful and humble? Courageous and persistent—and all the other virtuous traits that keep the little light of my life burning bright, bold, and lasting for Christ?

The wise virgins had prepared accordingly. But the foolish virgins dared to show up, knowing they weren't ready, hoping to coerce the ready to share their readiness. Not possible. They dared, indeed, to sleep while the bridegroom was delayed. Then when he suddenly appeared, they scurried around, trying vainly to borrow oil—then rushing off to buy oil, but returning too late.

The door was locked. Is that your fate? Or mine? Rather than worry, vow to live each day in a spirit of readiness, eager to see Jesus—prepared and glowing. Confident. Light shining. 🕯️

Be prepared.
LORD BADEN POWELL

Going Deeper

So be on your guard, not asleep like the others.
1 Thessalonians 5:6

The word *preparation* shares a root with the word *parent*. What connection do you see between these two words? Explain.

What's your personality style—deliberate or spontaneous? When you prepare, how does it impact your goals or activities?

What special insight has God taught you this week about the virtue of preparation?

If you'd like, write a prayer that reflects your needs regarding the virtue of preparation.

To be prepared is half the victory.
MIGUEL DE CERVANTES

PERSEVERANCE

His Promise

Patient endurance is what you need now,
so that you will continue to do God's will.
Then you will receive all that he has promised.
Hebrews 10:36

My Prayer

I thank You today, blessed Lord,
for Your reminder to endure with perseverance.
Through life. Through work. Through it all.
Then bless me to do Your will
as I receive all that You have promised.

Perseverance: In Believing God

At just the right time we will reap a harvest of blessing if we don't give up.
Galatians 6:9

George Müller. Let's put his name on the table. Right on top. In any talk about perseverance, Müller surely stands with the best. His familiar story of redemption, inspiration, and endurance in prayer deserves regular retelling, to be sure.

So here's Müller, a ne'er-do-well gambler and thief. As young as ten, say biographers, he was stealing government money from his father, a Prussian tax collector. At fourteen, while his mother lay dying, he was playing cards and drinking with friends.

Then came Jesus. Healing, restoring, forgiving Jesus. So Müller, seeing he needed salvation, gave his life to Christ—eventually working with his wife to start orphanages that would feed, educate, and house some ten thousand homeless, hungry children in Bristol, England. How'd Müller do it?

With prayer. Enduring, persevering, stubborn, never-give-up prayer.

For all his faith in a providing God, Müller must best be remembered for his determined, persistent, unwavering prayers to the God who meets needs in time.

Even for the starving. So while Müller said grace for breakfast, when he had no breakfast, this persevering servant led his wife and the orphans in thanking God for what they were about to receive, just as a baker knocked on the door—with enough fresh breakfast bread for all. Müller never asked others for anything, in fact. He only asked God.

So Müller prayed enduringly over fifty-two years for five former pals to accept Christ. Sure enough, one by one each came to the Lord—including the last friend who came to Jesus at Müller's funeral.

Give up? Müller, crying out across history, says no. Keep trying. Keep praying. Keep blessing God. Keep letting Him inspire and save. How? Don't stop believing. 🌱

> Patient, persevering, believing prayer, offered up to God, in the name of the Lord Jesus, has always, sooner or later, brought the blessing.
> GEORGE MÜLLER

Perseverance: By Believing God

So let's not get tired of doing what is good.
Galatians 6:9

They didn't get tired. Those persevering saints, some famous and some not, kept Christianity alive by their own determined faith. From George Müller to Richard Allen, Jim Elliot to Harriet Tubman, Nate Saint to Amy Carmichael, Mildred Cable to William Wilberforce, and countless others—Christian history is blessed with legions of servants who simply refused to give up.

So I search for them this morning, scouring the Internet for their histories, amazed at their stories and sacrifices. But I pause to reflect on two: John Wycliffe and William Tyndale. Church reformers and Bible translators, they gave their all so you and I could hold our Bibles this morning and read the blessed truth of God's Word.

John Wycliffe, called the "Morning Star of the Reformation," dared to defy false teaching and clerical abuses by diligently translating the Bible from the Latin Vulgate into handwritten English—so literate people could read it for themselves.

Hounded in life and declared a heretic in death, Wycliffe was still deemed dangerous when, thirty-four years after his 1394 death, his writings and books were ordered burned and his remains were dug up, crushed, and burned.

Tyndale, meantime, was hunted for eleven years by papal authorities for producing the first printed version of the Bible, his English-language translation of Greek and Hebrew—a work forming much of the King James Version, among others. Betrayed by a supposed friend, Tyndale was arrested, tried for heresy, strangled, and burned at the stake. His dying words: "Lord! Open the King of England's eyes!"

Just four years later, in fact, King Henry VIII did allow four English translations of the Bible to be printed and published in England. All were based on Tyndale's persevering work. So how should we bless the memory of these two reformers?

Diligently read God's Word today. Then let's not get tired of what they died for. 🌿

If all the world be against us, God's word is stronger than the world.
WILLIAM TYNDALE

Perseverance: In Praying for the Lost

*For when your endurance is fully developed, you will be
perfect and complete, needing nothing.*
James 1:4

Thirty years? Would you pray that long? Believe that long? Trust God that long? *Work* that long? The Wycliffe Bible translators did.

Thirty years ago, their translations of the New Testament Scriptures included the Central Ifugao language, one of 170 languages spoken in the Philippines. Thus, a Filipino village priest named Pugong heard the gospel, but he refused to accept Christ. "I'm going to accept Christ," he often said. "But I'm still afraid of what the spirits will do to me."

As described in an issue of *One Passion,* the Wycliffe Bible Translators magazine, Pugong believed spirits determined his villagers' fate—and also his. So he kept an altar to the spirits in his home, sometimes returning home late after drinking large amounts of alcohol as part of his ritual and priestly duties.

But he would see a lamp burning in the dwelling of Wycliffe translator Anne West, knowing "she was always waiting to see that he was safe." As she worked on the Old Testament translation in Central Ifugao, she kept encouraging Pugong to accept Christ. Indeed, nine of his children, his son-in-law, and many neighbors already had.

Then one September day, thirty years after the New Testament translation came to his village, Pugong came to Jesus. When a church group came to his home, he asked to be baptized. "I'm ready to accept Christ."

"Wait until a pastor comes!" someone said. But not Pugong. "I can pray now."

But can you? Pray now, after decades, for an unsaved family member or neighbor? Pray now to get the Bible into the hands of the lost even if it takes thirty years?

Such endurance knows that, to God, "a thousand years are as a passing day, as brief as a few night hours" (Psalm 90:4).

And thirty years? Not too long for enduring servants to believe. 🔥

Success seems to be largely a matter of hanging on after others have let go.
WILLIAM FEATHER

Perseverance: By God's Spirit

For when your endurance is fully developed, you will be
perfect and complete, needing nothing.
James 1:4

Perseverance is hard. So we get tired. So here I am, just forty-six weeks into writing a fifty-two-week devotional—a task I craved doing and love completing. But this week? As I reflect on perseverance, I struggle. I'm exhausted. With only six weeks of a year's devotionals left to go, and with the light shining brightly at the end of a long tunnel, that light on this day seems as far as the farthest sun in the farthest universe. Ever been there?

So you know, as I now see, what the theologians mean when they say perseverance isn't about toughing it out.

"It's toughening in."

My husband says this today. He's not a theologian by training. But he's handed me pep talks all along, listening every day for a year to my writing worries and thoughts, hearing me out on my weekly topics. Then, across the breakfast table on this cold and chilly fall day, he says what I overlooked.

"It's about God's Spirit."

"God's Spirit," I repeat, determined to hear him.

"Perseverance," he says, munching toast. "It's toughening *in.*"

I could hug him. And I do. Because it's exactly what a tired servant of God needs to hear. That is, we read the stories of Tyndale and Wycliffe and Elliot and Müller and the other heroic saints, and in comparison we feel weak and incapable. Not able to tough it.

But it's not our strength that carries us over, or that starts us.

Not by power. Not by might. "But by my Spirit, says the LORD of Heaven's Armies" (Zechariah 4:6). When we know this, believing it and walking in it, says James, our endurance will be complete. Perfect. Then we will need nothing else. Instead, by God's Spirit we will bless Him with our obedient perseverance to go the last mile.

So I surrender today. By His Spirit, I'll see this fine work to its holy end. 🔥

Saints are sinners who kept on going.
ROBERT LOUIS STEVENSON

Perseverance: That Inspires Others

So take a new grip with your tired hands and stand firm on your
shaky legs. . . . Then those who follow you, though they are
weak and lame, will not stumble.
Hebrews 12:12-13

Michelangelo didn't paint the Sistine Chapel ceiling lying on his back—a common myth. Still, he set an artistic record by persevering through four neck-grinding years—between 1508 and 1512—to complete "an artistic vision without precedent."

That's how one critic struggled to describe the more than three hundred lushly painted figures, scenes, and two-dimensional architectural moldings that dress the ceiling. Covering a frescoed surface well over five thousand square feet, all this work makes for a masterpiece of such iconic scale, artistry, vision, and complexity that the artist and the art have become legendary.

Yet at several points during this project for Pope Julius II, it wasn't clear if Michelangelo would even get paid. (A "warrior pope," the pontiff was financing a long war.)

But Michelangelo kept plastering and painting—outlasting mold and damp, grueling hours, bending backwards and looking up while paint dripped into his eyes, ruining them for life, he later said. But he didn't stop. Not until he painted the last stroke.

The result? We're inspired. Some five hundred years later, we're inspired—still awed and amazed that, as Michelangelo pored over and over the Old Testament Scriptures looking for inspiration, he found the power to tell God's story and not quit.

Perseverance does that. When *you* keep going, *I'm* inspired too. "So take a new grip with your tired hands," wrote the author of Hebrews. "Then those who follow you, though they are weak and lame, will not stumble and fall but will become strong" (v. 13). Did Michelangelo intend to bless us today with such persevering strength? Perhaps. But as we reflect with awe on his work, let's remember its bigger godly lesson: don't stop. 🖌

Genius is eternal patience.
MICHELANGELO

Perseverance: That Follows Jesus

*We do this by keeping our eyes on Jesus, on whom our faith
depends from start to finish.*
Hebrews 12:2

Perseverance is no joke. No walk around the park. It's just flat-out hard. Why?

We're not bees. Or ants. Or dogs pulling sleds. Or salmon swimming upstream. Those creatures and critters persevere by instinct—without thinking.

But human beings have to think and choose. So our Christian heroes— Tyndale, Wycliffe, Elliot, Tubman, Müller, and more—decided deliberately to take on their cause for Christ, then to stick to it.

Life handed these ordinary believers situations, but they didn't fall and faint. They got up and hung on, determined to outlast difficulty. And you and I can too.

Today, in fact, we can.

In our own strength, that is, we probably won't feel like bending our necks back for four years to paint a seventy-foot-high Sistine ceiling, or pray for fifty-two years until a friend or family member finally comes to Christ.

How can we do it? Keep our eyes on Jesus— "on whom our faith depends from start to finish." So we think about all He endured.

When you and I run out of reasons and will, let's consider Christ. That's what we do on hard days. Seeing all the reasons to give out and give up—on ourselves, our loved ones, our friends, our churches, and our Lord. But, looking at Jesus, we remember that great cloud of witnesses cheering us on, urging us all: *don't stop.*

Let's bless God today by doing exactly that, looking for Him to do more in us. Indeed, He endured more. Looking to Him, we'll endure more too. For His people. For His Kingdom. All for Him. Pressing on. 🔥

Lord, grant that I may always desire more than I can accomplish.
MICHELANGELO

Perseverance: Going Deeper

Therefore, since we are surrounded by such a huge crowd of witnesses to the life of faith, let us strip off every weight that slows us down, especially the sin that so easily trips us up. And let us run with endurance the race God has set before us.
Hebrews 12:1

What goals have you set—spiritual or otherwise— that require your perseverance?

Are you succeeding at your goals? If not, what's slowing or weighing you down?

What may be stopping you from keeping your eyes on Jesus as you pursue your goals?

What special insight has God taught you this week about the virtue of perseverance?

If you'd like, write a prayer that reflects your needs regarding the virtue of perseverance.

Perseverance is not a long race; it is many short races one after another.
WALTER ELLIOTT

VIGILANCE

His Promise

*Keep a close watch on yourself. . . . Stay true to what is right,
and God will save you and those who hear you.*
1 Timothy 4:16

My Prayer

Keep me ever watchful and alert,
looking up to You, Blessed Father,
for my deliverance,
my salvation,
and my next opportunity to stand for You.

Vigilance: To See God's Healing

Woman, you are healed!
Luke 13:12

For eighteen years, a woman had been passing by a synagogue, crippled with an evil spirit, but looking for God's healing Word.

On this Sabbath, however, the one who could heal her saw her instead.

Jesus was busy teaching, so He could have ignored her. But as the Savior who came to heal, He stayed on the lookout for the sick. Vigilantly, in fact, He looked—as in the manner of Psalm 14:2: "The LORD looks down from heaven on the entire human race; he looks to see if anyone is truly wise, if anyone seeks God."

So He dared to stop His sermon, calling to her, declaring what's true for all believers: "You are healed!"

Is there any doubt, indeed, that Jesus heals those for whom He so vigilantly seeks? Such a question should challenge each of us today.

First, be comforted, knowing that Christ sees you. Second, start looking, as He looks, for sick and lost people you may have ignored. But look, as well, for your own healing in Christ. Vigilantly, He invites you to seek Him—as your Healer.

Vigilance, that is, seems a vital first step in healing where Jesus is concerned. So He vigilantly asked, "Who touched me?" when the woman with the issue of blood crawled vigilantly through a crowd to find Him (Luke 8:45). Or as He said so beseechingly to the blind man He treated at Bethsaida, "Can you see anything now?" (Mark 8:23). Lovely, healing questions. Yet can *we* see today? See Christ? See hope for His return? See the person needing our help and healing touch in the meantime? But also are we looking so hard we see the healing He offers to us?

If such vigilance seems pushy or presumptuous, look again at Jesus. Not only did He seek the sick and lost, He healed them, even on the Sabbath. So bless God today by seeking Him at all times. Then bless others by showing them the one who sees their needs and answers with love. His name? The Healer. 🌿

He is watchful while they are in peace, for they know
when their Shepherd is nigh.
WILLIAM BLAKE

Vigilance: To Stay Awake for Christ

Keep watch and pray, so that you will not give in to temptation.
For the spirit is willing, but the body is weak!
Matthew 26:41

Look. Watch. See. Live. In other words, wake up!

That's what Jesus told Peter, James, and John before praying on the night before He was crucified. Wake up, brothers! Keep watch! Start praying! Stay vigilant. Otherwise, we become the church pushing the snooze button.

Could that explain why church attendance, according to two respected pollsters—the Pew Forum on Religion and Public Life, and the Gallup-Healthways Well-Being Index—hasn't moved off the meter since the late 1960s? The Barna Group, another respected research team, sheds light on such behavior, reporting in 2007 that a full third of Americans, some 73 million adults in America, are "unchurched." Add in teens and children, and that's 100 million Americans who rarely if ever walk through a church door—or get as close as the parking lot.

Does the thought of church put them to sleep? Or are too many believers, like the disciples who fell asleep while Jesus prepared for death, sleeping too?

Imagine, instead, leaping up—wide awake—for Christ and for His cause.

What would we see with our wide-open eyes? Think of the service we'd discover, the work we'd find, the life we'd create, all because we finally woke up. No longer distracted by temptations and tests, our new vigilance would sharpen our vision to see Jesus and His exciting will for our lives. In our new vigilance, indeed, we'd have to pray: *Lord, keep me awake!* Stir in me the will to see others' needs, plus face my battles, and then to fight.

If that sounds like your prayer today, *pray it.* Vigilantly. Then let God's Spirit bless you with His power to stay awake. 🕯

The church is not a dormitory for sleepers, it is an institution for workers.
BILLY SUNDAY

Vigilance: To Guard Our Hearts from Temptation

Keep watch and pray, so that you will not give in to temptation.
For the spirit is willing, but the body is weak!
Matthew 26:41

Of course the vigilant get blessed. And not just sometimes. Daily they flee temptation, turn from sin, defeat disappointment, outlast terror, shun evil, keep covenants, walk in righteousness, never give up. And all that from keeping their eyes wide open for Christ as they pray.

They're wise, in other words, knowing that keeping watch for Jesus protects them from Satan—the same enemy who deceived Eve with his "cunning ways" (2 Corinthians 11:3), who prowls around constantly, working overtime to distract us with his devilish, sneaky ways.

But is he prowling around today? Only if we're not watching. Our enemy celebrates, in fact, when we're asleep with weakness, our truest nature. But it was Jesus who described it perfectly: "For from the heart come evil thoughts, murder, adultery, all sexual immorality, theft, lying, and slander. These are what defile you."

When Christ spoke these words in Matthew 15:19-20, He was talking to Peter, explaining to His disciple why true inner purity matters more than the ritual purity of hand washing or eating "clean" food.

Inner purity results from a heart that shuns its temptations, choosing instead to honor God by walking in His ways—not chasing lusts, breaking trusts, or snoozing.

So keep watch.

But don't just keep watch. Leap up today and pray—as if it's a matter of life and death, because it is. Indeed, are family members failing? Leap up and pray. Are church numbers falling? Leap up and pray. Ignore Satan's lie that watching and praying don't matter. Such vigilance saves lives and souls. So keep watch. Every minute. Every second, too. Then let the Holy Spirit bless you with His victorious presence as you watch, awake in Him, and vigilantly pray. 🔥

The safe place lies in obedience to God's Word,
singleness of heart and holy vigilance.
A. B. SIMPSON

Vigilance: To Watch Our Mouths

The words you say will either acquit you or condemn you.
Matthew 12:37

Idle talk. Gossip. Slander. Scheming. Judgment.

Jesus heard it all.

So He challenged the Pharisees. The hypocritical religious leaders dared to judge His power to heal a demon-possessed man, saying it came not from the Holy Spirit but from Satan, "the prince of demons" (Matthew 12:24).

Fighting words, yes.

But Jesus "knew their thoughts" (v. 25). So He answered with a challenge, not just for the Pharisees—but also for us:

> *If Satan is casting out Satan, he is divided and fighting against himself. His own kingdom will not survive. . . . But if I am casting out demons by the Spirit of God, then the Kingdom of God has arrived among you. For who is powerful enough to enter the house of a strong man like Satan and plunder his goods? Only someone even stronger—someone who could tie him up and then plunder his house.* (vv. 26, 28-29)

Thus, He explains what every believer today must know: that "every sin and blasphemy can be forgiven—except blasphemy against the Holy Spirit, which will never be forgiven" (v. 31). So watch your mouth? Absolutely. To be sure, Jesus was warning the blasphemous Pharisees, promising them that they must give an account on Judgment Day "for every idle word you speak" (v. 36).

Will we face the same test? Indeed, we will. So let's watch our mouths.

Vigilantly. In a world that tells Jesus jokes around watercoolers and on television, ridiculing the Holy Spirit and other things of God—while asking God's people to laugh along with the "fun"—let us watch our mouths. Let praises pass our lips today instead. Such vigilance blesses us now. Then it acquits us. How long? Forever. ❦

Beseech God to accompany our vigilance with his.
JOHN WESLEY

Vigilance: To Watch for the Blessings of Battle

Be careful! Watch out for attacks from the Devil, your great enemy. He prowls around like a roaring lion, looking for some victim to devour.
1 Peter 5:8

Watch for Jesus? We know to do that. But are we watching as hard for His blessings?

I ask that question today with conviction.

Among some believers today, the push for humility and self-denial has left many teaching that it's wrong to look to God for *any* good favor or blessing.

Satan affirms this false teaching. Busying us with vain self-denial, pumping us up to feel superior about it while roaring in our ears with lies and doubts, he works hard at devouring our hope in God's golden promises to bless His people. Yet be not dismayed, because God "cares about what happens to you," Peter writes in verse 7. As members of His royal priesthood, we can cast our anxieties on Him—and get blessed in the process.

This would be good news for the Gentile audience of this letter. Like new believers of today, they struggled with persecution from those questioning their faith. They did not yet understand how struggle develops both character and courage.

And what's the blessing after struggle? "After you have suffered a little while, he will restore, support, and strengthen you, *and* he will place you on a firm foundation" (v. 10, italics added).

Resist the devil—then get blessed. We're restored and stronger. We're supported by God, and in Him granted a firm place to stand. At work. At home. In the world. Resist bad and get blessed for right.

To nonbelievers, as we battle, we may look square and prudish, like weak "church people." But standing up to Satan is tough work. "From start to finish," said evangelist E. M. Bounds, "it is war."

God in His mercy, however, makes the fight worth it. So fight hard. But don't stop short of your blessing. 🌿

> Never neglect details. When everyone's mind is dulled or distracted . . .
> be doubly vigilant.
> COLIN POWELL

Vigilance: To Watch for Everyone's Salvation

Wake up, for our salvation is nearer now than when we first believed.
Romans 13:11

We wear pajamas—our sleeping clothes—when we sleep. We'd look silly wearing pajamas to work or to church. In fact, on "pajama day" at schools or workplaces, the whole day seems upside down and silly. Wear our sleeping pajamas when we're working or going to school? To most, it feels ridiculous.

Wearing evil is just as silly for those redeemed by Christ.

With one foot in our old life and one foot in our new—wearing both clothes of light and darkness—we show we're not ready for the gift of Christ's salvation.

But wake up.

"Time is running out" (v. 11).

Paul uses plain language, to be sure, to talk to new believers in the provinces of Rome. Calling themselves "saved" but acting unsaved in their lives—going to "wild parties," getting drunk, committing adultery, and engaging in "immoral living"—they'd fooled themselves into thinking that being a Christian in name counted for good (v. 13).

But wake up.

"The night is almost gone," Paul declares. "The day of salvation will soon be here. So don't live in darkness. Get rid of your evil deeds. Shed them like dirty clothes" (v. 12).

The blessing? "Everyone can approve of our behavior" (v. 13).

When we stop saying one thing and living another—when our declaration of being saved matches the way we live—then imagine: everyone can approve of Christ. So our salvation determines not just our place in eternity. It influences eternity for others.

So pray this today: *Wake me up, O God.* Then take off your pajamas—and put on your work clothes.

Then be light. All day. Why? Everyone depends on it.

Watch the way of the Spirit of God into thee.
JOHN DONNE

Going Deeper

Be on guard. Stand true to what you believe. Be courageous. Be strong.
And everything you do must be done with love.
1 Corinthians 16:13-14

What are your biggest temptations? Honestly describe them.

Are your temptations dangerous enough to cost you your salvation?
Or the salvation of others? Explain.

What should you do today to guard against those dangers that draw you
away from God?

What has God taught you this week about the virtue of godly vigilance?

If you'd like, write a prayer that reflects your needs regarding the virtue
of vigilance.

The battle, sir, is not to the strong alone. It is to the vigilant,
the active, the brave.
PATRICK HENRY

Commitment

His Promise

Listen, I am making a covenant with you
in the presence of all your people.
I will perform miracles that have never been
performed anywhere
in all the earth or in any nation. And all the people
around you will see the power
of the Lord—the awesome power
I will display for you.
Exodus 34:10

My Prayer

Bless Your Name, O Miracle-Working God,
for binding me to You in an unbreakable covenant
of promise and love,
forgiveness and grace,
wonder and power!

Commitment: That Gives Me God's Protection

Obey all the commands I am giving you today. Then I will surely drive out all those who stand in your way.
Exodus 34:11

Why do vows matter? Because they matter to God. His precious name, *the LORD*, is His covenant name. By this name, He offered the Israelites a binding, lasting contract to be His exclusive people. By this name, He offered protection, power, and peace. But repeatedly, they broke His laws. Ignored His mandates. Turned their backs. Worshiped idols—refusing to understand:

"You must worship no other gods, but *only the LORD*, for he is a God who is passionate about his relationship with you" (v. 14, italics added).

Passion like that, and the commitment that goes with it, comes with conditions, however. That's how contracts work. As He promised: obey my commands, "then I will surely drive out all those who stand in your way."

So stop struggling with enemies. Instead, stand up today and receive God's covenant-keeping love and promise to defeat them. How? Obey our God, then pray His promise back to Him:

Help me, promising God, to obey Your covenant, but also to believe. Then drive out my enemies—doubts, insecurity, worry, moral failure, spiritual mistrust, and more.

Pray *that*, indeed, daring today to test God's exclusive covenant with you.

When He vows, we can count on Him. We can stop, indeed, our meltdowns during life's trials. Instead, we can pray like George Müller, the saint who served ten thousand orphans in England by trusting God's promises and standing on them. Why not, indeed, trust a God whose very covenant-keeping name, *the LORD*, assures us He will keep His promises to us? Not to trust Him shows our failures, never His.

To be sure, if you commit to nothing else this day, commit to standing on God by renewing an unbreakable pact with Him. Then abide by His Spirit as He blesses your feeble heart to actually keep it. 🦋

There is no more blessed way of living than the life of faith
based upon a covenant-keeping God.
CHARLES SPURGEON

Commitment: That Honors My Marriage

So guard your heart; do not be unfaithful to your wife.
Malachi 2:16

Marriage is dead? So claimed the challenging *Time* magazine article "Who Needs Marriage?" A provocative look at a "changing institution," the article sought to explain why, in 2010, only about 50 percent of American adults were married—compared to nearly 70 percent in 1960. Meantime, eight times as many children were born out of wedlock in 2010 compared to 1960. That year, two-thirds of twentysomethings were married as compared to 2008 when just 26 percent were.

So is marriage obsolete? In a 2010 *Time* poll, nearly 40 percent of Americans agreed. That's the general opinion anyway. But what does God say?

We find one clear answer in the book of Malachi. The prophet, aiming hard at sinning priests and cynical believers, cut to the heart of their problem: wrong relationships. They were indifferent to God, sinning against spouses and cheating at business and within their community.

> *You cry out, "Why doesn't the LORD accept my worship?" I'll tell you why! Because the LORD witnessed the vows you and your wife made when you were young. But you have been unfaithful to her, though she remained your faithful partner, the wife of your marriage vows. Didn't the LORD make you one with your wife? (vv. 14-15)*

Marriage obsolete? Even the hint of the idea blasphemes God. Marriage, as created by God, strengthens home and heart, family and children, neighborhood and nation. "So guard your heart," Malachi declared. "Do not be unfaithful to your wife."

Marriage obsolete? Don't believe it. Not today. Not ever. Instead, believe God. Make your vow and keep it. The blessings of the Lord of Heaven's Armies will be the eternal reward for all. ❦

A successful marriage requires falling in love many times,
always with the same person.
MIGNON MCLAUGHLIN

Commitment: That Blesses My Spouse Forever

Give honor to marriage, and remain faithful to one another in marriage.
Hebrews 13:4

She had a marriage proposal, a ring—and cold feet. With a wedding date only a few months away, the young woman had "the dress" and "the guy." But the prospect left her terrified.

Her biggest worry: "What if I meet somebody else? Somebody better?"

"*After* you get married?" I asked.

She nodded—and I smiled. "Oh, you will! Every week. Maybe every day!" I laughed, and she tried to. But she understood.

Marriage isn't about feeling head over heels in love every day for the rest of your life. Marriage is about being committed to your spouse every day for the rest of your life. That's true for those times when you're feeling madly in love—or just feeling mad—but also when you meet "somebody better." So commitment says *stay faithful*. To your spouse. To your God.

That's what I tried to suggest to the nervous bride-to-be: that when wives and husbands start out knowing that marriage is first about commitment—not just about feelings—they're on their way to a marriage that will last.

A hard lesson? In fact, it's one of those basics that takes couples from failure to success. As marriage expert Seth Eisenberg told *Time* magazine, very few couples have had a chance to learn the rules of love and intimacy, "not because the rules are so difficult to learn, just because no one told them."

So open the Bible. From passion to practicalities, God's Word tells you everything you should know about commitment but perhaps were never taught. Commit first to God. Then when you commit to a spouse—to the godly person God chose for you, or to the not-so-godly spouse you're trying to love—you won't be nervous. Or frightened. Or overwhelmed. You'll be ready to give your marriage to God as He makes it right. 🖋

A happy marriage is the union of two good forgivers.
ROBERT QUILLEN

Commitment: That Supports My Community

*But all of you who were faithful to the LORD your God
are still alive today—every one of you.*
Deuteronomy 4:4

My next-door neighbor, a retired Marine, never breaks a promise. If I ask her to watch our house when I'm out of town, I return to a house that's still standing—but also with no pizza-shop flyers on the porch or stray newspapers cluttering the driveway.

She keeps promises. Then she goes the extra mile.

Even before the Marines, however, promises mattered to her. It seems she learned that from her father, who learned it from his father—who learned it during an era when a person's word was his bond. If somebody said it, you could count on it.

In God's Word, the book of Deuteronomy outlines the critical nature of such promise keeping. As we keep God's covenant, that is, obeying God's commandments and extending justice as God mandates, we "will live" (Deuteronomy 8:1) *and* enjoy "prosperous lives" (5:33) *and* "occupy the land" or territory God has promised (8:1), and enjoy all this *together*. As neighbors. As a nation.

So I sit with this idea today. Then I ask God to plant in my not-always-committed heart His amazing promise:

If I commit to do my small part, and so does everybody else, a whole nation prospers. "For what great nation has a god as near to them as the LORD our God is near to us whenever we call on him?" Moses asked. "And what great nation has decrees and regulations as righteous and fair as this body of instructions?" (4:7-8).

So how committed are you to your community, family, and God? Do you cut corners? Break promises? Go halfway? Tell half-truths? Say yes but do no? Talk big but act small? Or will you vow today to make promises you keep? By God's Spirit, a committed life can result. But the blessing won't only be yours. Everybody around you will praise God too. 🔥

We must not promise what we ought not, lest we be
called on to perform what we cannot.
ABRAHAM LINCOLN

Commitment: That Strengthens My Family

Most important of all, continue to show deep love for each other,
for love covers a multitude of sins.
1 Peter 4:8

My family isn't perfect, and neither am I. So I made a vow just to love all of us anyway, myself included. Why? To show I trust God? To believe that, despite being older, I don't have to try to control everything? That it matters more to my family's unity to let my grown children be their own adults? Indeed, to trust God in matters of disagreement—and to accept the things I can't change and stand in serenity about the things I can.

I've reflected on such things a lot in recent years.

After decades of parenting, I realized—long after my children were grown and gone—that it was time I stopped trying to be in charge and pass that baton of their lives, truly, to them. Indeed, my job at this point is simple: love.

Love God. Love family. Love everybody else.

(And not to give advice unless it's requested.)

Just love? It seems not quite enough. But love, says Peter, covers a multitude of sins. So love means I don't lose patience. Instead, I laugh. Or at least try to. So I go with the flow. I turn off my perfectionist questions *and* answers. So I see our good choices, hard work, long hours, tough challenges, generous hearts, and I have the wisdom not to ask for more.

Love deeply, Peter says. Such family love "displays our relationship with Christ," says my *NLT Study Bible.* Thus, such love declares that Christ is alive—and that we live in Him. Such love declares that Christ redeems—and we're redeemed by Him. Such love declares that Christ saves—and we're saved by Him. Such love declares that Christ is Love—and we love like Him.

And all that other stuff that parents could gripe about to grown children? Give it to God today. All of it. Then love deeply. Should I say more? I could. But love covers all. 🌿

You don't choose your family. They are God's gift to you, as you are to them.
DESMOND TUTU

Commitment: That Reflects Christ's Life-Giving Spirit

Under the new covenant, the Spirit gives life.
2 Corinthians 3:6

God doesn't make mistakes. So the old covenant between God and His people wasn't bad. And yet? "It lacked the power to enable people to do what it commanded," says my *NLT Study Bible*. That's surprising, but it's good and plain language. So I reflect on how the apostle Paul explained it: "The law of Moses was unable to save us because of the weakness of our sinful nature." So what did God do? "He sent his own Son in a body like the bodies we sinners have" (Romans 8:3).

I like this plain language, too. So I keep reading.

"And in that body God declared an end to sin's control over us by giving his Son as a sacrifice for our sins. He did this so that the just requirement of the law would be fully satisfied for us, who no longer follow our sinful nature but instead follow the Spirit" (Romans 8:3-4).

Yes, chasing after the Spirit. Then surrendering. That's how we finally commit to Christ.

So let go. Stop trying today, on your own, to obey those two great commandments: love God—and love everybody else as much as yourself.

Instead, by the power of God's Holy Spirit, allow God to help you love Him and others—becoming a minister of love, spreading God's love but also sharing His life.

"The old written covenant ends in death," says 2 Corinthians 3:6. "But under the new covenant, the Spirit gives life." Empowered but tender and wise and flexible and lasting life.

Does that describe your life yet? Or, by not following after His Spirit, are you failing at your commitment to enliven others through Christ? If so, pray for a fresh anointing of His Spirit. That's a prayer, indeed, that He won't turn down. So get ready to receive His answer—more Spirit-filled love and life—and the power to share it. 🍂

I myself do nothing. The Holy Spirit accomplishes all through me.
WILLIAM BLAKE

Going Deeper

I will be their God, and they will be my people.
Jeremiah 31:33

How do you feel when friends or loved ones break their promises to you?
Explain.

Commitments are important to God. What about you? Are you a promise
keeper? If not, what promises have you broken? What commitments do
you need to stick to and honor again?

Under God's old covenant, laws and commandments were constantly
broken by His people. Under the new covenant, Christ's death and
resurrection enable us to be promise keepers by the power of His Holy
Spirit. Do you feel empowered to keep God's new covenant?

What new insights has God given you this week about the virtue
of commitment?

If you'd like, write a prayer that reflects your needs regarding the virtue
of commitment.

Promise a lot and give even more.
ANTHONY J. D'ANGELO

SERVICE

His Promise

Just as the body is dead without breath,
so also faith is dead without good works.
James 2:26

My Prayer

Keep me alive, O Life-Giving God,
with the goodness of works
that serve and glorify You.

Service: That's Empowered by the Spirit

*Just as the body is dead without breath, so also faith is dead
without good works.*
James 2:26

On Thanksgiving week, all over this town, churches were busy feeding hungry people. Good work? Absolutely. Proper service? Without a doubt.

As servant Mother Teresa of Calcutta observed about hungry people: "I say to myself this is hungry Jesus. I must feed him. Give him some bread." So with my family, I arose early on Thanksgiving morning—not to wrestle with my own turkey and dressing, but to drive downtown to help serve somebody else a hot meal: turkey with all the fixings, plus hot corn bread.

Plates filled with food, served on this rainy morning, showed Jesus, to be sure.

But to change everybody's lives, including my own, we good church folk must do more. Starting with prayer, we must ask the Holy Spirit to give us life. Enough of walking-dead servanthood, that is.

The book of James takes on this problem, warning against the emptiness of believing in faith but not acting on it. "You say you have faith, for you believe that there is one God. Good for you! Even the demons believe this. . . . How foolish!" (2:19-20).

Instead, to demonstrate the substance of your faith, says James, get up today and serve life—and not just on Thanksgiving. True service, in other words, is *Spirit*-led. And God help us today, and throughout this year's holiday season, to remember that. But also to seek it.

So I'll dare to pray this: *I'm nothing today without Your Spirit, O God.*

Yes, I like that prayer. So I pray another: *Anoint me, Lord, to serve others with more than turkey. Help me instead to serve life. Well done. Every day.* 🕊

If you can't feed a hundred people, then feed just one.
MOTHER TERESA

Service: Without Picking Favorites

*Since I, your Lord and Teacher, have washed your feet,
you ought to wash each other's feet.*
John 13:14

Even Judas. The betrayer of Christ got his feet washed too.

Even Judas. The one whose feet would run to betrayal let Jesus wash off the dirt.

Even Judas, in that classic scene in the upper room at the Passover meal, let Jesus scrub off grime. To be sure, within hours, Judas would betray Jesus. Yet Jesus put on a servant's towel and washed the feet of all His disciples. Even Judas.

A small detail in this story? Or the most important?

This wondrous moment is always remembered for the example Christ set for His followers: first be a servant. Indeed, the idea of servant leadership never fails to captivate. But while we study it, let us remember its other hard lesson: no favorites.

A hard demand? Consider that it troubled even Jesus. As He told His disciples, "Now that you know these things [about servant leadership], God will bless you for doing them" (John 13:17). *But not all of you.* "I know the ones I have chosen," He declared. For Jesus had handpicked Judas, too. But "the one who eats my food has turned against me" (v. 18).

And yet? He washed the feet of all twelve.

Even Judas.

So while we're busy being good servant leaders, will we serve even our enemies? Backstabbers? Betrayers? The ones plotting against and gossiping about us even right now?

The real servant leader doesn't have a choice. So stand up today and go wash feet. Yes, every one assigned to you. Then bless God by leaving what happens next in His hands, standing fast on His unmovable promise: "Now that you know these things, God will bless you for doing them." Believe it? Then go serve all. 🕊

The highest form of worship is the worship of unselfish Christian service.
BILLY GRAHAM

Service: In Common Ways and Places

"No," Peter protested. . . . Jesus replied, "Unless I wash you,
you won't belong to me."
John 13:8

Coach Wayne Gordon "washes feet" in the inner city of Chicago's West Side. So some people think he's a bit crazy. Or courageous? In 1975, when Gordon graduated from Wheaton College in suburban Chicago, he took a coaching job at a high school in what was the fifteenth poorest neighborhood in the United States. But after seeing the incredible needs of his students in North Lawndale, he made a drastic choice: he moved with his young bride, Anne, into one of the city's "worst" blocks, and to his own surprise launched a church. A bit crazy?

In the manner of Jesus, that is, Gordon took off his suburban options and dressed in a servant's spirit to serve the inner-city poor. His church is now the vital spiritual home of about one hundred families—and a shining light in a neighborhood needing hope.

But Gordon saw potential. So he helped found the Lawndale Christian Health Center, which sees more than 120,000 patients per year. Then, as founding president of the Lawndale Christian Development Corporation, "Coach"—as he likes to be called—has led efforts to rehab more than four hundred units of abandoned housing, encouraging homeownership among residents.

A bit crazy? Humble service always is.

When Gordon took his bride to a "run-down" neighborhood to live, many questioned his choice, if not his sanity. But in addition to raising their own three children there, he has seen more than two hundred young people from North Lawndale graduate from college, with more than half returning to live and work in their neighborhood.

A bit crazy? Absolutely.

Glamorous? No, despite winning a Point of Light award from the White House, among other awards. But the greatest award for Coach Gordon? Just washing feet. It changes lives. 🌿

Good works do not make a good man, but a good man does good works.
MARTIN LUTHER

Service: That Starts with Family

"No," Peter protested. . . . Jesus replied, "Unless I wash you,
you won't belong to me."
John 13:8

Where to practice servanthood first? In the hardest place—right at home.

Jesus taught this lesson, not in the byways and highways of towns and villages, but in the bosom of His discipleship family. Right at the kitchen table.

He knew it's too easy to go across town and "serve" the poor when we haven't bothered to serve the people right at home.

Proud relatives would resist, for one thing.

So it embarrassed Peter, a beloved disciple, to receive from his Master the lowly work normally performed by a slave. Jesus even tied a slave's towel around His waist, laying aside His Lord clothes to pick up the foot-washing cloth of the lowliest servant.

Imagine your own most beloved relative—a grandparent or favorite aunt or uncle—kneeling on the ground before you to scrub off mud from your grimy, crusty feet.

But wait. That favorite grandparent did exactly that?

Or maybe it was a favorite teacher, camp counselor, or Sunday school teacher—that one golden person in your life who saw your need and gave all?

And now it's your turn. To suffer with a family member, performing the lowest tasks needed—like Jesus did.

Can you do it?

It will be hard. Unless you have a perfect family—and surely nobody does—it will be hard. Servanthood challenges ego and expertise. But Jesus set the standard. He gave all for people who weren't grateful. So let us, too, serve family, grateful or not. Then from that practice ground, let's go serve the world. God's reward, as He told Peter, will be His great blessing. 🕊

The family fireside is the best of schools.
ARNOLD GLASOW

Service: That Glorifies God through Our Good Deeds

*Let your light shine before others, that they may see your good deeds
and glorify your Father in heaven.*
Matthew 5:16, TNIV

In rural Kenya, young Evans Wadongo grew up reading by firelight. Sound romantic? Not when you're exposed to wood and kerosene smoke, as he was every day. His eyes were damaged for life because his family couldn't afford electricity.

So "I couldn't compete effectively with other kids who had access to lighting," he said on a CNN *Heroes* broadcast. "In every home in the village it was the same. Many children drop out of school for these reasons . . . so they remain poor for the rest of their life."

Evans recognized the solution: Give light. Safe and healthy light. Then the money villagers spent to buy kerosene could be used to buy food. Plus, children would have light to read and learn, leading to good jobs.

But where would Evans find light?

The answer came as the twenty-three-year-old college student in Kenya was fiddling around with a dorm experiment with LED (light-emitting diode) Christmas lights—and, literally, saw the light: solar power.

Then while walking home one day, he stumbled on a broken piece of solar panel, somebody else's throwaway. He used it to light a few LEDs, giving birth to a solar lantern that Evans called MwangaBora, Swahili for "good light."

And the rest is history. Now, because of Evans, some ten thousand households in rural Kenya enjoy light for free. Volunteers who make the solar-powered LED lanterns are paid a portion of production costs, providing funds to support their families too. And Evans? He eats one meal a day so more lanterns can be built. Then more will see his good light.

But why tell Evans's story? To inspire our own. For as we take light to a dark world, people in darkness will see God. 🌱

Fill the waterpots, stretch out your hand, distribute the loaves.
ELISABETH ELLIOT

Service: That Blesses Others with Gladness

Serve the Lord enthusiastically. Be glad for all God is planning for you.
Romans 12:11-12

The graying man was nice and friendly—and flawed. So the good church people trying to help him were getting annoyed. His clutter, his chaotic surroundings, his lack of focus, his inappropriate laughter and lack of protocol, and his lack of worry about any of it were turning the church "service project" into an exercise in patience and frustration.

But godly service isn't judging.

"Sometimes it's about giving away most what you need the most." That's how my pastor, Timothy Tyler, explained godly service at a Bible study. We were four or five weeks into the thirteenth chapter of John—Jesus' foot-washing lesson. But now came the nitty-gritty: what if we don't love the person we're serving?

"Sometimes you don't," Pastor Tyler said. "Not everybody we're supposed to love is lovable." But look at Jesus, Pastor urged.

"You can know you've become a servant when, like Jesus, you lay down your life anyway, taking the thing you love the most and giving it away—that is, yourself."

Even when you're annoyed.

So never approach service from the standpoint of seeing yourself as "better" than the person you serve, Pastor added. "In fact, being a servant may mean not giving a blessing, but being able to receive a blessing—even with gladness."

With the graying man, some of us tried to show we understood. When he laughed when somebody stumbled over his junk-filled floor, we laughed too. When we stopped judging, that is, we could serve with gladness—and even enthusiasm. Still it's hard, this mandate to serve. But a little humble laughter makes the work of loving go down easy. 🔥

If we don't work, God doesn't move. If we don't speak, God is silent.
TIMOTHY E. TYLER

Going Deeper

Well done, my good and faithful servant. You have been faithful
in handling this small amount, so now I will give you many
more responsibilities. Let's celebrate together!
Matthew 25:21

What service have you given to others this year? Did it make a difference?

Jesus put on a slave's towel to wash dirty feet. Do your good deeds humble you or put you on a pedestal, making you look good? Explain.

Kenyan college student Evans Wadongo has brought solar lighting to some ten thousand households in rural Kenya at no charge. What do you see in his character that led to the dramatic impact of his service to others?

What new insights has God given you this week about the virtue of service?

If you'd like, write a prayer that reflects your needs regarding the virtue of service.

Do all the good you can, by all the means you can, in all the ways you can, in all the places you can, at all the times you can, to all the people you can, as long as ever you can.
CHARLES WESLEY

THRIFT

His Promise

The LORD is my shepherd;
I have all that I need.
Psalm 23:1

My Prayer

You keep on providing, Generous Father,
and I am so thankful.
Now help me to be a godly steward
of Your every gift, giving back with grace,
for Your glory.

Thrift: That Honors God as Owner of All

LORD, you alone are my inheritance.
Psalm 16:5

God owns everything. For years, I'd heard this. For years, I didn't understand it. For years, I guess I didn't want to accept it. Then after decades of poor money management, as I sat one cold day in the parking lot of my bank, I vowed to renew my understanding of His ways, starting with money principle number one:

God owns everything. "The earth is the LORD's, and everything in it. The world and all its people belong to him," says Psalm 24:1. Adds Psalm 50:10, "For all the animals of the forest are mine, and I own the cattle on a thousand hills."

Moreover, "'The silver is mine, and the gold is mine,' says the LORD of Heaven's Armies," according to Haggai 2:8.

And me? I own nothing. Instead, I'm blessed to be a steward of God's vast resources. You are too. And once I finally understood *that*, I could praise God for two salient things:

First, since He owns everything, I will never go without. Second, as His beloved child, it's my job to take care of what He gives me to handle. Then I will wisely and prudently steward the resources He sends my way.

Suddenly, indeed, I began to understand what wise money-management experts like Ron Blue, Michelle Singletary, Dave Ramsey, the late Larry Burkett, and others have been teaching all these years: every spending or saving decision *is* a spiritual decision. But so is every life decision.

The details of our personal plans will differ, of course.

But before we start reading *Rich Dad, Poor Dad* or *The Millionaire Next Door* or *Total Money Makeover* or any of the scores of money-management books and guides available, we'd do better to make peace with God. Our sovereign Father owns everything. Even us. Let's bless Him by accepting that. Then we'll put money in its rightful place. 🌿

What I possess, God owns.
HOWARD DAYTON

Thrift: That Puts Money in Its Place

*For wisdom is more profitable than silver, and her wages
are better than gold.*
Proverbs 3:14

It's only money? So money isn't good or bad. Money isn't wonderful or evil.
Money isn't special or magical. It's only money—a medium for exchanging
what we buy or what we sell. So it doesn't control us, unless we let it.

And that, of course, is the problem. As Dave Ramsey, the bestselling money-
management expert, said in an interview with a Christian broadcaster: "The
weird thing about money in our culture is that we worship it."

Why? Because money buys stuff. And that's what we crave. More stuff.
New stuff. Better stuff. Ramsey, in fact, struggles with stuff. "I think that
God makes me teach this every day because I struggle with it. My name is
Dave and I like stuff."

It's in our DNA, psychologists say of this craving. We're hunters and gath-
erers, clamoring to get more to calm our anxiety about being without—or
not being cool if we don't get more. So we seek and buy more, piling up
debt, possessions, and misery.

Or we can get smart. Today. As we move through the Christmas-buying
season, we can be so smart we'll vow not to buy more of what we don't need,
not for us or for others.

Such thrift puts money in its place. Even better, it puts God back in first
place in our lives. And look at me, preaching about something I struggled
over for so long. But I praise God this morning for opening my feeble eyes
to see this: Thrift is not first about spending. Or not spending. Thrift is first
about enriching my relationship with God.

So thrift is surrendering, seeking, knocking, asking: *What, O Providing
Father, should I do with Your resources? This paycheck, home, talent, and body
are Yours. Use them for Your glory—then replace my craving for stuff with more
of You.* And *amen* for the prayer that puts money in its place. 🕯

The world asks, "What does a man own?" Christ asks, "How does he use it?"
ANDREW MURRAY

Thrift: That Calms My Anxiety about Money

*Don't wear yourself out trying to get rich. Be wise enough
to know when to quit.*
Proverbs 23:4

A million bucks needed for retirement. Ouch. We've all heard that number and other numbers even higher, depending on our incomes. All those zeroes generate enough anxiety to make us all a little crazy. But what does the Bible say, not just about saving for retirement, but about money in general?

Don't be crazy.

Don't wear yourself out trying to get rich. "In the blink of an eye wealth disappears, for it will sprout wings and fly away like an eagle," says Proverbs 23:5. Or as John D. Rockefeller, the world's first billionaire, put it: "If your only goal is to become rich, you will never achieve it."

So what in the world should we do about money? Methodist theologian John Wesley's simple approach: "Earn all you can, give all you can, save all you can."

Money management, in other words, is about calm goal setting, wise planning, and regular saving. Nothing fancy. "Take a lesson from the ants," says the writer of Proverbs. "Though they have no prince or governor or ruler to make them work, they labor hard all summer, gathering food for the winter" (6:6-8).

The old-fashioned way of working hard, tithing, and saving—with automatic payments deducted and deployed *before* you get your paycheck so it's a hands-off resource—will pay you and God's Kingdom handsomely in the long run.

Trying to go too fast won't work, says money expert Dave Ramsey. "Incrementally, step by step, by degrees, frustratingly slow—but that's how you win."

Like the ant. Earn all we can, give all we can, save all we can. But along the way, what else should we do? Let us praise and serve our wondrous and generous Lord. ❧

Be willing to be the tortoise. Every time I read the book, he beats the hare.
DAVE RAMSEY

Thrift: That Maximizes My Earnings

Wealth from get-rich-quick schemes quickly disappears;
wealth from hard work grows over time.
Proverbs 13:11

Christmas is coming soon, so my daily newspaper is printing a regular dose of feel-good, holiday-themed stories. Heart candy, I call them, with full respect. They taste sweet and feel good. One, however, captures my heart in a special way.

It's about a single mom of three, divorced and struggling to make ends meet, who's decided to stop scraping by and, instead, maximize her income. But not for the money. She's changing her life for her three girls. Then "when they got older," this young mom tells my local *Denver Post*, "they would always know I fought for myself and for them."

So she buckled down and went back to school, working at a fast-food restaurant to pay tuition to become a medical assistant.

So, no, this story isn't about a megazillionaire making even more bucks.

Instead, for the young mom in the news story, money was tight. Then it was gone. Then when she couldn't pay rent, she moved with the girls into a motel for a month, ditching her clunker car to ride the bus. Up before dawn, she and the girls caught a 5:30 a.m. bus to the babysitter. After school, she bundled up the kids and headed to the downtown Denver Public Library. The kids read and played in the children's section while the mom finished homework. Back at the motel, a church-lady friend watched the kids while the mom worked the late-night shift at the fast-food place, ending at 2 a.m.

Then her boss issued an ultimatum. School or job. She chose school, daring to take an unpaid internship in a physician's office to finish the last leg of her schooling.

And it all paid off. With only thirty dollars left in this woman's wallet, the physician called her in to say well done and to offer her a job. With real pay. Next for her? Nursing school. Next for us? Learning her simple lesson: to earn more, work hard. But the Bible said it first. 🔥

Good planning and hard work lead to prosperity.
PROVERBS 21:5

Thrift: That Maximizes My Giving

For God is the one who provides seed for the farmer and then bread to eat.
In the same way, he will provide and increase your resources and then
produce a great harvest of generosity in you.
2 Corinthians 9:10

When Paul taught this lesson on giving, he spoke of farming and seed stock and harvest—all concepts that meant something real to first-century Christians. His teaching can feel relevant to believers today, as well, if we listen closely.

Giving back money to God surely can challenge the best of us, especially if we're not living by biblical principles of thrift and money management, so our money supply always seems tight. But Paul offers this smart reminder: farmers always keep back a portion of seed from each harvest to plant for next year's crop.

The tithe operates the same way. Giving back to God that 10 percent off the top of our earnings—our firstfruits—shows Him to be our Provider of it all, the one alone who increases our resources in order to "produce a great harvest of generosity."

As Paul writes to the Corinthians, "the one who plants generously will get a generous crop" (2 Corinthians 9:6). But don't give reluctantly or under pressure. "For God loves a person who gives cheerfully" (v. 7). Or as Crown Financial Ministries, the Christian money-management organization, says about such matters: "The principle of tithing is just that—a principle . . . God is looking for the right attitude in a person's giving." Any distraction over the percentage misses the point. God doesn't own just the 10 percent; He owns the 90 percent left over, too. So as you and I tithe, let's pray over all of it.

And if you're in deep debt and tithing only 1 or 2 percent until you can give more, keep tithing cheerfully. Your attitude is what counts. Then watch your ability to earn *and* to give grow in kind. "Then you will always have everything you need," Paul says, "and plenty left over to share with others" (v. 8). And your harvest? As it grows, watch it glorify God. 🌿

It is a matter of the heart in giving to God.
CROWN FINANCIAL MINISTRIES

Thrift: That Maximizes My Saving

Yet true godliness with contentment is itself great wealth.
1 Timothy 6:6

Spend less than we earn. That's the secret. But here's the key: be content with what we have. That way we're not tempted to spend *more*.

But isn't that too simple?

In discussing faith-based money management, Christian financial-planning expert Ron Blue boils down this simple rule of thumb in just that way. As he says, everybody's question is, "Will I ever have enough? Secondly, will it continue to be enough? And then, by the way, how much is enough?"

Blue's wise answer: "The only way to have enough is to spend less than you earn and do it over a lifetime."

But isn't that too simple?

Blue, who has counseled thousands of people over a long and successful career in financial planning, says saving "enough" in a godly way amounts to just that. "Live within your income; set it aside a little bit over a long lifetime—[it] will always work out." He adds, "I have seen millionaires who you'd never, ever guess were millionaires. They just lived within their income. They were content with what they had. They were content with their life-style. And they ended up, in light of economic uncertainty, living really, really well."

But can such savings success be ours? Do we want it to be?

Blue and other Christian money experts remind us that the discipline of saving and stewarding God's resources according to Bible-based principles hinges, not on our account balance, but on our trust in the living God. As Blue says, "The best financial-planning question that can be asked is 'Lord, what would *you* have me to do?'"

About our savings. Our giving. Our earning. Let's pray that in faith, then look for His answers to grow savings that turn our financial life into a feast of worship. 🌿

Walking by faith means allowing God to be God.
RON BLUE

Going Deeper

*Don't store up treasures here on earth, where moths eat them and rust
destroys them, and where thieves break in and steal. Store your treasures
in heaven. . . . Wherever your treasure is, there the desires
of your heart will also be.*
Matthew 6:19-21

God owns everything. Is that true for everything in your life, including
money? Explain.

If you have anxiety about money, what's your biggest worry? You can
replace your worry about money with more trust in God, starting with
asking Him to enlarge your trust and then show you what to do about
your money. Pray that prayer now.

What new insights has God given you this week about the virtue of thrift?

If you'd like, write a prayer that reflects your needs regarding the virtue
of thrift.

If a person gets his attitude toward money straight,
it will help straighten out almost every other area in his life.
BILLY GRAHAM

ENTERPRISE
AND
INDUSTRY

His Promise

The diligent make use of everything they find.
Proverbs 12:27

My Prayer

Equip me to honor You, our hardworking God,
with a willing heart and hands that commit
to industry and enterprise in all You show me to do.

Enterprise and Industry:
That Turns My Work into Worship

Our sister, may you become the mother of many millions! May your
descendants be strong and conquer the cities of their enemies.
Genesis 24:60

The young mom came to America from Poland, working for ten years to earn her green card—then studying another three years to earn a master's degree, part of that time caring for her infant too. Her husband, also from Poland, did the same. Then came the day they both graduated and launched out into good jobs, evidence that industrious diligence pays off.

"This is still the best country in the world," she said in an interview on the radio program *Talk of the Nation.* As she put it: "When you can come from a country like Poland, when you don't speak English and after ten, fifteen years, you can go back to school and you can enjoy life in here. This is—cannot happen anywhere else."

How did she do it? She set a goal, got to work, gave extra, and didn't stop.

Her story reflects the story of another industrious young woman, Rebekah of the Holy Bible. She was chosen to be wife of Isaac, the beloved and rich son of Abraham—God's covenant leader—not just because she was beautiful but because she worked hard and gave more than asked.

Read her story today in Genesis 24. Abraham's servant, sent to find a wife for Isaac among Abraham's relatives, sees young women coming to draw water. In prayer, he decides the one who offers him a drink—as well as offers to water his camels—will be the right woman for Isaac. Sure enough, beautiful Rebekah shows hospitality and industry, kindly offering water to the servant but also to his thirsty camels—animals known to drink twenty-five gallons each. So her offer is no small gesture. Her reward? A blessing that rewarded millions, even as it still reminds us: go that extra mile today—for God. ✐

In the ordinary business of life, industry can do anything which genius can do,
and very many things which it cannot.
HENRY WARD BEECHER

Enterprise and Industry:
In Doing Business That Glorifies God

She goes to inspect a field and buys it; with her earnings she plants a
vineyard. . . . She makes sure her dealings are profitable;
her lamp burns late into the night.
Proverbs 31:16, 18

That virtuous wife of the Bible is many things. But more than all, to my surprise, she is enterprising. And I didn't expect that. Studying her a few years
back, daring to try to shape my life after hers, I sat down with paper and pen
and made a list of all her virtuous traits. From her trustworthy, hardworking,
time-watching ethic, she's a paragon of good works and wisdom. Her profile,
however, also includes the job of businesswoman.

Make that successful businesswoman.

It makes sense, in fact, that a woman who brings good to her husband,
finds wool and "busily" spins it—and gets up before dawn to prepare breakfast for her household, plus plans each day's work for her servants—would
then hunker down and do business. Enterprising business.

So, no, I refuse to get into the debate about her "superwoman" standard
being too high. Instead, I'm inspired by what she does inside her household
and beyond. In her case, the virtuous woman buys land. Selling it for profit,
she plants a vineyard, another steady stream of income. A seamstress, meantime, she also makes belted linen garments and sashes to sell to merchants.
Earning all she can, she helps the poor and needy too.

Of course, she makes a profit. Hard work pays off, the Bible promises. Yet
this woman's legacy is that, while her success speaks well for her husband and
family, it also glorifies God. *That* is the hallmark of an enterprising believer.

She's kind, indeed, and "suffers nothing from laziness" (v. 27). Thus, her
day-to-day enterprising lifestyle is itself a witness to the empowering God
she fearfully serves. A high standard? No higher than expected for a woman
whose life's labor speaks for God. ❧

Don't limit yourself.
MARY KAY ASH

Enterprise and Industry:
In Telling Others about Christ

Therefore, go and make disciples. . . . And be sure of this:
I am with you always, even to the end of the age.
Matthew 28:19-20

Why go into business? To tell more people about Christ. That's what Crown Financial Ministries teaches is the number one goal of a Christian business owner.

Not to make a profit?

That's what I asked myself as I looked over Crown's many informative articles about business ownership. While profit is important, Crown says it's not the first reason to be enterprising. Instead, profit allows Christian business owners to witness, by their Spirit-led actions and benefits, who Christ is—sharing Him first with a company's managers and supervisors. In turn, those managers and supervisors can witness, in their actions and benefits, to those working under their charge.

Which brings us to Hobby Lobby.

Many know the inspiring story of the two-billion-dollar company. Founder Dave Green, one of six children raised in a God-loving Oklahoma family, launched an art-framing store after earning a business degree. The business grew into the hobby, art, and crafts business, struggling to survive during the oil recession of the eighties, but reviving into a thriving retail chain, which, in 2010, numbered 462 stores in 39 states. Several related businesses, including Christian bookstore chain Mardel, are in the Hobby Lobby family.

The chain's strongest identity, however, may be its clear commitment to lift the name of Jesus. From its closed-on-Sundays store policy to its popular full-page newspaper ads at Christmas and Easter, Hobby Lobby stands unapologetically as a witness for the Lord. And so can we. No matter how big or small our enterprises, let's use them for excellence in showing the light of Jesus' love. Our success in evangelism will bless our industry with this empowering promise of Christ: I am with you always. Even in your business.

God visits industrious men with His favors.
MATTHEW HENRY

Enterprise and Industry: That's Small but Mighty

In this way, your generosity stores up a reward for you in heaven.
Luke 16:9

Not every business will be a two-billion-dollar megagiant like David Green's Hobby Lobby retail chain. But small can still be mighty.

That's what I'm thinking today as my husband, Dan, and I sit in a teeny biscuit café on a funny curved street with almost no parking space in south Denver.

Biscuits, indeed, are all they sell in this miniscule shop—that plus coffee, juice, and tea. Made with love and a light touch, the Southern-style biscuit is the star in this Lilliputian restaurant with its one table plus two leather stools against a wall.

Small, focused, simple. And mighty.

Our daily newspaper touted the place for its friendly service, low prices— "and, oh, those biscuits." As Dan and I enjoy our sackful, we think about the power *and* prosperity of such uncomplicated simplicity.

All over the world, in fact, such so-called mom-and-pop businesses continue to keep local economies alive. The argument that only large-scale business visions matter, as even respected business schools teach these days, overlooks what Jesus taught:

Start small and be faithful. But give big. And stay with it.

"If you are faithful in little things, you will be faithful in large ones" (Luke 16:10). Then whether your simplified business hits the two-billion-dollar mark, or stays as small as a one-table café, you can be trusted "with the true riches of heaven" (v. 11).

That's what Jesus urges in His lesson on being faithful in small things. In that way, the tiny but enterprising business operating well for God's glory honors Him, and in the sight of heaven is beyond measure. In fact, people will call it not small, but a giant. 🔥

There is nothing small if God is in it.
D. L. MOODY

Enterprise and Industry: That Doesn't Give Up

Work hard and become a leader; be lazy and become a slave.
Proverbs 12:24

Sarah Breedlove could have lived and died in Delta, Louisiana, never to be known by more than a few close relatives. But as the daughter of newly freed slaves, who both died when she was only seven, the hardworking African American girl took on life with a determination that transformed her from a cotton-field orphan to one of the first self-made female millionaires in America.

We know her now as Madam C. J. Walker, founder of a hair-care and cosmetics empire that, by 1917, employed nearly one thousand female sales agents across the country, operated its own manufacturing factory, and enabled Walker to become a visionary philanthropist.

In a Harvard Business School case, "Madam C. J. Walker: Entrepreneur, Leader, and Philanthropist," Professor Nancy Koehn described a key component of Walker's extraordinary success. Her church connections "formed the basis for her agent network and helped build word-of-mouth advertising for the products."

That strategy and her name change—in the manner of Estée Lauder and Elizabeth Arden, both of that same era—fueled Walker's God-fearing determination to help black women look and feel better.

And the world took notice. While other millionaires of her day were burning through their cash, Walker donated thousands to causes to improve life for others. She helped fund the building of a YMCA, promoted world peace after World War I, and joined other civic leaders in a meeting with President Woodrow Wilson to speak out against lynching. Her path? From the cotton fields to the White House.

"Work hard and become a leader," says Proverbs 12:24. Are you up for such a challenge? Why not start today to find out? ❧

Don't sit down and wait for opportunities to come;
you have to get up and make them.
MADAM C. J. WALKER

Enterprise and Industry: That Won't Stop Believing

Remember the LORD your God. He is the one who
gives you power to be successful.
Deuteronomy 8:18

The Lawndale Miracle should not have worked. As a business model it was all wrong. As a church, its members were mostly neighborhood kids—poor black kids, that is—and their young white pastor was a high school coach. The first church project? Put a washer and dryer in the church storefront so folks in the area had a safe place to wash clothes.

A washer and dryer? That's how Pastor Wayne "Coach" Gordon—the pastor I introduced to you in early December—reacted as he set out to launch Lawndale Community Church in what is still one of the poorest neighborhoods anywhere in Chicago, or in America, for that matter.

But Gordon listened. He prayed. He believed God. Then a few days later he got a call out of the blue from a suburban man looking to donate his family's washer and dryer. The appliances worked fine, but the color didn't match the new color scheme of the man's home. To donate them, the donor agreed to deliver the two appliances right to the storefront-church door.

A miracle? Just one of the first for the North Lawndale church whose youth longed for a neighborhood recreation center but lacked funds. Then an empty auto parts store two doors from the church came up for sale. Price: $18,000. Too much. But before Gordon could say no, the owner dropped the price. "You're doing great things. I'll sell it to you for $10,000." Still too much for a church with only $6,000 and change in the bank and whose board refused to ever operate by going into debt. So Gordon again said no.

But the owner insisted. "Could you come up with six thousand dollars?"

A miracle? That's what a Chicago businessman must've thought. When he heard about the washer and dryer donation, he donated $10,000 to reimburse the church for buying the empty building, with enough extra for $2,000 or so in repairs. The Lawndale Community Church Recreation Center opened soon after.

Enterprising belief? Or believing enterprise? Either way, examine your enterprise today. Then ask if what's missing is a belief in the God of big miracles. 🔥

Belief is power.
FREDERICK W. ROBERTSON

Going Deeper

Always work enthusiastically for the Lord, for you know that
nothing you do for the Lord is ever useless.
1 Corinthians 15:58

As a child, what were you taught about business and hard work? How do those childhood lessons line up with what the Bible says about such matters?

Does God bless business operations? What does His Word say to you about this?

If you've ever dreamed of starting your own business or ministry, what has stopped you? What do you need to do to act on this dream?

What new insights has God given you this week about the virtue of industrious enterprise?

If you'd like, write a prayer that reflects your needs regarding the virtue of enterprising industry.

Hell itself must yield to industry.
BEN JONSON

COMPLETION

His Promise

And I am certain that God,
who began the good work within you,
will continue his work until it is finally finished
on the day when Christ Jesus returns.
Philippians 1:6

My Prayer

Thank You for Your certainty, O Blessed God,
that the work You have started in me
will be fine-tuned, but also ready,
when Jesus our anointed Christ
returns in victory.

Completion: That Lets God Keep Working in Me

God, who began the good work within you, will continue
his work until it is finally finished.
Philippians 1:6

And now we come to the end?

We could say that about completion, this last topic in our year of studying and praying, growing and asking. But as with a commencement exercise at any school—from pre-K, high school, college, or university—the word *commencement* actually means "to begin."

So here in December, this last month of the year, we don't as believers observe the last days of the life of our Christ. We celebrate His birth.

In fact, in this darkest part of the calendar year, we don't wring our hands in despair, giving in to the gloom of dark mornings and inky nights. Instead, we sing with joy, celebrating our Jesus, the incandescent, always-shining Light of the World.

Paul teaches this same principle, of beginning again at the end, in his letter to the faithful new believers in Philippi. Paul, thus, declares that God, "who began the good work [of salvation] within you, will continue" it. Until January? Until next summer? Actually, "until it is finally finished on the day when Christ Jesus returns."

So I feel myself drawn back to my day-at-a-time *One Year* yes-I-can Bible, but not to put it away on a shelf forever. I'm eager instead to read it again, confident the work of completion in me continues. I look in my next year's mirror and see, indeed, what I still need to learn. How to serve better, love deeper, surrender sooner. To be sure, this finishing work of growing in grace and peace, as Paul puts it, is exciting.

For "every time I think of you," Paul writes so longingly, "I give thanks to my God" (1:3)—because God looks at me and doesn't give up. In fact, He makes what should be the end, for all of us, a new beginning. Will you accept that truth? If you will, you'll measure today, not by what you still aren't, but by what God promises to continue to do in you. 🕯

Imagine you wake up with a second chance.
RITA DOVE

Completion: That Reflects the Glory of Christ

You have tested us, O God; you have purified us like silver.
Psalm 66:10

Our favorite Christmas tree ornaments take center stage. For most of us, a homemade tree bob made by a beloved child—a son, daughter, niece, nephew, grandchild, student, or neighbor—gets hung on our tree every year with great love. With thanks to my wonderful children, I have more than a few of those myself.

But my most unique piece to hang on our tree? It's an heirloom silver ball with a bell inside—a wedding present—inscribed with the year my husband and I were married.

We were married a few days before Christmas, many years ago, and that silver ball has traveled from house to house, city to city, neighborhood to neighborhood, across three-plus decades of married life.

Was every year easy? No. Married life never is, not consistently. But many more good days than bad make up our story. So every year, I unwrap the ball from its flannel-cloth covering, apply silver polish and give it a deep shine, then hang it on an evergreen branch. And all that symbolism shines with a deep glow all Christmas long.

The shine and beauty of silver is hard wrought, indeed. To extract silver from other ores takes screamingly intense heat, and sometimes even acid, for the culling. In sheet-metal form, silver still undergoes all manner of hammering, annealing (more heat), forging and forming, planishing and burnishing—among other steps—before a piece is finished and deemed ready for use.

It ain't easy, in other words, to become a piece of usable silver. It's a journey that seems to mirror this process called life, married or otherwise. Then there's that iconic anecdote describing how the craftsman knows when a piece of silver is finally ready. Says the silversmith in that story: "It's ready when I can see my reflection in it." And in that way, may we on this Christmas Day, and all the new year, reflect the glory of our burnishing Christ. 🕯

Radiant beams from thy holy face, With the dawn of redeeming grace;
Jesus, Lord, at thy birth—Jesus, Lord, at thy birth.
JOSEPH MOHR

Completion: That Gets the Job Done

It would be good for you to finish what you started.
2 Corinthians 8:10

I'm doing a brisk mile on the treadmill, eyes glued to a home renovation show called *Disaster DIY*. On this episode, the host is helping a retired mom "who started a thousand DIY [do it yourself] projects," says her daughter, "and she hasn't finished any of it." So the house is a disaster, for sure.

Kitchen floor? Loose tiles in place but never plastered down. Cabinets? Nailed in position, but the countertops wobble on top, unattached. Backsplash? Glass tiles are cut, but they're hanging on the wall with tape.

"Tape?" asks the show host, laughing with a wink.

But laughs turn to groans when he sees the bathroom, with its floor tiles "dry fit" but never installed and a bathtub with a plastic bag for a shower curtain. The biggest problem with this homeowner?

"Confidence," says the host.

The homeowner agrees. "And fear," she adds. Power tools and wet saws terrify her. So she stops short. Never completing anything.

The entire mess, however, makes me think about how, as believers, we struggle to finish this Christian walk with victory.

I reflect on the matter, in fact, as the HGTV host shows this homeowner how to chalk a plumb line across her kitchen floor before laying tile. Like our plumb line that is Christ, the chalk will mark the straight path to follow to achieve a tile floor that's right.

Can't find a friend to hold the other end of the line before snapping it? "Hang it on a nail." I listen to this advice, letting the words sink in. To be sure, if my life is attached to our Lord's crucifixion, I'll stay on track, walking this journey and finishing.

In that way, the homeowner "made a bit of a mess," as we do in life, "but she put her back into" the tasks and she finished. Beautiful kitchen? Even better, she earned a beautiful life. "I feel empowered," she said. Even better, in Christ, as we take on the tasks of life, we'll finish with beauty and grace. 🍃

The important thing is doing it.
BRYAN BAEUMLER

Completion: That Honors the Sacrifice of Christ

*For by that one offering he forever made perfect those
who are being made holy.*
Hebrews 10:14

Today I see a bright light. Not so big a light, but it's mighty. In a sea of bad news—that says only 68.8 percent of high school students in the United States graduate in four years—I discover the Urban Prep charter school in inner-city Chicago.

In one of the toughest neighborhoods in the nation, Urban Prep CEO Tim King and a determined faculty will see 100 percent of their 2010 senior class—that's 107 boys in the all-black, all-male school's first graduating group—finish on top. So every Urban Prep graduate in 2010 was accepted to a four-year college—Northwestern University, Morehouse College, Howard University, Trinity College, and the University of Virginia, among others, reported the Associated Press.

What fueled such achievement and completion? Hard work and sacrifice, plus an extended school day that's two hours longer than most, and for good measure, students were assigned double periods of English.

Could we do as much in our living for Christ? To be sure, for graduate Kishaun Branch, who arrived at Urban Prep with Ds and truancies, the road to becoming president of the school's student government association was all sacrifice.

"I knew I was going down the wrong path," he told the Associated Press. "I had to graduate or my life was going to be nothing."

The result of his sacrifice? "My personality changed. My posture changed. My speech changed. A lot about me has changed."

Sound familiar? As followers of Christ, when we sacrifice our all to reach a goal, we, too, will discover a fresh walk, graduating from old ways to new change. As new creatures in the Lord, we even look different. Our great inspiration, indeed, is Christ. Let us bless Him today by pursuing a goal that honors His selfless, finalizing sacrifice. Then let's finish it. ❧

He finished it when He couldn't, but He did.
LESTER ROLOFF

Completion: That Keeps Step with God's Pace

The fastest runner doesn't always win the race.
Ecclesiastes 9:11

Are you still in a hurry? Frustrated with the end-of-year pace of your mission or ministry? Impatient with your business plan or goals, your relationships or realities? Even fed up with yourself—and others, too? If so, consider a wiser path to completion in Christ.

Eugene Peterson, in his compelling and unique way, says this as well as anybody.

"The Christian life is the lifelong practice of attending to the details of congruence—congruence between ends and means, congruence between what we do and the way we do it." Or as Peterson, in his classic reflection on spiritual theology, *Christ Plays in Ten Thousand Places*, concludes: "Only when we do the Jesus truth in the Jesus way do we get the Jesus life."

And Jesus isn't in a rush. Neither should we be with life, or with Christ— or with ourselves. "The fastest runner doesn't always win the race," says the writer of Ecclesiastes, as recorded in chapter 9, verse 11. Then Martin Luther expressed the same thing this way, while talking about prayer: "I have so much to do this day that I shall spend the first three hours in prayer."

So let us slow down. If we didn't accomplish all we planned to achieve this year, we slow down, trusting that the God of good timing and second chances will give us another go. Another turn? That, in fact, is exactly what is needed, Peterson adds, noting: "This is slow work and cannot be hurried. It is also urgent work and can't be procrastinated." So we need to slow ourselves down and get in step with the pace of the Holy One to get it right.

Today, let us first just seek Him. And listen to Him. And abide in Him. Then we can work with Him. But not on our own agenda. Instead, let's listen, abide, and work to colabor with God on His plan. So it probably won't be fast.

Getting right with God and with others, and for His Kingdom, takes much good time. But imagine this: in the slowness of His pace, we finish well. Then we win. 🌿

There are no shortcuts to becoming the persons we're created to be.
EUGENE PETERSON

Completion:
That Turns My Feet toward the New Year

Understand what really matters, so that you may live pure and blameless lives until the day of Christ's return.
Philippians 1:10

Somebody's waiting for us? As the year prepares to turn, somebody precious is waiting for you and me to get up and get moving for His Kingdom.

How do I know? Because on the afternoon I write these closing words, my phone rings. It's a caller from the Bible translation company, Wycliffe, not asking for a year-end donation. Instead, the caller asks if I need prayer. I am moved by her offer and we talk awhile. So I ask her to pray for this last page of thoughts. Then our chat turns to the Bible translation accomplished this year—some of it achieved on the ground, with plain elbow grease and tears, and some with pretty cool technology that wasn't even around the year before. So the ministry's outreach workers around the world completed more translations, making the Bible now available to thirty-seven million more people than a year ago.

Exciting, wondrous news.

Within an hour, however, I'm drawn to the *New York Times* website, only to see that Christians in Iraq are facing unspeakable persecution, including the massacre a few weeks before of fifty-one worshipers and two priests in a Baghdad church. On this day, says the *Times*, Christians are fleeing the violence in droves, leaving behind jobs and cars and household possessions, only to face more trials as they try to start over in the Kurdish area of Erbil.

And somebody is waiting for us.

As we look to the New Year, we could make a personal list of resolutions for ourselves. Or we could compose a prayer, asking the Lord to show us how, by His Spirit, to bless, love, and lift others—both near and far. For certain, we've learned that while it's astounding to be blessed by God, it's even better to bless others in His name. Thus we can know, as Paul said, "what really matters." It's simple and good:

Go be His servant. 🌿

Spend life for something which outlasts it.
WILLIAM JAMES

Completion: That Closes the Year with His Love

I pray that your love will overflow more and more, and that you will keep on growing in knowledge and understanding.
Philippians 1:9

One amazing year ends. Another year waits. But how do we tie the two together?

How about with love? Topped off with peace and grace?

Instead of wrestling over a year's worth of Christian virtues, wondering how to weave them into this Christian life so they bless going and coming, what if we gave this year back to God—walking into next year with one simple goal? To share more of Him.

That's what our wise road travelers recommend. Says Eugene Peterson, for example, "To begin with, the Christian life is not about us; it is about God." He adds: "Christian spirituality is not a life-project for becoming a better person, it is not about developing a so-called 'deeper life.' We are in on it, to be sure. But we are not the subject."

Our blessed walk this year, in other words, wasn't for us. As wondrous as the great blessings from God are, they don't stop with us—because they aren't just for us. "I pray," says Paul, "that your love will overflow." And not just a little bit. "More and more."

So we take what we learned, experienced, and struggled with this year. We reflect and pray, praising God for all. But we pass it on by giving to others His love and peace.

One day at a time, I can just try this. To listen with generosity and patience. To love with mercy and hope. To obey with humility and repentance. To seek justice and discipline and industry with truth and passion, but also with grace. Balance marks this life. So I can love with abandon, but also with wisdom. And if I fail? In Christ, there is no failure—there's only trying again to bless Him along this way. Together. 🌿

Beginning well is a momentary thing; finishing well is a lifelong thing.
RAVI ZACHARIAS

Going Deeper

It is finished!
John 19:30

Have you left any key projects unfinished this year? If so, what mental or spiritual obstacle stands in your way to completing your goal?

Jesus went to the Cross, knowing what He would endure, but He went anyway, finally declaring, "It is finished!" In light of His sacrifice, what tough challenge in your life can you vow to complete in the coming months? In the coming years?

"The fastest runner doesn't always win the race," says Ecclesiastes 9:11. Why do you think this is true?

What special insight has the Lord given you about the virtue of completion?

If you'd like, write a prayer that reflects your needs regarding the virtue of completion.

Live like it's important.
ELIZABETH EDWARDS

ENDNOTES

INTRODUCTION

"the frivolous character" A. W. Tozer, *The Knowledge of the Holy* (New York: HarperCollins, 1961), 116.

JANUARY

3 *"I wait quietly"* Richard Foster, *Prayer: Finding the Heart's True Home* (New York: HarperCollins, 1992), 200.

4 *"There was none of that"* Dale Carnegie, *How to Win Friends and Influence People,* reissue ed. (New York: Simon & Schuster, 2009), 97.

6 *"In those days"* Helen Keller, *The Story of My Life: The Restored Edition* (New York: Modern Library Classics, 2004), 9–10.

8 *"simply imagine"* Curt Thompson, *Anatomy of the Soul* (Carol Stream, IL: Tyndale, 2010), 107, italics in original.

20 *"I know this sounds crazy"* Lisa Marshall, "The Gift of Sight for a Rwandan Orphan," *Denver Post,* February 23, 2010, http://www.denverpost.com /recommended/ci_14450423.

22 "Dear Amy" Amy Dickinson, "Teaching a 16-Year-Old Daughter to 'Play Nice,'" Ask Amy, *Denver Post,* March 1, 2010, http://www.denverpost.com /lifestyles/ci_14488584#ixzz1GEkKXUfc.

30 *"The sea feeds"* C. H. Spurgeon, "A Cheerful Giver Is Beloved of God," (sermon, Metropolitan Tabernacle, London, August 27, 1868), http://www .spurgeongems.org/vols13-15/chs835.pdf.

FEBRUARY

2 *"How can I help"* Story told in an interview with David Scott, "The Secret Life of Mother Teresa," Beliefnet.com, http://www.beliefnet.com/Faiths /Catholic/2005/03/The-Secret-Life-Of-Mother-Teresa.aspx?p=4.

9 *"Within days of the two gangs"* Suzanne Smalley, "2 Gangs Find Real Peace, in Secret; Officials' Summit Halts Bloodshed," *Boston Globe,* November 5, 2006.

10 *"were barely speaking"* Maria Cramer, "Truce and Reconciliation: Setting Example, Black Ministers Seek to End 'Clergy Wars,'" *Boston Globe,* February 14, 2009, http://www.boston.com/news/local/massachusetts /articles/2009/02/14/truce_and_reconciliation/.

16 *"This is just unbelievable"* "4 Weeks after Quake, Survivor Found," WPLG–Miami, February 9, 2010, http://www.justnews.com/news/22505430/detail .html#.

22 *"As we start on the miracle"* Lewis Smedes, *The Art of Forgiving: When You Need to Forgive and Don't Know How* (New York: Ballantine Books, 1996), 6.

23 *"To clear up some false notions"* Ibid., xiii.

23 *"we can be sure"* Ibid., 11.

26 *"don't ask Him to forgive"* R. C. Sproul, *The Intimate Marriage* (Phillipsburg, NJ: P&R Publishing, 1975), 127–128.

27 *"The quality of mercy"* William Shakespeare, *The Merchant of Venice*, act 4, scene 1.

MARCH

5 *"is to refuse"* Charles Spurgeon, *Morning and Evening*, trans. Alistair Begg, (Wheaton, IL: Crossway Books, 2003), 609.

5 *"the spiritual razzmatazz"* John Reed, "Luke," J. Reed's Christian Expositions, http://www.jrtalks.com/Luke/luke17v11to19.html.

9 *"The majority said"* "Why Men Cheat," *The Oprah Winfrey Show*, February 12, 2009, http://www.oprah.com/relationships/Why-Men-Cheat_2.

13 *"My prayer [hopes]"* Andrew Murray, *With Christ in the School of Prayer* (New Kensington, PA: Whitaker House, 1981), 165.

APRIL

16 *"Is he—quite safe?"* C. S. Lewis, *The Lion, the Witch and the Wardrobe* (New York: Macmillan, 1950), 64.

18 *"sees each moment"* David A. Hubbard, *Mastering the Old Testament 15A: Proverbs* (Dallas: Word, Inc., 1989), 48.

MAY

25 *"to glorify God"* Chick-fil-A, "Chick-fil-A's Closed-on-Sunday Policy," press release, http://www.chick-fil-a.com/Media/PDF/ClosedonSundaypolicy.pdf.

30 *"I would like to clarify"* Chief Arvol Looking Horse, statement on Sedona sweat lodge deaths, October 20, 2009, http://www.manataka.org/page108.html#October_20,_2009.

31 *"constitutional sins"* Arthur Pink, "Self Knowledge," *Studies in the Scriptures* 7 1934–35, 46.

JUNE

8 *The online dating industry* Patrick Danner, "Love Is Blind When Uninformed," *San Antonio Express News*, June 24, 2010, http://www.mysanantonio.com/business/local/article/Love-is-blind-when-uninformed-781503.php.

12 *"The take-home message of this study"* "Self-Control, and Lack of Self-Control, Is Contagious," *Science Daily*, January 18, 2010, http://www.sciencedaily.com/releases/2010/01/100113172359.htm.

22 *In fact, more than half* "Cosmetic Surgery and Makeover Wish List for 2010 Uncovered: Teeth Whitening, Tummy Tuck on Top," RealSelf.com, http://www.realself.com/cosmetic-surgery-wishlist.

23 *"the everlasting burden"* Richard Foster, *Celebration of Discipline: The Path to Spiritual Growth*, 3rd ed. (San Francisco: HarperSanFrancisco, 1988), 10.

26 *"the most popular living person"* Catharine Smith, "Facebook's Most Popular: The 50 Hottest People on Facebook," Huffington Post, July 9, 2010, http://www.huffingtonpost.com/2010/07/09/facebook-most-popular-the_n_640965 .html#s111758&title=1__Michael.

26 *"Celebrities are fascinating"* Carlin Flora, "Seeing by Starlight: Celebrity Obsession," *Psychology Today*, http://www.psychologytoday.com /articles/200407/seeing-starlight-celebrity-obsession.

28 *"Why not plant trees?"* "Taking Root: The Vision of Wangari Maathai," see video clip at http://moralheroes.org/wangari-maathai.

29 *"When choosing what to wear"* C. J. Mahaney, *Worldliness: Resisting the Seduction of a Fallen World* (Wheaton, IL: Crossway Books, 2008), 118.

29 *"Exalting God and not ourselves"* Ibid., 120.

29 *"Modesty is humility"* Ibid., 136.

30 *the number of abortions worldwide* See http://www.worldometers.info /abortions/.

JULY

3 *"Retire from the world"* A. W. Tozer, "Of God and Men: Cultivating the Divine/Human Relationship," *Christian Publications*, June 1995, 128–129.

4 *"ought to be commemorated"* Michael Medved, "Independence Day Messages from John Adams," Townhall.com, http://townhall.com/columnists /michaelmedved/2007/07/04/independence_day_messages_from_john_adams.

7 *"Why, if we are obeying"* Donald Whitney, *Spiritual Disciplines for the Christian Life* (Colorado Springs, CO: NavPress, 1991), 192.

11 *Americans have the highest levels* Jennifer Warner, "U.S. Leads the World in Illegal Drug Use," CBS News.com, July 1, 2008, http://www.cbsnews.com /stories/2008/07/01/health/webmd/main4222322.shtml.

12 *68 percent of adults* Centers for Disease Control and Prevention, "FastStats: Obesity and Overweight," http://www.cdc.gov/nchs/fastats/overwt.htm.

17 *Yet daily prayer, unlike five other faith habits* Barna Group, "Five Out of Seven Core Religious Behaviors Have Increased in the Past Decade According to Barna Survey," April 3, 2006, http://www.barna.org/barna-update/article /5-barna-update/156-five-out-of-seven-core-religious-behaviors-have-increased -in-the-past-decade-according-to-barna-survey?q=prayer.

26 *"creaturely activity"* Richard Foster, *Prayer: Finding the Heart's True Home* (New York: HarperOne, 1992), 101.

27 *ASA says primary insomnia* "Insomnia," American Sleep Association, http:// www.sleepassociation.org/index.php?p=aboutinsomnia.

28 *"We rested in God's love"* Lynne M. Baab, "The Gift of Rest," Kyria.com, originally published in *Today's Christian Woman*, September/October 2005, 36, http://www.kyria.com/topics/spiritualformation/theologyspiritualissues/7.36 .html.

31 *"a confession, which . . . comes too late"* John Newton, *Thoughts upon the African Slave Trade* (Ithaca, NY: Cornell University Library, 1788), 2. See also

Jonathan Aitken, *John Newton: From Disgrace to Amazing Grace* (Wheaton, IL: Crossway Books, 2007), 319.

AUGUST

6 *"Standing with my boots"* Gary Haugen, *Good News about Injustice: A Witness of Courage in a Hurting World*, 10th anniv. ed. (Downers Grove, IL: InterVarsity Press, 2009), 100.

11 *"I believe that there are hundreds"* Associated Press, "DNA Exonerates Dallas County Man after 26 Years in Prison," *Houston Chronicle*, January 3, 2008, http://www.chron.com/disp/story.mpl/headline/metro/5422726.html.

11 *In fact, if just one percent* See *The Innocence Project Annual Report 2010*, http://www.innocenceproject.org/news/Annual Report 2010.php.

16 *"Because deep down"* A Few Good Men, Castle Rock/Columbia Pictures (1992).

17 *"How'd you like"* Stephen J. Dubner, "Why Do You Lie? The Perils of Self-Reporting," *Freakonomics* (blog), June 23, 2008, http://www.freakonomics.com/2008/06/23/why-do-you-lie-the-perils-of-self-reporting/.

20 *"the reality, the substance"* Andrew Murray, *With Christ in the School of Prayer* (New Kensington, PA: Whitaker House, 1981), 20, italics in original.

20 *"not only a thing"* Ibid., 21.

23 *As delightful as an eleven-year-old* You can read about these stories at http://www.msnbc.msn.com/id/34455093/ns/us_news-wonderful_world/ and http://www.msnbc.msn.com/id/40630483/ns/us_news-wonderful_world/.

SEPTEMBER

6 *Then stand at "the intersection"* Max Lucado, *Cure for the Common Life* (Nashville: Thomas Nelson, 2008), 3.

8 *"will be the gauge by which"* Jim Cymbala, *Fresh Wind, Fresh Fire* (Grand Rapids, MI: Zondervan, 1997), 27.

15 *"People are threatening to break"* Eamon McNiff, Elisa Roupenian, and Lee Ferran, "Exclusive: After Broken Arm, Boy Cheerleader Still Threatened," ABCNews.com, September 29, 2010, http://abcnews.go.com/GMA/TheLaw/exclusive-broken-arm-boy-cheerleader-threatened/story?id=11753915.

17 *one of the 365 songs of the century* See http://michaelcard.com/awardshonors.html.

17 *"we have not the slightest idea"* Michael Card, *Scribbling in the Sand: Christ and Creativity* (Downers Grove, IL: IVP Books, 2004), 13.

17 *"not the only world"* Ibid., 14.

18 *"for survival, not for navigation"* NLT Study Bible (Carol Stream, IL: Tyndale House Publishers, 2008), 33.

19 *"are merely creative"* Aaron Lee, review of *Scribbling in the Sand: Christ and Creativity*, by Michael Card, CreateLeVoyage.com, March 22, 2006, http://createlevoyage.com/backstage/literaryarts/2006/03/book-scribbling-in-sand-christ-and.html.

22 *"Commit your work"* C. J. Darlington, "Francine Rivers Interview," *TitleTrakk*

.com (blog), http://www.titletrakk.com/author-interviews/francine-rivers
-interview.htm.

22 *"had been in poor health"* Associated Press, "Kansas City Man Accused of
Throwing Ailing Wife from Balcony," *Missourian*, last updated July 22, 2008,
http://ww.columbiamissourian.com/stories/2007/08/16
/kansas-city-man-accused-throwing-ailing-wife-balco/.

24 *"love the brethren"* Andrew Murray, *Abide in Christ: Thoughts on the Blessed
Life of Fellowship with the Son of God* (Philadelphia: The Rodgers Company,
Philadelphia, n.d.), 183.

26 *"While some may see this"* Pastor Scott Distler, "When Churches Cooperate,"
Folks, Listen! (blog), March 17, 2010, http://folkslisten.blogspot
.com/2010_03_01_archive.html.

29 *"but working together"* Associated Press, "Chile: Trapped Miners Get Movies,
Censored News," *USA Today*, September 27, 2010, http://www.usatoday.com
/news/world/2010-09-27-Miners-Chile_N.htm.

OCTOBER

1 *Religious attendance, said a 2006 study* "Weekly Religious Attendance Nearly
as Effective as Statins and Exercise in Extending Life," *Science Daily*, April 3,
2006, http://www.sciencedaily.com/releases/2006/04/060403132753.htm.

5 *"It is exactly this balance"* "Enjoying God's Gifts" in *NLT Study Bible* (Carol
Stream, IL: Tyndale House Publishers, 2008), 1077.

11 *"God is using Rachel"* S. C. Gwynne and Timothy Roche, "The Columbine
Tapes: An Act of God?" *Time*, December 20, 1999, http://www.time.com
/time/magazine/article/0,9171,992875,00.html.

13 *"But our courage"* "God Provides Refuge" in *Precepts for Living: The UMI
Annual Sunday School Commentary 2010-2011*, vol. 13 (Chicago: Urban
Ministries, 2010), 83.

19 *"My prayer will depend"* Andrew Murray, *With Christ in the School of Prayer*
(New Kensington, PA: Whitaker House, 1981), 165.

22 *"About a million people"* "Loving the Job You Hate," *Forbes* on msnbc.com,
updated December 7, 2005, http://www.msnbc.msn.com/id/10372274/ns
/business-forbescom/.

24 *"These findings"* Ted Baehr, *So You Want to Be in Pictures* (Nashville: Broadman
and Holman Publishers, 2005), 67.

30 *Temperance* Benjamin Franklin, "Ben's 13 Virtues," PBS.org, accessed April 8,
2011, http://www.pbs.org/benfranklin/pop_virtues_list.html?.

31 *"Learning self-discipline"* John MacArthur, *The Pillars of Christian Character:
The Basic Essentials of a Living Faith* (Wheaton, IL: Crossway Books, 1998),
139.

NOVEMBER

7 *"The bottom line on planning"* Larry Burkett, *Business by the Book: Complete
Guide of Biblical Principles for the Workplace* (Nashville: Thomas Nelson,
2006), 42.

14 *"I'm going to accept Christ"* Matt Petersen, ed., "Freedom from Fear," *One Passion* 2, no. 1, 12, http://content.yudu.com/Library/A1p9bl/OnePassion /resources/index.htm?referrerUrl=http%3A%2F%2Fwww.yudu.com%2Fitem %2Fdetails%2F222922%2FOne-Passion.

16 *"an artistic vision"* "Sistine Chapel Ceiling," Wikipedia, last modified March 27, 2011, http://en.wikipedia.org/wiki/Sistine_Chapel_ceiling.

20 *a full third of Americans* Barna Group, "Unchurched Population Nears 100 Million in the U.S.," March 19, 2007, http://www.barna.org/barna-update /article/12-faithspirituality/107-unchurched-population-nears-100-million-in -the-us.

23 *"From start to finish"* E. M. Bounds, *The Necessity of Prayer* (Radford, VA: Wilder Publications, 2008), 61.

27 *only about 50 percent of American adults* Belinda Luscombe, "Who Needs Marriage?" *Time*, November 18, 2010, http://www.time.com/time/nation /article/0,8599,2031962,00.html.

28 *"not because the rules"* Ibid.

30 *"displays our relationship"* NLT *Study Bible* (Carol Stream, IL: Tyndale, 2008), 2129.

DECEMBER

1 *"It lacked the power"* NLT *Study Bible* (Carol Stream, IL: Tyndale, 2008), 1263.

3 *"I say to myself"* See http://www.motherteresa.org/13_anni /Reactionsandcomments.html.

5 For more on the Lawndale Community Church story, see Wayne Gordon with Randall Frame, *Real Hope in Chicago* (Grand Rapids, MI: Zondervan, 1995).

7 *"I couldn't compete effectively"* "Saving Lives with Solar-Powered Lights," CNN *Heroes*, February 12, 2010, http://www.cnn.com/2010/LIVING/02/11 /cnnheroes.wadongo/index.html#.

11 *"The weird thing about money"* Chris Carpenter, "The Total Money Makeover: An Interview with Dave Ramsey," CBN.com, http://www.cbn.com/family /familyadvice/carpenter-daveramseymoneymakeover.aspx.

12 *"Incrementally, step by step"* Ibid.

13 *"when they got older"* Bill Johnson, "Divorced Mother's Determination, Sacrifice Led to Better Life," *Denver Post*, December 3, 2010, http://www. denverpost .com/billjohnson/ci_16765338.

14 *"The principle of tithing"* Crown Financial Ministries, "Tithing Outside of the Local Church," http://www.crown.org/library/ViewArticle.aspx?ArticleId=572.

15 *"Will I ever have enough?"* See video clip "Ron Blue on Faith-Based Family Finances" at http://tyndale.com/Ron-Blue/bio.

17 *"This is still the best country"* Neil Conan, "Count on Envy to Drive the U.S. Economy," *Talk of the Nation*, PBS, December 6, 2010, http://www.npr.org /2010/12/06/131853959/op-ed-count-on-envy-to-drive-the-u-s-economy.

20 *"and, oh, those biscuits"* William Porter, "Eat Local: Rise & Shine Biscuit Kitchen," *Denver Post*, April 21, 2010, http://www.denverpost.com/restaurants /ci_14915927.

21 *"formed the basis"* Martha Lagace, "HBS Cases: Beauty Entrepreneur Madam Walker," *HBS Working Knowledge*, June 25, 2007, http://hbswk.hbs.edu /item/5662.html.

22 *"A washer and dryer?"* Wayne Gordon with Randall Frame, *Real Hope in Chicago* (Grand Rapids, MI: Zondervan, 1995), 70–71.

26 *a retired mom "who started a thousand"* "Tiling Crackdown: Episode HDDIY-402H," *Disaster DIY*, HGTV, http://www.hgtv.com/disaster-diy /tiling-crackdown/index.html.

27 *"I knew I was going"* Sharon Cohen, "100 Percent of Urban Prep's First Class College-Bound," Associated Press, June 28, 2010.

28 *"The Christian life is the lifelong practice"* Eugene H. Peterson, *Christ Plays in Ten Thousand Places: A Conversation in Spiritual Theology* (Grand Rapids, MI/ Cambridge, U.K.: William B. Eerdmans Publishing Company, 2005), 333–334.

28 *"This is slow work"* Ibid., 337.

29 *Christians in Iraq are facing* Steven Lee Myers, "More Christians Flee Iraq after New Violence," *New York Times*, December 12, 2010, http://www.nytimes .com/2010/12/13/world/middleeast/13iraq.html?_r=1&scp=1&sq=Christians %2C+Erbil&st=nyt.

30 *"To begin with"* Peterson, *Christ Plays in Ten Thousand Places*, 335.

SCRIPTURE INDEX
Arranged Alphabetically by Topic, with Dates

Generosity *January 29–February 4*
Deuteronomy 15:7-11; 1 Chronicles 29:12-14; Proverbs 11:24, 25; Matthew 10:8; Mark 12:41-43; Luke 6:38; John 3:16

Gratitude *March 5–March 11*
Genesis 50:19-20; Psalm 50:23; Psalm 100:3-5; Mark 14:22-23; Luke 17:11-19; Philippians 1:3; Philemon 1:3-5

Hard Work *October 22–October 28*
1 Samuel 16:10-13; Proverbs 12:11; Proverbs 21:5; Ecclesiastes 5:8-12; Ephesians 4:25-32; Colossians 3:16-24; 2 Thessalonians 3:11-15; 2 Timothy 2:15

Honesty and Integrity *August 20–August 26*
Psalm 119:1-8; Proverbs 2:6-8; Proverbs 10:8-10; Proverbs 11:1-3; Proverbs 20:7-11; Proverbs 28:6

Hope *March 12–March 18*
Ezra 10:1-2; Job 11:18; Psalm 33:22; Psalm 37; Psalm 118:5-7; Jeremiah 29:10-14; Zechariah 9:11-13

Hospitality *April 9–April 15*
1 Kings 17:8-24; Luke 10:5; Luke 24:28-38; Hebrews 13:2; 1 Peter 4:9-11

Humility *May 7–May 13*
Psalm 37:11; Proverbs 3:33-35; Proverbs 11:1-2; Proverbs 15:33; Proverbs 22:4; Matthew 5:15; Luke 14:11; 2 Corinthians 12:7-10

Joy *April 2–April 8*
Nehemiah 8:9-12; Psalm 16:11; Psalm 34:8; Psalm 51; Matthew 25:14-30; John 15:10-12; Romans 14:17

Justice *August 6–August 12*
Exodus 23:1-9; Deuteronomy 24:14-22; Deuteronomy 32:1-4; Psalm 33:5; Psalm 34:18; Psalm 37:27-28; Proverbs 2:8; Romans 12:17-21

Kindness *January 22–January 28*
Genesis 50:21; Ruth 3:9-11; Proverbs 11:16-17; Jeremiah 9:23-24; Romans 11:17-24; 2 Peter 1:5-11

Knowledge *May 28–June 3*
Proverbs 2:3-6; Proverbs 9:9-10; Proverbs 11:9; Proverbs 17:2-27; Proverbs 22:12; Daniel 11:32; Matthew 11:29; Colossians 1:9-10; 2 Peter 1:2-8

Listening *January 1–January 7*
Deuteronomy 30:19-20; Nehemiah 8:1-6; Proverbs 1:1-9; Proverbs 8:32-34; Luke 11:28

Loving *January 8–January 14*
Proverbs 21:21; Zephaniah 3:16-20; Luke 6:27-35; John 14:31;
1 Corinthians 8; 1 Corinthians 12:31; 1 Corinthians 13:1-13; Ephesians
5:22-28; Colossians 3:14

Mercy *February 26–March 4*
Exodus 33:18-19; Psalm 23; Psalm 103:11; Micah 6:8; Matthew 5:7;
Matthew 18:32-33; Luke 1:46-50

Obedience *April 23–April 29*
Leviticus 26:3-13; Deuteronomy 28:1; Luke 5:27-28; John 14:15-25;
Acts 5:29

Order and Discipline *October 29–November 4*
Genesis 1:27-31; Proverbs 13:1-3; Luke 16:10-13; 1 Corinthians
10:29-31; 2 Corinthians 9:6-12; Ephesians 5:15; Philippians 4:6-9;
1 Timothy 4:8

Passion and Zeal *September 3–September 9*
Exodus 34:5-9; Psalm 107:9; Isaiah 56:7; Matthew 21:12-13; John 2:15-17;
1 Corinthians 12:4-11; 1 Corinthians 14:22-25; 2 Corinthians 8:6-12;
2 Corinthians 9:2, 6-16; James 5:13-18

Patience *February 12–February 18*
Exodus 34:4-7; Romans 15:2-7; 2 Corinthians 6:6; Galatians 5:19-23;
1 Timothy 1:12-16; James 5:10-11; 2 Peter 3:14-15

Peace *February 5–February 11*
Judges 6:11-24; Job 22:21-25; Psalm 29:11; Matthew 5:9; Ephesians
2:11-14; 2 Thessalonians 3:16; James 3:17-18

Perseverance *November 12–November 18*
Galatians 6:9-10; Hebrews 10:36; Hebrews 12:1-4, 12-13; James 1:2-4

Persistence *October 15–October 21*
1 Chronicles 16:7-11; Isaiah 30:18-22; Matthew 10:22; Matthew
24:4-13; 1 Corinthians 15:56-58; Galatians 6:1-9; Hebrews 12:2; James
5:16

Praise *March 19–March 25*
2 Samuel 22:1-4; 2 Chronicles 20:20-24; Psalm 5:11; Psalm 22:3-4, 25-28;
Psalm 81:10; Acts 16:23-26

Preparation *November 5–November 11*
Judges 6:33-40; 1 Samuel 17:32-47; Esther 4:15-17; Proverbs 6:6-11;
Proverbs 16:3; Matthew 25:1-10; Luke 3:4, 6; John 14:1-6;
1 Thessalonians 5:6

Prudence   *June 4–June 10*
Proverbs 14:8, 15-16, 18; Proverbs 19:14; Proverbs 22:3; Amos 5:13

Purity   *May 14–May 20*
Matthew 5:8; 1 Thessalonians 4:3-8; 2 Timothy 2:21-22; Titus 1:15-16;
James 4:8; 1 John 1:5-9; 1 John 3:2-3

Repentance   *August 27–September 2*
Psalm 51; Daniel 9:20-23; Daniel 10:10-19; Acts 3:17-20; 2 Corinthians
7:8-10, 11-13

Rest   *July 23–July 29*
Psalm 4:6-8; Psalm 23; Psalm 91; Psalm 116:1-7; Psalm 127; Isaiah 32:18;
Matthew 11:28-30

Reverence and Fear of God   *April 16–April 22*
Psalm 25:11-15; Psalm 31:19; Psalm 34:7-9; Psalm 103:13; Psalm 112:1;
Proverbs 1:5-7; Proverbs 3:7-8; Proverbs 9:10-11; Proverbs 22:1-4

Righteousness   *April 30–May 6*
Psalm 34:15; Proverbs 2:6-7; Proverbs 3:31-35; Isaiah 32:9-17; Hosea
10:12; Matthew 5:6; 1 John 1:8-10

Sacrifice   *July 16–July 22*
Genesis 22:9-17; 1 Samuel 15:22; Psalm 51; Jeremiah 33:1-3; Romans
12:1-2; Romans 15:15-20; Philippians 2:17; Hebrews 13:15-16

Self-Control   *June 11–June 17*
Proverbs 16:32; Proverbs 25:27-28; Galatians 2:17-21; Galatians 5:19-22;
Ephesians 5:15-18; 2 Peter 1:5-11

Service   *December 3–December 9*
Matthew 5:14-16; Matthew 25:21; John 13:8-17; Romans 12:9-12; James
2:18-26

Silence and Solitude   *July 2–July 8*
1 Kings 19:11-13; Psalm 62:1-5; Proverbs 17:27; Isaiah 30:15;
Lamentations 3:22-26; Zechariah 2:10-13; Luke 4:1, 14-15; Luke 6:12-16

Strength and Vigor   *September 10–September 16*
1 Chronicles 29:10-12, 18; Psalm 8; Psalm 138:1-3; Isaiah 40:29;
Daniel 1:12-17; 1 Corinthians 1:8; 2 Corinthians 12:7-10; Philippians
4:11-13

Temperance   *July 9–July 15*
Proverbs 23:2, 4; Proverbs 25:16; Ecclesiastes 6:7-9; Matthew 4:1-4,
18-21; John 3:23-30; Galatians 5:19-26

Thrift   *December 10–December 16*
Psalm 16; Psalm 23:1; Proverbs 3:13-18; Proverbs 13:4-11; Proverbs 21:5; Proverbs 23:4-5; Matthew 6:19-21; 2 Corinthians 9:6-15; 1 Timothy 6:6-10

Trust   *May 21–May 27*
Genesis 6:9-22; Genesis 9:1; Psalm 9:10; Psalm 32:10; Psalm 34:8-10; Psalm 37:1-3; Psalm 125:1; Isaiah 26:2-3

Truth   *August 13–August 19*
Proverbs 12:19; Jeremiah 4:1-2; John 8:31-32; Ephesians 1:12-14; Ephesians 4:11-16; Colossians 3:9-11; 2 Timothy 1:12-14; Revelation 22:13

Unity   *September 24–September 30*
Psalm 68:6; Psalm 133:1, 3; Ecclesiastes 4:9-12; John 17:20-24; Romans 15:5-7; Ephesians 4:11-16

Vigilance   *November 19–November 25*
Matthew 12:31-37; Matthew 26:36-46; Luke 13:10-17; Romans 13:11-13; 1 Corinthians 16:13-14; 1 Timothy 4:16; 1 Peter 5:6-10

Vision   *July 30–August 5*
Psalm 34:8; Habakkuk 1:1-5; Habakkuk 2:1-3; Matthew 5:8; Mark 8:22-26; Mark 10:46-52; Acts 9:10-18; Acts 10:1-36; 1 Corinthians 13:12

Wisdom   *October 1–October 7*
Proverbs 2:6, 11; Proverbs 3:1-8, 13; Proverbs 4:1-7; Proverbs 15:31; 1 Corinthians 1:24-25; James 1:5; James 3:17-18

ENJOY A TESTIMONY TO THE ENDURING FAITH OF THE AFRICAN AMERICAN PEOPLE THROUGH HYMNS, ARTWORK, AND GOD'S TIMELESS WORDS.

Visually representing a slice of America's musical and spiritual history, the *Bound for Glory Parallel Bible* contains:

- The full text of the popular NLT and KJV Bible translations
- A new introduction giving a history of the King James Version's heritage and legacy in honor of its 400th anniversary
- Sixteen pages of calligraphic artwork from the *Bound for Glory* collection by Timothy R. Botts
- Complete lyrics from selected spirituals

978-1-4143-4988-6 (Hardcover)
978-1-4143-4989-3 (LeatherLike)

The *Bound for Glory* book features a collection of 52 calligraphic works by Timothy R. Botts. Offering striking visual interpretations of African American spiritual songs, *Bound for Glory* also includes reflective readings from Botts and writer and speaker Patricia Raybon.

978-1-4143-5453-8

CP0491